Crime Linkage

Theory, Research, and Practice

Advances in Police Theory and Practice Series

Series Editor: Dilip K. Das

Crime Linkage: Theory, Research, and Practice
Jessica Woodhams and Craig Bennell

Policing White Collar Crime: Characteristics of White Collar Criminals
Petter Gottschalk

Honor-Based Violence: Policing and Prevention
Karl Anton Roberts, Gerry Campbell, and Glen Lloyd

Policing and the Mentally Ill: International Perspectives
Duncan Chappell

Security Governance, Policing, and Local Capacity
Jan Froestad with Clifford D. Shearing

Policing in Hong Kong: History and Reform
Kam C. Wong

Police Performance Appraisals: A Comparative Perspective
Serdar Kenan Gul and Paul O'Connell

Los Angeles Police Department Meltdown: The Fall of the Professional-Reform Model of Policing
James Lasley

Financial Crimes: A Global Threat
Maximillian Edelbacher, Peter Kratcoski, and Michael Theil

Police Integrity Management in Australia: Global Lessons for Combating Police Misconduct
Louise Porter and Tim Prenzler

The Crime Numbers Game: Management by Manipulation
John A. Eterno and Eli B. Silverman

The International Trafficking of Human Organs: A Multidisciplinary Perspective
Leonard Territo and Rande Matteson

Police Reform in China
Kam C. Wong

Mission-Based Policing
John P. Crank, Dawn M. Irlbeck, Rebecca K. Murray, and Mark Sundermeier

The New Khaki: The Evolving Nature of Policing in India
Arvind Verma

Cold Cases: An Evaluation Model with Follow-up Strategies for Investigators
James M. Adcock and Sarah L. Stein

Policing Organized Crime: Intelligence Strategy Implementation
Petter Gottschalk

Security in Post-Conflict Africa: The Role of Nonstate Policing
Bruce Baker

Community Policing and Peacekeeping
Peter Grabosky

Community Policing: International Patterns and Comparative Perspectives
Dominique Wisler and Ihekwoaba D. Onwudiwe

Police Corruption: Preventing Misconduct and Maintaining Integrity
Tim Prenzler

FORTHCOMING

Police Investigative Interviews and Interpreting: Context, Challenges, and Strategies
Sedat Mulayim, Miranda Lai, and Caroline Norma

Cold Cases: Evaluation Models with Follow-up Strategies for Investigators, Second Edition
James M. Adcock and Sarah L. Stein

Democratic Policing
Darren Palmer

Corruption, Fraud, Organized Crime, and the Shadow Economy
Maximilian Edelbacher, Peter C. Kratcoski, and Bojan Dobovsek

Female Criminals: An Examination and Interpretation of Female Offending
Venessa Garcia

Women in Policing: An International Perspective
Venessa Garcia

Policing in Hong Kong: History and Reform
Kam C. Wong

Policing Terrorism: Research Studies into Police Counter-terrorism Investigations
David Lowe

Collaborative Policing: Police, Academics, Professionals, and Communities Working Together for Education, Training, and Program Implementation
Peter C. Kratcoski and Maximilian Edelbacher

Crime Linkage

Theory, Research, and Practice

Edited by

Jessica Woodhams

Craig Bennell

CRC Press
Taylor & Francis Group
Boca Raton London New York

CRC Press is an imprint of the
Taylor & Francis Group, an **informa** business

CRC Press
Taylor & Francis Group
6000 Broken Sound Parkway NW, Suite 300
Boca Raton, FL 33487-2742

First issued in paperback 2019

ISBN-13: 978-1-4665-0675-6 (hbk)
ISBN-13: 978-0-367-86707-2 (pbk)

Library of Congress Cataloging-in-Publication Data

Crime linkage : theory, research, and practice / editors, Jessica Woodhams, Craig Bennell.
pages cm. -- (Advances in police theory and practice series)
Includes bibliographical references and index.
ISBN 978-1-4665-0675-6 (hardcover : alk. paper) 1. Criminal behavior. 2. Criminal methods. 3. Crime analysis. 4. Criminal behavior, Prediction of. 5. Criminal investigation. I. Woodhams, Jessica. II. Bennell, Craig.

HV6080.C685 2015
364.3--dc23 2014027964

Visit the Taylor & Francis Web site at
http://www.taylorandfrancis.com

and the CRC Press Web site at
http://www.crcpress.com

This book is dedicated to my dad, Rick Woodhams. An internationally renowned Shihan, my lessons in Karate from you from age five taught me discipline and pressure points. Both have served me well in academia!

Jessica Woodhams

This book is dedicated to my wife, Cindy, and our two wonderful boys, Noah and Elijah. Thank you for bringing so much love and happiness into my life.

Craig Bennell

Contents

Series Editor's Preface xiii
Prologue xv
Editors xvii
Contributors xix
Acknowledgments xxv

1 Introduction: Time to Consolidate and Reflect 1
JESSICA WOODHAMS AND CRAIG BENNELL

2 Consistency and Distinctiveness of Criminal Behavior 11
JESSICA WOODHAMS AND CRAIG BENNELL

3 Sex Crime Linkage: Sexual Fantasy and Offense Plasticity 33
DION GEE AND ALEKSANDRA BELOFASTOV

4 The Effect of Mental Disorder on Crime Scene Behavior, Its Consistency, and Variability 55
JESSICA WOODHAMS AND KINGA KOMARZYNSKA

5 Linking Crimes with Spatial Behavior: A Need to Tackle Some Remaining Methodological Concerns 83
BRENT SNOOK, KIRK LUTHER, AND SARAH MACDONALD

6 **Testing the Theories Underpinning Crime Linkage** **107**
MATTHEW TONKIN

7 **A Cross-National Comparison of Behavioral Consistency in Serial Homicide** **141**
C. GABRIELLE SALFATI

8 **A Practitioner's Perspective: Theory, Practice, and Research** **173**
LEE RAINBOW

9 **The Use of Linkage Analysis Evidence in Serial Offense Trials** **197**
GÉRARD LABUSCHAGNE

10 **Crime Linkage as Expert Evidence: Making a Case for the *Daubert* Standard** **225**
TOM PAKKANEN, PEKKA SANTTILA, AND DARIO BOSCO

11 **The Ability of Human Judges to Link Crimes Using Behavioral Information: Current Knowledge and Unresolved Issues** **251**
REBECCA MUGFORD AND MELISSA MARTINEAU

12 **Extending Crime Linkage to Versatile Offenders** **279**
MATTHEW TONKIN

13 **Exploring If (Situation) … Then (Behavior) Contingencies in Interpersonal Crimes** **303**
JAN M. WINTER

14 **Informing Practice: Research Methods in Crime Linkage Analysis** **337**

CRAIG BENNELL, ALASDAIR M. GOODWILL, AND ANNIE CHINNECK

15 **Crime Linkage Research: Where to From Here?** **369**

CRAIG BENNELL AND JESSICA WOODHAMS

Index **373**

A Call for Authors **383**

Advances in Police Theory and Practice **385**

Series Editor's Preface

Although the literature on police and allied subjects is growing exponentially, its impact upon day-to-day policing remains small. The two worlds of research and practice of policing remain disconnected even though cooperation between the two is growing. A major reason is that the two groups speak in different languages. On the one hand, the research work is published in hard-to-access journals and presented in a manner that is difficult to comprehend for a lay person. On the other hand, the police practitioners tend not to mix with researchers and remain secretive about their work. Consequently, there is little dialogue between the two and almost no attempt to learn from one another. Dialog across the globe, among researchers and practitioners situated in different continents, is of course even more limited.

I attempted to address this problem by starting the IPES, www.ipes.info, where a common platform has brought the two groups together. IPES is now in its 17th year. The annual meetings which constitute the most major annual event of the organization have been hosted in all parts of the world. Several publications have come out of these deliberations, and a new collaborative community of scholars and police officers has been created whose membership runs into several hundreds.

Another attempt was to begin a new journal, aptly called *Police Practice & Research: An International Journal* (PPR) that has opened the gate to practitioners to share their work and experiences. The journal has attempted to focus upon issues that help bring the two groups on a single platform. PPR is completing its 15 years in 2014. It is certainly an evidence of growing collaboration between police research and practice that PPR, which began with four issues a year, expanded into five issues in its fourth year, and now, it is issued six times a year.

Clearly, these attempts, despite their success, remain limited. Conferences and journal publications do help create a body of knowledge and an association of police activists but cannot address substantial issues in depth. The limitations of time and space preclude larger discussions and more authoritative expositions that can provide stronger and broader linkages between the two worlds.

It is this realization of the increasing dialogue between police research and practice that has encouraged many of us—my close colleagues and I connected closely with IPES and PPR across the world—to conceive and implement a new attempt in this direction. I am now embarking on a book series, *Advances in Police Theory and Practice*, that seeks to attract writers from all parts of the world. Further, the attempt is to find practitioner contributors. The objective is to make the series a serious contribution to our knowledge of the police as well as to improve police practices. The focus is not only in work that describes the best and successful police practices but also one that challenges current paradigms and breaks new ground to prepare a police for the twenty-first century. The series seeks for comparative analysis that highlights achievements in distant parts of the world as well as one that encourages an in-depth examination of specific problems confronting a particular police force.

It is hoped that through this series it will be possible to accelerate the process of building knowledge about policing and help bridge the gap between the two worlds—the world of police research and police practice. This is an invitation to police scholars and practitioners across the world to come and join in this venture.

Dilip K. Das
Founding President,
International Police Executive Symposium,
http://www.ipes.info

Series Editor,
Advances in Police Theory and Practice,
CRC Press/Taylor & Francis Group.

Series Editor,
Interviews with Global Leaders in Police, Courts, and Prisons,
CRC Press/Taylor & Francis Group.

Series Editor,
PPR Special Issues as Books,
Routledge/Taylor & Francis Group.

Founding Editor-in-Chief,
Police Practice and Research: An International Journal,
Routledge/Taylor & Francis Group.
http://www.tandfonline.com/GPPR

International Police Executive Symposium

Police Practice & Research
An International Journal

Prologue

A decade ago, little was being written on the topic of crime linkage, despite practitioners across the world utilizing it with a range of crime types. Since then, a modest but significant literature on the topic has amassed making this an opportune time to collate and evaluate what has been done to date and look forward to where research and practice might go in the future.

The chapters contained within this book have been written by key researchers and practitioners in the field. Our authors come from various parts of the world and they speak to the diversity of issues that are currently being examined and debated in the crime linkage field, making this the most authoritative book on the topic. Many of the chapters examine crime linkage from a purely theoretical perspective. They explore the conditions under which criminals behave in ways that might allow their crimes to be accurately linked; they consider the relevance of psychological and criminological theory to the crime linkage problem, and they examine how crime linkage has been studied by researchers. Some chapters speak to more practical issues, such as how crimes can actually be linked within investigative settings, how courts of law might perceive crime linkage testimony, and how research in this area can be modified to make it more practically relevant.

Rarely in the crime linkage field have attempts been made to bridge the gap between researchers and practitioners. In our experience, researchers in this field usually adopt some sort of theoretical, methodological, and analytical approach to examine a chosen topic. Most researchers that we spoke to hope that their results will say something interesting about the behavior of serial criminals, and that their results will ultimately assist practitioners in their attempts to link crimes to research findings. However, as far as we are aware, researchers and practitioners do not frequently speak to one another with the goal of increasing the utility of crime linkage research. In accordance with the mandate of the book series to which this volume belongs, *Crime Linkage: Theory, Research, and Practice* represents an initial step in this direction.

Ultimately, our goal was to write a book that is a collaborative effort between researchers and practitioners. When initially discussing this book, we hoped that the end product would provide an account of the current thinking in this field with the goal of better informing both groups (researchers and practitioners) about what the other group is doing. We also hoped that this book would create a set of conditions that would promote further researcher–practitioner collaboration so that crime linkage research conducted in the future could be more scientifically rigorous and also more practically relevant. With respect to these goals, we believe that we have been successful, though only time will tell for sure. We hope that readers of this book agree.

Editors

Jessica Woodhams
School of Psychology
University of Birmingham
Birmingham, UK

Dr. Jessica Woodhams is a forensic psychologist and a senior lecturer in forensic psychology at the University of Birmingham (UK). Her PhD thesis focused on investigating juvenile sex offending and included a large section on crime linkage, reflecting her employment as a crime analyst prior to entering academia in 2002. She has published many articles, book chapters, and magazine articles on the topic of crime linkage, and in 2013, she founded C-LINK, an international network of practitioners and researchers of crime linkage. In 2012, she co-edited a special issue of the *Journal of Investigative Psychology and Offender Profiling* with Craig Bennell. She is regularly invited to speak at international conferences regarding crime linkage and sexual offending. As well as conducting research on crime linkage, her expertise has been sought by organizations such as the Metropolitan Police Service and the Scottish Crown Office on matters pertaining to crime linkage and behavioral similarity.

Craig Bennell
Department of Psychology
Carleton University
Ottawa, Ontario, Canada

Dr. Craig Bennell is a professor of psychology at Carleton University. He is also the director of the Police Research Lab at Carleton and editor of *Journal of Police and Criminal Psychology*. Craig completed his BSc in psychology at the University of Alberta (Canada) and his MSc and PhD in psychology at the University of Liverpool (UK). His primary line of research examines the reliability, validity, and usefulness of psychologically based investigative techniques, including methods used to link serial crimes. He also studies police decision-making, especially in use of force encounters. He is a founding member of the Crime Linkage International Network (C-LINK), which intends to build academic–practitioner partnerships for the purpose of making crime linkage research more operationally relevant.

Contributors

Aleksandra Belofastov
Australasian Psychology Services
Professional Assessment, Treatment & Consultation
Melbourne, Australia

Dr. Aleksandra Belofastov has a PhD in clinical psychology (with a specialization in forensic psychology) from Monash University in Victoria, Australia. She has worked in forensic mental health settings both in the United Kingdom and Australia for the past 10 years. Her clinical work involves the assessment, treatment, and consultation of individuals with mental illnesses and severe personality disorders, who have come into contact with the criminal justice system, including those who have committed sexual offences. Clinical and research interests include treatment of personality disorders, psychological understandings of symptoms of mental illness and their potential relationships to criminal behavior, and victim-related issues including the impact of trauma.

Dario Bosco
University Federico II Naples
Napoli, Italy

Dr. Dario Bosco is a criminal lawyer. He has been working within the Italian Criminal Courts for more than 10 years. He has an MD in forensic science and criminology, and he has done research in the field of criminal profiling, crime linkage, and forensic science and their application in court. He has published on forensic science, criminal profiling, psychology, and law, criminology, and criminal justice in and outside of Italy. He is a visiting professor of forensic science and criminology in many universities in Italy. He is also a member of the Centro Scienze Forensi in Turin, Italy.

Annie Chinneck
Department of Psychology and Neuroscience
Dalhousie University
Halifax, Nova Scotia, Canada

Annie Chinneck is currently pursuing a PhD in clinical psychology at Dalhousie University (Canada). She graduated with a BA (Honours) in psychology from Carleton University (Canada). Her clinical and research interests lie in the field of forensic psychology, and she is particularly interested in studying substance abuse and other behavioral addictions, such as gambling. She has also conducted research related to crime linkage analysis, police burnout, and the myths and misconceptions surrounding sex offenders.

Dion Gee
Australasian Psychology Services
Professional Assessment, Treatment & Consultation
Melbourne, Australia

Dr. Dion Gee is a registered psychologist in Australia with specialist endorsement in forensic psychology. He is currently a director of Australasian Psychology Services and is employed by the Victorian Institute of Forensic Mental Health (Forensicare) working within the Acute Assessment Unit of the Melbourne Assessment Prison. Since 2000, he has specialized in forensic mental health within Australia and the United Kingdom, where he has received postdoctoral training in the assessment, treatment, and risk management of diverse offender populations. His areas of expertise include the assessment and risk management of sexual/violent offenders, cognitively/intellectually impaired offenders, offenders with personality disorders, and offenders presenting with impaired mental functioning. Clinical and research interests include psychological profiling, deviant sexual fantasy, personality disorders, risk assessment/management, clinical implementation of Verdin's sentencing principles, and the impact of long-term segregation on prisoner mental health.

Alasdair M. Goodwill
Department of Psychology
Ryerson University
Toronto, Canada

Dr. Alasdair Goodwill is the director of the Criminal and Investigative Research and Analysis Group at Ryerson University (Toronto, Canada). Alasdair received his BSc (Hons) from McMaster University (Canada), his MSc from the University of Liverpool (UK), and his PhD from the University of Birmingham (UK). He is an associate professor in the Department of Psychology, a chartered psychologist (UK), a fellow of the Royal Statistical Society, and an associate fellow of the British Psychological Society. His primary areas of research include (1) the research and application of behavioral and criminal investigative analysis in sexual offending and (2) the development of pragmatic multiphasic methods of crime scene behavioral analysis in sexual and violent criminal investigations. Part of his research is currently funded by the Ontario Mental Health Foundation (OMHF) of Canada.

Kinga Komarzynska
HM prison
West Midlands, UK

Dr. Kinga Komarzynska obtained her degree in clinical psychology from the University of Wrocław in Poland. Following this, she was awarded a forensic psychology practice doctorate from the University of Birmingham (UK). She is a chartered psychologist and a registered forensic psychologist with the UK's Health and Care Professions Council. She has experience of working with sex offenders and violent offenders in both Special Hospitals as well as in the Prison Service. Clinical and research interests include investigative psychology, assessment and treatment of sex offenders and violent offenders.

Gérard Labuschagne
Investigative Psychology Section
Forensic Services Division
South African Police Service
and
Department of Police Practice
College of Law
University of South Africa
Pretoria, South Africa

Division of Forensic Medicine and Pathology
Faculty of Health Sciences
University of the Witwatersrand
Johannesburg, South Africa

Brigadier Gérard Labuschagne, PhD, is the section head of the South African Police Service's (SAPS) Investigative Psychology Section (IPS). The IPS is responsible for assisting the SAPS with investigations of psychologically motivated crimes such as serial sex offences. He is a clinical psychologist with the Health Professions Council of South Africa. He is an adjunct faculty member of the California School of Forensic Studies at Alliant International University in the United States and also a Professor *Extraordinarius* at the Department of Police Practice at the University of South Africa. He also holds an honorary associate professorship in the Division of Forensic Medicine and Pathology at the University of the Witwatersrand in South Africa. Over the past 12 years, he has assisted in the investigation of over 110 serial murderers and over 200 serial rapists. He has vast experience in crime linkage based on *modus operandi* and often testifies about crime linkage in court.

Kirk Luther
Psychology Department
Memorial University of Newfoundland
St. John's, Newfoundland, Canada

Kirk Luther is a PhD student at Memorial University of Newfoundland (Canada). His research interests include the cognitive processes underlying judgment and decision making, crime linkage systems, and police interviewing and interrogation methods. His other research interests include the interaction patterns in police interviews and caution comprehension.

Sarah MacDonald
Psychology Department
Memorial University of Newfoundland
St. John's, Newfoundland, Canada

Sarah MacDonald is a PhD student at Memorial University of Newfoundland (Canada). She obtained her MSc at Memorial University of Newfoundland in 2011 and her BSc (Honours) at Dalhousie University (Canada) in 2009. Her general research interests include investigative interviewing practices and deception detection.

Melissa Martineau
Royal Canadian Mounted Police
Canadian Police Centre for Missing and Exploited Children
and Behavioural Sciences Branch
Ottawa, Ontario, Canada

Melissa Martineau is a senior research specialist in behavioral sciences with the Royal Canadian Mounted Police. Melissa completed her BSc in criminology and sociology and her master of criminology at the University of Ottawa (Canada). Her primary research interests include serial and sexual homicide, detection of deception, threat and risk assessment and crime linkage. She has authored numerous technical reports and journal articles and provided advice within the Canadian police community regarding the application of empirical research to police investigation.

Rebecca Mugford
Department of Psychology
Carleton University
Ottawa, Ontario, Canada

Rebecca Mugford is a PhD student in experimental psychology at Carleton University (Canada). Her primary research interests include evaluating the validity, reliability, and utility of psychologically based police investigative techniques (e.g., crime linkage analysis) and examining factors that impact police investigative and use-of-force decision making.

Tom Pakkanen
Abo Akademi University
Turku, Finland

Tom Pakkanen is a PhD student of forensic psychology at the Abo Akademi University, Turku, Finland. He has years of experience working full time assisting the police and the judicial system, mainly in the Helsinki Metropolitan Area, with forensic investigations of suspected child sexual and physical abuse. He has been training the police at the Police College of Finland for a decade, and he is a sought-after lecturer on topics of applied forensic psychology. In his spare time, he is finishing his doctoral thesis on crime linkage. His research interests include crime linkage, criminal profiling, decision-making processes, and the application of forensic psychology in the court room and in pretrial investigations.

Lee Rainbow
BIA—Head of Profession
National Crime Agency, UK

Lee Rainbow is the head of profession for Behavioral Investigative Advice within the National Crime Agency (UK) and a member of the Association of Chief Police Officers Behavioral Science Committee. After gaining an MSc in investigative psychology in 1996, he subsequently worked within Cleveland Constabulary as a criminal intelligence analyst and Surrey Police as a behavioral science consultant before being employed by the National Crime Faculty as the first-ever full-time Behavioral Investigative Adviser. He has produced over 300 written reports in support of serious crime enquiries and has supported many of the most high profile cases in the United Kingdom, as well as cases in Europe and the Caribbean. He has played a leading role in the national coordination of behavioral investigative advice within the United Kingdom and has contributed significantly to the enhanced professionalization of the discipline from both a tactical and strategic perspective.

C. Gabrielle Salfati
Department of Psychology
John Jay College of Criminal Justice
City University of New York, New York

Dr. C. Gabrielle Salfati is a professor of psychology at John Jay College of Criminal Justice (US) where she directs the Investigative Psychology Research Unit. She is part of the first group of people who emerged within the new field of investigative psychology and was instrumental in its development as an international research field, in particular in the advancement of the science of offender profiling and the empirical analysis of violent criminal behavior. Her main areas of expertise relate to the methodology of research in offender profiling and linking serial crimes, specifically with a focus on interpersonal violence and victimization patterns in homicide and violent sexual crimes. This work is being developed within an international framework through collaboration with law enforcement agencies internationally. She has presented and published her work widely both nationally and internationally, and she provides training to law enforcement, crime analysts, and other criminal justice professionals internationally.

Pekka Santtila
Department of Psychology
Abo Akademi University
Turku, Finland

Dr. Pekka Santtila is a professor of legal psychology at the Abo Akademi University, Turku, Finland. He has conducted research on predicting offender characteristics from crime scene behavior, geographical profiling as well as crime linkage. In addition to this work, he has published widely on different aspects of child sexual abuse including interviewing techniques, decision-making processes, prevalence as well as diagnosing pedophilic interest and its etiology. Professor Santtila has consulted on numerous court cases both in Finland and abroad.

Brent Snook
Department of Psychology
Memorial University
St. John's, Newfoundland, Canada

Dr. Brent Snook is a professor of psychology at Memorial University of Newfoundland (Canada). He holds a PhD in psychology from The University of Liverpool (UK). His research aims to advance scientific literacy within the criminal justice system and improve the administration of justice. His specific research interests pertain to decision making, investigative practices (e.g., interviewing), and eradicating pseudoscience in the criminal justice system. In addition to the implementation of PEACE in Canada, his current body of work involves how people understand their legal rights and testing the effectiveness of the PEACE model of interviewing.

Matthew Tonkin
Birmingham City University
Birmingham, UK

Dr. Matthew Tonkin is a lecturer in forensic psychology at Birmingham City University (UK). He gained his PhD at The University of Leicester in 2012 and has published numerous peer-reviewed articles in the area of investigative psychology. In particular, his research has focused on the linking of crimes using offender crime scene behavior, geographical profiling, and offender profiling. Dr. Tonkin is also one of the founding members of the recently established

C-LINK network who are currently seeking to drive forward research and practice in the area of behavioral case linkage. Dr. Tonkin also researches the social climate of prisons and forensic psychiatric hospitals. In collaboration with colleagues from England, Germany, and Australia, he has been seeking to develop and test a short and psychometrically sound questionnaire to measure the social climate in secure settings. This questionnaire is called the Essen Climate Evaluation Schema (EssenCES).

Jan M. Winter
Central Operational Cooperation Division (DLOS)
Dutch National Police
Zoetermeer, The Netherlands

Department of Clinical and Life Span Psychology (KLEP)
Vrije Universiteit Brussel
Brussels, Belgium

Jan M. Winter works full time as an investigative psychologist in a team of Behavioral Investigative Advisors with the Dutch National Police. He advises predominantly on stalking, violent and sexual offending. He received his MSc in clinical psychology from the Vrije Universiteit Brussel (VUB, i.e., Free University of Brussels, Belgium). He also holds an MSc in investigative psychology from the University of Liverpool (UK) and a postgraduate diploma in investigative psychology from the Rino Group (The Netherlands). He is a PhD student with the VUB, attempting to dissect the effects of the offender–victim interaction in serious sexual assaults.

Acknowledgments

We thank Carolyn Spence and Marsha Pronin (Taylor & Francis Group), Dilip Das, and Scott Phillips for assisting us in the production of this text. We were delighted that they liked our proposal for the book and we hope they are as pleased with the finished product as we are.

We also thank Rebecca Mugford for assisting with proofreading various chapters, Brittany Blaskovits for doing a great job on formatting the chapters, and Holly Ellingwood for chasing down references.

Finally, we thank our contributors, for putting together important chapters in such a timely manner and for being so responsive to reviews. Your contributions to this book will hopefully allow the field of crime linkage to advance in useful directions.

Introduction
Time to Consolidate and Reflect

1

JESSICA WOODHAMS AND
CRAIG BENNELL

Contents

What Is Crime Linkage? 1
Crime Linkage: An Umbrella Term 2
Academic–Practitioner Collaboration 5
The Structure of the Book 5
References 9

What Is Crime Linkage?

Crime linkage is a police practice whereby crimes that may be the work of the same offender(s) are identified from an analysis of crime scene behaviors. The analysis attempts to uncover similarities across the potential series that are also relatively distinct from behavior exhibited in other crimes (of the same type). It, therefore, rests on two underlying principles: the principles of behavioral consistency (Canter, 1995) and behavioral distinctiveness (also referred to as differentiation and interindividual variation; Bennell & Canter, 2002). The first principle requires offenders to show some consistency in the way they commit their offenses. The second requires that the crimes of one offender are relatively distinctive from the crimes of another offender such that it is possible to distinguish a crime series from crimes being committed by other offenders (Woodhams & Grant, 2006).

Crime linkage is rooted in the discipline of psychology where (non-criminal) behavioral consistency and distinctiveness have been the subject of much study for many decades. Crime linkage has been the subject of empirical research since the 1970s (e.g., Green, Booth, & Biderman, 1976); however, it is only since the year 2000 that research on this practice has really taken off. Throughout these last 14 years, crime linkage research has evolved from studying the principles of crime linkage under the umbrella of offender profiling research, to researching it as a practice in its own right.

This emergence of crime linkage as a topic of importance and the subsequent critical mass of literature on the topic prompted the writing of this book. Both editors have been working in the field since around 2000 and have witnessed the interest in this topic grow. We felt that research on the topic had reached a critical point whereby it was time to consolidate what we had learnt into one volume, take stock of where we are, and identify issues that require further development and research. Our decision to develop this book coincided with two significant events. The first was a special issue of the *Journal of Investigative Psychology and Offender Profiling* on behavioral linking that we coedited, for which we received a considerable number of papers (too many for the one issue we had been allocated). The second event was a successful application to the Leverhulme Trust to set up a network for academic–practitioner collaboration (C-LINK, Crime Linkage International NetworK) that would allow these groups to work together on developing crime linkage as an applied field of research.

Crime Linkage: An Umbrella Term

Although the term *crime linkage* has been adopted for the title of this book, we recognize that this is an umbrella term capturing different practices and nomenclature. The literature on crime linkage has not always recognized this and hence this is a topic raised in several chapters of the book. It is also apparent throughout the chapters where authors note variations in practice and the terms used to describe those variations.

In terms of nomenclature, the academic and practitioner literature regularly use terms such as *comparative case analysis*, *linkage analysis*, *case linkage*, *behavioral linking*, and *behavioral analysis*, to describe the process of linking crimes through behaviour, to name just a few (see Chapter 8). However, in some jurisdictions, variations in the terms used reflect real differences in the actual task facing the practitioner. For example, for some, *crime linkage* or *case linkage* is reserved for those situations where a practitioner is presented with a predefined set of crimes and their opinion is sought as to whether the set represents a linked series. In contrast, some use *comparative case analysis* to refer to situations where a practitioner is notified by an investigating officer of a query offense (or offenses) that they suspect may be part of a series, with the accompanying request that the practitioner look for any similar offenses. The crime linkage practitioner, having completing his or her analysis, then provides the investigating officer with information of cases that share similar behaviors to the index offense (or offenses) where any are found. A further variation in practice is situations where a crime linkage practitioner proactively interrogates a police database for offenses that share marked similarities, which are then fed back to the investigating officer(s).

This variation in scenarios in which a practitioner uses information about behavioral similarity and distinctiveness to advise police investigations has not been given explicit attention by researchers. Instead, research papers use the full range of terms interchangeably. The fact that these nuances are not recognized in the research literature is likely due to two reasons. First, regardless of the linking task facing the practitioner, the underlying assumptions arguably remain the same (and as described above). Since much of the research conducted to date has been concerned with evaluating the validity of the assumptions underlying crime linkage, differences in the linking scenario have not been a pressing concern for researchers. Second, practitioners themselves have rarely articulated the way in which they conduct the linking task (see Hazelwood & Warren, 2004; Labuschagne, 2006; Woodhams, Bull, & Hollin, 2007; Chapter 8, as exceptions), nor have they drawn explicit attention to the variations that can exist.

While we recognize that there are different ways in which the linking task is conducted both within and between countries, for the sake of simplicity we have included all practices under the umbrella term of "crime linkage" for the title of the book. However, what variations in practice mean for applying research findings to real-world police investigations is a topic that is returned to later in the book.

The international nature of crime linkage no doubt also contributes to the range of nomenclature used. Crime linkage is practiced in many different countries, including those in Europe and North America, Australia and New Zealand, and Japan and South Africa. Not only do the terms used to describe the crime linkage process vary by country, but there is also variation between countries in terms of practice. For example, in some countries, specialist units exist that conduct crime linkage on the most serious of crimes (e.g., homicide and sexual offenses). Police forces in some of these countries have invested in large-scale databases that can be used by the linkage practitioner in their analyses (e.g., the Violent Crime Linkage Analysis System, ViCLAS). In other countries, such resources are simply not available. Even within countries, there are differences in how crime linkage is practiced, often reflecting the formalization of crime linkage depending on whether a crime is considered "serious" or not. In the United Kingdom, for instance, many crime analysts working in police forces on a local level identify crime series, often of volume crime, but do not use large-scale databases to support their work.

We are pleased that we were able to reflect the international nature of crime linkage research and practice in the authors who contributed to this volume. Having said this, much of the research on crime linkage is limited to studies from Europe and North America. As editors, while we tried to seek as wide a contributor base as possible, it is apparent from the author biographies that Europe and North America are still overrepresented in this book. In recognition of the variation in nomenclature and methods used around the world, we did not require chapter authors to adopt any particular term in their writing. Due to their different locations around the world, the methods they use for crime linkage will vary and chapter authors were simply asked to provide sufficient descriptions of their method within their chapters.

Despite these variations in nomenclature and methods, there are some basic steps to crime linkage that are outlined here to describe to readers who are new to the field what crime linkage typically involves (Woodhams et al., 2007):

1. The practitioner must collate all relevant information about the case(s) of interest. The case (or cases) may have been brought to the attention of the practitioner by an investigating officer or a bordering force, or they may have proactively identified a potential series. The nature of the material that is collated will vary depending on the crime type under consideration, but could include victim/witness accounts, closed-circuit television footage, autopsy reports, and forensic examination reports.
2. Once all the information is collated, the practitioner needs to spend sufficient time familiarizing himself or herself with the details of the case(s).
3. Having done so, the next step is to identify the salient behaviors within the case(s) of interest. This may involve selecting behaviors that the practitioner has noted to be common across crimes or it may involve coding all offenses against a standardized checklist of behaviors. We advocate the latter approach.
4. At this point, the practitioner may search for other crimes that appear similar (with respect to behaviors) to the case(s) of interest, and this search may be conducted with the support of a large-scale database. However, if the practitioner has been presented with a potential series to consider in isolation, this step may not take place.
5. The practitioner must next map the similarities between the cases under analysis. This could involve drawing a chart and visually indicating where there are similarities and differences across the crimes being examined, or it could involve statistically calculating a measure of how similar each pair of crimes in the set is to one another.
6. Where differences in behavior exist between crimes in the set, the practitioner needs to consider how they might be explained. For example, the practitioner would want to consider whether the differences indicate that some of the crimes in the set are the work of a different offender or whether the differences are due to situational influence, learning, maturation, and so on.
7. Finally, the practitioner must assess behaviors that appear across two or more crimes in the potential series for their distinctiveness.

> This means that for each behavior that is shared by two or more crimes, the practitioner must consider how rare or common that behavior is in general within the crime type under consideration (e.g., how common it is for an offender to kiss a victim during stranger rapes in general). Decision making at this stage might be supported by base rates calculated from a large-scale police database (e.g., the percentage of stranger rapes in the database where kissing of the victim by the offender occurs). Some practitioners may also calculate the percentage of stranger rapes in a database, which share the same *combination* of behaviors.

Academic–Practitioner Collaboration

Since 2000, there have been some notable court cases in which crime linkage analysis has featured. There have also been important developments in practice over this time period, some of which have been discussed in the academic literature in articles authored by practitioners. More recently, debates have been taking place in the literature about how crime linkage is conducted. Given all of these things, it seemed to us both that the time was ripe to work more closely with our practitioner colleagues and take stock of where we are in terms of crime linkage practice. By having practitioners contribute their thoughts to this volume, they have been able to consider the state of crime linkage research and also suggest where this research is lacking (from an application perspective). Our hope is that this will give impetus to new strands of research activity. It was very important to us both that our practitioner colleagues had a voice within this book and we are very pleased that this was realized. This book therefore represents a collaborative effort between us and all of our chapter authors to bring to the reader a comprehensive account of where the research and practice of crime linkage is at present, as well as our thoughts and suggestions on where we need to go next as researchers and practitioners working within this field.

The Structure of the Book

The book is arranged around four core themes. The first three chapters consider theoretical explanations for how, when, and why we may (or may not) see similarity in a person's crime scene behavior. In Chapter 2, Woodhams and Bennell outline models and research findings from the fields of personality and social psychology that relate to behavioral consistency and distinctiveness, and explain how these models and theories relate to the underlying principles of crime linkage and crime linkage research to date. They argue that there are striking differences in the data sources and methods adopted in the fields of personality and social psychology, and crime linkage research. However, despite these differences, they suggest that new insights into the study of behavioral consistency and distinctiveness, and new avenues for future research, can be identified by giving explicit attention to how such research has evolved in personality and social psychology.

Following on from this are two chapters that focus specifically on consistency and distinctiveness in sexual offending. In Chapter 3, Gee and Belofastov explain the various ways in which sexual fantasy can influence sexual offending behavior. They consider how sexual fantasies can help account for both stability and instability in crime scene behavior within a series (e.g., in terms of cross-over in victim type, and change in *modus operandi*) and why change might be observed at particular points in a series. Chapter 4, by Woodhams and Komarzynska, also focuses on sexual offending, but describes how mental illness and disorder might affect behavioral consistency and distinctiveness. The limited research on how mental illness/disorder can manifest in crime scene behavior is described, and the issues of how schizophrenia and personality disorder may affect consistency in offending behavior are explored. Within this chapter, the first two studies of behavioral (in)consistency and distinctiveness with mentally disordered sex offenders are presented.

The next three chapters provide an overview of crime linkage research conducted to date. In Chapter 5, Snook, Luther, and MacDonald review crime linkage research that has studied the effectiveness of using inter-crime distance to make linking decisions across a broad range of offense types. They provide a theoretical account for why offenders might be consistent in their spatial decision making. They also provide a compelling critique of the research studies to date and suggest important avenues for future research. In Chapter 6, Tonkin summarizes the existing research on behavioral consistency and distinctiveness in the criminal domain and describes the main approaches that have been used by researchers to examine the assumptions underlying crime linkage. He highlights a number of key limitations of the research conducted to date and reflects on the directions in which the research now needs to move. Chapter 7 by Salfati focuses on serial homicide and makes a timely assessment of whether findings generated in one country can be applied to another. Bearing in mind the dominance of UK and US samples in much of the crime linkage research, the question of generalizability is an important one. Salfati provides an overview of the research conducted in the United States and compares and contrasts this with research on (serial) homicide from non-US countries in terms of general behavioral trends and, more specifically, in terms of behavioral consistency.

As noted above, it was important to us that the book also allows readers to reflect on where we are in the field of crime linkage from a practitioner perspective. Chapters 8 through 11 represent the third core theme of the book, which examines the use of crime linkage in practice. This section starts with Chapter 8 by Rainbow in which he questions the applicability of crime linkage research to date to the work engaged in by at least some practitioners. Having outlined the different scenarios in which a practitioner might assess similarity in behavior between two or more crimes, he provides an account of crime linkage practice in the United Kingdom and the context in which it occurs. He illustrates this with an extract from a genuine crime linkage report. Having outlined how crime linkage analysis is practiced in the United Kingdom, he proposes likelihood ratios as a preferred method to adopt in crime linkage analysis in the future and sets out a research agenda that would be more responsive to practitioner needs.

This chapter is followed by Chapter 9, also authored by a renowned practitioner in the field of crime linkage. Labuschagne provides an account of how crime linkage analysis is used in Republic of South Africa, both as an investigative support tool and as evidence in South African courts. Labuschagne accompanies his discussion with illustrative examples. He describes various legal principles, which might impact the use of linkage analysis in court with reference to existing legal cases. Following this, he provides some words of caution about using crime linkage analysis in legal proceedings. He concludes his chapter by presenting two crime linkage analysis case studies from Republic of South Africa.

The use of crime linkage analysis in legal proceedings is given further attention in Chapter 10 where Pakkanen, Santtila, and Bosco provide a review of court decisions where crime linkage analysis was entered as evidence. They outline the requirements for crime linkage analysis testimony, were it to be given in a jurisdiction where the *Daubert* criteria apply. For the remainder of the chapter, they adopt the *Daubert* criteria as their standard of choice, against which they evaluate past and current approaches to crime linkage. They present the argument that crime linkage practitioners should strive to make the practice of crime linkage more scientific and use the *Daubert* criteria as a guide for their discussion around this issue. In recognition of the need for researcher–practitioner collaboration in reaching this standard, they outline key areas for future research collaboration.

The growing volume of research on the principles underpinning crime linkage (as outlined in Chapters 4, 6, and 7) stands in stark contrast to the research conducted on human decision making during crime linkage tasks. In Chapter 11, Mugford and Martineau detail the research on this topic, noting its often limited ecological validity. Having identified the strengths and limitations of existing research, they outline a number of avenues for researchers to pursue in the future. In doing so, they also give consideration to how practitioners might be supported in their work with the findings of empirical research (e.g., through the development of structured professional judgment tools).

While each chapter author has made efforts to suggest where research or practice needs to move next, there are some obvious areas of innovation to which we wanted to dedicate chapters. The remaining three chapters represent the fourth core theme of the book: new directions for research and practice. In Chapter 12, Tonkin outlines a new strand of research investigating the feasibility of linking across crime types. Crime linkage studies typically limit themselves to just one type of crime (e.g., linking within rapes or within robberies), however, more recently, Tonkin and colleagues have begun to investigate whether it is possible to link across types (e.g., linking a rape to a robbery), thereby extending the potential suspect pool.

At the start of the book (Chapter 2), the reader is introduced to theories from personality and social psychology, which include arguments that the situation has an important role to play in influencing behavior. Winter picks up on this argument in Chapter 13, where he outlines how practitioners currently take account of situational influence in their decision making about whether a given set of crimes are linked or not. Indeed, this is mentioned explicitly in chapters by our practitioner authors and publications by other authors (e.g., Hazelwood & Warren, 2004). Despite this recognition that situational influences are important to consider, attempts to incorporate situational factors in crime linkage research have been minimal. As Winter explains, this no doubt is at least partially explained by the limited availability of statistical methods that can be used to study this. However, following recent statistical developments, we are now at a point where we can start to study the role of the situation in influencing the degree to which serial offenders display behavioral consistency/distinctiveness. Winter describes the handful of studies that have adopted these methods (including his own research) and outlines the findings to date.

The final chapter within this section, Chapter 14, by Bennell, Goodwill, and Chinneck, reviews the range of statistical methods used in research of the crime linkage principles, giving particular attention to recent innovations in this area. The variation that can exist in the practice of crime linkage, as outlined in earlier chapters, is given explicit attention in this chapter as the authors describe how different statistical techniques might lend themselves to the study of different linking scenarios/problems. The chapter concludes by providing a constructive critique of the research designs used to date and outlining some key issues that researchers in this area might want to consider when conducting future studies to assess the feasibility of crime linkage analysis.

The book closes with a concluding chapter, Chapter 15, written by Bennell and Woodhams. They take stock of the considerable progress made over the last decade in this field while also noting how far, and where, we still have to go. In editing this book, it was extremely important to us that differences in opinion were not suppressed or hidden and that opportunity be given for different viewpoints to be heard. The concluding chapter notes that while we have reached consensus in some areas of crime linkage research (e.g., of the nature of the assumptions), there are other areas where little consensus exists (e.g., in agreeing operational standards and research methods). It is unclear at this point if individuals working within this field will reach agreement on the range of issues discussed in this chapter, or if it is even desirable that agreement be reached in all cases. However, in the spirit of this book, we feel strongly that progress will only be made by continuing to critically reflect on the research being conducted through active collaborations with one another.

References

Bennell, C., & Canter, D. V. (2002). Linking commercial burglaries by *modus operandi*: Tests using regression and ROC analysis. *Science & Justice, 42*, 153–164.

Canter, D. (1995). Psychology of offender profiling. In R. Bull & D. Carson (Eds.), *Handbook of psychology in legal contexts* (pp. 343–355). Chichester, England: Wiley.

Green, E. J., Booth, C. E., & Biderman, M. D. (1976). Cluster analysis of burglary M/Os. *Journal of Police Science and Administration, 4*, 382–388.

Hazelwood, R. R., & Warren, J. I. (2004). Linkage analysis: Modus operandi, ritual, and signature in serial sexual crime. *Aggression and Violent Behavior, 9*, 307–318.

Labuschagne, G. N. (2006). The use of linkage analysis as evidence in the conviction of the Newcastle serial murderer, South Africa. *Journal of Investigative Psychology and Offender Profiling, 3*, 183–191.

Woodhams, J., Bull, R., & Hollin, C. R. (2007). Case linkage: Identifying crimes committed by the same offender. In R. N. Kocsis (Ed.), *Criminal profiling: International theory, research, and practice* (pp. 117–133). Totowa, NJ: Humana Press.

Woodhams, J., & Grant, T. (2006). Developing a categorization system for rapists' speech. *Psychology, Crime & Law, 22*, 245–260.

Consistency and Distinctiveness of Criminal Behavior

2

JESSICA WOODHAMS AND
CRAIG BENNELL

Contents

Introduction	11
Behavioral Consistency and Personality and Social Psychology	12
Mischel and Shoda's (1995) CAPS	13
Similarities and Differences between Personality Psychology and Investigative Psychology	15
Concepts	16
Data	16
Methodology	17
Applying the CAPS to Criminal Events	20
Situational Similarity	20
Type of Behavior	22
Expertise	23
Time Elapsed	24
Age of the Individual	24
Psychopathology	25
Conclusion	26
References	28

Introduction

As was outlined in Chapter 1, crime linkage rests on the assumptions of consistency (Canter, 1995) and distinctiveness in criminal behavior (Woodhams, Hollin, & Bull, 2007). As is described in Chapter 6, much of the research in the field of crime linkage has been concerned with testing the validity of these two principles. Generally speaking, this research supports the view that serial offenders display enough behavioral consistency and distinctiveness across their crimes to allow for at least a moderate degree of linkage accuracy, though the extent to which this is true varies across the conditions that have been tested (e.g., linkage accuracy tends to vary as a function of the behaviors under examination; Bennell, Mugford, Ellingwood, & Woodhams, 2014).

There are several reasons why we might see variation in crime linkage accuracy across studies, crime types, individual criminals, and with in the same individual at different time points. This chapter describes models and research findings from personality and social psychology concerned with non criminal behavior to explain why and when we might see variation in crime linkage effectiveness. It also gives explicit consideration to the similarities and differences between crime linkage research and personality and social psychology research in terms of the concepts we use, our data, and the methods we employ.

Behavioral Consistency and Personality and Social Psychology

The study of behavioral consistency has a long history in the fields of personality and social psychology. For some time, personality psychologists and social psychologists struggled to reconcile beliefs that personality should result in the stability of an individual's behavior over time and across situations with research findings that suggested the opposite (Shoda & Smith, 2004). The dominant theories at the time that would have predicted such stability were the trait theories of personality psychology and psychodynamic–psychoanalytic models (Mischel, 2009). The personality psychologist's method for studying consistency often included measuring trait indicators (e.g., behaviors assumed to represent the underlying trait of conscientiousness, or sociability, or aggressiveness), often through questionnaires or behavioral observations, and rank ordering people within a sample depending upon their scores. Behaviors of interest were measured over multiple time intervals, or across different situations, with the expectation that the participants' positions in the ranking would remain the same. However, this expectation was not borne out in the results of studies. Personality psychologists, on the one hand, attempted to reconcile the findings by critically considering their methods of study to try and design out what was assumed to be "error" (the influence of the situation; e.g., Epstein, 1979, 1980). Social psychologists, on the other hand, saw the results as proof of the greater power of the situation in influencing behavior (Mischel, 1973, 2009). This mismatch between theory and empirical findings was referred to as the personality paradox (Barenbaum & Winter, 2008; Mischel & Peake, 1983).

Rather than viewing *either* the person *or* the situation as influential in the production of behavior, it was argued by some (e.g., Mischel, 1973) that psychologists needed to turn their attention to the interaction of the person and the situation in producing behavior. The recognition that the situation and the person interact with one another to produce behavior is referred to as interactionism in personality psychology (Griffo & Colvin, 2009). It was formalized in Mischel and Shoda's (1995) Cognitive–Affective Personality System (CAPS); however, as Griffo and Colvin (2009) and Mischel (2009) have recently noted, concepts of interactionism predated even the personality paradox of the 1970s.

Mischel and Shoda's (1995) CAPS

> If we include the situation as it is perceived by the person, and analyze behavior in this situational context, the consistencies that characterize the person, rather than disappearing as had been assumed, would be seen. (Mischel, 2009, p. 284)

The model of personality most frequently cited in the literature on crime linkage is Mischel and Shoda's (1995) CAPS (see Figure 2.1). The favor shown to the CAPS in crime linkage literature likely originates from the ability of this model to accommodate both behavioral consistency and distinctiveness

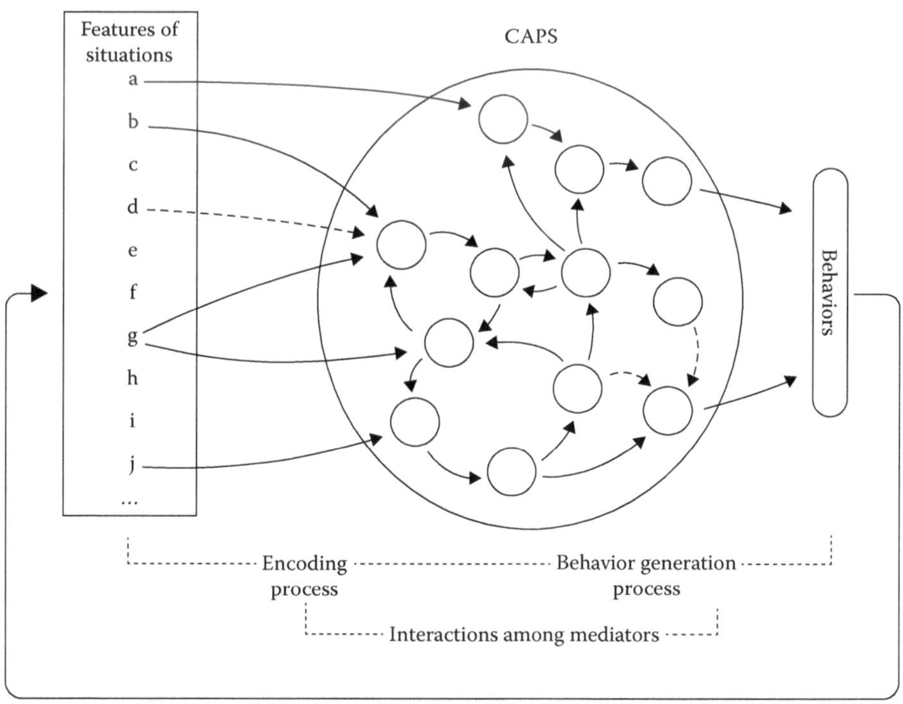

Figure 2.1 The cognitive-affective personality system. (From Mischel, W. and Shoda, Y., *Psychological Review,* 102, 246–268, 1995. American Psychological Association. Reprinted with permission.)

(the two key assumptions of crime linkage). In addition, it provides useful predictions as to when behavioral consistency and distinctiveness is most likely to be observed, which can then be subjected to empirical investigation to determine their applicability to criminal behavior and their relevance to the crime linkage practitioner.

This model proposes that the situations we all encounter in our daily life contain features that are psychologically salient to the individual and that these features trigger internal reactions (cognitive and affective) within the person. What reactions are triggered in a given person's CAPS depends on their learning history, their expectations, and how they interpret the situational cues. The personality system is proposed to consist of mental representations, or cognitive–affective units, that are activated by situational features and through whose activation behavior it is produced (Mischel & Shoda, 1995). Activation can be triggered by external events as well as internal events (such as fantasizing and planning) (Mischel, 1999; how these two activities are implicated in criminal behavior is considered in Chapters 3 and 4).

The types of units or mental representations included within CAPS are (1) constructs for the self (e.g., I am God's gift or I am worthless), people (e.g., other people cannot be trusted), and situations; (2) expectancies and beliefs (about the social world, behavioral outcomes, and self-efficacy); (3) affects (including affective responses and physiological reactions); (4) goals and values; and (5) competencies and self-regulatory plans. It is thought that these units do not exist in isolation to produce behavior, but interact with one another and are influenced by one another through a stable network of interconnections—as Mischel and Shoda (1995) state, "Within any individual a rich system of relationships among the cognitive and affective units guides and constrains further activation of other units throughout the network, ultimately activating plans, strategies and potential behaviors in the behavior generation process" (p. 254). The exact structure of these interconnections is proposed to result from the individual's accumulated learning experiences, and therefore, the structure of the network is unique to each individual.

The pattern of associations between the mental representations is believed to determine how a person interprets and responds to social information. These associations between situational triggers and subsequent behavior are expressed within the CAPS as *if (situation) … then (behavior)* contingencies; for example, *if (someone insults me) … then (I withdraw)*. Because the patterns of activation that produce behavior in a given situation are based on a person's accumulated biology and learning history, the system not only allows for interindividual differences in *if … then* situation contingencies, but also allows for change within the structure of the system as new experiences (and therefore functionally different situations) are encountered. A person's CAPS can therefore evolve with time.

The model predicts consistency in behavior when a person encounters psychologically similar situations. Similar situations will contain similar psychological triggers, which will produce a similar pattern of activation within the person's CAPS, and therefore the same resulting behavior (Mischel, 2009). Interindividual variation in behavioral responses to the same situation (or triggers) is also accommodated within the model: such variation would be a result of differences in how the same situation is processed and understood as a result of different people's psycho social, biological, and/or learning histories (Mischel, 2009), which would impact the availability of cognitions and affects for activation and the patterns and strengths of associations between them (Zayas, Shoda, & Ayduk, 2002).

The model also predicts interindividual differences in behavioral consistency itself, which result from individual differences in characteristics such as attributional biases (selectively attending to particular cues or processing social information in a biased manner, such as interpreting hostility from ambiguous cues), discriminative faculty (the ability to make fine-grained distinctions between situations), and response tendencies (Mischel, 2009; van Mechelen, 2009; Walters, 2000). For example, people with broad response tendencies are not sensitive to situational differences and therefore may behave consistently across functionally different situations (Mischel, 2009).

The CAPS is further differentiated into a "hot" emotional system and a "cool" cognitive system. According to Mischel (2009), "The hot emotional system is specialized for quick emotional processing and responding based on unconditional or conditional trigger features.... In contrast, the cool cognitive system is specialized for complex spatiotemporal and episodic representation and thought" (p. 288). These two systems closely interact with one another and their balance can be upset in favor of the hot system in times of situational stress, thereby undermining self-control and planning. Their relative balance is also dependent on the developmental stage of the cool system, which is thought to become more established as one matures. In terms of what this means for behavioral consistency, behaviors that are more impulsive and which are less cognitively mediated (automatic) are likely to show greater consistency over time and across situations (Furr & Funder, 2004). Individual differences in self-regulatory ability (i.e., impulse control) would also be predicted to result in interindividual differences with respect to behavioral consistency across situations.

Similarities and Differences between Personality Psychology and Investigative Psychology

As explained above, the CAPS has been the favored model for crime linkage researchers because it lends itself to predictions about the conditions under which behavioral consistency and distinctiveness will be observed in *criminal* behavior (Woodhams, Hollin, et al., 2007; Woodhams, Hollin, & Bull, 2008).

Before outlining what the model might mean for crime linkage practice and research, and what crime linkage research has found thus far, it is useful to first reflect on the key similarities and differences between research in personality psychology and what is possible in investigative psychology.

Concepts

Both crime linkage researchers and personality psychologists are concerned with the question of whether there is stability in individual differences in behavior over time. Also, in their research, personality psychologists recognize that people can demonstrate behavioral consistency in a normative way (i.e., someone responds to a situation in a stable manner, but that is typical to the responses of others) or in an atypical way. In crime linkage research, this translates into the question of whether criminals behave consistently in their response to a situation over time (the assumption of consistency) *and* whether this behavioral response is similar (typical) or relatively distinctive (atypical) to the responses of his/her criminal peers (the assumption of distinctiveness). The second assumption is crucial to the success of crime linkage because only if this condition is met can the crimes of one individual be accurately distinguished from the crimes of another person. The questions of interest to researchers in both fields are therefore conceptually similar if phrased differently. However, although personality psychologists study the patterns of response produced by an individual over time and across situations, crime linkage researchers thus far have tended to assess the principles of consistency and distinctiveness at a group level, using only aggregate measures. This has been because crime linkage researchers have been mindful to assess the validity of these assumptions in general, across the population of criminals, because in practice crime linkage methods are often applied to databases or samples of crimes where it is not known who is responsible for which criminal events. The assumptions therefore need to stand for all individuals, to a lesser or greater degree.

Data

Personality psychologists who study behavioral consistency often sample *direct* observations of behavior (e.g., using video cameras or observational ratings) repeatedly as it naturally occurs across different situations (Mischel, 2009) or rely on repeated self-ratings of behavior across different situations over time (Furr, 2009). This is fundamentally different when compared to research conducted within investigative psychology. Crime linkage researchers cannot directly observe criminal behavior. The intention of most offenders is obviously to commit their offenses without observation by third parties, and thus, most crimes do not lend themselves to overt (or even covert) observation. Even if this were possible, it would be unethical to do so without intervening when one considers the type of crimes under study (e.g., burglary, robbery, rape). Instead, crime linkage researchers must rely on secondhand accounts of an offender's behavior at the crime scene, typically using the reports provided by victims in cases involving certain interpersonal crimes (e.g., rape), or thirdhand police reports for crimes committed in the absence of a witness (e.g., a burglary) or where the victim/witness is deceased (e.g., a homicide). Secondary accounts are likely to be imperfect records of how an offender behaved for a number of reasons including the fact that victims may have a poor memory of the event (e.g., in the case of drug-assisted sexual assault) or they may distort their account by suppressing or exaggerating details (Alison, Snook, & Stein, 2001). Even if the victim's memory is complete and they are able to provide a coherent and accurate account of the event, errors or omissions can occur when police interview the victim or take his/her statement (Woodhams, Bull, & Hollin, 2007). Accounts of offender behavior, which are derived from reports of crime scene officers, can also be highly problematic, given the range of inferences that must be drawn from a crime scene when reconstructing what actually occurred.

Methodology

The situations studied in personality psychology can be contrived as in an experimental laboratory setting (e.g., requiring two participants of the opposite sex to sit together on a sofa for a predetermined amount of time during which they are observed; Furr & Funder, 2004). Alternatively, the situations studied by personality psychologists can be naturally occurring, but intentionally selected for observation because they differ in a psychologically meaningful manner, such as when Shoda, Mischel, and Wright (1993) rated situations for the types of competencies they demanded of the children who were being observed.

These types of studies allow personality psychologists to investigate the stability in the way people respond (e.g., being aggressive) over time in similar situations (i.e., on repeated occasions of being teased) and whether the same response is exhibited in response to different situations (i.e., when being teased by a peer compared to when being warned by an adult). These methods of study also allow personality psychologists to determine on average how a person compares to others in terms of their expression of a behavioral response (e.g., overall, are they more or less aggressive than their peers), as well as providing an understanding of the degree to which an individual varies in his/her expression of a behavior across different situations. Personality psychologists can also use these methods to collect data, which allow them to determine whether a given person deviates from the norm (with respect to their behavior) in a stable manner across different situations.

The situation in the field of crime linkage research is quite different. Crime linkage researchers sample crimes from series that have come to the attention of the police and that have been identified as a series on the basis of a conviction (therefore the offender's identity is known) or through DNA scene-to-scene hits (where the identity of the offender may or may not be known). Because the criminals represented in crime linkage datasets have instigated these criminal events themselves, it is they who have dictated the situations available for study. This means it is not possible to control the psychological features present in the criminal events in the sample or indeed, to make sure that each criminal has been exposed to situations of the same valence, demand characteristics, and so on. On the one hand, this likely introduces considerable error into our measurements. On the other hand, according to the CAPS, people select and create situations that suit their personality system (Mischel & Shoda, 1995; Sherman, Nave, & Funder, 2010), which may increase the likelihood of criminals encountering similar situations over time. If this is true, within the datasets of criminal events used for crime linkage research, it is possible that each series represents situations of at least some psychological similarity.

Beyond these differences between the fields of personality and investigative psychology, there is also another methodological issue that is important to discuss. As explained above, personality psychologists often measure behavioral consistency in terms of how someone responds to situations in reference to the rest of the cohort (rank-order consistency). For example, they might examine whether a person is consistently more aggressive than his/her peers across a series of situations. In contrast, due to practical constraints and the need to determine whether particular crimes have been committed by specific offenders, crime linkage researchers assess what personality psychologists would term *absolute behavioral consistency*, that is, whether the same behavior, or set of behaviors, is displayed across time and situations (Sherman et al., 2010). Having obtained a sample of crime series, each crime in the dataset is coded against a behavioral checklist consisting of behaviors that are known to occur in events making up the crime type (e.g., the offender displayed a knife, the offender complemented the victim). If a behavior was displayed by the offender in the crime in question it is scored 1, whereas if the behavior did not occur, or this is not known, it is scored as 0. This binary coding forms the basis for subsequent statistical analysis, which quantifies the degree of behavioral similarity between two criminal events. With regard to absolute behavioral consistency, personality psychologists have concluded that "this type of consistency is not a fruitful target for research because there is scant evidence that absolute consistency exists" (Sherman et al., 2010, p. 332). As will be outlined in Chapter 6, contrary to this assertion, evidence for absolute consistency has been found in the field of crime linkage, although this evidence varies across studies (Bennell, Mugford, et al., 2014).

Having coded the crimes in each series against the behavioral checklists, crime linkage researchers tend to assess the assumptions of behavioral consistency and distinctiveness using one of two methodologies (Bennell, Woodhams, & Mugford, 2014). The first was published by Bennell and Canter (2002) and involves calculating behavioral similarity scores for pairs of crimes that have either been committed by the same (serial) offender (linked pairs) or different offenders (unlinked pairs). Most often Jaccard's coefficient, which ranges from 0 (no similarity) to 1 (perfect similarity), has been used to quantify behavioral similarity. A statistical procedure, such as logistic regression analysis, is then used to determine the degree to which these similarity scores discriminate between the two types of crime pairs. The accuracy with which this can be achieved is quantified using a measure known as the area under the curve (AUC), derived from receiver operating characteristic analysis, which usually varies from 0.50 (chance accuracy) to 1.00 (perfect accuracy). An alternative approach is to use statistical clustering techniques (e.g., multidimensional scaling) to group crime scene behaviors into psychological themes (or dimensions; Santtila, Junkkila, & Sandnabba, 2005). Scores on these themes act as independent variables, which are used to make predictions as to which series a crime belongs to, or which other crimes in the dataset score similarly enough to belong to the same series as the crime in question. The accuracy of these decisions is then calculated by comparing predictions to series membership in reality.

Bennell's method of creating linked and unlinked crime pairs for comparison has some similarities to what Furr (2008) refers to as sample-level analysis, whereby people's behavioral profiles that should be complementary (e.g., the profile of a target and his/her informant) are compared to two randomly paired profiles, which act as a baseline for comparison. As Furr says, "the average similarity between 'true' pairs is then contrasted with the average similarity between random pairs" (p. 1273). The latter, theme-based approach, has some similarities with trait research in personality psychology (Barenbaum & Winter, 2008) where there is thought to be a common set of traits on which a person's position would be unique in a cumulative sense (i.e., the pattern of their positions across the traits would be unique to them). For crime linkage, the themes or dimensions that are derived to represent criminal behavior would be expected to apply to all criminals and to capture the range of behavior in each criminal event. If such dimensions are to have practical utility, each criminal's position (in a cumulative sense) across the dimensions would need to stay stable over time and would also need to be unique to allow for differentiation from his/her peers.

Another area where there are differences between personality psychology and crime linkage is in consideration of motive. Personality psychologists give explicit recognition to the role of motive in determining behavior in that behavior is viewed as goal-oriented (Barenbaum & Winter, 2008).

In contrast, the crime linkage literature has avoided incorporating motive into its analyses, preferring to focus on behaviors solely. In personality psychology, the same motive can be served by different behaviors, and one action can have the potential to fulfil different motives. This difficulty of inferring the "correct" motive from a behavior, which is unable to be observed directly, is probably why motive has not been considered in crime linkage research.

In summary, comparisons of concepts, data, and methods used in personality psychology and crime linkage research reveal both similarities and differences. The most striking difference is in the lack of control crime linkage researchers have over the data available to them for study and the amount of "noise" this introduces into measures of behavioral similarity across crimes.

Applying the CAPS to Criminal Events

Returning to the CAPS proposed by Mischel and Shoda (1995), and what it might mean for crime linkage practice and research, this model predicts several conditions under which we might expect to observe greater consistency (and distinctiveness) in criminal behavior.

Situational Similarity

The features of a situation that make it psychologically salient are those which activate thoughts or feelings in the CAPS (Shoda & Mischel, 2000). As noted above, the features that have been studied and manipulated in personality psychology include valence (negative and face-threatening vs. positive and face-saving; Shoda et al., 1993), task demands (social, cognitive, self-regulatory, physical, and motor control demands; Shoda et al., 1993), task type (competitive vs. cooperative; Furr & Funder, 2004), and type of interaction partner (e.g., extroverted vs. introverted, or peer vs. adult; Furr & Funder, 2004; Shoda et al., 1993). Because personality psychologists can exercise control over the types of situations participants encounter, they have been able to assess whether situational similarity results in greater behavioral consistency. Greater behavioral consistency has been found in situations that are psychologically similar to each other (as determined using the features above, when they are assessed by self-ratings or rated by independent judges; Funder & Colvin, 1991; Furr & Funder, 2004; Sherman et al., 2010; Shoda et al., 1993).

Most of the findings that have emerged from personality psychology come from studies that personality psychologists themselves have labeled as "contrived" experimental settings (Sherman et al., 2010). Whether the findings will generalize to criminal events is therefore questionable, but certainly worthy of study. As Alison, Bennell, Mokros, and Ormerod (2002) explained, the situations under study in investigative psychology typically "involve intense, relatively short-lived, and potentially traumatic interactions that are generally characterized by the diametrically opposed interests of the offender and victim" (p. 123). Criminal events are, therefore, quite different than the types of situations studied by personality psychologists (e.g., cooperative tasks, being teased, being praised, sitting with a member of the opposite sex).

Defining situational similarity in the investigative context might appear challenging compared to the personality context. However, initial attempts at this (Woodhams et al., 2008) suggest that this task should be possible. On the face of things, because serial offending typically represents multiple crimes against *different* victims, we would assume that each crime in a series represents a different situation to the offender that could come with different task demands and be characterized by differing levels of valence. Using the terms of personality psychologists, each crime would also have a different interaction partner therefore introducing further situational dissimilarity. However, there are other features of serial offending which make it feasible that different crimes in a series may be more similar than initially thought. For example, offenders have some choice when it comes to target selection and they can exert some control over this potential for variation thereby increasing situational similarity. A burglar, for instance, may scope out potential properties in advance, assessing them for ease of entry and choosing those that suit his/her skills and experience. Similarly, rapists may select victims who are inebriated to minimize resistant behaviors or victims who are introverted. An offender's own initial actions during a crime can enhance similarity, such as when a blitz rapist uses immediate, disabling force thereby incapacitating the victim. Crimes in a series are also similar in terms of task type—whether we are referring to serial rape, murder, robbery, or burglary, all represent competitive tasks because the goal of the offender is opposed to the goal of the victim. Finally, although in interpersonal crimes the offender is typically interacting with a different victim for each crime in the series, there is only a finite range of behaviors a victim can engage in and some reactions are more typical than others. This therefore places a limit on the range of task demands an offender could face and subsequently the degree of situational dissimilarity. Although Woodhams, Hollin, Bull, and Cooke (2012) found an impressive range of victim behaviors within their sample of stranger sex offenses, the five most common behaviors in the maintenance stage of the offense were struggling (57%), seeking help verbally (40%), giving the offender an order (e.g., "get off me"; 35%), compliance (24%), and requesting a behavior of the offender (20%). Some situations encountered by violent criminals will therefore be more typical than others (Alison et al., 2002), increasing situational similarity in terms of victim behavior.

However, having outlined reasons for why we might see greater behavioral similarity within a series than you might initially expect, it is important to note that behavior is produced from an interaction between the situation and the person. In terms of rapist behavior, there are anecdotal reports of rapists changing the way they interact with victims within a series for reasons other than victim resistance (Davies, 1992). These include encountering a victim who is perceived to be different to previous victims (in terms of perceived class), which resulted in the offender displaying quite different behavior. Similarly, in attempted homicides and robberies, offender behavior is reported to vary depending on how much the offender values the victim (Fritzon & Ridgway, 2001; Luckenbill, 1981). Even where victim behavior was the same within a series, and thus situational similarity as defined in this manner would be high, inconsistency in offender behavior is still a possibility.

Because of the issues outlined here, and because of the nature of data available to study, it is questionable whether a similar relationship between situational similarity and behavioral consistency found in personality psychology research could be found with data consisting of criminal events. There has been only one study conducted on this topic thus far (Woodhams et al., 2008). Woodhams and her colleagues defined situational similarity in terms of the similarity in victim behavior between crimes within the same series. No evidence for a relationship between situational similarity and behavioral consistency was found. However, several potential reasons for this finding were put forward, including the way the researchers conceptualized situational similarity (i.e., similarity in victim behavior) not representing the way in which it is construed by offenders and that there may be factors other than victim behavior that have a greater impact on perceived situational similarity (e.g., victims' physical appearance, offender mood, and mental state). There are many ways in which we can conceptualize and investigate situational similarity in criminal events, which could lead to higher levels of observed consistency within series.

Type of Behavior

The CAPS predicts that activation of the hot emotional system will result in automatic behaviors that are hypothesized to be exhibited more consistently across situations. Research findings have confirmed this. For example, Furr and Funder (2004) found greater consistency for the automatic behaviors of laughing and gesturing compared to more planned behaviors. Similarly, greater consistency has been found for behaviors that are spontaneous and emitted by the individual rather than elicited from the environment (Funder & Colvin, 1991) and for behaviors under "primary control," which are goal directed and reflect the needs/desires of the individual (Hettema & Hol, 1998).

This line of research suggests that similar behaviors (e.g., those emerging from the hot system and those under primary control) may be exhibited in a more consistent fashion by criminals across their crimes. Indeed, most research in the crime linkage area bears this out. For example, drawing on the research conducted by Funder and Colvin (1991), Bennell and Canter (2002) suggested that behaviors exhibited by serial burglars may vary with respect to the degree of control the offender has in exhibiting the behavior; some residential burglary behaviors appear to be largely determined by the burglar, such as choosing the location of the targeted house, whereas other behaviors appear to be largely situation determined, such as the type of property that the burglar can steal (which depends entirely on what items are available to steal). It is thought that this variation in *degree of control* largely explains commonly reported findings in the crime linkage literature, such as the superior performance of inter-crime distance as a predictor of whether two crimes are linked, compared to similarity measures based on behaviors such as property stolen (see Chapters 5 and 6 for a review of these studies).

Similarly, in crime linkage studies where the behaviors of offenders are classified into domains to reflect their underlying function, *control behaviors*, which reflect actions designed to exert control over victims/witnesses/the environment, are typically exhibited in a more consistent and distinct fashion than other sorts of behaviors. Indeed, several studies have found predictions of series membership based on such behaviors to be more accurate compared to other aspects of offenders' *modus operandi* (Bateman & Salfati, 2007; Grubin, Kelly, & Brunsdon, 2001; Woodhams & Toye, 2007). This may be because the *control domain* incorporates behaviors that are automatic, spontaneous, and/or under the influence of the hot emotional system.

Expertise

According to the CAPS, when a person repeatedly encounters the same type of situation, the same networks of mental representations will be activated each time. It has been proposed that this strengthens activation pathways, which in turn increases the likelihood that the same pathways will be activated again in the future (Greene, 1989). In this way, expertise and familiarity with a particular type of situation can develop, resulting in behavioral consistency (Hettema & van Bakel, 1997). Most criminals are versatile in the types of crime they commit, particularly younger offenders (Klein, 1984; Warr, 1996); however, research has shown that they do develop expertise in offending (e.g., see Nee & Meenaghan, 2006 for the development of expertise in burglary). Because expertise develops over time and with experience, Woodhams, Hollin, et al. (2007) suggested that greater behavioral consistency might be found toward the end of a crime series compared to at the start.

Two studies have investigated whether this is true. More specifically, these studies examined whether pairs of crimes at the start of an offender's series have smaller Jaccard's coefficients (representing less behavioral consistency) than those at the end of a series (Tonkin, Grant, & Bond, 2008; Woodhams

& Labuschagne, 2012). These two studies produced conflicting results, and thus, it is currently unclear whether expertise in criminal offending results in greater across-crime consistency in behavior. With regard to expertise in sexual offending in particular, there are factors that could counteract the stabilizing effect of expertise on behavior. For example, see Chapter 3, which discusses how fantasy can destabilize crime scene behavior (see also Gee & Belofastov, 2007).

Time Elapsed

As was explained above, the CAPS allows for alteration to the associative links between mental representations as new situations are encountered. Therefore, the CAPS would predict that behavioral inconsistency is more likely to occur when measurements of behavior are separated by significant time periods because this affords more time for changes to the CAPS. Personality psychologists have certainly found behavioral consistency to reduce when more time has elapsed between observations (Pervin, 2002). For the crime linkage practitioner, this means that series comprised of offenses that have occurred in close succession should be characterized by greater behavioral consistency (Woodhams, Hollin, et al., 2007). Similarly, within a series, crime pairs that are separated in time by fewer days should, in theory, be more similar.

Crime linkage researchers have put this proposition to the test by calculating the number of days elapsed between crimes from the same series to see if those occurring closer together in time are more similar in behavior (Markson, Woodhams, & Bond, 2010; Tonkin et al., 2008; Woodhams & Labuschagne, 2012; Woodhams et al., 2008). To date, little evidence for such a relationship has emerged. One explanation for this is that police records are unlikely to be a complete and accurate record of a person's offending; therefore, in reality, the crimes representing the series in current datasets would likely be interspersed with other, at present, unattributed crimes. Of course, this would make the calculations of how much time has elapsed between offenses incorrect.

Age of the Individual

It has been shown that a person's CAPS can change over time, but during childhood and adolescence it is hypothesized to change at a faster rate (Mischel, 1999). As reported in the previous subsection, it is believed that changes in the CAPS can result in behavioral inconsistency, and thus, it would follow that the behavior of children and adolescents should be less consistent over time and situations compared to adults (Pervin, 2002). This line of reasoning might suggest the need to exercise caution if conducting crime linkage analysis with juvenile offenders (Woodhams, Hollin, et al., 2007). Conversely, however, the CAPS also suggests that the hot emotional system responsible for automatic (and consistent) behaviors is more dominant in younger people (Mischel, 2009), suggesting that at least for some types of behaviors, consistency may be observed among the young. As an example, research by personality psychologists has shown children to be consistent in their aggressive behavior across similar situations (e.g., Shoda et al., 1993). In the investigative context, recent research with juvenile serial stranger sex offenders found levels of behavioral consistency that are equivalent to those of adult serial rapists (Woodhams, Hollin, & Bull, submitted).

Psychopathology

Various forms of psychopathology can impact behavioral consistency by affecting how people select, attend to, and process situational cues, and by affecting the behavioral responses available to the individual (Eaton, South, & Krueger, 2009; Mischel, 1973; van Mechelen, 2009). For example, serious deficits in discriminative faculty can prevent people from differentiating between situations adequately and result in indiscriminate responses and consistency over functionally different situations (Mischel, 1973). Other individuals can have very limited behavioral repertoires, which can manifest in behavioral consistency across radically different situations (Eaton et al., 2009). Severe hostile attribution bias, for example, can result in the indiscriminate production of aggressive responses (Walters, 2000). See Chapter 4 for a discussion of how personality disorders can affect behavioral consistency and what this might mean for linking the crimes of such offenders.

These kinds of deficits in social information processing have been found in criminal populations (Collie, Vess, & Murdoch, 2007; Farrow, Kelly, & Wilkinson, 2007; McGuire, 2005). Because these deficits can all result in consistent behavior being exhibited across functionally different situations, this suggests that criminals in general may show behavioral consistency in the way they commit their offenses regardless of changes in situational cues (such as differences in victim behavior within a series). As far as we are aware, no research has yet to investigate how the degree of behavioral consistency might be associated with psychological characteristics, such as deficits in social information processing. However, as will be outlined in Chapter 6, some studies of criminal behavioral consistency find quite impressive support for behavioral consistency and distinctiveness, which may in part be due to serial offenders possessing various forms of psychopathology.

Conclusion

This chapter aimed to ground the study of criminal behavioral consistency in a broader theoretical framework, namely, the field of personality psychology, which has a more established history than crime linkage. The commonly referenced CAPS was described to illustrate how situational cues are processed to produce behavior and how this might apply to criminal behavior. This model, and other theory developed by personality psychologists, suggests several conditions under which we might expect to see greater behavioral consistency. As we have both asserted for some time (e.g., Bennell & Canter, 2002; Woodhams, Hollin, et al., 2007), an examination of these conditions is warranted because they may well impact the efficacy of crime linkage practice.

That being said, although theory and research from personality psychology provide a useful means for reflecting on existing crime linkage research and considering future avenues of investigation, there are fundamental differences between how research is conducted by personality psychologists and how research can be conducted by investigative psychologists given the serious constraints within which crime linkage researchers work. Yet, it may be these constraints that lead to the most interesting findings. For example, for practical reasons, crime linkage researchers must examine forms of consistency, which personality psychologists would likely define as *absolute* (vs. *relative*). Although personality psychologists have abandoned their search for absolute consistency (Sherman et al., 2010), crime linkage research is arguably uncovering evidence of absolute consistency in criminal behavior (although not perfect consistency, nor displayed by all individuals). This is intriguing considering the poor quality of data with which we work (Bennell & Canter, 2002) and may suggest that crime linkage research has something to offer the field of personality psychology.

In fact, as we have outlined in this chapter, there are several possible explanations for why some criminals display relatively high levels of behavioral consistency across situations, and a greater understanding of these explanations may provide interesting possibilities for the study of personality. One reason could be because researchers who study crime linkage sample situations that the criminals have themselves created and selected, rather than exposing them to situations selected by the researcher, as in personality psychology research. The CAPS predicts that people will select and create situations that suit their personalities, resulting in self-induced exposure to similar situations (Mischel & Shoda, 1995), something that may not be occurring in mainstream personality research.

The personality psychology literature also reports that individuals with psychopathology, such as social-information-processing deficits, behave more consistently across situations (Eaton et al., 2009; Mischel, 1973; van Mechelen, 2009; Walters, 2000). As we have outlined, these types of deficits have been found in criminal populations and are thought to contribute to their offending behavior. As is explained in more detail in Chapter 4, criminals with some forms of psychopathology (e.g., personality disorder and psychopathy) are likely to come to the attention of crime linkage practitioners more often due to the types of offenses they commit and the frequency with which they commit them. Given that the samples upon which crime linkage researchers base their studies come from this pool of criminals, the offenders we examine in our studies may be predisposed to behaving in a more consistent manner.

Finally, if a person encounters a situation that demands competencies that they are lacking, the individual can experience stress. This stress can then result in the activation of the hot emotional system within CAPS (Shoda et al., 1993). Given this, it may be that the reasonably high levels of behavioral consistency reported in the crime linkage literature (see Bennell, Mugford, et al., 2014) results from the fact that the hot emotional system in offenders (or certain types of offenders) is often activated. This idea leads to interesting possibilities for understanding findings from the crime linkage literature. For example, the type of stress described above is arguably more likely to be experienced by offenders committing interpersonal crimes versus property crimes. Unlike crimes such as burglary, interpersonal crimes are characterized by situations where the offender and victim's goals are diametrically opposed, and thus, we might expect these criminal events to be characterized by more automatic behaviors on the part of the offenders, which should result in greater consistency within such series. This might account for the higher levels of linkage accuracy that are often reported for interpersonal crimes compared to property crimes (see Chapter 6 and Bennell, Mugford, et al., 2014, for more details). This finding may also suggest that there is value in examining how typical participants studied in traditional personality psychology studies behave across situations that are characterized as stressful.

It should also go without saying that research conducted in the field of personality psychology should continue to provide direction to crime linkage researchers. Such research can provide us with ways to better understand our research findings while also providing direction on how we might more effectively carry out our research. For example, the personality psychologists' use of case studies to more fully understand why people display (or do not display) their individual differences in a consistent fashion over time (e.g., Barenbaum & Winter, 2008) may also be a useful way to gain insight into the conditions under which offenders are most likely to display consistency. In addition, given that crime linkage researchers study issues that are so similar to the issues tackled by personality psychologists, we might also learn lessons from debates taking place in that field. Ongoing debates about the appropriateness of applying group-derived factors (traits) to individual cases (Barenbaum & Winter, 2008) are likely relevant to much of the work currently being conducted in the crime linkage field, as are the debates around how to most effectively capture the important elements of person–situation interactions in the search for behavioral consistency (e.g., Sherman et al., 2010).

References

Alison, L. J., Bennell, C., Mokros, A., & Ormerod, D. (2002). The personality paradox in offender profiling: A theoretical review of the processes involved in deriving background characteristics from crime scene actions. *Psychology, Public Policy, and Law, 8*, 115–135.

Alison, L. J., Snook, B., & Stein, K. (2001). Unobtrusive measurement: Using police information for forensic research. *Qualitative Research, 1*, 241–254.

Barenbaum, N. B., & Winter, D. G. (2008). History of modern personality theory and research. In O. P. John, R. W. Robins, & L. A. Pervin (Eds.), *Handbook of personality: Theory and research* (pp. 3–26). New York, NY: The Guilford Press.

Bateman, A., & Salfati, G. (2007). An examination of behavioral consistency using individual behaviors or groups of behaviors in serial homicide. *Behavioral Sciences & the Law, 25*, 527–544.

Bennell, C., & Canter, D. V. (2002). Linking commercial burglaries by modus operandi: Tests using regression and ROC analysis. *Science & Justice, 42*, 1–12.

Bennell, C., Mugford, R., Ellingwood, H., & Woodhams, J. (2014). Linking crimes using behavioural clues: Current levels of linking accuracy and strategies for moving forward. *Journal of Investigative Psychology and Offender Profiling, 11*, 29–56.

Bennell, C., Woodhams, J., & Mugford, R. (2014). Linkage analysis. In G. J. N. Bruinsma & D. L. Weisburd (Eds.), *Encyclopaedia of criminology and criminal justice* (pp. 2947–2953). New York, NY: Springer.

Canter, D. (1995). Psychology of offender profiling. In R. Bull & D. Carson (Eds.), *Handbook of psychology in legal contexts* (pp. 343–355). Chichester, England: Wiley.

Collie, R. M., Vess, M., & Murdoch, S. (2007). Violence-related cognition: Current research. In T. A. Gannon, T. Ward, A. R. Beech, & D. Fisher (Eds.), *Aggressive offenders' cognition: Theory, research and practice* (pp. 179–198). Chichester, England: Wiley.

Davies, A. (1992). Rapists' behaviour: A three-aspect model as a basis for analysis and the identification of serial crime. *Forensic Science International, 55*, 173–194.

Eaton, N. R., South, S. C., & Krueger, R. F. (2009). The cognitive-affective processing system (CAPS) approach to personality and the concept of personality disorder: Integrating clinical and social-cognitive research. *Journal of Research in Personality, 43*, 208–217.

Epstein, S. (1979). The stability of behavior: On predicting most of the people much of the time. *Journal of Personality and Social Psychology, 37*, 1097–1126.

Epstein, S. (1980). The stability of behavior: II. Implications for psychological research. *American Psychologist, 35*, 790–806.

Farrow, K., Kelly, G., & Wilkinson, B. (2007). *Offenders in focus: Risk, responsivity and diversity*. Bristol, England: The Policy Press.

Fritzon, K., & Ridgway, J. (2001). Near-death experience: The role of victim reaction in attempted homicide. *Journal of Interpersonal Violence, 16*, 679–696.
Funder, D. C., & Colvin, C. R. (1991). Explorations in behavioral consistency: Properties of persons, situations and behaviors. *Journal of Personality and Social Psychology, 60*, 773–794.
Furr, R. M. (2008). A framework for profile similarity: Integrating similarity, normativeness and distinctiveness. *Journal of Personality, 76*, 1267–1316.
Furr, R. M. (2009). Profile analysis in person-situation integration. *Journal of Research in Personality, 43*, 196–207.
Furr, R. M., & Funder, D. C. (2004). Situational similarity and behavioral consistency: Subjective, objective, variable-centered, and person-centered approaches. *Journal of Research in Personality, 38*, 421–447.
Gee, D., & Belofastov, A. (2007). Profiling sexual fantasy: Fantasy in sexual offending and the implications for offender profiling. In R. N. Kocsis (Ed.), *Criminal profiling: International theory, research and practice* (pp. 49–71). Totowa, NJ: Humana Press.
Greene, J. O. (1989). The stability of non-verbal behaviour: An action-production approach to problems of cross-situational consistency and discriminativeness. *Journal of Language and Social Psychology, 8*, 193–220.
Griffo, R., & Colvin, C. R. (2009). A brief look at interactionism: Past and present. *Journal of Research in Personality, 43*, 243–244.
Grubin, D., Kelly, P., & Brunsdon, C. (2001). *Linking serious sexual assaults through behaviour: HORS 215*. London, England: Home Office Research Development and Statistics Directorate.
Hettema, J., & Hol, D. P. (1998). Primary control and the consistency of interpersonal behaviour across different situations. *European Journal of Personality, 12*, 231–247.
Hettema, J., & van Bakel, A. P. (1997). Cross-situational consistency in a mastery condition. *Journal of Research in Personality, 31*, 222–239.
Klein, M. W. (1984). Offence specialization and versatility among juveniles. *British Journal of Criminology, 24*, 185–194.
Luckenbill, D. F. (1981). Generating compliance: The case of robbery. *Journal of Contemporary Ethnography, 10*, 25–46.
Markson, L., Woodhams, J., & Bond, J. (2010). Linking serial residential burglary: Comparing the utility of modus operandi behaviours, geographical proximity and temporal proximity. *Journal of Investigative Psychology and Offender Profiling, 7*, 91–107.
McGuire, J. (2005). Social problem solving: Basic concepts, research and applications. In M. McMurran & J. McGuire (Eds.), *Social problem solving and offending: Evidence, evaluation and evolution* (pp. 3–30). Chichester, England: Wiley.
Mischel, W. (1973). Toward a cognitive social learning reconceptualization of personality. *Psychological Review, 80*, 252–283.
Mischel, W. (1999). Personality coherence and dispositions in a cognitive affective personality system (CAPS). In D. Cervone & Y. Shoda (Eds.), *The coherence of personality: Social cognitive bases of consistency, variability and organisation* (pp. 37–60). London, England: Guilford Press.
Mischel, W. (2009). From *personality and assessment* (1968) to personality science (2009). *Journal of Research in Personality, 43*, 282–290.

Mischel, W., & Peake, P. K. (1983). Analyzing the construction of consistency in personality. In M. M. Page (Ed.), *Nebraska symposium on motivation, 1982: Personality—Current theory and research* (Vol. 30, pp. 233–262). Lincoln, NE: University of Nebraska Press.

Mischel, W., & Shoda, Y. (1995). A cognitive-affective system theory of personality: Reconceptualizing situations, dispositions, dynamics and invariance in personality structure. *Psychological Review, 102*, 246–268.

Nee, C., & Meenaghan, A. (2006). Expert decision-making in burglars. *British Journal of Criminology, 46*, 935–949.

Pervin, L. A. (2002). *Current controversies and issues in personality* (3rd ed.). New York, NY: Wiley.

Santtila, P., Junkkila, J., & Sandnabba, N. K. (2005). Behavioural linking of stranger rapes. *Journal of Investigative Psychology and Offender Profiling, 2*, 87–103.

Sherman, R. A., Nave, C. S., & Funder, D. C. (2010). Situational similarity and personality predict behavioral consistency. *Journal of Personality and Social Psychology, 99*, 330–343.

Shoda, Y., & Mischel, W. (2000). Reconciling contextualism with the core assumptions of personality psychology. *European Journal of Personality, 14*, 407–428.

Shoda, Y., Mischel, W., & Wright, J. C. (1993). The role of situational demands and cognitive competencies in behaviour. *Journal of Personality and Social Psychology, 65*, 1023–1035.

Shoda, Y., & Smith, R. E. (2004). Conceptualizing personality as a cognitive-affective processing system: A framework for models of maladaptive behavior patterns and change. *Behavior Therapy, 35*, 147–165.

Tonkin, M., Grant, T., & Bond, J. (2008). To link or not to link: A test of the case linkage principles using serial car theft data. *Journal of Investigative Psychology and Offender Profiling, 5*, 59–77.

van Mechelen, I. (2009). A royal road to understanding the mechanisms underlying person-in-context behavior. *Journal of Research in Personality, 43*, 179–186.

Walters, G. D. (2000). Disposed to aggress? In search of the violence-prone personality. *Aggression and Violent Behavior, 5*, 177–190.

Warr, M. (1996). Organization and instigation in delinquent groups. *Criminology, 34*, 11–37.

Woodhams, J., Bull, R., & Hollin, C. R. (2007). Case linkage: Identifying crimes committed by the same offender. In R. N. Kocsis (Ed.), *Criminal profiling: International theory, research and practice* (pp. 117–133). Totowa, NJ: The Humana Press.

Woodhams, J., Hollin, C. R., & Bull, R. (2007). The psychology of linking crimes: A review of the evidence. *Legal and Criminological Psychology, 12*, 233–249.

Woodhams, J., Hollin, C. R., & Bull, R. (2008). Incorporating context in linking crimes: An exploratory study of the relationship between behavioural consistency and situational similarity. *Journal of Investigative Psychology and Offender Profiling, 5*, 1–23.

Woodhams, J., Hollin, C. R., & Bull, R. (submitted). The consistency and distinctiveness of adolescent serial stranger sex offending. *Manuscript submitted for publication.*

Woodhams, J., Hollin, C. R., Bull, R., & Cooke, C. (2012). Behavior displayed by female victims during rapes committed by lone and multiple perpetrators. *Psychology, Public Policy, and Law, 18*, 415–452.

Woodhams, J., & Labuschagne, G. (2012). A test of case linkage principles with solved and unsolved serial rapes. *Journal of Police and Criminal Psychology, 27*, 85–98.

Woodhams, J., & Toye, K. (2007). An empirical test of the assumptions of case linkage and offender profiling with serial commercial robberies. *Psychology, Public Policy, and Law, 13*, 59–85.

Zayas, V., Shoda, Y., & Ayduk, O. N. (2002). Personality in context: An interpersonal systems perspective. *Journal of Personality and Social Psychology, 70*, 851–900.

Sex Crime Linkage
Sexual Fantasy and Offense Plasticity

3

DION GEE AND
ALEKSANDRA BELOFASTOV

Contents

Introduction 33
The Evolution of Crime Linkage 34
Crime Linkage 35
Offense Plasticity in Crime Linkage 36
Modus Operandi 38
Signature/Rituals 40
Staging 41
Sexual Fantasy and Offense Plasticity 41
Offense-Focused Fantasy and Temporal Shift 44
Conclusion 47
References 48

Introduction

Historically, one of the primary aims of criminal investigative analysis (CIA), as devised by S. A. Howard Teten and S. A. Pat Mullany, was to aid in the linkage of previously unconnected cases, a proposition that seemingly underpins the more contemporary focus on crime linkage (see Woodhams, Bull, & Hollin, 2007 for a review). Noting that in some jurisdictions, such as the United Kingdom, crime linkage is often conducted without consideration of motive, it can be argued that such a practice significantly limits the utility of crime linkage analysis when attempting to connect crimes that are based more in the subjective/internal world of the perpetrator (e.g., serial sex crimes, sexual sadism, sexual homicide, serial arson) than those based in the physical/external environment (e.g., burglary, robbery, vehicle theft). Indeed, Gee and Belofastov (2007) have previously advocated that the construct of sexual fantasy is, and should be, considered central to the process of linking sexual crimes, despite a current lack of rigorous empirical evidence in support of this.

In the following sections, we also advance that sexual fantasy plays a fundamental role in offense plasticity, that is, malleability within and across an offender's aberrant behavior. Thus, by explicating the influence of sexual fantasy in the offense process, particularly as it relates to crime linkage, investigators may more readily account for the shifting patterns of offense behavior noted in the career pathways of many recidivist sexual offenders (Gee & Belofastov, 2007; Ward, Bickley, Webster, Fisher, Beech, & Eldridge, 2004; Ward, Yates, & Long, 2006; Yates, Kingston, & Ward, 2009). We further contend that, with a comprehensive understanding of sexual fantasy, one can better understand the internal world of an offender; as well as the means by which their offense fantasies are transformed into aberrant sexual behavior.

The current chapter opens with a brief account of CIA, placing particular emphasis on crime linkage. It then summarizes contemporary literature concerning offense plasticity, noting the impact of behavioral consistency, distinctiveness, and crime-switching behavior on crime linkage. Next, we shift to the construct of sexual fantasy, highlighting its integral role in the maintenance of serial sex crimes. Finally, offense-focused sexual fantasies are used to elucidate the role of fantasy scripts in the temporal shift of crime scene behavior for serial sex offenders.

The Evolution of Crime Linkage

In 1972, the Behavioral Sciences Unit (as part of the Federal Bureau of Investigation) coined the phrase *criminal investigative analysis* to describe an *ideal investigative strategy* for analyzing and identifying the major personality and behavioral characteristics of an offender, based on the crimes they had committed (Turvey, 1997). Originally conceptualized as a deductive, analytical process grounded in physical evidence, the primary aim of CIA was to provide investigators with a tool to aid in the solving of previously unsolved crime and for the linkage of previously unlinked cases (Turvey, 1998b). Built on the notion that investigators use multiple sources of data [i.e., evaluations of the criminal act; evaluations of the details of a crime scene(s); analyses of the victim; evaluations of preliminary police reports; and evaluations of autopsy protocols (Burgess, Burgess, Douglas, & Ressler, 1997)], the CIA process was intended to aid in the development of a profile by outlining an offender's critical characteristics and providing investigative strategies fashioned from that profile.

Broadly speaking, CIA connotes the application of psychological theory and behavioral evidence analysis to the forensic examination and reconstruction of physical evidence as it relates to a particular offender's crime scene characteristics, victimology, motivation, and behavior patterns. It attempts to explain the behaviors and motivations of a specific offender at a specific crime scene(s) by analyzing the unique facets of a crime to make hypotheses, which draw from broad datasets in combination with theory.

Crime Linkage

By definition, crime linkage involves those procedures which aim to identify crimes committed by the same suspect through behavioral similarities across crimes (Woodhams et al., 2007), similarities which some refer to as the *modus operandi* (MO; Bennell & Jones, 2005). Recently, Woodhams et al. (2007) opined that crime linkage, while sharing several features in common with criminal profiling, is distinguishable from the latter because it does not ascribe to the assumption of *homology*, a principle which holds that offenders sharing similar criminal behaviors should share similar demographic characteristics (Mokros & Alison, 2002).

Generally speaking, for two crimes to be linked to a common offender, an individual's crime scene behavior must be similar in some way from one crime to the next, while maintaining a degree of individuality that allows it to be distinguished from the crime scene behavior of another offender (Bateman & Salfati, 2007; Woodhams & Toye, 2007). More specifically, crime linkage is predicated on two key hypotheses, that is, crimes by the same offender share both consistency and distinctiveness. The offender consistency hypothesis (Canter, 1995) reflects a form of cross-situation behavioral consistency, asserting that criminals demonstrate consistency in the ways in which they behave during the commission of their crimes across a series. In other words, crime linkage focuses on the similarities of an individual's aberrant behaviors across their offending career and within their crime type (e.g., murder, sexual offenses).

To date, a large body of research supports the notion of behavioral consistency in sexually aberrant behavior, with Woodhams and Labuschagne (2012a) recently suggesting that sexual fantasy may be one reason for such observed consistency. This latter contention reflects earlier theory positing that crime scripts (Cornish & Clarke, 2002) or offense scripts (i.e., a set of rules for predicting, interpreting, responding to, and controlling a set of interpersonal scenes that are meaningful to an individual; Ward & Hudson, 2000b) play an important role in shaping offense behavior. Research has also demonstrated that there is a lack of uniformity in relation to the stability of offense behaviors longitudinally, with numerous factors (such as intoxication, offender mood, experience, temporal proximity, and victim behavior) believed to moderate behavioral consistency across multiple crimes (see Sorochinski & Salfati, 2010; Tonkin, Grant, & Bond, 2008 for reviews).

The second key principle of crime linkage is behavioral distinctiveness; an assumption advancing that offenders display a degree of uniqueness in their pattern of aberrant behavior across a series that will be distinguishable, or differentiate them, from others committing similar types of crime (Bennell & Canter, 2002). Although less researched, several studies have found evidence for behavioral distinctiveness in an offender's career (see Tonkin et al., 2008 and Chapter 6).

Accepting that the above-mentioned constructs bear on the process of crime linkage (making inferential reasoning about crime scene behavior somewhat nebulous), numerous writers (e.g., Gee & Belofastov, 2007; Turvey, 1999; Woodhams et al., 2007; Woodhams, Hollin, & Bull, 2008) have posited that a number of core assumptions guide the crime linkage analysis process. Specifically, these assumptions include the following: (1) Human behavior develops uniquely over time and in response to environmental, situational, and biological factors; (2) No offender acts without motivation, though at times the precise motivation will only be known to the offender; (3) Different offenders exhibit the same or similar behaviors oftentimes for completely different reasons; (4) The nature of human behavior, interpersonal interactions, and environmental influences sees no two cases being completely alike; (5) An offender may have various motives during the commission of a single offense and/or over the commission of multiple offenses; and (6) Both MO and signature behaviors can evolve, devolve, or remain stable over time and across the commission of multiple offenses.

Offense Plasticity in Crime Linkage

Central to the process of crime linkage is the construct of offense plasticity. As evidenced within the personality literature, human behavior is not an all-or-nothing phenomenon, but instead is contingent upon personal, situational, and environmental factors. Importantly, as highlighted by Funder and Colvin (1991), constancy in human behavior across situations may be less about a specific behavioral display and more about the underlying psychological disposition of the individual, a disposition which can be expressed behaviorally in a variety of ways. That is, the specific behaviors of offenders may be interpreted as psychologically interchangeable, despite their outward dissimilarity (Funder & Colvin, 1991). Showers and Cantor (1985) further suggest that individuals use a variety of goal-dependent cognitive strategies for interpreting situations, adopting behaviors that enable them to achieve their desired outcomes within a given context.

Embedded within such cognitive strategies are meaningful patterns of behavioral variation, patterns that reportedly alter in accordance with an individual's goals and situational contingencies (Showers & Cantor, 1985). Hence, behavioral change is rooted within the changing cognitive strategies that offenders use to reach their ultimate goal (Sorochinski & Salfati, 2010), which in turn is influenced by environmental circumstances at the commission of the offense (Davies, 1992; Lundrigan, Czarnomski, & Wilson, 2010). It has therefore been argued that crime linkage should rely more on the "process of offending" than on a specific offender and his or her behavior (Meier, Kennedy, & Sacco, 2001), that is, by examining the interplay between the offender, the victim, and the context of the aberrant behavior. Further, Tonkin et al. (2008) have contended that one must not only consider whether criminals display patterns in their crime scene behaviors, but also *when* and *why* such patterns occur.

In light of the above, and reflecting the recent assertion by Sorochinski and Salfati (2010), it is argued that examining behavioral patterns as opposed to discrete behavioral episodes would be a more fruitful way of unpacking offense plasticity in serial sex crimes. This is especially the case given the *crime-switching* behaviors evident in some serial offenders. To illustrate, Beauregard (2010) noted that recidivist sexual offenders can seemingly "switch" offending patterns and victim selection across their criminal career, adapting their behaviors and developing different victim preferences along multiple dimensions (e.g., victim's age, gender, relationship to the offender, nature of acts committed by the offender, and crime location) (see also Beauregard, Proulx, Rossmo, Leclerc, & Allaire, 2009; Beauregard, Rebocho, & Rossmo, 2010; Lussier, Leclerc, Healey, & Proulx, 2007). Thus, although some sexual offenders display "specialization" within their offending (used here to connote offenders who confine themselves to one type of victim) (Cann, Friendship, & Gozna, 2007; Guay, Proulx, Cusson, & Ouimet, 2001; Simon, 1997, 2000), the consensus appears to be that sexual offenders are both "generalists" and "specialists" simultaneously (Soothill, Francis, Sanderson, & Ackerley, 2000), displaying both consistency and versatility (Beauregard, 2010).

Historically, sexual offenders have been regarded as a discrete subgroup of individuals exhibiting specific offense behaviors and preferences that are stable over time (Canter & Kirby, 1995; Ward, Hudson, & McCormack, 1997). This idea appeared to be based on the notion that sexual deviance is a stable construct and acts as a prime motivator in sexual offending (Hanson & Bussiere, 1998). More contemporary studies of sexual offender specialization, however, have reached diverse conclusions around both the exclusivity with which sexual offenders commit aberrant behavior and the stability of MO in specific sexual offenses (Sjostedt, Langstrom, Sturidsson, & Grann, 2004; Ward & Hudson, 2000a), particularly in relation to the heterogeneity and variability of victim preferences and offense types (Simon, 1997, 2000; Studer, Clelland, Aylwin, Reddon, & Monro, 2000).

In addition to consistency, distinctiveness, and crime-switching behavior, offense plasticity is further complicated by the impact of MO, signature/rituals, and staging on the offense process. These topics will be elucidated below.

Modus Operandi

MO encapsulates a pattern of behaviors committed by an offender that serves the purpose of protecting the perpetrator's identity, procuring a victim, ensuring success in their crime, facilitating escape, and avoiding detection (Burgess et al., 1997; Cornish & Clarke, 1987; Hazelwood & Warren, 1995; Leclerc, Proulx, & Beauregard, 2009). MO can be quite simple or very complex (Hazelwood & Warren, 2003), comprising of a dynamic and malleable cluster of learned behaviors that are functionally significant and context dependent (Alison, Goodwill, & Alison, 2005). These behaviors can develop over time as the offender becomes more experienced, sophisticated, and confident (Douglas & Munn, 1992; Salfati, 2008; Turvey, 1998c). This evolution, based in the repetitive and automatic nature of serial crime, allows the perpetrator to refine perceived flaws in their offense script (Geberth, 1996), seemingly affording a sense of familiarity and control that allows them to focus more intently on the motives underpinning their aberrant behavior (Hazelwood & Warren, 2003).

Gee and Belofastov (2007) contended that knowledge of sexual fantasy is integral to understanding the crime scenes of serial sex offenders, particularly when attempting to link crimes through MO behavior, that is, sexual fantasy acts to shape the core aspects of MO behavior by reinforcing the development of the offense script and providing the mental sketchpad upon which to relive previous crimes and plan subsequent offending. Specifically, fantasy provides an offender with the means to explore which aspects/components of a potential crime (e.g., context of the offense, victim type, method of approach, control process) will best fulfil the core functions and/or goals implicit within the offense process.

Accepting that the core fantasy themes to which an offender's sexual responses become conditioned are essentially static and that a nexus exists between an offender's sexual fantasies and the means by which their crimes are transposed into reality, it is unlikely that the context of an individual's aberrant behavior will change fundamentally, unless the MO behavior and underlying fantasy script fail to fulfil the motives underpinning the offense. It is at such points where a dramatic shift in MO behavior can occur (as can be noted between the initial and subsequent crimes of some offenders) or a gradual evolution away from those aspects of a crime that are no longer gratifying/rewarding is seen to occur. Thus, it is argued that the stability of these fantasies can, in part, help explain both the consistency of an offender's MO behavior across time, as well as the distinctiveness (or uniqueness) of sex crime behavior perpetrated by a specific individual.

MO may also devolve over time, becoming less organized, competent, or skillful, decompensating by virtue of the offender's emerging mental illness (such as psychosis or depression); increased use of controlled substances; overconfidence in their ability to avoid detection; personality pathology; and/or the presence of extraneous variables (e.g., unavailability of a victim, behavioral responses of the victim, presence of witnesses). All these factors may result in the need for improvisation or offender retreat (Douglas, Burgess, Burgess, & Ressler, 1992; Geberth, 1996; Hazelwood & Warren, 2003; Woodhams & Labuschagne, 2012a, 2012b), facets that are distinguishable from the processes that can underpin a disorganized MO. Here, disorganization refers to the unplanned, impulsive, and spontaneous nature of offense behavior that can signal a lack of criminal sophistication, the youthfulness of the offender, and/or intellectual deficiency (Douglas et al., 1992). Further, unlike personality, *mental state* is not seen to be static across time, and therefore, in some instances, an offender's MO may reflect their mental state at the time of the offense, rather than enduring personality functioning and/or psychopathology. For example, the "inexplicable" crime scene behaviors that can occur within the context of a brief psychotic disorder or drug-induced psychosis can have little resemblance to those demonstrated by the offender when their mental state is not so compromised (see Chapter 4 for further discussion of the sexual offending of mentally disordered offenders).

Importantly, in light of the foregoing, it has been found that some of the more traditional MO behaviors are apparently less useful in linking crime scenes, because their expression is, in large part, dependent on situational factors (Markson, Woodhams, & Bond, 2010). Specifically, research by Leclerc et al. (2009) has shown that MO is particularly influenced by the age and gender of the victim, the offender–victim relationship, and the presence of deviant sexual fantasies before the crime (see below). Of note, however, it is also plausible that such influences are only *quasi-situational*, instead highlighting the ability of some offense scripts to accommodate extraneous variables *on the fly*, while still maintaining close links to the core goals underpinning an offense. As noted above, this latter proposition finds further support in the research of Funder and Colvin (1991), wherein it was contended that divergent MO behaviors may in fact be psychologically interchangeable, despite their outward dissimilarity. Given the foregoing, the motives underlying the sexual offense script are seemingly not only responsible for specific offense behaviors, but appear to have increased salience in guiding variability within an offender's MO behavior.

Signature/Rituals

Signature behaviors have been conceptualized as a distinctive pattern of actions that are characteristic of, and satisfy the, emotional and psychological needs of an offender (Turvey, 1998a), with the behavioral display going beyond what is sufficient to accomplish a crime (Burgess et al., 1997; Keppel, 1995). These behaviors purportedly emanate from an offender's personality structure, lifestyle, and developmental experiences. As such, they are psychologically significant rather than context dependent (Alison et al., 2005) and can evolve, devolve, or remain stable across multiple offenses (Brown, 1997; Geberth, 1996; Turvey, 1998c). Signature behaviors may include such things as the taking of mementos; having a victim say or do pre-scripted actions; the sequencing of offense behaviors; or seeking out/altering a crime scene prior to an offense to ensure that it conforms to an offender's "idealized" image of the environment in which the offense will occur.

Signature behaviors are symbolic in nature rather than functional, reflecting those aspects of the offender's mental life that are pivotal in expressing the primary motivation or purpose of the criminal act (Hazelwood & Warren, 2003). In essence, signature behaviors account for *why* an offender commits a particular crime—although its presence may not always be easily discernible—and are therefore an integral component in the process of offending (Gee & Belofastov, 2007). As noted by Gee and Belofastov (2007), the attribution of psychological motives to crime scene behavior is difficult, a task that is further complicated by the fact that, unlike personality, mental state is not constant across time. Therefore, as is the case with MO, apparent signature behaviors might be more reflective of an offender's psychological/mental state at the time of the offense than of motives embedded within their personality structure or enduring psychopathology (see also Schlesinger, 2004, 2009).

Previous research has suggested that when signature behaviors are evident in an offender's repertoire (i.e., ritualistic behaviors, such as postmortem object insertion and binding and gagging with victim's own clothes), these behaviors were more often found to be consistent than that of MO behaviors (Harbort & Mokros, 2001). Importantly, as suggested by Gee and Belofastov (2007), such consistency could potentially evolve from the sexual fantasies that accompany aberrant sexual behavior and the mechanisms by which the motivations underpinning an offender's core sexual fantasy content are translated into aberrant behavior.

Staging

Douglas and Munn (1992) defined the staging of a crime scene as the deliberate effort by an offender to alter the crime scene prior to the arrival of police (e.g., making a crime scene appear careless and/or disorganized). These are actions that signify criminal or precautionary intent that are distinguishable from alterations of a crime scene by the victim's loved ones. Generally, staging reflects an attempt to redirect the investigation away from the most logical suspect; to protect the victim's dignity and/or that of their family (Geberth, 1996); or to communicate a symbolic message through the crime (Douglas & Olshaker, 1996). Further, as noted by Douglas et al. (1992), perpetrators may stage secondary criminal activities (such as a robbery) in an attempt to conceal the primary motive for an offense (e.g., home-invasion rape).

Gee and Belofastov (2007) advanced that post-offense staging might also signify an attempt by an offender to escape the realization of their behavior and/or avoid the consequent negative affect (e.g., denial, shame, guilt) in the immediate post-offense period, that is, as an outgrowth of offense-focused fantasy, the apparent "undoing" of a crime scene may serve a broader coping function, which could help explain why a rapist might subsequently ask his victim for a date or why a corpse is dressed following a sexual assault and murder.

Sexual Fantasy and Offense Plasticity

Sexual fantasy has been conceptualized as an imaginative thought process accompanied by a deliberate withdrawal from the immediate demands of the external world and a narrowing in focus of an individual's internal world (Leitenberg & Henning, 1995). Such a process allows an individual to create an elaborate, emotionally anchored, mental picture that has its origins in daydreaming and involves erotica that creates or intensifies sexual arousal (Carlson & Havelock-Coleman, 1977; Rokach, 1990). Furthermore, research has distinguished between sexual fantasy and deviant sexual fantasy, with the latter containing imagery that involves the intentional infliction of harm in a sadistic/sexually aggressive way (Prentky et al., 1989) or themes depicting illegal (e.g., rape, child sexual offenses) and/or socially marginal behaviors (e.g., exhibitionism, humiliation, voyeurism, degradation). Moreover, within an offending context, the notion of *offense-focused fantasy* has been adopted to distinguish the offense-based and preparatory sexual fantasies evident within sexual offender populations from those otherwise aberrant sexual fantasy themes observed in nonoffending populations (see Gee & Belofastov, 2007; Gee, Devilly, & Ward, 2004).

An individual's core sexual fantasies are believed to be organized around a small number of basic themes laid down early in life (Person, 1995). Through repetition, incongruous sexual imagery becomes consolidated into a coherent sexual fantasy script, that is, a collection of rules for predicting, interpreting, responding to, and controlling a set of interpersonal scenes that are meaningful to an individual (Ward & Hudson, 2000a, 2000b). Generally, such scripts comprise a number of salient facets (Gee et al., 2004; Hazelwood & Warren, 1995), including a behavioral component (i.e., the sexual behavior that occurs within the fantasy); a situational component (i.e., the context in which the fantasized activity is occurring); a relational component (i.e., how the various participants are related within the fantasy); a demographic component (i.e., the characteristics of the fantasized other); and a perceptual component (i.e., how the individual perceives themselves within the fantasy). Furthermore, source material for sexual fantasies can be drawn from internal (i.e., content that stems purely from imaginary processes) and/or external sources (i.e., an individual's own childhood abuse, pornography, previous sexual experiences, modeled experience, and/or the media; Gee, Ward, Belofastov, & Beech, 2006).

The development of offense-focused sexual fantasies, coupled with the resultant mental picture, constitutes the formation of an offense script that, together with mental simulations, provides an offender with an automatic, goal-dependent action plan (Ward & Hudson, 2000a). By using the psychological processes of mental simulation (Taylor & Pham, 1996), cognitive rehearsal (Ward, 2000), and covert modeling (Marshall, Jones, Ward, Johnston, & Barbaree, 1991), individuals can modify those aspects of fantasy that become "boring" or unstimulating, while "zeroing in" on the most pleasurable parts of the mental representation. This in turn provides more powerful imagery that can be used as sexual stimuli.

Earlier research attempted to tease out the potential role(s) of fantasy in sexual offending (see, e.g., Hazelwood, Dietz, & Warren, 1995; MacCulloch, Snowden, Wood, & Mills, 1983; Prentky & Burgess, 1991), whereas more contemporary investigations have specifically focused on the function of sexual fantasy within the context of aberrant sexual behavior (Gee, Ward, & Eccelston, 2003; Howitt, 2004; Meloy, 2000). In particular, sexual fantasy, especially offense-focused fantasy, is seen to provide an offender with a mental *sketchpad* to plan and rehearse future offending through simulation. This affords the offender with a sense of control, a means of dissociation, a way of inducing or enhancing arousal, a means of coping, and a way to regulate affect (see Gee et al., 2003 for a review).

Perhaps the most concerning function sexual fantasy serves within the context of aberrant sexual behavior is its potential to act as a "blueprint," or offense script, which facilitates the enactment of fantasy themes. Researchers generally agree that when offense-focused sexual fantasies become part of the offense chain, an individual moves closer to the point where acting on aberrant sexual fantasy becomes a reality (Carabellese, Maniglio, Greco, & Catanesi, 2011; Gee & Belofastov, 2007; Leitenberg & Henning, 1995; Prentky et al., 1989). As fantasy scenarios are repeated or rehearsed, each offense, victim experience, and/or sexual behavior becomes incorporated into the offender's collective fantasy, resulting in a qualitative shift in fantasy content away from the innocuous sexual themes present in nonoffending populations (Gee et al., 2004; Ward & Hudson, 2000b). When offense-focused sexual fantasy escalates to a point whereby the incorporation of new fantasy material fails to produce the desired changes in attention, arousal, or the environment, individuals may attempt to transform their fantasy into reality through offending behavior. Moreover, the element of novelty associated with sexual desire may diminish with the repeated activation of the sexual fantasy (Meloy, 2002), leading to the incorporation of more diverse/explicit sexual acts and/or a wider variety of victims into the offense script (Gee & Belofastov, 2007; Skovran, Huss, & Scalora, 2010).

Reenactment of fantasy scripts, along with providing a means of arousal, affords an opportunity to plan and simulate escalatory behavior, whereby the individual can preview anticipated experiences, prepare for alternatives, and attempt to resolve notable obstacles. Indeed, as shown by Dandescu and Wolfe (2003), sexual offenders often report more masturbatory fantasies following their first offense, suggesting that for some individuals offense-focused fantasies are less important in the etiology of deviant sexual preferences, although become increasingly central in its maintenance. Importantly, although very few sexual offenders appear to entertain offense-focused fantasies in their early developmental years, those that do appear to display more predatory and/or sadistic offense behaviors (Gee et al., 2004).

Given the above, Leclerc, Beauregard, and Proulx's (2008) study used the *Modus Operandi* Questionnaire (Kaufman, 1994) to investigate the offense behaviors of adolescent sexual offenders. Although exploratory, and accepting there were only minor differences between the types of victim–offender relationship and MO strategies, Leclerc et al. (2008) found that the presence of victim-specific fantasies prior to an offense was strongly associated with MO strategies exhibited by the perpetrator. That is, conscious planning occurred, with the offender making explicit decisions about which strategies would be used under what situations. Moreover, those offenders entertaining victim-specific fantasies were seen to be more strategic, highly motivated to commit offenses, and consequently more willing to adopt a variety of strategies in their repertoire to reach their offense goals (Leclerc et al., 2008).

The foregoing findings resonate with earlier research by Gee et al. (2004), wherein it was found that the majority of offenders used victim-specific offense fantasies in the targeting/grooming process, especially during relapse offenses. Moreover, for some offenders, fantasy provided a means to actively manipulate their "reality," whereby offenders could transform consensual sexual experiences into an offense-focused experience by substituting a partner's characteristics for those of a current/future victim within their fantasy (Gee et al., 2004).

In summary, the above research suggests that offense-focused sexual fantasies may structure and/or influence an offender's choice of MO (Beauregard, Lussier, & Proulx, 2005; Leclerc et al., 2008), that is, there may be a direct relationship between the content of fantasy and the behaviors engaged in during a crime (Gee et al., 2004; Keppel, 1995, 2000; Keppel & Birnes, 2009; Schlesinger, 2004). Specifically, sexual fantasy appears to provide a "stepping stone" to offending, allowing a means by which innocuous sexual imagery can be transformed into nonspecific offense fantasies, which in turn may fuel a progression into offense-specific fantasy themes (Gee & Belofastov, 2007). Fantasy rehearsal seemingly results in the desensitization and normalization of aberrant sexual fantasy, which, after pairing with sexual arousal through masturbation, can increase sexual deviance and the potential for future behavioral enactment. Even where a direct nexus between fantasy and offense behavior is seemingly absent, Baumgartner, Scalora, and Huss (2002) have contended that the motivations underlying aberrant sexual behavior are likely influenced by sexual fantasies, again highlighting the complex relationship between sexual fantasy and the process of offending. The authors argued for a more comprehensive account of the offense process than that provided by the offender's MO alone (Leclerc et al., 2009).

Offense-Focused Fantasy and Temporal Shift

Investigators have recently advanced that sexual fantasy might provide one plausible explanation for the consistency observed in the offense behavior of sexual offenders (Woodhams & Labuschagne, 2012a). Support for this hypothesis is found in the writings of Hettema and colleagues (Hettema & Hol, 1998; Hettema & Van Bakel, 1997), where it was posited that those behaviors over which an individual exerts more control (i.e., are situation-independent) should be displayed with higher degrees of consistency. This notion is supported by research in relation to both spatial patterns (i.e., crime location) (e.g., Bennell & Jones, 2005; Leclerc et al., 2008) and temporal proximity/crime behavior (e.g., Lundrigan et al., 2010; Markson et al., 2010; Sorochinski & Salfati, 2010). Further, Hettema and Van Bakel (1997) have argued that experience and expertise with a situation fosters an ability to adapt and transform such situations—that is, experience fosters behavioral control—hence behaviors observed in familiar situations are more likely to be those that reflect an offender's desires, rather than environmental adaptation. These propositions can potentially help explain fantasy's influence within the process of offending, given that fantasy is both under an offender's explicit control and the individual has considerable experience/expertise with its enactment. It is therefore not surprising that a high concordance of offense paralleling occurs between offense-focused sexual fantasy and an offender's criminal behavior (see Gee & Belofastov, 2007).

Accepting the limited evidence in support of an exclusive association between sexual fantasy and offending (Gray, Watt, Hassan, & Macculloch, 2003), coupled with the notion that sexual fantasy varies in its causal nexus to aberrant behavior, it is acknowledged that both stability and evolution can coexist within a crime series, a situation that makes crime linkage all the more difficult. Recently, Sorochinski and Salfati (2010) posited that the evolvement of the offender's fantasy life may account for pattern shifts in crime scene behavior, reinforcing Salfati's (2008) earlier assertion that crime linkage would greatly benefit from considering behavioral change patterns in a temporal context. Specifically, Sorochinski and Salfati (2010) contended that early in an offense series, an offender's fantasy script might not correspond to the situational factors they encounter during the commission of their offenses, and as such, they require new strategies and behaviors to allow for the gradual fulfilment of their fantasy. This inability to fulfil one's fantasy could also lead to frustration and a subsequent loss of control, invoking change in the offender's risk-taking and planning behaviors (Hickey, 2006).

Further evidence of behavioral shift is found in research by Harbort and Mokros (2001), where it was noted that offenders' behaviors changed most from their first to second offense, and their third offense was often similar to their initial planning style. Importantly, it was also posited that, for some rapists, the observed escalation of violence between the first and second offense was highly correlated with evolving sadistic fantasies (Harbort & Mokros, 2001).

In line with Sorochinski and Salfati's (2010) contention, research incorporating a temporal dimension to sexual fantasy has recently explicated how this phenomenon can change across the offense process (Gee & Belofastov, 2007). The development of a tripartite model of sexual fantasy for sexual offenders has elucidated the function (Gee et al., 2003), content (Gee et al., 2004), and structural properties (Gee et al., 2006) of sexual fantasy across the process of sexual offending. As highlighted by Gee and Belofastov (2007), constancy and change in sexual fantasy is not only dependent on which stage of the offense chain/process an offender is in (i.e., the five time-sequenced stages of background, pre-lapse, lapse, initial offense, and post-offense; see Laws, Hudson, & Ward, 2000 for a comprehensive account of each phase), but also on whether the perpetrator was committing his or her first offense (i.e., the initial offense chain), was committing a subsequent offense (i.e., a relapse offense cycle/chain), or was in the post-offending period (i.e., the point at which an offender moves out of the offending context, which may or may not involve incarceration).

Specifically, the tripartite model noted a temporal shift in fantasy content away from the ill-defined and circumscribed nonspecific offense fantasies evident prior to an offender's initial offense, onto more complex, coherent, and encompassing offense-focused fantasies as an offender cycled through relapse offenses, that is, the beginning of a relapse cycle coincided with a qualitative escalation in the five identified components evident within a sexual fantasy script (i.e., behavioral, situational, relational, demographic, and perceptual), whereupon offense-focused fantasies content gained complexity, detail, and intensity, as well as broadening in scope. It can therefore be hypothesized that during the initial offense, very few offenders possess the requisite offense fantasy scripts required to adapt their offense behavior "on the fly." However, through behavioral tryout, simulation, and cognitive rehearsal, fantasy can be used to develop and refine more adaptable offense scripts.

Taken to their extreme, offense-focused fantasy scripts can also contribute to the devolution in an offender's crime scene behavior, that is, as offense-specific fantasy gains in complexity and becomes more intricate, the potential for behavioral "slippage" within the offense behavior increases (Gee & Belofastov, 2007). To illustrate, as an offender's sexual fantasy gains in complexity and becomes more intricate, the successful completion of a crime that conforms to the fantasy script becomes increasingly difficult. The overutilization of sexual fantasy in the development of offense scripts may afford an offender unrealistic expectations of the offense process, leading to considerable discrepancy between an offender's fantasy and the way an offense unfolds. An example would be how the three interpersonal foci of offending, that is, mutual, self, and other (Ward, Fon, Hudson, & McCormack, 1998), are incorporated into an offense-focused fantasy and the consideration given to the interplay between the various parties, that is, some fantasies have a "mutual" focus, whereby the offender considers the perspectives of all the individuals involved in the fantasy. In some instances, this may mean that all of the parties within a fantasy actively participated in and enjoyed the experience, whereas in others, it means that one party (usually the perpetrator) enjoyed the fantasized experience while the other individual(s) did not, for instance, fantasies that are more often present for adult rapists and/or where there is a controlling/sadistic quality to the offense process. In other instances, fantasies can be more narrowly focused, with the perpetrator focusing purely on the *self* during the fantasy or solely on the *other* victims within the fantasy. If it were the case that an offender used a mutual or other-focused approach (wherein both parties are actively participating, or the victim is perceived as enjoying the experience), the offender may not be prepared if he met with victim resistance during the actual commission of the offense.

A second plausible explanation to account for pattern shifts in offense behavior is changes that occur as a result of the shifting nature of an offender's implicit goals and the motivations linked to their aberrant fantasy scripts (Sorochinski & Salfati, 2010). In addition, acknowledging the interconnectedness of the various functions of sexual fantasy, recent research has noted that offenders do not consistently use fantasy for any one specific reason over the course of the offense chain (Gee & Belofastov, 2007). Instead, sexual fantasy functions more dynamically across the offense/relapse process, appearing less "tied" to the offense chain than it is to the underlying sexual scripts that guide sexual interactions. Hence, as an offender's initial offense fantasies are achieved, a perpetrator may readjust their fantasy scripts through the setting of new goals, subsequently modifying their offense script (i.e., cognitive and behavioral strategies) in order to match their changing intentions (Sorochinski & Salfati, 2010).

The aforementioned explanation might also go some way to understanding the pattern shifts in the expression of signature behavior for some serial sexual offenders, that is, the interplay between personality, psychopathology, and sexual fantasy might help account for temporal shifts in identified signature behaviors. As the underlying motivation for offending changes, the expression of such motives through the fantasy script would also arguably change. For example, an adult rapist whose offending initially incorporates a mutual interpersonal focus might shift their behavioral pattern after confronting victim resistance that cannot be accommodated within the distorted perception of the offense process expressed through their fantasy script. In such circumstances, an offender may resort to blaming the victim for the unsuccessful completion of the offense script, thus incorporating more controlling, violent, or retaliatory themes into the fantasy script to ensure its successful completion. Alternatively, the perpetrator's goal may switch onto more self-focused behavior, in which an opportunistic victim is merely an object used by the perpetrator to express the motives underpinning their fantasy behavior.

Conclusion

Crime linkage is the examination of crime scene behaviors with the focus on identifying similarities across different offenses thought to be committed by the same person. In this way, the investigator analyses for consistency and distinctiveness across crime scenes in an endeavor to understand the MO of the offender. In cases of sex crimes, an explicit consideration of the role of sexual fantasy in the commission of discrete offenses may provide invaluable insights into the mind and motives of the perpetrator. Patterns of behavior (e.g., consistency in victimology, offense approach/pathway) can reveal intrinsic information regarding the offender's internal fantasy scripts and ultimately their core psychological drives, impulses, and aberrations. As described above, these fantasy scripts tend to remain largely stable across time through a process of rehearsal, (re)enactment, and reinforcement. Although a certain degree of offense plasticity is anticipated and related adaptations or "refinements" to the offense-focused fantasy may be seen (usually observable as developments in the situational/environmental factors of the crime scene), at its core, the script will contain the same or similar underlying psychological motivations of the offender (e.g., desire for control and power, humiliation, sadism). To use a metaphor, although someone may change the outfit he wears, he still remains the same person underneath. Therefore, investigators can use their knowledge of core psychological constructs to link particular sex crime scenes, ultimately developing a psychological profile of the offender while simultaneously narrowing and refining their analyses.

This chapter explored one of the more salient tasks of CIA within the arena of sexual offending, namely, sex crime linkage. Particular attention was paid to the role of sexual fantasy in offense plasticity, drawing on contemporary research investigating behavioral consistency, distinctiveness, and crime-switching within the offense process. The notions of crime scene stability and change were used to demonstrate the importance of sexual fantasy, especially offense-focused fantasy, in the etiology and maintenance of serial sex crimes. Underpinned by personal, situational, and environmental factors, sexual fantasy plays an integral role in the evolution and devolution of offending behavior, which arguably accounts for much of the temporal shift patterns evident across the careers of serial sex offenders. By better understanding the importance of sexual fantasy within the process of sexual offending, investigators will have a better vantage point from which to consider the complex relationship between sexual fantasy and crime linkage. In particular, the challenge for those investigating (serial) sex crimes concerns the inherent dilemmas associated with drawing offense-paralleling behaviors from fantasy, the latter of which is, by its very nature, dynamic and evolving across time. Despite this dilemma, the perpetrator maintains a *thread* of consistency in their fantasizing (as mirrored in their offending), that is, at its core, their penultimate sexual perversion, and that which offers us the greatest insights into their psyche.

References

Alison, L. J., Goodwill, A., & Alison, E. (2005). Guidelines for profilers. In L. J. Alison (Ed.), *The forensic psychologists' casebook: Psychological profiling and criminal investigation* (pp. 235–277). Devon, England: Willan.

Bateman, A. L., & Salfati, C. G. (2007). An examination of behavioral consistency using individual behaviors or groups of behaviors in serial homicide. *Behavioral Sciences & the Law, 25*, 527–544.

Baumgartner, J. V., Scalora, M. J., & Huss, M. T. (2002). Assessment of the Wilson sex fantasy questionnaire among child molesters and non-sexual forensic offenders. *Sexual Abuse: A Journal of Research and Treatment, 14*, 19–33.

Beauregard, E. (2010). Rape and sexual assault in investigative psychology: The contribution of sex offenders' research to offender profiling. *Journal of Investigative Psychology and Offender Profiling, 7*, 1–13.

Beauregard, E., Lussier, P., & Proulx, J. (2005). The role of sexual interests and situational factors on rapists' modus operandi: Implications for offender profiling. *Legal and Criminological Psychology, 10*, 265–278.

Beauregard, E., Proulx, J., Rossmo, D. K., Leclerc, B., & Allaire, J. F. (2009). A script analysis of patterns in the hunting process of serial sex offenders. *Criminal Justice and Behavior, 34*, 1069–1084.

Beauregard, E., Rebocho, M. F., & Rossmo, K. D. (2010). Target selection patterns in rape. *Journal of Investigative Psychology and Offender Profiling, 7*, 137–152.

Bennell, C., & Canter, D. (2002). Linking commercial burglaries by modus operandi: Tests using regression and ROC analysis. *Science & Justice, 42*, 1–12.

Bennell, C., & Jones, N. J. (2005). Between a ROC and a hard place: A method for linking serial burglaries by modus operandi. *Journal of Investigative Psychology and Offender Profiling, 2*, 23–41.

Brown, K. L. (1997, June 4). The signature aspect of crime scenes. *Corpus Delicti: The Knowledge Solutions Newsletter*. Retrieved from http://www.corpus-delicti.com/newsletters/june/Brown_K_CP101May97.html

Burgess, A. W., Burgess, A. G., Douglas, J. E., & Ressler, R. K. (Eds.). (1997). *Crime classification manual*. San Francisco, CA: Jossey-Bass.

Cann, J., Friendship, C., & Gozna, L. (2007). Assessing crossover in a sample of sexual offenders with multiple victims. *Legal and Criminological Psychology, 12*, 149–163.

Canter, D. (1995). Psychology of offender profiling. In R. Bull & D. Carson (Eds.), *Handbook of psychology in legal contexts* (pp. 343–355). Chichester, England: John Wiley and Sons.

Canter, D., & Kirby, S. (1995). Prior convictions of child molesters. *Journal of Science & Justice, 35*, 73–78.

Carabellese, F., Maniglio, R., Greco, O., & Catanesi, R. (2011). The role of fantasy in a serial sexual offender: A brief review of the literature and a case report. *Journal of Forensic Sciences, 56*, 256–260.

Carlson, E. R., & Havelock-Coleman, C. E. (1977). Experimental and motivational determinants of the richness of an induced sexual fantasy. *Journal of Personality, 45*, 528–541.

Cornish, D. B., & Clarke, R. V. (1987). Understanding crime displacement: An application of rational choice theory. *Criminology, 25*, 901–916.

Cornish, D. B., & Clarke, R. V. (2002). Analyzing organized crimes. In A. R. Piquero & S. G. Tibbetts (Eds.), *Rational choice and criminal behaviour: Recent research and future challenges* (pp. 41–63). New York, NY: Routledge.

Dandescu, A., & Wolfe, R. (2003). Considerations on fantasy use by child molesters and exhibitionists. *Sexual Abuse: A Journal of Research and Treatment, 15*, 297–307.

Davies, A. (1992). Rapists' behaviour: A three aspect model as a basis for analysis and the identification of serial crime. *Forensic Science International, 55*, 173–194.

Douglas, J. E., Burgess, A. W., Burgess, A. G., & Ressler, R. K. (Eds.). (1992). *Crime classification manual*. New York, NY: Lexington Books.

Douglas, J., & Munn, C. (1992). Violent crime scene analysis: Modus operandi, signature, and staging. *FBI Law Enforcement Bulletin, 61*, 1–10.

Douglas, J., & Olshaker, M. (1996). *Mindhunter*. London, England: Heinemann.

Funder, D. C., & Colvin, C. R. (1991). Explorations in behavioral consistency: Properties of persons, situations, and behaviors. *Journal of Personality and Social Psychology, 60*, 773–794.

Geberth, V. (1996). *Practical homicide investigation: Tactics, procedures, and forensic techniques* (3rd ed.). Boca Raton, FL: CRC Press.

Gee, D. G., & Belofastov, A. (2007). Profiling sexual fantasy: Fantasy in sexual offending and the implications for criminal profiling. In R. N. Kocsis (Ed.), *Criminal profiling: International theory, practice, and research* (pp. 49–71). Totowa, NJ: Humana Press.

Gee, D. G., Devilly, G., & Ward, T. (2004). The content of sexual fantasies for sexual offenders. *Sexual Abuse: A Journal of Research and Treatment, 16*, 315–331.

Gee, D. G., Ward, T., Belofastov, A., & Beech, T. (2006). The structural properties of sexual fantasies for sexual offenders: A preliminary model. *Journal of Sexual Aggression, 12*, 213–226.

Gee, D. G., Ward, T., & Eccelston, L. (2003). The function of sexual fantasies for sexual offenders: A preliminary model. *Behaviour Change, 20*, 44–60.

Gray, N. S., Watt, A., Hassan, S., & Macculloch, M. J. (2003). Behavioral indicators of sadistic sexual murder predict the presence of sadistic sexual fantasy in a normative sample. *Journal of Interpersonal Violence, 18*, 1018–1034.

Guay, J., Proulx, J., Cusson, M., & Ouimet, M. (2001). Victim-choice polymorphia among serious sex offenders. *Archives of Sexual Behavior, 30*, 521–533.

Hanson, R. K., & Bussiere, M. T. (1998). Predicting relapse: A meta-analysis of sexual offender recidivism studies. *Journal of Consulting and Clinical Psychology, 66*, 348–362.

Harbort, S., & Mokros, A. (2001). Serial murderers in Germany from 1945 to 1995: A descriptive study. *Homicide Studies, 5*, 311–334.

Hazelwood, R. R., Dietz, P. E., & Warren, J. I. (1995). The criminal sexual sadist. In R. R. Hazelwood & A. W. Burgess (Eds.), *Practical aspects of rape investigation: A multidisciplinary approach* (2nd ed., pp. 361–371). New York, NY: CRC Press.

Hazelwood, R. R., & Warren, J. I. (1995). The relevance of fantasy in serial sex crime investigation. In R. R. Hazelwood & A. W. Burgess (Eds.), *Practical aspects of rape investigation: A multidisciplinary approach* (2nd ed., pp. 127–138). New York, NY: CRC Press.

Hazelwood, R. R., & Warren, J. I. (2003). Linkage analysis: Modus operandi, ritual, and signature in serial sexual crime. *Aggression and Violent Behavior, 8*, 587–598.

Hettema, J., & Hol, D. P. (1998). Primary control and the consistency of interpersonal behaviour across different situations. *European Journal of Personality, 12*, 231–247.

Hettema, J., & Van Bakel, A. P. (1997). Cross-situational consistency in a mastery condition. *Journal of Research in Personality, 31*, 222–239.

Hickey, E. (2006). *Sex crimes and paraphilia*. Upper Saddle River, NJ: Prentice Hall.

Howitt, D. (2004). What is the role of fantasy in sex offending? *Criminal Behaviour and Mental Health, 14*, 182–188.

Kaufman, K. L. (1994). *Modus operandi questionnaire: Revised version*. Columbus, OH: Author (Children's Hospital).

Keppel, R. (1995). Signature murder: A report of several related cases. *Journal of Forensic Sciences, 40*, 670–674.

Keppel, R. D. (2000). Investigation of the serial offender: Linking cases through modus operandi and signature. In L. B. Schlesinger (Ed.), *Serial offenders: Current thought, recent findings* (pp. 121–134). Boca Raton, FL: CRC Press.

Keppel, R. D., & Birnes, W. J. (2009). *Serial violence: Analysis of modus operandi and signature characteristics of killers*. Boca Raton, FL: CRC Press.

Laws, D. R., Hudson, S. M., & Ward, T. (2000). *Remaking relapse prevention with sex offenders: A sourcebook*. Thousand Oaks, CA: Sage Publications.

Leclerc, B., Beauregard, E., & Proulx, J. (2008). Modus operandi and situational aspects in adolescent sexual offenses against children: A further examination. *International Journal of Offender Therapy and Comparative Criminology, 52*, 46–61.

Leclerc, B., Proulx, J., & Beauregard, E. (2009). Examining the modus operandi of sexual offenders against children and its practical implications. *Aggression and Violent Behavior, 14*, 5–12.

Leitenberg, H., & Henning, K. (1995). Sexual fantasy. *Psychological Bulletin, 117*, 469–496.

Lundrigan, S., Czarnomski, S., & Wilson, M. (2010). Spatial and environmental consistency in serial sexual assault. *Journal of Investigative Psychology and Offender Profiling, 7*, 15–30.

Lussier, P., Leclerc, B., Healey, J., & Proulx, J. (2007). Generality of deviance and predation: Crime-switching and specialization patterns in persistent sexual offenders. In M. Delisi & P. J. Conis (Eds.), *Violent offenders: Theory, research, public policy, and practice* (pp. 97–118). London, England: Jones & Bartlett.

MacCulloch, M. J., Snowden, P. R., Wood, P. J., & Mills, H. E. (1983). Sadistic fantasy, sadistic behaviour and offending. *British Journal of Psychiatry, 143*, 20–29.

Markson, L., Woodhams, J., & Bond, J. (2010). Linking serial residential burglary: Comparing the utility of modus operandi behaviours, geographical proximity and temporal proximity. *Journal of Investigative Psychology and Offender Profiling, 7*, 91–107.

Marshall, W. L., Jones, R., Ward, T., Johnston, P., & Barbaree, H. E. (1991). Treatment outcomes with sex offenders. *Clinical Psychology Review, 11*, 465–485.

Meier, R. F., Kennedy, L. W., & Sacco, V. F. (2001). Crime and the criminal event perspective. In R. F. Meier, L. W. Kennedy, & V. F. Sacco (Eds.), *The process and structure of crime* (pp. 1–28). New Brunswick, Canada: Transaction.

Meloy, J. R. (2000). The nature and dynamics of sexual homicide: An integrative review. *Aggression and Violent Behavior, 5*, 1–22.

Meloy, J. R. (2002). Pathologies of attachment, violence, and criminality. In A. Goldstein (Ed.), *Handbook of psychology, Vol. 11. Forensic psychology* (pp. 509–526). New York, NY: Wiley.

Mokros, A., & Alison, L. J. (2002). Is offender profiling possible? Testing the predicted homology of crime scene actions and background characteristics in a sample of rapists. *Legal and Criminological Psychology, 7*, 25–43.

Person, E. S. (1995). *The force of fantasy: Its role, its benefits and what it reveals about our lives*. London, England: Harper Collins.

Prentky, R. A., & Burgess, A. (1991). Hypothetical biological substrates of a fantasy-based drive mechanism for repetitive sexual aggression. In A. W. Burgess (Ed.), *Rape and sexual assault* (pp. 235–256). New York, NY: Garland.

Prentky, R., Burgess, A., Rokous, F., Lee, A., Hartman, C., Ressler, R., & Douglas, J. (1989). The presumptive role of fantasy in serial sexual homicide. *American Journal of Psychiatry, 146*, 887–891.

Rokach, A. (1990). Content analysis of sexual fantasies of males and females. *Journal of Psychology, 124*, 427–436.

Salfati, C. G. (2008). Offender profiling: Psychological and methodological issues of testing for behavioural consistency. *Issues in Forensic Psychology: Investigative Psychology, 8*, 68–81.

Schlesinger, L. B. (2004). *Sexual murder, catathymic and compulsive homicides*. Boca Raton, FL: CRC Press.

Schlesinger, L. B. (2009). Psychological profiling: Investigative implications for crime scene analysis. *The Journal of Psychiatry & Law, 37*, 73–84.

Showers, C., & Cantor, N. (1985). Social cognition: A look at motivated strategies. *Annual Review of Psychology, 36*, 275–305.

Simon, L. M. J. (1997). Do criminal offenders specialize in crime types? *Applied & Preventive Psychology, 6*, 35–53.

Simon, L. M. J. (2000). An examination of the assumptions of specialization, mental disorder, and dangerousness in sex offenders. *Behavioral Sciences & the Law, 18*, 275–308.

Sjostedt, G., Langstrom, N., Sturidsson, K., & Grann, M. (2004). Stability of modus operandi in sexual offending. *Criminal Justice and Behavior, 31*, 609–623.

Skovran, L. C., Huss, M. T., & Scalora, M. J. (2010). Sexual fantasies and sensation seeking among psychopathic sexual offenders. *Psychology, Crime & Law, 16*, 617–629.

Soothill, K., Francis, B., Sanderson, B., & Ackerley, E. (2000). Sex offenders: Specialists, generalists, or both? *British Journal of Criminology, 40*, 56–67.

Sorochinski, M., & Salfati, G. C. (2010). The consistency of inconsistency in serial homicide: Patterns of behavioural change across series. *Journal of Investigative Psychology and Offender Profiling, 7*, 109–136.

Studer, L. H., Clelland, S. R., Aylwin, A. S., Reddon, J. R., & Monro, A. (2000). Rethinking risk assessment for incest offenders. *International Journal of Law and Psychiatry, 23*, 15–22.

Taylor, S. E., & Pham, L. B. (1996). Mental simulation, motivation, and action. In P. M. Gollwitzer & J. A. Bargh (Eds.), *The psychology of action: Linking cognition and motivation to behaviour* (pp. 219–235). New York, NY: Guilford.

Tonkin, M., Grant, T., & Bond, J. W. (2008). To link or not to link? A test of the case linkage principles using serial car theft data. *Journal of Investigative Psychology and Offender Profiling, 5*, 59–77.

Turvey, B. (1997). What is criminal profiling? *Knowledge Solutions Newsletter, 31*, 7. Retrieved from http://www.corpus-delicti.com/KSNL_031797.html

Turvey, B. (1998a). *Deductive criminal profiling: Comparing applied methodologies between inductive and deductive criminal profiling techniques* [Knowledge Solutions Library]. Retrieved from http://www.corpus-delicti.com/Profiling_law.html

Turvey, B. (1998b). *Definitions of criminal profiling* [SAMPLE lesson plan from CP501: Criminal profiling. Knowledge Solutions Lecture Series]. Retrieved from http://www.corpus-delicti.com/demo.html

Turvey, B. (1998c). *Offender modus operandi, signature and the law* [Knowledge Solutions Library]. Retrieved from http://www.corpus-delicti.com/signature_law.html

Turvey, B. (1999). *Criminal profiling: An introduction to behavioural evidence analysis.* London, England: Academic Press.

Ward, T. (2000). Sexual offenders' cognitive distortions as implicit theories. *Aggression and Violent Behavior, 5*, 491–507.

Ward, T., Bickley, J., Webster, S. D., Fisher, D., Beech, A., & Eldridge, H. (2004). *The self-regulation model of the offense and re-offense process—Volume I: Assessment.* Victoria, BC: Pacific Psychological Assessment Corporation.

Ward, T., Fon, C., Hudson, S. M., & McCormack, J. (1998). A descriptive model of dysfunctional cognitions in child molesters. *Journal of Interpersonal Violence, 13*, 129–155.

Ward, T., & Hudson, S. M. (2000a). A self-regulation model of relapse prevention. In D. R. Laws, S. M. Hudson, & T. Ward (Eds.), *Remaking relapse prevention with sex offenders: A sourcebook* (pp. 79–101). Thousand Oaks, CA: Sage Publications.

Ward, T., & Hudson, S. M. (2000b). Sexual offenders' implicit planning: A conceptual model. *Sexual Abuse: A Journal of Research and Treatment, 12*, 189–202.

Ward, T., Hudson, S. M., & McCormack, J. (1997). The assessment of rapists. *Behaviour Change, 14*, 39–54.

Ward, T., Yates, P. M., & Long, C. (2006). *The self-regulation model of the offense and re-offense process—Volume II: Treatment.* Victoria, BC: Pacific Psychological Assessment Corporation.

Woodhams, J., Bull, R., & Hollin, C. (2007). Case linkage: Identifying crimes committed by the same offender. In R. N. Kocsis (Ed.), *Criminal profiling: International theory, research, and practice* (pp. 113–117). Totowa, NJ: Humana Press.

Woodhams, J., Hollin, C., & Bull, R. (2008). Incorporating context in linking crimes: An exploratory study of situational similarity and if-then contingencies. *Journal of Investigative Psychology and Offender Profiling, 5*, 1–23.

Woodhams, J., & Labuschagne, G. N. (2012a). A test of case linkage principles with solved and unsolved serial rapes. *Journal of Police and Criminal Psychology, 27*, 85–98.

Woodhams, J., & Labuschagne, G. N. (2012b). South African serial rapists: The offenders, their victims and their offences. *Sexual Abuse: A Journal of Research and Treatment, 24*, 544–574.

Woodhams, J., & Toye, K. (2007). An empirical test of the assumptions of case linkage and offender profiling within serial commercial robberies. *Psychology, Public Policy, and Law, 13*, 59–85.

Yates, P. M., Kingston, D., & Ward, T. (2009). *The self-regulation model of the offense and re-offense process—Volume III: A guide to assessment and treatment planning using the integrated good lives/self-regulation model of sexual offending.* Victoria, BC: Pacific Psychological Assessment Corporation.

The Effect of Mental Disorder on Crime Scene Behavior, Its Consistency, and Variability

4

JESSICA WOODHAMS AND
KINGA KOMARZYNSKA

Contents

Introduction 56
The Incidence of Mental Disorder in the Sex Offender Population 56
Schizophrenia and Sexual Offending 57
Personality Disorder and Sexual Offending 58
Testing the Assumptions of Crime Linkage with Mentally Disordered Rapists 60
Factors Affecting Stability and Change in the Offending Behavior of Mentally Disordered Serial Sex Offenders 64
Situational Factors 67
Victim Behavior and Victim Characteristics 67
The Offense Environment 67
Employment 68
Social Network 68
Presence of a Co-Offender 68
Third Party Interruption 69
Personal Factors 69
Sexual Fantasy 69
Motive/Mood 71
Experience 72
Physiological 74
Planning/Preparation 74
Attitudes and Beliefs 75
Summary 77
Conclusion 79
References 79

Introduction

Mentally disordered individuals have been reported to show more consistent offense behavior than individuals without such disorders (Argyle, 1967, as cited in Davies, 1992). Indeed, within the crime linkage literature, it has been proposed that offenders with more severe pathology will be more consistent in their offending behavior (Santtila et al., 2008). Consistency in offense behavior by mentally disordered individuals following hospitalization is also a subject of research in its own right, in terms of the literature on offense-paralleling behavior (Daffern, Jones, & Shine, 2010). If mental disorder or illness results in greater consistency in offense behavior, as suggested, this could enhance crime analysts' abilities to link offenses by such offenders, providing that they also show distinctiveness in their crime scene behavior.

All of the research on crime linkage that has been conducted to date focused on samples of serial offenders who do not suffer from a mental illness or disorder, or for whom mental health status was unknown. In contrast, this chapter focuses on this issue. First, we consider the incidence of mental illness/disorder in sex offender samples. Following this, we review opinions and research as to the effect that such conditions might have on crime scene behavior. We then present findings from the first studies of the behavioral consistency and distinctiveness of serial sex offenders with a known mental illness/disorder. Throughout this chapter, for the sake of brevity, we use the term *mental disorder* to refer to both mental illness and mental disorder. This chapter gives particular attention to sexual offenders with a mental disorder because it is this population that has received the most speculation in terms of the potential effects of mental disorder on offending behavior (e.g., Kocsis, Cooksey, & Irwin, 2002; Smith, 2000) and because crime linkage analysis is often conducted on stranger sex offenses in practice.

The Incidence of Mental Disorder in the Sex Offender Population

Historically, sexual offending, particularly rape, was thought to be a result of some form of psychopathology (Scully & Marolla, 1984). In addition, the small but significant association between mental disorder and violent behavior (Drake & Pathe, 2004) could suggest such a link. Studies of sex offenders conducted within prisons or forensic psychiatric institutions report diagnoses of mental disorder to be common (Harsch, Bergk, Steinert, Keller, & Jockusch, 2006; Heasman, 2005; Novak, McDermott, Scott, & Guillory, 2007). However, within the prison environment at least, the prevalence of mental disorder is thought to be higher than it is in the general population (Fazel & Danesh, 2002), which could lead to overestimation of the comorbidity between offending and mental disorder if research relies only on samples of incarcerated sex offenders when gauging prevalence rather than assessing this relationship using a community sample.

Regarding the types of mental disorder commonly associated with sexual offending, research suggests a particular link between schizophrenia and sexual offending (Drake & Pathe, 2004; Novak et al., 2007) and personality disorder and rape (Davison & Janca, 2012; Rigonatti, Serafim, Caires, Guerra, & Arboleda-Florez, 2006), even with national samples of community-dwelling adults (Hoertel, Le Strat, Schuster, & Limonsin, 2012). We therefore selected these two forms of mental disorder for specific attention in this chapter.

Schizophrenia and Sexual Offending

As reported, a particular association has been noted between schizophrenia and sexual offending; however, it should also be noted that schizophrenic sex offenders are thought to account for less than 10% of sex offenses (Sahota & Chesterman, 1998, as cited in Drake & Pathe, 2004). Schizophrenia is thought to contribute to sexual offending via several pathways: by having a disinhibitory effect on thoughts and urges, through offense-related delusions and hallucinations, and via social withdrawal and cognitive deterioration, which may prevent the offender achieving physical intimacy with others in socially appropriate ways (Drake & Pathe, 2004).

In terms of how schizophrenia might affect the behavior displayed by an offender at the crime scene, the association that has been reported between psychosis and violence (Khalid, Ford, & Maughan, 2012) could suggest that psychotic sex offenders might show a greater propensity for physical violence within their offending (Kocsis et al., 2002). One study comparing schizophrenic and nonschizophrenic sex offenders also noted a tendency for schizophrenic sex offenders to show a preference for targeting female adult victims (Alish et al., 2007).

In addition, it has been speculated that schizophrenic offenders may also show more disorganization* in their offending and be more opportunistic (Kocsis et al., 2002). There is also a popular view that their offense behavior will be bizarre or odd (Smith, 2000). Studies of the motivation driving sexual offending by psychotic individuals suggest that most are motivated by opportunism and sexual desire (Greenhall & West, 2007; Smith, 2000). Disorganization and opportunism could result in greater intra-individual variation in offending, which would suggest that crime series by

* Here, Kocsis and colleagues (2002) are referring to the Federal Bureau of Investigation's organized–disorganized typology (Ressler, Burgess, & Douglas, 1988), where disorganized crime behavior is haphazard and random in nature.

schizophrenic rapists would be harder for crime linkage practitioners to detect. Paradoxically, bizarre behavior that is idiosyncratic in nature could help identify a crime series.

However, such behaviors would likely only be displayed during an offense when the offender has been actively psychotic. It has been estimated that only 5% of sex offenders who suffer from mental illness are actively psychotic at the time of their offense (Abel, Becker, & Skinner, 1980). This finding suggests that the majority of sex offenders with schizophrenia will commit their crimes when their symptoms are in remission and therefore characterizations of disorganization, violence, and opportunism would be relevant only for the small minority of mentally ill sex offenders. Indeed, Smith (2000) investigated differences in the offense behavior of rapists who were psychotic at the time of their offense compared to those who were not. Smith's sample consisted of 80 sex offenders in the United Kingdom who committed their offense alone against a lone female victim. Sixty-one percent of these men assaulted a woman who was a stranger to them. Of the stranger rapists, most used a surprise approach to obtain their victim and most offenses occurred outdoors. Most of the 80 men (76%) used just sufficient force to facilitate the assault rather than engaging in excessive violence. Most offenders (61%) related to their victim in an impersonal manner. Some of the men did show bizarre behavior during the offense, but this constituted a minority of the sample (20%). Examples of such behavior included shouting at auditory hallucinations; displaying irrational, delusional speech; and making robotic or other strange bodily movements. The findings of Smith (2000) do not therefore support the popular view that psychotic rapists will show violent behavior any more so than rapists who are not psychotic, and only a minority of these actively psychotic men displayed bizarre behavior. The latter point needs to be considered alongside Abel et al.'s (1980) findings that only 5% of mentally ill sex offenders are actively psychotic at the time of the offense. Bizarre behavioral acts might be useful for identifying rape series, but it should not be assumed that it is typically displayed by psychotic rapists. Smith (2000) argues that like rapists without a mental disorder, his sample's offending was driven by cognitive distortions, deviant fantasy, and poor sexual knowledge. Consequently, we might expect a level of consistency in schizophrenic rapists' crime scene behavior that is similar to that we have observed with existing samples where mental health status was unknown. The limited potential for bizarre behavior within this subsample of rapists might assist crime linkage by assisting with the differentiation of offenders.

Personality Disorder and Sexual Offending

Like mentally ill and schizophrenic rapists, personality-disordered and psychopathic rapists have been reported to be motivated to sexually offend by sexual desire and opportunism; however, they are also more likely to be motivated by pervasive anger, sexual sadism, and vindictiveness (Greenhall & West, 2007). In terms of how this might manifest in offense behavior, Greenhall and West noted a tendency for their English psychopathic offenders* to be more violent toward their victims. Proulx, Aubut, Perron, and McKibben (1994, as cited in Mokros & Alison, 2002) have made similar observations for personality-disordered offenders with antisocial and paranoid tendencies.

Personality disorders have the potential to impact quite significantly on behavioral consistency and distinctiveness. As noted by Eaton, South, and Krueger (2009), personality disorders endure once they develop during adolescent years, and they are "pervasive and inflexible across a wide range of functioning" (p. 208). Unlike the potential influence of schizophrenia on crime scene behavior being limited to periods of active psychosis, the influence of personality disorders would be hypothesized to be continuously present.

Using Mischel and Shoda's (1995) cognitive–affective personality system (CAPS) as a reference point, Eaton and colleagues (2009) make a number of predictions about how personality disorders, when conceptualized using the CAPS, could result in behavioral stability and change (see Chapter 2 for an introduction to the CAPS). These predictions are as follows: (1) People with a personality disorder could interpret the same situation differently when compared to people without a personality disorder (due to cognitive and affective distortions associated with the disorder); (2) personality disorders may also result in people being unable to differentiate situations effectively leading to the same response being produced in psychologically different situations; (3) people with personality disorder can have a more limited behavioral repertoire or may struggle to make full use of their behavioral repertoire due to inflexibility; and (4) the CAPS of people with personality disorder can be more greatly influenced by self-related factors resulting in the individual recreating the same situation over time.

In terms of trying to behaviorally link the crimes of offenders, point (1) above suggests that there should be some variability between offenders in how they react to the same environmental stimuli, which would allow for some differentiation between the crimes of different offenders. Points (2), (3), and (4) imply that offenders with personality disorders may show greater consistency in behavior across their crimes than offenders without such pathology. It follows that crime linkage could be more effective when an attempt is made to link the crimes of offenders with such personality pathology. With regard

* These stranger rapists were not diagnosed as psychopathic according to the PCL-R (Hare, 2003) but according to the Mental Health Act 1983 and would have displayed a range of personality disorders.

to sex offenders in particular, the beliefs of mentally disordered sex offenders have been argued to be more persistent and enduring over time (Drake & Pathe, 2004). The role of beliefs within the CAPS, in terms of affecting behavior, would suggest further evidence for behavioral consistency over time.

Although, as Eaton et al. (2009) note, personality disorders are believed to become enduring during adolescence, there is also some evidence that pathological personality dispositions (such as deceitfulness, selfishness, and remorselessness associated with adult psychopathy) emerge during childhood and show moderate-to-substantial consistency during childhood and adolescence (Loney, Taylor, Butler, & Iacono, 2007; Obradovic, Pardini, Long, & Loeber, 2007; van Baardewijk, Vermeiren, Stegge, & Doreleijers, 2011). The consistency and distinctiveness we might expect to see in the crimes of adult personality-disordered offenders may also be reflected in the crimes of youngsters.

It has been suggested that the number of sex offenders with a mental disorder that would come to the attention of a crime linkage practitioner would be small (Davies, 1992); however, some research on offending behavior by rapists with psychopathy suggests that their offenses may come to the attention of the police and crime linkage practitioners a disproportionate amount of the time compared to those of offenders with other mental disorders. For example, psychopathic and personality-disordered rapists are more likely to target adults and stranger victims (Rigonatti et al., 2006; Skovran, Huss, & Scalora, 2010), the latter being the crime type most likely to be the subject of crime linkage. Furthermore, their sex offenses are perpetrated more frequently and involve more severe forms of sexual violence (Skovran et al., 2010), which would make them a particular policing priority.

In summary, the presence of active psychosis or a personality disorder may affect the degree of behavioral consistency and distinctiveness shown by a sex offender across his or her series. Although it is thought that only a minority of sex offenses are committed by offenders with a mental disorder, it is possible that due to their characteristics they may disproportionately come to the attention of crime linkage practitioners. If this is the case, it is important for us to have a good understanding of the degree of consistency and distinctiveness they show in their offense behavior.

Testing the Assumptions of Crime Linkage with Mentally Disordered Rapists

As reported in other chapters (e.g., Chapters 5 and 6), crime linkage researchers tend to sample a set of crime series for which the identity of each offender has been established through conviction or DNA evidence. This practice allows the researcher to make predictions about which crimes are part of the same series and which are from a different series, against which actual series membership can be compared. In our first study of the behavioral consistency and distinctiveness of mentally disordered offenders, we sampled 20 adult male patients (aged ≥18 years) from a high security hospital in the United Kingdom. All 20 patients had committed two or more sexual offenses, as established by conviction. In total, these 20 men had committed 69 sexual offenses. All of the men had a diagnosis of schizophrenia and/or personality disorder according to the *DSM-IV-TR* classification (American Psychiatric Association, 2000). Table 4.1 shows a breakdown of the men's primary, and if relevant, secondary diagnoses.

Hospital files for each offender were accessed following the offender's consent to participate in the study, and all relevant documents and reports that described their offense behavior were viewed. Using these sources of information, each offense was coded against a checklist of offenders' crime scene behavior in a binary fashion (0 = behavior not present or unknown if it was displayed, 1 = behavior present in the offense). The checklist used was from Woodhams and Labuschagne (2012), with some amendments made due to additional behaviors being present in this sample.

As will be outlined in Chapter 6, a procedure first proposed by Bennell and Canter (2002) is commonly used to test the two underlying assumptions of crime linkage (behavioral consistency and distinctiveness). This procedure involves creating linked and unlinked crime pairs from the sample of crime series and comparing these for their degree of similarity in offense behavior. Typically, this procedure is quantified using Jaccard's coefficient, as was the case here. All possible linked and unlinked crime pairs were created from the 20 series resulting in 2346 crime pairs, of which 109 were linked and 2237 were unlinked.

Tests of difference for the linked and the unlinked pairs indicated that the linked crime pairs were significantly more similar in terms of offense behavior compared to the unlinked crime pairs. The magnitude of the

Table 4.1 Diagnostic Profile of 20 Serial Sex Offenders Including Comorbidity

Primary Diagnosis	Secondary Diagnosis	Number of Patients
Schizophrenia	None	4
	Specific learning difficulties	2
	Personality disorder(s)	2
Personality disorder(s)	None	2
	Elevated PCL-R scores (>25)	8
	Other mental disorder (e.g., anxiety disorder)	4

Note: PCL-R refers to the Psychopathy Checklist-Revised (Hare, 2003), a measure of psychopathy.

difference was much larger than has been observed in other studies of serial rapists. For example, with our sample, the linked crime pairs had an average Jaccard's coefficient of 0.76 and the unlinked pairs had an average of 0.29. In comparison, the figures reported by Woodhams and Labuschagne (2012) were 0.52 and 0.34, respectively, and for Bennell, Jones, and Melnyk (2009), they were 0.41 and 0.27.

In line with previous studies of crime linkage with serial rape, how well the linked crime pairs could be differentiated from the unlinked crime pairs on the basis of behavioral similarity was assessed using receiver operating characteristic analysis. This analysis produces a measure of discrimination accuracy, the area under the curve (AUC), which in crime linkage studies refers to how well linked and unlinked crime pairs can be discriminated using Jaccard's coefficients. The larger the AUC, the more accurately linked and unlinked crime pairs can be differentiated. The AUC produced by the receiver operating characteristic analysis was 0.996, which was statistically significant. According to published guidelines used to interpret the size of an AUC, this value would correspond with an exceptional or high level of discrimination accuracy (Hosmer & Lemeshow, 2000; Swets, 1988). Again, this figure is much higher than has been observed in existing samples of serial rapists. For example, with Woodhams and Labuschagne's (2012) sample of serial rapists from the Republic of South Africa, an AUC of 0.88 was reported, and Bennell et al. (2009) found an AUC of 0.75 with their UK sample.

Further analyses were conducted comparing those serial rapists who had a primary diagnosis of schizophrenia versus those with a primary diagnosis of personality disorder in case there were differences in their degree of behavioral consistency (see Table 4.2). Although the personality-disordered serial rapists appeared to show a slightly higher degree of behavioral similarity across their series compared to the schizophrenic rapists, a significant difference in behavioral similarity between the two groups was not found. However, the number of rapists with a primary diagnosis of schizophrenia was small; therefore, the analyses likely lacked power. An effect size calculation indicated that there was a medium-sized effect present ($d = 0.40$) (Cohen, 1988). A *post hoc* power calculation using G-Power 3.1.5 (Faul, Erdfelder, Lang, & Buchner, 2007) produced a power of 0.17. Therefore, with larger subsamples a significant difference would likely be found.

This research study therefore provides support for the assumptions of behavioral consistency and distinctiveness for a sample of mentally disordered serial sex offenders. In fact, at first glance, the levels of behavioral consistency and distinctiveness within this sample seem far superior to those from existing samples of serial rapists. It would be tempting to speculate that these differences emerge because of the mentally disordered nature of the serial rapists in the sample, particularly the high prevalence of personality disorders, which, as explained in Section Personality Disorder and Sexual

Table 4.2 Degree of Behavioral Consistency Observed within Series for Rapists with Schizophrenia and Those with Personality Disorder

Primary diagnosis	Series Number	Degree of Behavioral Similarity (Jaccard Coefficient) Mean (Range)[a]
Schizophrenia	3	0.62 (0.47–0.84)
	7	0.77 (0.67–0.88)
	9	0.81 (0.66–0.97)
	12	0.74 (0.62–0.87)
	13	0.80 (0.74–0.90)
	17	0.89 (0.83–0.90)
	20	0.59
	Overall group mean	0.75 (0.11)
Personality disorder	1	0.75
	2	0.93
	4	0.82 (0.74–0.93)
	5	0.70
	6	0.65 (0.45–0.82)
	8	0.74 (0.64–0.90)
	10	0.71 (0.58–0.93)
	11	0.97 (0.96–1.00)
	14	0.65
	15	0.88 (0.75–1.00)
	16	0.80 (0.71–0.88)
	18	0.74
	19	0.82 (0.78–0.90)
	Overall group mean	0.78 (0.10)

[a] For series of just two offenses, only one Jaccard's value can be calculated.

Offending, is related to rigid thinking and behavior, as well as variability in reaction to environmental stimuli, such as victim behavior. However, there is also a key difference between this study and studies conducted previously with serial rapists. This difference lies in the nature of the data source about the offending behavior of the sample. In existing studies of crime linkage with serial rapists, police files or entries from police databases are used as the source of information about crime scene behavior. Typically, it is the victim's account of the crime that is relied upon by the police and is therefore the source of information in these crime linkage studies. In contrast, in this study, we had access to hospital files that in some cases contained more information than would be held in a police file. This was not the case for all of the offenders, though; in some cases, the researcher had access only to the court report, a witness statement, or the police report. It is therefore possible that it is the richer data available for some of the offenders in the sample that has led to larger estimates of behavioral consistency across a series than seen previously.

Disentangling these two competing explanations would require a collaborative study between both the police and forensic mental health institutions. Ideally, a research study would be designed, whereby a sample of serial rapists with mental disorders was identified from the data held by forensic mental health institutions. Having identified a potential sample, the relevant police force or agency would need to be contacted to access the police data held regarding the offense behavior of each individual as displayed in each offense. Although possible, such a study will be challenging to conduct.

When comparing within our sample, there was a nonsignificant trend suggesting serial rapists with a personality disorder showed a higher degree of behavioral consistency across their series when compared to the serial rapists with schizophrenia. In theory, greater behavioral consistency should be observed only for those schizophrenic serial rapists who are actively psychotic at the time of offense, whereas personality disorders and their effect on the stability of crime scene behavior should be more persistent. It was not possible within the current study to determine whether the schizophrenic rapists were actively psychotic at the time of offense; however, from Table 4.2, it is clear that some individuals within the schizophrenia subsample displayed relatively lower levels of behavioral consistency (e.g., 0.59) compared to others (e.g., 0.89), and it may be that these differences reflect the influence of active psychotic symptoms. Future studies that are able to determine period of active psychosis would be able to assess this impact on offending.

Factors Affecting Stability and Change in the Offending Behavior of Mentally Disordered Serial Sex Offenders

Much of the research on crime linkage has investigated the principles of behavioral consistency and distinctiveness with serial sex offenses (Bennell et al., 2009; Canter et al., 1991; Grubin, Kelly, & Brunsdon, 2001; Lundrigan, Czarnomski, & Wilson, 2010; Santtila, Junkkila, & Sandnabba, 2005; Woodhams, Grant, & Price, 2007; Woodhams & Labuschagne, 2012; Yokota, Fujita, Watanabe, Yoshimoto, & Wachi, 2007). However, there is very little research in this area (or with other crime types) that investigates the factors that influence the display of certain crime scene behaviors and, importantly, how these factors might result in stability or change in behavior across a series, although the need for such research was identified more than 10 years ago

(Grubin et al., 2001). To address this gap in our knowledge, we interviewed four mentally disordered serial sex offenders about the offenses they had committed and the factors that they thought had influenced their behavior during each offense and across the series. We gave specific attention to their perceptions of behavioral stability and change and the causes of both.

Fourteen hours of interviews were conducted by the second author with four White British male patients held in a high security hospital in the United Kingdom. These men were aged between 27 and 47 years old. All had committed at least two separate sexual offenses against different adult women, therefore meeting the common definition of a serial offender (Federal Bureau of Investigation, 2008; Grubin et al., 2001; Santtila et al., 2005). The length of the participants' series ranged from 2 to 15 sexual offenses; however, their offending history was not limited to sexual offending and included violent and acquisitive offenses. The sexual offenses included rape and, in some cases, sexual homicide. All four participants had been diagnosed with personality disorders (Clusters A and B)* and all met the diagnosis for antisocial personality disorder (American Psychiatric Association, 2000). All had also been assessed using Hare's (2003) Psychopathy Checklist-Revised and had received scores above the UK cutoff of 25 (Olver & Wang, 2006; Semple, 2005).

A semistructured interview schedule was devised drawing on existing literature of factors that influence sexual offending behavior (e.g., sexual fantasies, attitudes, psychological and emotional state at the time of the offense). However, the interviews also asked questions about significant event characteristics pre-, during, and post-offense, allowing the participants to raise other factors that were relevant to their individual offending. The characteristics of the offenders, in terms of the nature of their mental disorders, meant that a flexible manner was required during interviews. Prompts were regularly used to bring the interview back "on topic." The number of interviews varied in each case due to participants' presentation, readiness to talk about sensitive issues, as well as the volume of material to cover during the sessions. The number of sessions per participant ranged from two to six. Prior to each set of interviews with a participant, the second author reviewed the case files for each individual so that she already had a good understanding of the nature and scope of their sexual offending behavior.

The interviews were transcribed on the secure site so that any information taken off-site was anonymized. This was achieved by replacing any

* The types of personality disorders are grouped, according to the characteristics of their traits, into three clusters: Cluster A (odd and eccentric), which includes schizoid, schizotypal, and paranoid personality disorder; Cluster B (dramatic and emotional), which includes the diagnosis of antisocial, histrionic, narcissistic, and borderline personality disorders; and Cluster C (anxious and fearful), which includes avoidant, dependant, and obsessive–compulsive disorders (American Psychiatric Association, 2000).

names with pseudonyms. Template analysis (King, 2004), a type of qualitative analysis, was used to identify themes within the participants' accounts. This form of analysis involves various stages typical of forms of thematic qualitative analysis, including familiarization with the data, development of an initial coding template, refinement of codes, charting, and memoing. The template that is produced from the analysis can consist of lower- and higher-order themes and can, in part, include some a priori themes.

Our coding template consisted of two higher-order themes (personal factors and situational factors) under which lower-order themes were arranged. These themes can be seen in Table 4.3. Each theme is described below with regard to whether it was related to consistency, change, or both and is illustrated with relevant quotes from the interviews.*

Table 4.3 The 25 Lower-Order Codes Arranged into Themes Representing Factors Affecting the Stability and Change of Crime Scene Behavior for Mentally Disordered Serial Sex Offenders

Personal	Situational
• Sexual fantasy	• Victim
• Motive/mood	• Victim behavior
• Anger	• Victim characteristics
• Desire	• Physical environment
• Boredom/excitement	• Employment
• Anxiety	• Social network
• Experience	• Presence of a co-offender
• Being a victim of abuse	• Third party interruption
• Offending against others	
• Observational learning	
• Physiological	
• Planning/preparation	
• Reconnaissance	
• Rehearsal	
• Familiarity	
• Attitudes/beliefs	
• About self	
• About victim	
• About offending	
• About Police/Justice system	
• About world	
• Associated with personality disorder	

* The quotes are not attributed to particular offenders, as would normally be the case when presenting qualitative research. This is to avoid a series or offender being identified from his quotes being pieced together.

Situational Factors

Victim Behavior and Victim Characteristics

All four offenders described how the behavior of the victim had resulted in behavioral change during their series. This description included reports that victim resistance had deterred the offender or that he had accommodated her behavior to an extent. One of the offenders altered his future offending behavior as a result of a victim's reaction therefore introducing behavioral variation between two time-adjacent offenses:

> I could hear her crying. I could hear the effect of what I had done to her ... as soon as she started crying I knew that I had hurt her emotionally, which was extremely pleasing for me ... next offence was more about that.

This finding replicates anecdotal reports from other researchers that victim behavior can alter behavior of the offender (e.g., Davies, 1992) and reflects what would be expected from theories of behavioral consistency, which would suggest that situational change (in this case, as defined by victim behavior) results in behavioral change (Woodhams, Hollin, & Bull, 2008).

Victim characteristics were reported to result in both behavioral consistency and variation. In terms of consistency, one offender reported targeting victims of a particular appearance; however, most indicated that it was perceived vulnerability that was more relevant for their targeting rather than actual physical looks. Unexpected conditions resulted in behavioral change. For example, one offender changed his behavior when he realized the victim was menstruating.

The Offense Environment

All four of the participants indicated some degree of consistency with regard to the environment in which they chose to offend. The reasons for their choice included the area being isolated, the area having good escape routes, or their having easy access to weapons (i.e., in a victim's home). One offender reported repeatedly choosing areas that were overlooked because he found this sexually arousing:

> being overlooked ... that gave me a sense of thrill, sense of the excitement ... the risk element made me feel that I might get caught here. That was exciting, that was thrilling ....

For this offender, his preference for such locations meant that he returned to the exact same location to reoffend:

> I actually found an area the first time around and ... I went back to the same spot.

These findings are not surprising when we consider the number of studies of crime linkage principles that have indicated the utility of inter-crime distance as a predictor of linkage status (see Chapter 5 for a critical discussion of this research), whereby crimes committed by the same offender are often located closer together than crimes committed by two different offenders.

One offender reported changing his offense location preference during his series because an outdoor environment presented too much risk of being unsuccessful in his offending:

> So I preferred ... her place ... I knew I can do whatever I wanted and this time, no one is going to interrupt me.

Employment

The offender's choice of employment was based on facilitating access to victims in two cases, resulting in consistency in the short term in how victims were approached by the offender, in offense location, and in victimology.

> I was thinking that this [referring to his choice of job] would be the easiest way to have access to the young girls without raising suspicion.

However, all the offenders interviewed reported varied histories of employment. Therefore, although accessing victims via their employment remained a stable part of the offenders' *modus operandi*, the exact nature of their employment changed across series.

Other offenders were in a position of trust in their employment, and their work uniform provided them with a method of approach, in terms of gaining the victim's trust, as well as a means of avoiding drawing attention to themselves. For example:

> I was wearing my security uniform so it wouldn't draw too much suspicion to me.

Social Network

Instead of using employment as a means to access victims, one participant selected victims from his social circle. His choice of social circle was intentional so that he could access his desired victim type, which was a consistent aspect of his offending:

> hanging around much younger people ... I always knew where to be ... my friend told me once that if there is a group of 15 year old girls on the street corner when he walked passed he knew somewhere I am going to be there.

Presence of a Co-Offender

Two participants reported that their initial offenses were committed with another person, but that they progressed to become a lone offender. In both cases, the presence of a co-offender resulted in different behavior in the initial offense compared to their later offenses. The participants reported that the presence of a co-offender introduced unpredictability and that having to consider someone else's "agendas" affected their offending behavior. For example, in the case of one offender, the circumstances of his first offense were dictated by his co-offender, whereby the offense occurred outdoors with the victim being obtained through a surprise approach. This offense contrasted dramatically with his later (lone) offending. Another offender identified himself as the catalyst for the group sex offense, but there were still behavioral differences between the group offense and his later offence in that he was concerned with showing off to his co-offender in the first offense.

Third Party Interruption

Two of the four participants reported being interrupted by somebody during the offense, which naturally introduced change in *modus operandi*. Moreover, this interruption produced a change in the future behavior of one participant, as he was interrupted on two occasions. This caused him to change the location of his offending from an isolated outdoor area to indoors.

> I heard someone in the alleyway ... that was one of my escape routes ... I panicked ... as soon as I heard somebody I thought "oh shit! I am going to get caught!"

The other offender was interrupted by a third party on one occasion. However, apart from being forced to abandon his plans for offending (short-term changes), this incident did not alter his offending behavior in the long term.

Personal Factors

Sexual Fantasy

Deviant sexual fantasy is unquestionably one of the most recognized factors associated with sexual offending (Carabellese, Maniglio, Greco, & Catanesi, 2011; see also Chapter 3). The analysis of this theme highlighted the dynamic nature of sexual fantasy, as well as its multilayered relationship with moods, motives, and offense planning (rehearsing). This theme seemed to reinforce certain behaviors of participants, which resulted in behavioral stability, yet instigated new behaviors in other circumstances.

All four participants reported evolution in their sexual fantasies, which included various kinds of scenarios depending on their mood and personal circumstances. This content variation resulted in alteration of their *modus operandi* across offense series.

> They would range from … I can make an approach and make sexual advances towards her that would be: "well, we've already started so we may as well finish" type, to: I would grab hold of her, drag her to an area, I would then forcibly take her … I would rape her and if she was not agreeing with something I really wanted, I would end up killing her and that's where the fantasies kind of went … having sex with …, to raping and killing … that whole range depending on how upset, how angry, how happy I suppose I was.

The fantasies were also modified with time due to the offender gaining experience and developing more specific interest and aims:

> I was thinking about what I had done in the first one then I went for the second one and then thinking in my head, adding things.

Two participants reported escalation of violence in their fantasies over time, which also increased in their frequency. Both of them reflected on parallel escalation at the time in their offending behavior.

> My fantasies changed to be more violent, physically violent, the sexual violence is self evident in terms of that I am forcing somebody to do what I want … but the fact that I was more aroused at being physically violent whilst performing sexual acts against someone …, that was something … that was highly arousing to me … it started with me doing more stuff, to involve punching while having sex or whatever.

In other cases, sexual fantasies either contributed toward the stability of behavior at the crime scene in terms of reinforcing the pleasurable behavior and desired outcome of previous offenses

> I thought about sex with women … they were pretty violent, yeah, similar to what I was doing to victims …,

or toward victim targeting, where the object of the offender's fantasy shared characteristics with the victims selected (e.g., being of a young age).

For one participant, whose sadistic interests and feeling in complete control over the offense situation were crucial, sadistic sexual fantasy was also an opportunity for rehearsal.

> In terms of fantasy … it is remembering … it is not so much fantasy but remembered sexual experience. I would replay in my mind what I have already done. I would be fantasising about it, while I was following her … about what I am going to do to her and how I am going to make her feel.

This individual's sexual fantasies tended to be very detailed and tailored for each offense in order to "prepare" for all possible challenges. Although his fantasies were adapted to each offense, they would still include similar elements that were responsible for this participant's behavioral consistency.

Motive/Mood

This theme incorporated the affective factors that can be identified as drive and motive for the offense. For all four participants, motive/mood was one of the most powerful themes responsible for both stability and change in their behavior. Several lower-order themes described the various moods/motives—anger, desire, boredom (looking for excitement), and anxiousness. The first two subthemes (anger and desire) have been reported in other studies of sex offenders with personality disorders (Greenhall & West, 2007; Proulx et al., 1994, as cited in Mokros & Alison, 2002).

All four participants highlighted that some degree of anger was always present during their offenses, and all stated that most of the time it was a necessary component to justify their offending behavior.

> I had to dislike them to do it. If I liked them I couldn't hurt them but I had to get to that stage where I disliked them and disliked them enough.

For two participants, revenge for being rejected (often by their victims) led to consistency in their perception of the victim and offense, as well as consistency in their offense behavior.

> I think that the anger was already there and the rejection caused even more anger and at that moment the dislike of that person ... because they don't like me was permission giving and I just said "fuck you, I will do what I want" and that was true about all my offences.

The analysis of transcripts suggested that the mood/motive in all four cases was never limited to only one kind. Apart from anger, desire was the other common drive related to sexual offending. This theme incorporated aspects around sexual preoccupation and looking for sexual gratification and/or intimacy. All four participants stated that sexual pleasure/gratification was one of their most important aims.

For three participants, desire was responsible mainly for stable features in their offending, often the repertoire of sexual acts that they would find enjoyable (e.g., anal or oral sex, kissing, fondling breasts). For the remaining participant, desire had a different impact, because his sexual interest was strongly and solely influenced by his sadistic preferences. Although a certain range of behaviors would remain fairly consistent in his case, in the long term he incorporated more violent and odd acts into his *modus operandi*:

> It was more about pain and suffering ... emotional as well as physical pain ... if I had not been caught ... if I am honest, I think I would have probably ended up killing someone.

All four participants referred to feeling anxious when committing offenses early in their series. In all cases, this initial lack of confidence compared to the confidence experienced with later offenses resulted in behavioral instability within the series:

> I couldn't perform the act of intercourse with the first girl because I was petrified.
>
> My confidence was building ... for the second one when I was coming up to the door, a difference to the first one was this was early morning ... so it was quite light. The other one was at night time so I think that shows the confidence or stupidity at that time.

This confidence along with anger resulted in reckless behavior, which in all four cases led to their arrest by the police.

> The first offence I didn't want to be caught ... the second offence I didn't care.

This recklessness seemed to result in some consistency, as the more an offender felt that "he could do whatever he wanted," the more likely he was to engage in similar behaviors over time that he found pleasurable:

> I was getting more and more blasé about the whole situation and just doing what I wanted to do even more, not really caring about the consequences.

Two offenders reported changes in mood during an offense (e.g., being forceful and angry at the beginning of the offense, but feeling anxious or ashamed post-offense). One offender in particular noted the acute sense of anxiety he experienced in the closure stage of a rape, when he feared he would be caught. He explained that this sense of anxiety resulted in specific "caring" post-offense behavior (e.g., giving the victim advice about getting home safely or giving her money for a taxi) in an attempt to influence his victims into not reporting the offense:

> The reality is it is not because he has got empathy with the victim but because it is self preservation, you know. I didn't want to go to prison at all.

Experience

Another theme that influenced the behavior of all four participants was related to their previous experiences. This experience could relate to having been a victim of abuse themselves, their previous offending, or "observational learning."

All four participants disclosed being subjected to sexual abuse as children and all of them were able to link their offending behavior with some elements of their past victimization. This experience contributed toward stability in offending behavior for two offenders:

> From my own experience that was a very painful thing to happen … so I knew that this would cause more pain and that was the whole point.
>
> Conning … partially I learned that from that incident … I included that into my own behavior. The fact that I never complained about the offences committed to me … I thought: "well people are not going to talk about it because I have never."

However, the experience of being abused in the other two cases was associated with behavioral change within a series. Their memories of their own abuse were triggered during a particular offense, resulting in extreme emotional reactions and significant change in their *modus operandi*.

> The trigger to the violence, to the extreme violence, was that the whole thing reminded me of what happened to me when I was a child.

Experience from the sex offenses they had previously committed resulted in both behavioral stability and change within a series. One offender who engaged in elaborate con approaches reported becoming "more skilful" in constructing his con to suit the needs of new victims. Although the content of the con evolved to meet the new circumstances, the use of a con approach remained consistent. Another offender reported using the same tactic to isolate his second and third victim:

> The first one was something that just happened—I didn't think about it, the second one I knew that I could use the fact that she wanted something from me [to isolate her] and the third one was the same: she wanted something—I told her that I can give her a job.

In contrast, experience resulted in behavioral change for the offender who reported sadistic preferences:

> I got more sexual pleasure from the offence where I didn't rape my victim, compared to the one when I did—I wanted the victim of my next offence to be very vocal about how much it was hurting.

The *experience* theme also included *observational learning*, whereby offenders incorporated into their *modus operandi* new knowledge they had acquired from directly observing others, from overhearing conversations, or from other sources such as television or the Internet. For all three participants who reported observational learning, it resulted in behavioral change within their series. However, rather than accurately mirroring the incident they had learned about, the information was more likely to be used as an idea for future modifications to their own offending:

> One guy I met ... he got superglue and he glued their hands behind their backs, so they could not do anything and that is something I heard about in prison and ... I mean I quite liked the idea of vulnerability ....

In addition, various sources of information (films, books, inmates from institutions where they were serving their sentence) improved participants' knowledge about the justice system and legal aspects of their crimes that they went on to consider in their future offending (e.g., age of consent affecting future victim targeting).

Physiological

Based on the statements of two participants, a *physiological* theme was identified. These two participants reported that they experienced one or more episodes of erectile dysfunction or premature ejaculation (e.g., due to anxiety). In both cases, this resulted in different sexual behavior in at least one offense in the series.

Planning/Preparation

During the analysis of the interviews, three subthemes emerged related to planning and preparation for the offense that all offenders employed differently: reconnaissance, rehearsing, and familiarization. Reconnaissance was identified from the interviews of just one offender and related to in-depth investigation of the location of potential crime scenes (e.g., location, surroundings, escape routes) or of the victim (e.g., her routine, habits, behaviors, personality) pre-offense. By engaging in these sophisticated assessments, he took an individualized approach to each victim. However, due to his feeling "in control" of the environment and his ability to control the victim, he also displayed high levels of confidence, which allowed him to introduce some actions in his *modus operandi* that were similar across the series.

Rehearsing the crime pre-offense was discussed by all four participants during interviews. Rehearsal involved thinking about the most effective ways of approaching the victim, planning their behavior during the offense, gaining control over the victim, and giving consideration to bringing a weapon and other items to the crime scene. Rehearsal resulted in both behavioral stability and change across series. Stability came from reintroducing certain elements of a previous offense that had proved effective (e.g., a method of approach, faking an alibi) or desirable (e.g., sex acts). All four participants talked about consistent patterns in their offending behavior due to previously rehearsed plans.

All four participants also discussed modifications that they had made following rehearsal. This modification was due to either developing interests or wanting to improve the effectiveness of their plan:

> My first victim was in the wrong place at the wrong time. The only thing I hadn't planned was who my victim was going to be. But after this offence, straight away … I was already planning the offence that would happen [number] weeks later. I was angry that I didn't complete that offence, in terms that I didn't get to ejaculate … I also wanted the victim of my next offence to be very vocal about how much it was hurting … I knew exactly who my next victim was going to be.

Rehearsal was modified to suit a new mood/motive in two cases. For example, one offender said:

> I am going to do something which was very different to the way I thought before … yeah it was violent before but it was also about pleasing them before … this time I only felt rage, I just wanted to hurt them.

A third type of planning/preparation was labeled *familiarity.* Two participants stated that in the process of planning their offenses, familiarity played an important role and contributed to behavioral stability across their series. Familiarity included choosing locations well known to the offender, victims that he knew of, or weapons that he had used in other types of offending with which he had felt comfortable:

> I actually found an area the first time around and … I went back to the same spot.
>
> I have been carrying a knife since I was seven so I knew what a knife could do and I knew what sort of power that had and what sort of fear it can evoke and fear has one of two effects—either makes someone run or makes someone freeze.

As noted above, for two offenders their first offense was committed in the company of another person. In both cases, the offenders reported engaging in no planning with their co-offender. These offenses were described as more opportunistic, precluding the occurrence of at least the first two forms of preparation noted here.

Attitudes and Beliefs

All participants identified the crucial and complex role of their personal belief system and attitudes on their offending behavior. Within this theme, lower-order themes emerged that grouped the attitudes accordingly: attitudes and beliefs about self, about the victim, offending, police/justice system, and the world. Additionally, the analysis identified cognitions that corresponded with participants' diagnoses of personality disorders.

Stability was apparent for all four offenders as a result of beliefs that they were "entitled to have sex" or "invincible." Such beliefs encouraged behavior they were interested in, and, as explained above, the resulting recklessness was associated with stability in behavior. Beliefs about their victims also could result in behavioral stability across a series. For example, one offender targeted young, impressionable girls because he believed his employment would result in their desiring him and so he would purposefully play on this and make them feel special until he had managed to isolate them for the rape to occur.

All four participants discussed their attitudes and beliefs about their offending behavior within the interviews, and for all of them, the attitudes remained consistent throughout their criminal history. These attitudes related to supporting their behavior, justifying their decisions, and minimizing the consequences of their actions.

> I am just going to have sex with you, I have never seen that as rape. I've always seen it as being a little bit pushy.
>
> The way I interpreted sex and the way I related to sex was about control, about dominance, and about taking what I wanted rather than giving ... I can do what I like with you ... you are mine ....

Two participants discussed the role that their attitudes about police work or the justice system played in their offending behavior. This theme related to their awareness of the potential consequences for them and it contributed toward behavioral stability as well as change in their offending series.

All participants identified that their attitudes about the world (rules, expectations about life) and other people (how they think and behave), in a similar manner to the attitudes regarding themselves and their victims, reinforced and maintained their offending behavior. These attitudes were stable across their offending history, and they had a strong association with previously discussed cognitions as well as emotions.

> I am going to take what I want. Nobody gives a shit about me. I was so angry with the world and myself and everything else ....

Finally, it is unsurprising, considering the sample for this study, that attitudes linked to diagnoses of personality disorder were also found. Given that the symptoms of different personality disorders within the same cluster are very similar (e.g., impulsivity for diagnoses of borderline and antisocial personality disorder within Cluster B), the attitudes that can be linked with these disorders were identified without clustering them into specific types of disorder (Ullrich & Marneros, 2004). All four participants' attitudes corresponded with their diagnosis, and in all four cases, these attitudes were stable throughout their lives, contributing toward stability in their offending behavior. For example, attitudes consistent with narcissism and antisocial tendencies existed:

> I thought that I am a romancer, somebody that is clearly attractive … Mr "God's gift" for women.
>
> I will take what I want, I didn't really care … I didn't care, because I wanted to rape her. I don't care about the law, fuck the law.

Summary

Our interviews with the four participants produced very rich data on reasons why offenders use particular *modus operandi* behaviors, as well as explanations for both consistency and change within a series. Personal characteristics as well as situational factors were implicated in the production of offense behavior and whether the offense was consistently reproduced or not over a series. Several of the themes identified can be found within Mischel and Shoda's (1995) CAPS, including attitudes and beliefs, memories of real or imagined events (fantasy), and emotions (see Chapter 2 for more details of this model).

The interviews with these four individuals were challenging for several reasons, including the characteristics of the offenders themselves (e.g., psychopathy and going off topic) and because they required the offender to have sufficient insight into his own behavior and the reasons for it. Our participants did have insight into some aspects of their offending, which had likely been aided through their participation in sex offender treatment programs*; however, this was not always the case. We therefore had to draw inferences, at times, from their responses to interview questions, and it is important to acknowledge this limitation.

The method of interview we adopted was to ask the offenders to describe each of their offenses in the sequence they occurred before asking more direct questions about consistency and change between offenses. This method allowed us to observe behavioral consistency in their responses, of which they themselves were unaware. Often, when asked in what ways they thought they were consistent in their behavior, the offenders responded that they were not consistent. It was unclear to us whether they truly could not see their own consistency or whether they did not wish to appear predictable. The former explanation would be of greater appeal to crime linkage practitioners because it suggests that offenders can be consistent in their behavior without being aware of it, therefore making it less likely that they will take steps to conceal their offending through intentional behavior change.

* This is in itself problematic because the offenders may be reporting reasons for their offending that have been suggested to them in therapy rather than representing their thinking at the time of the offence.

From the interviews, it was also apparent that at times the offenders drew on experiences of non-sex offending to inform their sexual offending behavior. This repetition of *modus operandi* behaviors across sex and non-sex offending suggests there may be some potential for across-crime linkage, not just with inter-crime distance and temporal proximity (as will be seen in Chapter 12) but with *modus operandi* behaviors as well.

Although each offender disclosed accounts of behavioral consistency across their series in all cases, there was also behavioral change. This change was due to a range of factors, as described. If we can generalize from this very small sample, even sex offenders with personality disorders, who would be expected to show greater consistency than offenders without such disorders (as argued earlier), will not show perfect consistency in their offending behavior. It was also apparent from their accounts that the offenders displayed consistency in different ways (i.e., in different types of behavior). This finding suggests that, when conducting crime linkage with such offenders, focusing on any one behavior domain could result in failure to identify linked series.

Although there are studies that have adopted an interview approach with sex offenders to better understand their decision making (e.g., Beauregard & Leclerc, 2007), it is a rarity in the field of crime linkage research. Much of the knowledge regarding the principles of crime linkage has been generated from the statistical analysis of samples of solved crime series. Although this is informative in testing the underlying assumptions of this practice, it is only able to tell us about degrees of consistency across crime series and whether some types of behavior are more consistently observed than others. It cannot assist us in understanding when and why consistency is or is not observed. Crime linkage researchers have proposed explanations to account for variation in consistency (e.g., Bennell & Canter, 2002; Woodhams & Labuschagne, 2012), but without adopting a new research paradigm, these propositions cannot be put to the test. We would therefore encourage other researchers in the field of crime linkage to consider complementing the typical quantitative approach with qualitative methodologies.

A more qualitative approach, however, is not without its problems. Clearly, what we learn from interviewing offenders will be idiosyncratic, subject to the biases of self-report, and will also suffer from the same limitations as typical crime linkage research on solved crime series (i.e., that knowledge generated from apprehended offenders might have limited generalizability to offenders that remain at large). Generalizability is even more limited with the current sample, where the four individuals who agreed to be interviewed have personality disorders. Interviews such as these are also very time consuming, which limits sample size. Samples sizes for crime linkage studies in general are often not large, particularly when rarer crime types such as serial stranger rape or serial homicide are studied, and this problem is compounded when one tries to interview the individuals responsible for these offenses, who will be incarcerated in prisons or undergoing treatment in secure mental health facilities. However, despite these limitations, there is still great merit in adopting this alternative approach.

Conclusion

For several decades, there has been speculation that mentally disordered offenders will show greater consistency in their crime scene behavior than offenders without such disorders. It was argued in this chapter that although mentally disordered offenders account for the minority of sex offenses, they may come to the attention of crime linkage practitioners disproportionately due to the nature of their offending and the victims they target.

We reported the first studies of the behavioral consistency, distinctiveness, and change of mentally disordered serial sex offenders. The first study adopted a traditional methodology for crime linkage research, assessing the assumptions of consistency and distinctiveness of crime scene behavior by contrasting the behavioral similarity of linked and unlinked crime pairs. Linked crime pairs could be distinguished from unlinked crime pairs with a very high level of accuracy, lending support to hypotheses of greater consistency and distinctiveness in the behavior of mentally disordered sex offenders. However, it is as yet unclear whether this is an artifact, at least in part, of the data sampled; future research will need to rule out this explanation.

The second study used a qualitative methodology to better understand the factors that affect the display of consistency or variability in behavior across the series of mentally disordered sex offenders. In-depth interviews with four individuals with personality disorders followed by template analysis revealed both personal and situational factors that produced consistency and change in behavior over time. We conclude by noting the utility of a qualitative approach in advancing crime linkage research in the future.

References

Abel, G. G., Becker, J. V., & Skinner, L. J. (1980). Aggressive behaviour and sex. *Psychiatric Clinics of North America, 3*, 133–151.

Alish, Y., Birger, M., Manor, N., Kertzman, S., Zerzion, M., Kotler, M., & Stous, R. (2007). Schizophrenic sex offenders: A clinical and epidemiological comparison study. *International Journal of Law and Psychiatry, 30*, 459–466.

American Psychiatric Association. (2000). *Diagnostic and statistical manual of mental disorders* (4th ed.), *text revision (DSM-IV-TR)*. Washington, DC: American Psychiatric Association.

Beauregard, E., & Leclerc, B. (2007). An application of the rational choice approach to the offending process of sex offenders: A closer look at the decision-making. *Sexual Abuse: A Journal of Research and Treatment, 19*, 115–133.

Bennell, C., & Canter, D. V. (2002). Linking commercial burglaries by modus operandi: Tests using regression and ROC analysis. *Science & Justice, 42*, 1–12.

Bennell, C., Jones, N. J., & Melnyk, T. (2009). Addressing problems with traditional crime linking methods using receiver operating characteristic analysis. *Legal and Criminological Psychology, 14*, 293–310.

Canter, D., Heritage, R., Wilson, M., Davies, A., Kirby, S., Holden, R., … Donald, I. (1991). *A facet approach to offender profiling* (Vol. 1). Guilford, England: University of Surrey, Psychology Department.

Carabellese, F., Maniglio, R., Greco, O., & Catanesi, R. (2011). The role of fantasy in a serial sexual offender: A brief review of the literature and a case report. *Journal of Forensic Sciences, 56*, 256–260.

Cohen, J. (1988). *Statistical power analysis for the behavioral sciences* (2nd ed.). Hillsdale, NJ: Lawrence Erlbaum Associates.

Daffern, M., Jones, L., & Shine, J. (2010). *Offence paralleling behaviour: A case formulation approach to offender assessment and intervention*. Chichester, England: Wiley.

Davies, A. (1992). Rapists' behaviour: A three aspect model as a basis for analysis and the identification of serial crime. *Forensic Science International, 55*, 173–194.

Davison, S., & Janca, A. (2012). Personality disorder and criminal behaviour: What is the nature of the relationship? *Current Opinion in Psychiatry, 25*, 39–45.

Drake, C. R., & Pathe, M. (2004). Understanding sexual offending in schizophrenia. *Criminal Behaviour and Mental Health, 14*, 108–120.

Eaton, N. R., South, S. C., & Krueger, R. F. (2009). The cognitive-affective processing system (CAPS) approach to personality and the concept of personality disorder: Integrating clinical and social-cognitive research. *Journal of Research in Personality, 43*, 208–217.

Faul, F., Erdfelder, E., Lang, A. G., & Buchner, A. (2007). G*Power 3: A flexible statistical power analysis program for the social, behavioral, and biomedical sciences. *Behavior Research Methods, 39*, 175–191.

Fazel, S., & Danesh, J. (2002). Serious mental disorder in 23000 prisoners: A systematic review of 62 surveys. *Lancet, 359*, 545–550.

Federal Bureau of Investigation. (2008). *Serial murder: Multi-disciplinary perspectives for investigators*. Washington, DC: US Department of Justice.

Greenhall, P. V., & West, A. G. (2007). A study of stranger rapists from the English high security hospitals. *Journal of Sexual Aggression, 13*, 151–167.

Grubin, D., Kelly, P., & Brunsdon, C. (2001). *Linking serious sexual assaults through behaviour.* Home Office Research Study 215. London: Home Office.

Hare, R. D. (2003). *Manual for the revised psychopathy checklist* (2nd ed.). North Tonawanda, NY: Multi-Health Systems.

Harsch, S., Bergk, J. E., Steinert, T., Keller, F., & Jockusch, U. (2006). Prevalence of mental disorders among sexual offenders in forensic psychiatry and prison. *International Journal of Law and Psychiatry, 29*, 443–449.

Heasman, A. (2005). Personality and psychiatric disorders. Comorbidity in sex offenders. In E. W. Hickey (Ed.), *Sex crimes and paraphilia* (pp. 25–32). Upper Saddle River, NJ: Prentice Hall.

Hoertel, N., Le Strat, Y., Schuster, J. P., & Limonsin, F. (2012). Sexual assaulters in the United States: Prevalence and psychiatric correlates of in a national sample. *Archives of Sexual Behavior, 41* (6), 1379–1387.

Hosmer, D. W., & Lemeshow, S. (2000). *Applied logistic regression* (2nd ed.). New York: Wiley.

Khalid, F. N., Ford, T., & Maughan, B. (2012). Aggressive behaviour and psychosis in a clinically referred child and adolescent sample. *Social Psychiatry and Psychiatric Epidemiology, 47* (11), 1795–1806.

King, N. (2004). Using templates in the thematic analysis of text. In C. Cassell, & G. Symon (Eds.), *Essential guide to qualitative methods in organizational research* (pp. 11–22). London: Sage.

Kocsis, R. N., Cooksey, R. W., & Irwin, H. J. (2002). Psychological profiling of offender characteristic from crime behaviors in serial rape offences. *International Journal of Offender Therapy and Comparative Criminology, 46*, 144–169.

Loney, B. R., Taylor, J., Butler, M. A., & Iacono, W. G. (2007). Adolescent psychopathy features: 6 year temporal stability and the prediction of externalising symptoms during the transition to adulthood. *Aggressive Behavior, 33*, 242–252.

Lundrigan, S., Czarnomski, S., & Wilson, M. (2010). Spatial and environmental consistency in serial sexual assault. *Journal of Investigative Psychology and Offender Profiling, 7*, 15–30.

Mischel, W., & Shoda, Y. (1995). A cognitive–affective system theory of personality: Reconceptualizing situations, dispositions, dynamics and invariance in personality structure. *Psychological Review, 102*, 246–268.

Mokros, A., & Alison, L. J. (2002). Is offender profiling possible? Testing the predicted homology of crime scene actions and background characteristics in a sample of rapists. *Legal and Criminological Psychology, 7*, 25–43.

Novak, B., McDermott, E., Scott, C. L., & Guillory, S. (2007). Sex offenders and insanity: An examination of 42 individuals found not guilty by reason of insanity. *The Journal of the American Academy of Psychiatry and the Law, 35*, 444–450.

Obradovic, J., Pardini, D. A., Long, J. D., & Loeber, R. (2007). Measuring interpersonal callousness in boys from childhood to adolescence: An examination of longitudinal invariance and temporal stability. *Journal of Clinical Child & Adolescent Psychology, 36*, 276–292.

Olver, M. E., & Wang, S. C. P. (2006). Psychopathy, sexual deviance, and recidivism among sex offenders. *Sexual Abuse: A Journal of Research and Treatment, 18*, 65–82.

Ressler, R. K., Burgess, A. W., & Douglas, J. E. (1988). *Sexual homicide: Patterns and motives*. Lexington, MA: Lexington Books.

Rigonatti, S. P., Serafim, A. P., Caires, M. A. F., Guerra A. H., & Arboleda-Florez, J. (2006). Personality disorders in rapists and murderers from a maximum security prison in Brazil. *International Journal of Law and Psychiatry, 29*, 361–369.

Santtila, P., Junkkila, J., & Sandnabba, N. K. (2005). Behavioral linking of stranger rapes. *Journal of Investigative Psychology and Offender Profiling, 2*, 87–103.

Santtila, P., Pakkanen, T., Zappalà, A., Bosco, D., Valkama, M., & Mokros, A. (2008). Behavioural crime linking in serial homicide. *Psychology, Crime & Law, 14*, 245–265.

Scully, D., & Marolla, J. (1984). Convicted rapists' vocabulary of motive: Excuses and justifications. *Social Problems, 31*, 530–543.

Semple, D. (2005). *The Oxford handbook of psychiatry*. Oxford: Oxford University Press.

Skovran, L. C., Huss, M. T., & Scalora, M. J. (2010). Sexual fantasies and sensation seeking among psychopathic sexual offenders. *Psychology, Crime & Law, 16*, 617–629.

Smith, A. D. (2000). Offence characteristics of psychotic men who sexually assault women. *Medicine, Science and the Law, 40*, 223–228.

Swets, J. A. (1988). Measuring the accuracy of diagnostic systems. *Science, 240*, 1285–1293.

Ullrich, S., & Marneros, A. (2004). Dimensions of personality disorders in offenders. *Criminal Behaviour and Mental Health, 14*, 202–213.

van Baardewijk, Y., Vermeiren, R., Stegge, H., & Doreleijers, T. (2011). Self-reported psychopathic traits in children: Their stability and concurrent and prospective association with conduct problems and aggression. *Journal of Psychopathology and Behavioural Assessment, 33*, 236–245.

Woodhams, J., Grant, T., & Price, A. (2007). From marine ecology to crime analysis: Improving the detection of serial sexual offences using a taxonomic similarity measure. *Journal of Investigative Psychology and Offender Profiling, 4*, 17–27.

Woodhams, J., Hollin, C. R., & Bull, R. (2008). Incorporating context in linking crimes: An exploratory study of situational similarity and if-then contingencies. *Journal of Investigative Psychology and Offender Profiling, 5*, 1–23.

Woodhams, J., & Labuschagne, G. N. (2012). A test of crime linkage principles with solved and unsolved serial rapes. *Journal of Police and Criminal Psychology, 27*, 85–98.

Yokota, K., Fujita, G., Watanabe, K., Yoshimoto, K., & Wachi, T. (2007). Application of the behavioral investigative support system for profiling perpetrators of serial sexual assaults. *Behavioral Sciences & the Law, 25*, 841–856.

Linking Crimes with Spatial Behavior

A Need to Tackle Some Remaining Methodological Concerns

5

BRENT SNOOK,
KIRK LUTHER, AND
SARAH MACDONALD

Contents

Introduction 84
A Review of the Empirical Linking Studies That Have Examined Spatial Behavior 84
The Bennell and Canter (2002) Study 84
The Santtila, Korpela, and Häkkänen (2004) Study 85
The Bennell and Jones (2005) Study 85
The Goodwill and Alison (2006) Study 86
The Woodhams and Toye (2007) Study 86
The Tonkin, Grant, and Bond (2008) Study 87
The Bennell, Bloomfield, Snook, Taylor, and Barnes (2010) Study 87
The Markson, Woodhams, and Bond (2010) Study 88
The Tonkin, Woodhams, Bull, Bond, and Palmer (2011) Study 88
The Burrell, Bull, and Bond (2012) Study 89
The Davies, Tonkin, Bull, and Bond (2012) Study 90
The Tonkin, Santtila, and Bull (2012a) Study 90
The Tonkin, Woodhams, Bull, and Bond (2012b) Study 91
The Tonkin, Woodhams, Bull, Bond, and Santtila (2012c) Study 91
Theoretical Explanations 92
Theory of Personality 92
Rational Choice Theory 93
Crime Pattern Theory 94
Bounded Rationality 95

Methodological Concerns and Explanations 96
Threats to Validity 96
Threats to Reliability 99
Conclusion 101
References 102

Introduction

Crime linkage analysis research suggests that offender spatial behavior is one of the best predictors of whether or not the same offender committed two crimes (Bennell & Canter, 2002). A review of the linking studies that includes spatial behavior as one of its predictors shows that it is the only cue that differentiates linked and unlinked crimes consistently. Specifically, it has been shown that a decrease in the distance between two crime locations increases the probability that the same offender committed those crimes. Although a seemingly robust finding, it is our contention that a number of methodological concerns need to be tackled before it is possible to conclude with any degree of certainty that spatial behavior (as a linking cue) is of practical value to law enforcement officers or that other cues are relatively inferior for connecting crimes.

In this chapter, we review the empirical linking studies that have included offender spatial behavior among the cues tested. We then review some of the theories that may account for the regular observation that spatial behavior is a useful predictor of whether crimes are linked and that other cues are less valuable. We then highlight some methodological issues that need to be tackled and conclude with a brief commentary regarding the sort of linking research that needs to be conducted.

A Review of the Empirical Linking Studies That Have Examined Spatial Behavior

Below is a review of 14 studies on crime linkage analysis that have considered spatial behavior as one of the cues used to predict linked crimes. As will be seen, the general trend in these various studies is that offender spatial behavior is a potentially useful variable for linking crimes and that other cues tend to be inferior to spatial behavior.

The Bennell and Canter (2002) Study

Bennell and Canter (2002) examined the possibility of linking serial commercial burglaries. From a large database of crimes from a metropolitan police organization in the United Kingdom, they selected two solved crimes randomly from the series of 43 serial burglars (for a total of 86 crimes) as their training sample. For each of these crimes, they coded police records for the presence of behaviors pertaining to the following five domains: entry behaviors (e.g., kicked in rear door), target selection choices (e.g., pharmacy), property stolen (e.g., drugs), internal behaviors (e.g., ransacked drawers), and spatial behavior (e.g., inter-crime distance). For each of the four behavioral domains, a behavioral similarity analysis was conducted by calculating Jaccard's coefficient between each possible pair of (linked and unlinked) crimes in the sample (where 0 = no similarity across crimes and 1 = perfect similarity across crimes). The resulting four Jaccard's correlations and inter-crime distance were entered into a stepwise logistic regression to predict the linked crimes. The results showed that, when each variable was tested alone, inter-crime distance was the single best predictor. Specifically, they found that the probability that two crimes were committed by the same offender increased as distance between the crimes decreased. When all predictors were entered into the regression analysis, the optimal model contained inter-crime distance and entry behaviors.

Receiver operating characteristic (ROC) analyses were then used on a test sample to estimate the performance of the models. They found that the one-cue model containing inter-crime distance resulted in high levels of discrimination accuracy, and all of the other one-cue models had substantially lower discrimination accuracy than inter-crime distance. They also found that the one-cue inter-crime distance model was almost as accurate as the optimal model.

The Santtila, Korpela, and Häkkänen (2004) Study

Santtila and colleagues (2004) examined the ability of nine experienced vehicle offense investigators, nine experienced general investigators, seven novice general investigators, and eight naïve participants to link vehicle offenses. The participants were presented with crime reports of vehicle offenses and asked to link 30 offenses committed by 10 offenders. Participants were also given a map that contained the locations where the vehicle thefts occurred. They found that experienced vehicle offense investigators performed better on the linking task compared to naïve participants. There was no significant difference in the linking accuracy of the experienced vehicle offense investigators, experienced general investigators, and novice general investigators. The ability to link the vehicle offenses successfully was often associated with participants paying close attention to the offender spatial behavior, the type of vehicle, and the time at which an offense was committed.

The Bennell and Jones (2005) Study

Bennell and Jones (2005) examined the ability to link crimes within two different crime types—commercial and residential burglary. They selected solved burglaries from three different police districts and from a wider time frame than that used in Bennell and Canter's study (2002; 5 years vs. 1 year). Their sample consisted of three solved crimes from the series of 51 serial residential burglars and 57 serial commercial burglars. The authors examined the discrimination accuracy of entry behaviors, target characteristics, items stolen, and spatial behavior. Using a similar procedure to that used by Bennell and Canter (2002), they found that both linked commercial burglaries and linked residential burglaries had much shorter inter-crime distances than their unlinked counterparts. The results of their logistic regression analyses showed that, when the variables were tested individually, inter-crime distance resulted in substantially higher levels of predictive accuracy than entry behaviors, target characteristics, and items stolen. A model that contained inter-crime distance on its own was shown to be almost as accurate as optimal models.

ROC analyses further showed that inter-crime distance resulted in much higher levels of discrimination accuracy than entry behaviors, target characteristics, or items stolen. Furthermore, there was no discernible difference in discrimination accuracy (for residential or commercial burglaries) between optimal models and a model that only contained inter-crime distance.

The Goodwill and Alison (2006) Study

Goodwill and Alison (2006) examined the actions of 43 serial burglars in the United Kingdom. They extracted the first five offenses for each burglar contained in a centralized police database. They conducted analyses on a number of spatial, temporal, behavioral, and dwelling variables. For the spatial analyses, they examined the mean interpoint distance (MID). The interpoint distance is simply the distance between any two crimes' locations (often referred to as inter-crime distance). The MID is the average of the interpoint distances for a single offender; with five offenses, there would be a total of 10 interpoint distances used to calculate the MID. Lastly, the mean MID (MMID) is the average MID for all 43 serial burglars. Goodwill and Alison applied the MMID to each of the 215 burglary locations. Any crimes located within the MMID that were committed by the same offender were considered a correct link and any crimes located within that circular area that were committed by a different offender was considered an incorrect link. They found that the MMID linked the offender's crimes correctly 72.3% of the time. In addition, they were unable to link the crimes of serial offenders beyond chance levels when temporal proximity, behavioral information, and dwelling information were used.

The Woodhams and Toye (2007) Study

Woodhams and Toye (2007) scanned police records (dated between 1998 and 2003) from two UK police forces to identify commercial robbery series. Eighty solved serial commercial robberies (based on conviction or physical evidence) were extracted from police records, and the two most recent offenses per offender were selected for analyses. The records were coded for behaviors used to control the victim(s), target selection behaviors, behaviors that reflected planning, and inter-crime distance. The authors also created a comparison set of unlinked commercial robberies from the same 160 offenses. Their similarity analysis showed that linked crimes were more similar than unlinked crimes with respect to target selection and control behaviors. A stepwise logistic regression revealed that the best model for linking crimes included the domains of control, planning, and inter-crime distance. ROC analyses further showed that discrimination accuracy was highest for control behaviors, but that the difference in accuracy between control behaviors and inter-crime distance was not significant. The optimal model containing three cues (control behaviors, planning behaviors, and inter-crime distances) resulted in the highest level of discrimination accuracy. No cross-validation of the models was conducted to assess the level of overfitting for the various models.

The Tonkin, Grant, and Bond (2008) Study

Tonkin and colleagues (2008) examined a sample of 386 solved vehicle thefts in the United Kingdom committed between January 2004 and May 2007 by 193 serial car thieves. The two most recent crimes from each offender were selected and coded for target selection, target acquisition, and disposal behaviors. Information was also collected on inter-crime distance, inter-dump distance (i.e., distance between where the offenders discarded the stolen cars), offender experience (i.e., how prolific the offenders were), and temporal proximity (i.e., how close together in time the crimes were committed). Using Jaccard's coefficient, logistic regression, and ROC analyses, Tonkin and colleagues found that inter-crime and inter-dump distances were the most successful predictors for linking crimes. Target selection, target acquisition, disposal behaviors, and temporal proximity had limited predictive power. No cross-validation of the models was conducted to assess the level of overfitting for the various models.

The Bennell, Bloomfield, Snook, Taylor, and Barnes (2010) Study

Bennell and colleagues (2010) compared university students, police professionals, and a logistic regression model on their ability to link serial burglaries. Their sample comprised 40 undergraduate students and 31 police professionals from the United States, the United Kingdom, and Canada. Approximately one-half of the university students and one-half of the police professionals received crime linkage training (i.e., they were informed that as inter-crime distance decreases, the likelihood of crimes being linked increases), whereas the other half received no training regarding the best way to link crimes. Participants were provided with 38 pairs of commercial burglaries from the United Kingdom that were extracted from the same database used in the Bennell and Canter (2002) study. Participants were also provided with additional information, including (1) a map consisting of all offense locations, (2) the straight line distance (in kilometers) between the offenses, (3) the method of entry used by the offender, (4) target building characteristics, and (5) a list of property stolen from buildings.

Bennell and colleagues found that, although both students and professionals performed at above chance levels, students had a higher accuracy rate compared to the police professionals. Furthermore, the participants who were told about the value of using inter-crime distance to link crimes outperformed those that were not provided with this information. The results also showed that using inter-crime distance in a reliable way (i.e., via a logistic regression model) resulted in significantly better performance than when it was not used at all or used sporadically by human judges.

The Markson, Woodhams, and Bond (2010) Study

Markson and colleagues (2010) examined the ability to link serial burglaries committed in Northamptonshire, UK, between 2006 and 2008. They used a sample of 80 serial offenders (160 crimes in total) and examined behavioral similarity, geographical proximity, and temporal proximity of pairs of crimes committed by the same offender and pairs of crimes committed by different offenders. Inter-rater reliability was assessed on 10% of the sample. Their results showed that linked crimes were committed closer together in location and time than unlinked crimes. Similarity analyses indicated that linked crimes were significantly more similar when a combination of *modus operandi* (MO) behaviors was used to calculate Jaccard's coefficients. Their logistic regression showed that inter-crime distance and temporal proximity were the only significant predictors of linked crimes (80% and 76%, respectively, and 87% accuracy when the two variables were combined). Follow-up ROC analyses indicated that inter-crime distance was the most useful variable in predicting whether crime pairs were linked or unlinked. ROC analyses on all MO behaviors yielded a low level of predictive accuracy (see Swets, 1988). No cross-validation of the models was conducted to assess the level of overfitting for the various models.

The Tonkin, Woodhams, Bull, Bond, and Palmer (2011) Study

Tonkin and colleagues (2011) examined the discrimination accuracy of inter-crime distance and temporal proximity across different crime categories (e.g., robbery compared to burglary), for the same crime categories (e.g., personal robbery and commercial robbery), and for the same specific crime (i.e., personal robbery and personal robbery). The authors obtained case file information from a UK police force concerning 537 serial offenders. The results of Friedman's analysis of variance (ANOVA) tests and logistic regression analyses showed that linking accuracy could be achieved across the three levels of inquiry (i.e., different crime categories, same crime category, and same specific crime) with both the inter-crime distance and temporal proximity variables. There was no significant difference between the three levels of inquiry; however, the results showed that inter-crime distance resulted in greater linking accuracy compared to temporal proximity.

The authors also conducted ROC analyses on both the training and test datasets. Across both datasets, they found that inter-crime distance and temporal proximity had significant discrimination accuracy across the three levels of inquiry. Specifically, the ROC analyses indicated that the predictive accuracy of inter-crime distance was high for the different crime categories, same crime category, and same specific crime category. There was no significant difference between the three levels of inquiry. However, consistent with the ANOVA findings, the results showed that inter-crime distance resulted in greater accuracy compared to temporal proximity.

The Burrell, Bull, and Bond (2012) Study

Burrell and colleagues (2012) examined a sample of serial (personal) robberies that occurred over a two-year period (2005–2007) in Northamptonshire, UK. Two crimes per offender from a sample of 83 offenders were used to conduct their analyses. The authors extracted a total of 48 variables; 15 of them were subjected to inter-rater reliability analysis (and were coded reliably) and 33 of them were not subjected to inter-rater reliability analysis. Each variable was then assigned to one of the following five domains: target selection, control, property, inter-crime distance, and temporal proximity.

A similarity analysis showed that smaller inter-crime distances and fewer days between crimes were associated more with linked crimes than the other four domains and that this effect was larger for force-wide than borough-wide (local level) crime analysis. Interestingly, their results also showed that the target selection, control, property, and combined domains were more useful for linking purposes when considering smaller geographic regions (i.e., boroughs) rather than larger ones (i.e., force-wide).

The results of their regression analyses showed that inter-crime distance was the best predictor of linked crimes at the force-wide level and that little was to be gained through the use of an optimal model that contained inter-crime distance and target selection. They also found that target selection and inter-crime distance were the best predictors of linked crimes for the borough-wide analysis and that combining these two variables led to an increase in predictive accuracy. Further, the cross-validation using ROC analyses showed that inter-crime distance had the highest discrimination accuracy for the force-wide analysis and outperformed an optimal model. Although an optimal model resulted in the largest discrimination accuracy for the borough-wide analysis, inter-crime distance was nearly as accurate.

The Davies, Tonkin, Bull, and Bond (2012) Study

Davies and colleagues (2012) investigated the role of criminal behaviors, inter-crime distance, and temporal proximity in predicting crime linkages. They collected 258 crime pairs (129 linked and 129 randomly generated unlinked pairs) pertaining to car thefts from the Northamptonshire Police Force in the United Kingdom over the period 2007–2011. The two most recent crimes per offender were selected for the analyses. The results indicated that the single-cue regression models containing inter-crime distance, inter-dump distance, and temporal proximity were each able to predict whether crime pairs were linked or not linked. However, an optimal regression model containing four cues outperformed each of the single cues substantially. Interestingly, the results of the cross-validation showed that a model containing only inter-crime distance performed as well as the four-cue optimal model.

The Tonkin, Santtila, and Bull (2012a) Study

Tonkin and colleagues (2012a) created two datasets from a larger dataset of burglaries in Finland. The first dataset contained 117 serial burglars who committed two crimes each (i.e., linked crimes). The second dataset contained 117 pairs of crimes committed by different offenders (i.e., unlinked crimes). The information collected by the authors included crime scene location, date of crime, type of property stolen, entry method, search behavior, and type and cost of property stolen. This information was grouped into six behavioral categories, which included target characteristics, entry behaviors, internal behaviors, property stolen, inter-crime distance, and a combined domain that included the target, entry, internal, and property categories. Logistic regression analyses showed that, although all models were significant, the single best predictor used to link crimes was inter-crime distance, followed by the combined domain (i.e., target, entry, internal, property behaviors) and then temporal proximity.

Cross-validation (using ROC analyses) showed that, with the exception of property behaviors, the discrimination accuracy for all behavioral categories continued to be significant. When the accuracy of individual variables was tested, inter-crime distance produced the largest discrimination accuracy. Although the two optimal models (containing three and two cues) produced the highest discrimination accuracy scores, they were only slightly better than when inter-crime distance was used by itself.

The Tonkin, Woodhams, Bull, and Bond (2012b) Study

Tonkin and colleagues (2012b) examined both a sample of unsolved crimes and a sample of solved crimes from Northamptonshire, UK. The crimes chosen for the study were linked via DNA evidence. The authors obtained a sample of 132 police records of serial offenders (two crimes per offender). The authors compared three different types of crime pairs that included (1) across crime categories, (2) across crime types, and (3) within crime types. ROC analyses showed that both inter-crime distance and temporal proximity were successful in discriminating between linked and unlinked crimes. Across the three different types of crime pairs (across crime categories, across crime types, and within crime types), the predictive accuracy of inter-crime distance was high. The results suggest that inter-crime distance can be used to link crimes across crime categories, across crime types, and within crime types. Temporal proximity was shown to be successful for within crime types, but was of little value when discriminating between linked and unlinked crimes across crime types and crime categories.

The Tonkin, Woodhams, Bull, Bond, and Santtila (2012c) Study

Tonkin and colleagues (2012c) obtained data on 80 serial burglars operating in Helsinki, Finland, between 1990 and 2001. The authors also obtained data on 188 serial car thieves between 2004 and 2007 from Northamptonshire, UK. Tonkin et al. then created behavioral domains on which to conduct their analyses. In regard to the burglaries, the authors examined target characteristics, entry behaviors, internal behaviors, property stolen, inter-crime distance, and a combined behavioral domain that included variables from the target, entry, internal, and property domains. A logistic regression analysis showed that all models on a training dataset were statistically significant. When the variables were tested individually, their results showed that inter-crime distance was the best predictor, and the difference in accuracy between inter-crime distance and an optimal model (containing inter-crime distance, entry behaviors, and internal behaviors) was minimal. Of more importance, however, was the finding that inter-crime distance by itself had a level of discrimination accuracy that was comparable to the optimal model (inter-crime distance, entry behaviors, and internal behaviors) when tested on an unseen set of data.

In regard to the car thefts, Tonkin et al. (2012c) examined target selection choices, target acquisition, disposal behavior, inter-crime distance, and a combined domain (target selection, target acquisition, and disposal behaviors). The logistic regression analyses on the training dataset showed that all models had significant discrimination accuracy, except for target acquisition. Inter-crime distance again had the largest accuracy when the variables were tested individually. As with the burglary data, the optimal regression model (i.e., inter-crime distance, target selection, and disposal behaviors) was the most accurate. Most importantly, however, inter-crime distance by itself resulted in the largest discriminative accuracy when all variables and models were applied to unseen data (i.e., a test dataset). It is also worth noting that the cross-validation revealed little over fitting of the data for inter-crime distance.

Theoretical Explanations

Below we review four competing theoretical explanations for the regular observation that spatial behavior is useful for linking crimes and relatively more useful than other cues.

Theory of Personality

One explanation for the finding that spatial behavior is a relatively more useful variable for linking crimes relates to personality dispositions and situational factors. The assumption that it is possible to link crimes originates from the view that people are predisposed to behave in a particular way (Cervone & Shoda, 1999). If personal traits are the primary determinant of behavior, people should exhibit distinctive patterns of behavior in a stable fashion across situations. However, research has shown that high levels of behavioral consistency are not often found in noncriminal domains because situational factors play a key role in determining how people behave (Mischel, 1968). When stable patterns of behavioral distinctiveness are found, they are most often encountered across situations that are viewed as psychologically similar by the individual being observed (e.g., Shoda, Mischel, & Wright, 1994) or for behaviors that are largely under the control of the individual rather than a product of the situation (e.g., Funder & Colvin, 1991).

According to this theory, spatial behavior is the best variable for linking crimes because the choice of crime location is more under the control of the offender and less a product of the situation. For example, in Bennell and Canter's (2002) study of serial commercial burglary, a high level of consistency was found for crime site selection choice. However, very low levels of consistency were observed for behaviors related to what the offender was able to steal or how they entered a building—two domains that are dependent on the situation that the offender encounters. As indicated above, similar results (i.e., relatively high levels of consistency for crime site selection but low levels for other types of behaviors) have been reported for residential burglary (Bennell & Jones, 2005) and commercial robbery (Woodhams & Toye, 2007).

It should be noted that the choice of a crime location is not entirely devoid of situational influences. The availability of a target at a predetermined location, the presence of an alarm system, the presence of witnesses, and so on may all have an impact on whether the desired target is selected or not. Although the choice of where to offend appears on the surface to be less influenced by situational factors, there has not been much development of this theory to explain why spatial choices are less influenced by situational factors than other criminal behaviors. Given what is known about defensible space theory (see Newman, 1972), some environmental psychologists might argue that the choice of target locations is influenced heavily by situational factors (Cohen & Felson, 1979). Specifically, in situations where there is a sense of community or "watchful" presence, the offender may feel less secure when committing a crime.

Rational Choice Theory

Rational choice theory (RCT) relies on the idea that a person who commits a crime does so by making rational choices about whether or not to do so (Clarke & Cornish, 1985). Across three time periods (before, during, and after committing a criminal act), offenders make decisions about a number of factors that affect their behavior. A decision model created by Cornish and Clarke (1986) outlines two stages where the offender makes decisions—decisions regarding *involvement* in the crime and decisions pertaining to the actual *event*. At the first stage, prior to committing a crime, offenders' involvement decisions are affected by various factors, such as offender demographics (e.g., gender, age), previous experience, an assessment of needs (e.g., money), and potential solutions (e.g., committing a crime to get what the offender wants vs. pursuing a legitimate job). In addition, the offender makes a decision about their readiness to commit the crime and makes the decision to actually carry out the criminal act.

The second stage involves making decisions after a commitment to carry out a crime has been made by the offender. For example, this theory assumes that target selection decisions are based on an evaluation of all of the costs and benefits associated with available targets. In the case of a burglar, a home located in a secluded wooded environment may be a more desirable target compared to a suburban home located in a highly populated area with many neighbors. RCT assumes that an offender will make decisions that maximize benefits while minimizing costs. The finding that inter-crime distance is small for individual offenders suggests they are consistent in their calculation of the costs and benefits of choosing crime locations that are close together (and often close to their home location). Travelling large distances between crimes requires additional time, money, and possibly extra planning that may be estimated consistently to be too costly.

The theoretical assumptions of RCT mean that the lower level of discrimination accuracy associated with other cues that could be used to link crimes (e.g., entry behaviors) also results from an assessment of costs and benefits carried out by offenders when they consider performing a particular action. For instance, the cost of entering the front door of a building may be viewed as lower than entering a second floor window for the first crime in a series committed by an offender and then reversed for the second crime in that offender's series. In other words, the lack of stability associated with some behavioral domains may be due to the fluctuating nature of the costs and benefits assigned to different actions that comprise that domain.

Crime Pattern Theory

Crime pattern theory attempts to explain criminal spatial behavior through an analysis of the offender's environment (Brantingham & Brantingham, 1993; Lersch, 2007). This theory posits that the commission of a crime is influenced by an individual's movements throughout their environment (Brantingham & Brantingham, 2008). Crime pattern theorists assume that cognitive maps (i.e., mental maps of the environment) are formed when potential offenders carry out their daily activities, or routines (e.g., go from home to work; Lersch, 2007), and that these routines provide a framework of opportunities for potential offenders (Felson, 1987). A component of this theory is that offenders are more likely to commit a crime when a suitable target falls within their cognitive map or their awareness area (Brantingham & Brantingham, 2008; Lersch, 2007).

Crime pattern theory provides support for why spatial behavior may be a significant predictor for linking serial crimes. Once an offender has established their daily routine, they are more likely to offend within this geographical area—where they feel more comfortable and familiar with the surroundings and also have knowledge of potential targets. The studies reviewed above support the ideas that (1) offenders remain relatively consistent in where they commit crimes and (2) offenders do not travel large distances between crimes. The selection of crimes within a bounded geographical area would result in consistent spatial behavior and would likely be distinctive from other offenders who are likely to have a different bounded geographic area (i.e., it is assumed that the routines of different offenders would not overlap often).

Although crime pattern theory does not outline why nonspatial behaviors are less consistent than spatial behaviors, one possible explanation for the observed lack of consistency would be due to natural variations in the targets that are being selected within the bounded geographic area. For example, a commercial robber would be viewed as inconsistent in their choice of target if the only three commercial targets available within their awareness space were a coffee shop, a gas station, and a convenience store. The lack of stability in some of the behavioral domains that are evident in crime linking studies may be due to the varying characteristics of targets that are available within an offender's bounded awareness space (and how this might impact entry points, types of property to be stolen, etc.).

Bounded Rationality

According to RCT, a criminal would have to search indefinitely for endless amounts of information on decision options, have knowledge of every relevant aspect of each option, weigh all the available information according to importance, and finally perform intractable mathematical and statistical calculations that would result in the optimal option being chosen. Nobel Prize-winning economist and cognitive scientist, Herbert Simon, argued that rational choice models represent an impractical standard for assessing human judgment and rationality (Gilovich & Griffin, 2002). According to Simon's (1955, 1956) view, judgment and decision making is constrained by the processing limitations of the mind so humans have evolved to use "simple" strategies (i.e., heuristics) that can handle complex information (see also Kahneman, 1973; Miller, 1956).

In recent years, Gigerenzer and his colleagues (e.g., Gigerenzer, Hoffrage, & Kleinbolting, 1991; Gigerenzer & Selten, 2001; Gigerenzer & Todd, 1999; Todd & Gigerenzer, 2003) have argued that heuristic reasoning strategies have evolved over time to deal effectively with everyday judgments and decisions in a complex world and that the mind is an *adaptive toolbox*. Like a carpenter's toolbox, they have argued that the mind is equipped with a repertoire of simple mental tools that are well-suited for certain judgments and decisions. These mental tools are *fast and frugal* heuristics that have evolved to allow people to make smart decisions. The heuristics are fast because they do not involve much calculation or integration of information, and frugal because they ignore some of the available information, thus sparing mental resources.

Like RCT, the theory of bounded rationality can be applied directly to criminal decision making. In fact, a criminal's environment can best be characterized as a naturalistic decision setting where there are time pressures, high stakes, inadequate information, ill-defined goals, stress, dynamic conditions, coordination of individuals, interruptions, and distractions (see Klein, 2001; Orasanu & Salas, 1993). When an offender decides to commit a crime, he or she may begin a search for information to identify and locate a primary target through physical (e.g., walking around a neighborhood) and mental (e.g., thinking about potential targets) sources. In a world without limits, an offender could conduct an infinitely large search of all information available in the universe. In reality, however, offenders are like nonoffenders who do not have the luxury of unlimited search time, resources required to search for targets, cognitive ability to process endless amounts of information, or (potentially) knowledge on how to commit crimes.

The theory of bounded rationality offers one potential explanation as to why spatial behavior is a useful predictor for linking crimes. According to this theory, offenders are likely to be using simple cognitive strategies to deal with the limits of their available time, knowledge, and resources. The observation that offenders tend to commit crimes located close together would result from spatial decisions that are guided by simple cognitive strategies. For instance, an offender may simply use a satisficing heuristic, whereby offenders select targets that are "close enough" and "good enough." Although rational choice theorists and bounded rationality theorists would likely agree that the spatial decision is derived from cognitive processes, they would disagree as to how offenders reach those spatial decisions. As with RCT then, the lack of stability of some behavioral domains may be due to the fluctuating nature of the cues that guide various heuristic-led criminal decisions.

Like any field of study, subsequent controlled experimental research will ultimately determine which of the above theories (if any) is best able to account for the finding that spatial behavior is more consistent and distinctive than other behaviors used to link crimes. However, we believe that a number of methodological concerns need to be tackled before too much effort is put into theoretical developments.

Methodological Concerns and Explanations

As mentioned, the findings from crime linkage analysis research suggest that (1) inter-crime distance is a useful cue for linking crimes and (2) other behavioral variables, that have been studied thus far, such as *entry behaviors*, are of relatively less value for such a task. It is worth noting, however, that some of the variables that define crimes yet to be investigated in linking studies may prove to be of value for the linking task.

Our review of the linking research has revealed a number of methodological concerns—some of which have been acknowledged by authors of crime linkage studies—that may preclude the two aforementioned conclusions. In particular, we discuss concerns related to validity and reliability.

Threats to Validity

A methodological problem facing crime linkage analysis studies is validity. The first issue under this heading pertains to whether or not the data entered into police record systems are *accurate*. We are unaware of any research that shows that the data collected by the police—which ultimately are used in crime linkage studies—are an accurate reflection of what occurred during the criminal event. We are also unaware of any research showing that the data being used in linking studies are an accurate reflection of what exists in police records. In fact, none of the linking studies reviewed above provide any information about the accuracy of their data. It struck us that each variable provides an opportunity for an error to creep into police files and also research databases. In fact, some research suggests that the potentially lengthy and repetitive nature of the data entry process in this context could result in an unreasonably high number of errors (Healy, Kole, Buck-Gengler, & Bourne, 2004). The implicit assumption that police data are accurate is highly consequential because the quality of the information generated from studies using such data is only as good as the data that are used (Morley & Parker, 2009). The old adage "garbage in garbage out" may be directly applicable to the data being used in linking studies. Although concerns about data accuracy may be greater for *subjective* variables (i.e., variables whose presence in a database rests entirely with the interpretation of a particular individual, such as whether the entry location was through an open window) than *objective* variables (i.e., variables whose presence in a database are less open to interpretation, such as the XY coordinates of a crime location), evidence that all types of variables can be coded accurately needs to be tackled in this field.

A second issue relates to whether or not the conclusion that *these two offenses were committed by the same offender* is correct. Forensic psychologists, criminologists, and police officers are acutely aware that some offenders admit to crimes that they did not in fact commit (i.e., false confessions; Kassin, 2008; Kassin et al., 2010; Kassin & Kiechel, 1996) or are convicted of crimes that they did not commit (i.e., wrongful convictions; Appleby, Hasel, & Kassin, 2013). For instance, it has been acknowledged by some UK police organizations that they engage in a practice known as *taken into consideration* (TIC). A TIC refers to the police asking a suspect or accused person to admit to having committed other crimes so that the police can enhance their clearance rates. Under this practice, the person who agrees to confess to additional crimes is afforded potential benefits, such as allowing the accused person to put their past criminal offenses behind them (and avoid prosecution for these crimes in the future) and minimizing the overall severity of punishment by receiving a sentence for all of the crimes that is smaller compared to a sentence based on the addition of each individual crime. For instance, in a BBC News article published in November 2011, it was reported that one person was asked to confess to an additional 400 crimes, nearly 70,000 cleared crimes (approximately 6% of all crimes cleared in 2010) were due to TICs, and 35% of all detected burglaries and 25% of all detected car crimes were due to TICs (BBC News, 2011). If we revisit the aforementioned linking studies, we see that nearly all of the studies used data that were collected from UK police organizations, with many of the datasets pertaining to burglaries or car crimes.

The third validity issue pertains to attempts to assign criminal actions to the decision-making offender. Research suggests that crimes are often committed in groups (Juodis, Woodworth, Porter, & ten Brinke, 2009; Woodhams, Hollin, Bull, & Cooke, 2012). For instance, Fox and Zawitz (2007) estimated that 20% of homicides in the United States involved multiple perpetrators. Further, it is estimated that as much as 23% of sexual assaults in the United Kingdom were perpetrated by more than one individual (Woodhams, Cooke, Harkins, & da Silva, 2012). Regardless of prevalence rates, the fact that some crimes are committed by groups of offenders raises questions about whether it is possible to state conclusively that a particular profile of criminal actions can be assigned exclusively to one person. Even if it is possible to connect all criminal actions to a single individual (i.e., group members simply watched), there are questions about whether or not police officers and/or researchers can attribute the criminal actions to the correct group member. Although speculative, it might be the case that consistency in behaviors would increase from the levels reported in the 14 studies reviewed above if there were assurances that the across-crime similarity scores being calculated were attributable to the same offender. The problem is that we are unable to estimate the depth of this issue (and it is mentioned rarely in the linking literature) but it is certainly one that requires consideration if conclusions are going to be made about the cues that are useful or not useful for linking crimes.

A fourth issue pertains to the potential artificial nature of the data used in crime linkage analysis studies. It seems from reading crime linkage articles that the researchers trawl police datasets to identify serial offenders (and sometimes, offenders who commit one offense) and select those serial offenses from a narrow period of time (e.g., within 1 year). For the majority of linking studies, subsets of the crimes are then selected to create pairs of linked and unlinked crimes. For example, the researchers may choose to select their data from a database of 1000 crimes. Within this database, there might be 50 serial offenders who were responsible for committing 400 crimes. Six hundred different offenders are responsible for the remaining 600 crimes. From this data, 50 pairs of linked crimes and 50 pairs of unlinked crimes might be selected. In total, 200 crimes out of 1000 crimes are used in the study. This filtering process leads to a reduction of noise in the data. For instance, deciding which crimes are linked and unlinked when viewing a map with 1000 locations would likely be a more difficult task than viewing a map containing just 200 locations. It seems to us that including all of the data that the police have to contend with on a normal basis would result in a different set of conclusions than those made using cleansed data. In addition, putting relatively tight temporal bounds on data collection further increases the artificiality of research compared to a true linking scenario where wider bounds are likely to exist. In all of the studies reviewed above, researchers used cleansed data from a narrow time period, which raises a legitimate question about whether or not inter-crime distance and (other behaviors) really have predictive ability; especially because many of the accuracy rates in linking studies are low to moderate. Clearly, studies that are more ecologically valid would provide a better understanding of the true predictive ability of the various cues used to link crimes.

So, what do these four concerns about validity mean for what we know about crime linkage analysis and the conclusion that spatial behavior, relative to other cues, is a superior cue for linking crimes? In terms of data accuracy, our concerns should be obvious because inaccurate data will result in inaccurate conclusions being drawn. Spatial behavior may be less susceptible to accuracy concerns than other variables (e.g., temporal, MO behavior) as many of the studies collected data from police organizations that used a global positioning system (GPS) to obtain accurate coordinates. Having said this, on a go forward basis, we encourage all crime linking researchers to be explicit about how the crime locations were recorded. For instance, it is important to clarify if GPS coordinates are used, or whether a more crude measure, such as postal/zip code, is used. In terms of the other behavioral variables, such as entry behaviors when studying burglary, ensuring data accuracy is imperative because it may turn out that accurately reported entry behaviors end up being better predictors of crime linkages compared to spatial behavior. Even if spatial behavior continues to be a useful predictor, ensuring data accuracy gives a clearer picture of what is possible when it comes to crime linkage analysis.

Unfortunately, our concerns about TICs and ecological validity are applicable to all crime linkage behaviors. Until such time that researchers can ensure that their datasets do not contain crimes that were solved due to TICs and that more realistic scenarios are employed during the linking studies that reflect the way that real linking tasks work, it is prudent to remain cautious about the findings and recommendations emanating from the crime linkage literature.

Threats to Reliability

A second broad methodological concern in most linkage analysis studies pertains to the reliability of the data. Knowing how reliable data are in these studies is critical because the conclusion that spatial behavior is superior to other behaviors depends on a high degree of inter-rater reliability. A test of inter-rater reliability involves determining the extent to which two (or more) police officers interpret information about a crime in the same way (e.g., both police officers agree that a television was stolen). In addition, assuming that the police officers are in agreement, a second test of inter-rater reliability is needed whereby two (or more) researchers code the same information about a case from police records (e.g., both police officers agree that the item stolen was recorded as a television). Of course, the second test of inter-rater reliability that researchers would be responsible for carrying out would be impossible if the police officer's information is already stored in a database as coded data, as opposed to being stored in a computer system in a written format that requires coding.

In scientific research, a minimum level of 80% agreement is typically deemed acceptable before the inferences and conclusions drawn from coded data are trusted (e.g., Hartmann, 1977). None of the studies reviewed above provided the results of a police inter-rater reliability analysis, and only one of them provided a complete researcher inter-rater reliability analysis. A partial inter-rater reliability analysis was, however, reported for two of the studies. It may be the case that reliability is consistently over 80% agreement, but we have no way of knowing as of now. In one of those studies (Burrell et al., 2012), only 15 of 48 variables were checked for inter-rater reliability. Although Tonkin et al. (2012a) reported that the inter-rater reliability analysis resulted in a median Kappa, it would have been more instructive had the authors provided a range of Kappa values and indicated if any particular variables with low agreement values were removed from their analyses. The general lack of inter-rater reliability analysis raises questions about the trustworthiness of the conclusions drawn from linkage studies. Without evidence of reliable data, it is unclear if certain variables are not useful for linking crimes or simply unreliable.

Our concerns about conclusions being drawn in studies where we do not have any indication about data reliability are amplified when we consider the results of tests of inter-rater reliability in a related area. In one study that examined the inter-rater reliability of the sort of data entered into the Violent Crime Linkage Analysis System (ViCLAS) booklets (a computerized database that enables police officers to identify violent serial offenders), Martineau and Corey (2008) provided 237 police officers with either a sexual assault or homicide vignette (a two-page summary of the case) and asked them to complete a ViCLAS booklet. When Martineau and Corey (2008) calculated occurrence agreement values, inter-rater reliability agreement was 38% for the homicide case and 25% for the sexual assault case. These low percentages demonstrate that officers disagreed with each other about what was present in the vignettes more than they agreed.

In a second more recent study, Snook, Luther, House, Bennell, and Taylor (2012) tested 10 police officers to assess the inter-rater reliability associated with ViCLAS variables. Consistent with the results reported by Martineau and Corey (2008), the results indicated low levels of reliability. More specifically, of the 106 variables that were examined in this study, the average level of occurrence agreement was approximately 31%.

We are sympathetic to applied researchers who use police data to study various issues. We also realize that it is not always logistically possible (e.g., finding another researcher to code the data) or even legally possible (e.g., obtaining permission from participating police organizations for multiple people to view the police data) for researchers to carry out inter-rater reliability assessments. In the event that inter-rater is impossible to obtain, a warning about the weight given to the conclusions should be stated explicitly. Although a warning should be a minimum requirement, we have grave concerns that the effect of such cautions can wear off as citing researchers may choose not to emphasize the original authors' warnings or be unaware of how to draw upon the results of the studies while being mindful of the warnings. Further, there is an added concern that the warning labels do not get distributed to those who matter (e.g., the crime linkage analysts), or worse, the warnings are, for whatever reason, ignored.

Concerns over inter-rater reliability may be less applicable to spatial behavior than to other linking variables. Specifically, we have few concerns about inter-rater reliability of spatial data when crime locations are obtained using a GPS as to our knowledge this is currently the most accurate way to obtain location data. Having said that, some concerns about the precision of some geocoding methodologies have been raised (Ratcliffe, 2001). For example, in instances where crimes occur in large open spaces (e.g., a park), a precise location of the crime is unable to be noted. Inter-rater reliability would be an issue for spatial behavior if the researcher were extracting addresses in text format from police files that will be entered into some other program. Although this chapter focuses mainly on spatial behavior, it is important to point out that having good inter-rater reliability for all of the other variables is important so that the relative effectiveness of spatial behavior can be gauged properly. Assuming that spatial behavior is coded reliably, it is important to know if the predictive ability of spatial behavior can be supplemented by other variables.

Conclusion

Being able to conclude that it is possible to determine accurately that the same offender committed two different crimes would be important to investigators. The central trend from the body of research on this topic suggests to us that crime linkage, for the crime types that have been researched thus far, might be possible if this task was restricted to the use of inter-crime distance. Although a seemingly impressive finding, we argue that some fundamental methodological issues need to be tackled before it is possible to conclude with any certainty that inter-crime distance is a useful predictor and that it is the superior predictor. In particular, we advocate that studies examining the accuracy of police and researcher data be carried out. Every linkage analysis study in the future should report inter-rater reliability for every variable, regardless of how objective a variable may appear. This may seem like an extreme position because it is unlikely that researchers will ever be in the position to code crime scene information (and much information provided to researchers comes in the form of dichotomized data) and that much needed research would never be published. However, for any scientific findings to be considered useful, the data upon which those findings rest must be shown to be reliable. As it stands now, it is difficult to accept the conclusions in any crime linkage study where evidence of data reliability is not offered. At the very least, we expect researchers who are unable to report on inter-rater reliability, to be explicit about the caution that should be used when interpreting their results.

Police organizations have a wealth of data at their fingertips from criminal investigations. Such data provide a unique and cost-effective opportunity to improve their practices. Police organizations should therefore have a vested interest in ensuring that these data are reliable. For both investigative and research purposes, inter-rater reliability ought to be conducted routinely by police officers by having two officers (or civilians) code the variables from the same crime. In line with this solution, organizations need to develop manuals for officers to use when coding crime scene information. These coding manuals ought to contain clear and precise operational definitions of the variables to be coded to ensure a level of reliability that will allow the data to be usable. To ensure a high standard of reliability is upheld, officers should receive extensive training (and refresher training) on such coding manuals, and compliance and quality assurance checks must be carried out.

In addition, we encourage crime linkage researchers to continue to conduct studies that better mimic linking tasks in the real world by keeping the noise in the data. Further, research needs to be carried out to demonstrate that the TIC issue is not a threat to the validity of the findings from studies using data extracted from police organizations in the United Kingdom. On a go forward basis, we encourage researchers to continue to use cases where DNA has confirmed the identity of the offender (e.g., Tonkin et al., 2012b) and to rely more upon cases where the offender was convicted rather than merely arrested for an offense. Until such time as the methodological concerns raised above are tackled, we believe a skeptical stance toward the claims that it is possible to link crimes using inter-crime distance and that inter-crime distance is a superior predictor is justified.

References

Appleby, S. C., Hasel, L. E., & Kassin, S. M. (2013). Police-induced confessions: An empirical analysis of their content and impact. *Psychology, Crime & Law, 19*, 111–128.

BBC News (2011, November 1). Police "confession" crime detection rates revealed. Retrieved from http://www.bbc.co.uk/news/uk-15524569

Bennell, C., Bloomfield, S., Snook, B., Taylor, P., & Barnes, C. (2010). Linkage analysis in cases of serial burglary: Comparing the performance of university students, police professional, and a logistic regression model. *Psychology, Crime & Law, 16,* 507–524.

Bennell, C., & Canter, D. V. (2002). Linking commercial burglaries by *modus operandi*: Tests using regression and ROC analysis. *Science & Justice, 42,* 153–164.

Bennell, C., & Jones, N. J. (2005). Between a ROC and a hard place: A method for linking serial burglaries by *modus operandi*. *Journal of Investigative Psychology and Offender Profiling, 2,* 23–41.

Brantingham, P. L., & Brantingham, P. J. (1993). Environment, routine, and situation: Toward a pattern theory of crime. In R. V. Clarke & M. Felson (Eds.), *Routine activity and rational choice: Advances in criminological theory* (Vol. 5, pp. 259–294). New Brunswick, NJ: Transaction.

Brantingham, P. L., & Brantingham, P. J. (2008). Crime pattern theory. In R. Wortley & L. Mazerolle (Eds.), *Environmental criminology and crime analysis* (pp. 70–77). Portland, OR: Willan Publishing.

Burrell, A., Bull, R., & Bond, J. (2012). Linking personal robbery offences using offender behaviour. *Journal of Investigative Psychology and Offender Profiling, 9,* 199–295.

Cervone, D., & Shoda, Y. (1999). Beyond traits in the study of personality coherence. *Current Directions in Psychological Science, 8,* 27–32.

Clarke, R., & Cornish, D. (1985). Modeling offenders' decisions: A framework for policy and research. In M. Tonry & N. Morris (Eds.), *Crime and justice: An annual review of research* (Vol. 6, pp. 147–185). Chicago, IL: University of Chicago Press.

Cohen, L. E., & Felson, M. (1979). Social change and crime rate trends: A routine activity approach. *American Sociological Review, 44,* 588–608.

Cornish, D., & Clarke, R. (1986). *The reasoning criminal: Rational choice perspectives on offending*. New York, NY: Springer.

Davies, K., Tonkin, M., Bull, R., & Bond, J. W. (2012). The course of case linkage never did run smooth: A new investigation to tackle the behavioural changes in serial car theft. *Journal of Investigative Psychology and Offender Profiling, 9,* 274–295.

Felson, M. (1987). Routine activities and crime prevention in the developing metropolis. *Criminology, 25,* 911–931.

Fox, J. A., & Zawitz, M. W. (2007). Homicide trends in the United States. *Bureau of Justice Statistics*. Retrieved from http://bjs.ojp.usdoj.gov/content/pub/pdf/htius.pdf

Funder, D. C., & Colvin, C. (1991). Explorations in behavioral consistency: Properties of persons, situations, and behaviors. *Journal of Personality and Social Psychology, 60,* 773–794.

Gigerenzer, G., Hoffrage, U., & Kleinbolting, H. (1991). Probabilistic mental models: A Brunswikian theory of confidence. *Psychological Review, 98,* 506–528.

Gigerenzer, G., & Selten, R. (2001). *Bounded rationality*. London, England: The MIT Press.

Gigerenzer, G., & Todd, P. M. (1999). Fast and frugal heuristics: The adaptive toolbox. In G. Gigerenzer, P. M. Todd, & the ABC Research Group (Eds.), *Simple heuristics that make us smart* (pp. 3–34). New York, NY: Oxford University Press.

Gilovich, T., & Griffin, D. (2002). Heuristics and biases: Then and now. In T. Gilovich, D. Griffin, & D. Kahneman (Eds.), *Heuristics and biases: The psychology of intuitive judgment* (pp. 1–18). Cambridge, England: Cambridge University Press.

Goodwill, A. M., & Alison, L. J. (2006). The development of a filter model for prioritizing suspects in burglary offences. *Psychology, Crime & Law, 12,* 395–416.

Hartmann, D. P. (1977). Considerations in the choice of interobserver reliability estimates. *Journal of Applied Behavior Analysis, 10,* 103–116.

Healy, A. F., Kole, J. A., Buck-Gengler, C. J., & Bourne, L. E. (2004). Effects of prolonged work on data entry speed and accuracy. *Journal of Experimental Psychology: Applied, 10,* 188–199.

Juodis, M., Woodworth, M., Porter, S., & ten Brinke, L. (2009). Partners in crime: A comparison of individual and multi-perpetrator homicides. *Criminal Justice and Behavior, 36,* 824–839.

Kahneman, D. (1973). *Attention and effort.* Englewood Cliffs, NJ: Prentice Hall.

Kassin, S. M. (2008). False confessions: Causes, consequences, and implications for reform. *Current Directions in Psychological Science, 17,* 249–253.

Kassin, S. M., Drizin, S. A., Grisso, T., Gudjonsson, G. H., Leo, R. A., & Redlich, A. D. (2010). Police-induced confessions: Risk factors and recommendations. *Law and Human Behavior, 34,* 3–38.

Kassin, S. M., & Kiechel, K. L. (1996). The social psychology of false confessions: Compliance, internalization, and confabulation. *Psychological Science, 7,* 125–128.

Klein, G. (2001). *Sources of power: How people make decisions.* Cambridge, MA: The MIT Press.

Lersch, K. M. (2007). *Space, time, and crime.* Durham, NC: Carolina Academic Press.

Markson, L., Woodhams, J., & Bond, J. (2010). Linking serial residential burglary: Comparing the utility of modus operandi behaviours, geographical proximity and temporal proximity. *Journal of Investigative Psychology and Offender Profiling, 7,* 91–107.

Martineau, M., & Corey, S. (2008). Investigating the reliability of the violent crime linkage analysis system (ViCLAS) crime report. *Journal of Police and Criminal Psychology, 23,* 51–60.

Miller, G. A. (1956). The magic number seven, plus or minus two: Some limits on our capacity for processing information. *Psychological Review, 63,* 81–93.

Mischel, W. (1968). *Personality and assessment.* Hoboken, NJ: John Wiley & Sons.

Morley, D., & Parker, C. S. (2009). Databases and database management systems. In D. Morley & C. S. Parker (Eds.), *Understanding computers: Today and tomorrow* (pp. 588–627). Boston, MA: Cengage Learning.

Newman, O. (1972). *Defensible space: Crime prevention through urban design.* London, England: MacMillan.

Orasanu, M., & Salas, D. (1993). Team decision making in complex environments, In G. A. Klein, J. Orasanu, R. Calderwood, & C. E. Zsambok (Eds.), *Decision making in action: Models and methods* (pp. 327–345). Norwood, NJ: Ablex.

Ratcliffe, J. H. (2001). On the accuracy of TIGER-type geocoded address data in relation to cadastral and census areal units. *International Journal of Geographical Information Science, 15,* 473–485.

Santtila, P., Korpela, S., & Häkkänen, H. (2004). Expertise and decision-making in linking of car crime series. *Psychology, Crime & Law, 10,* 97–112.

Shoda, Y., Mischel, W., & Wright, J. C. (1994). Intraindividual stability in the organization and patterning of behavior: Incorporating psychological situations into the idiographic analysis of personality. *Journal of Personality and Social Psychology, 67,* 674–687.

Simon, H. A. (1955). A behavioral model of rational choice. *Quarterly Journal of Economics, 69,* 99–118.

Simon, H. A. (1956). Rational choice and the structure of the environment. *Psychological Review, 63,* 129–138.

Snook, B., Luther, K., House, J. C., Bennell, C., & Taylor, P. J. (2012). Violent crime linkage analysis system: A test of inter-rater reliability. *Criminal Justice and Behavior, 39,* 607–619.

Swets, J. A. (1988). Measuring the accuracy of diagnostic systems. *Science, 240,* 1285–1293.

Todd, P. M., & Gigerenzer, G. (2003). Bounding rationality to the world. *Journal of Economic Psychology, 24,* 143–165.

Tonkin, M., Grant, T., & Bond, J. W. (2008). To link or not to link: A test of the case linkage principles using serial car theft data. *Journal of Investigative Psychology and Offender Profiling, 5,* 59–77.

Tonkin, M., Santtila, P., & Bull, R. (2012a). The linking of burglary crimes using offender behaviour: Testing research cross-nationally and exploring methodology. *Legal and Criminological Psychology, 17,* 276–293.

Tonkin, M., Woodhams, J., Bull, R., & Bond, J. W. (2012b). Behavioural case linkage with solved and unsolved crimes. *Forensic Science International, 222,* 146–153.

Tonkin, M., Woodhams, J., Bull, R., Bond, J. W., & Palmer, E. J. (2011). Linking different types of crime using geographical and temporal proximity. *Criminal Justice and Behavior, 38,* 1069–1088.

Tonkin, M., Woodhams, J., Bull, R., Bond, J. W., & Santtila, P. (2012c). A comparison of logistic regression and classification tree analysis for behavioural case linkage. *Journal of Investigative Psychology and Offender Profiling, 9,* 235–258.

Woodhams, J., Cooke, C., Harkins, L., & da Silva, T. (2012). Leadership in multiple perpetrator stranger rape. *Journal of Interpersonal Violence, 27,* 728–752.

Woodhams, J., Hollin, C. R., Bull, R., & Cooke, C. (2012). Behavior displayed by female victims during rapes committed by lone and multiple perpetrators. *Psychology, Public Policy, and Law, 18,* 415–452.

Woodhams, J., & Toye, K. (2007). An empirical test of the assumptions of case linkage and offender profiling with serial commercial robberies. *Psychology, Public Policy, and Law, 13,* 59–85.

Testing the Theories Underpinning Crime Linkage

6

MATTHEW TONKIN

Contents

Introduction 108
Why Is It Important to Test the Principles of Crime Linkage? 108
The Principles of Crime Linkage: Behavioral Consistency and Distinctiveness 109
Empirical Tests of Behavioral Consistency and Distinctiveness 110
The Thematic Approach to Crime Linkage 111
The Bennell Approach to Crime Linkage 113
Automated Crime Linkage Systems 121
A Summary of the Evidence on Behavioral Consistency, Distinctiveness, and Discrimination Accuracy 122
The Limitations of Crime Linkage Research 123
Stage 1: Identify Sample and Behaviors 123
Over-Reliance on Solved Crime 123
Homogenous Samples of Crime 125
Small Number of Crimes Selected for Each Offender 126
How Offending Behavior Is Operationalized 126
Stage 2: Form Domains/Themes 127
No Comparison of Different Statistical and Nonstatistical/Intuitive Methods 127
Stage 3: Create Crime Pairs 128
Formation of the Unlinked Crime Pairs 128
Stage 4: Calculate Similarity Coefficients 129
Limited Exploration of Similarity Coefficients 129
Stage 5: Statistical Analyses to Test Discrimination Accuracy 130
Limited Comparison of Different Statistical Approaches to Discrimination Accuracy 130
Inappropriate Comparison Groups 131
Stage 6: Conclusions 133
Conclusions Limited by Geography, Time, and Methodology 133

General Limitations 134
Person × Situation Interactions 134
Moving Beyond Theoretical Tests of Crime Linkage 134
Conclusion 135
References 135

Introduction

The chapters included within this book demonstrate that crime linkage is becoming an increasing part of police investigations and subsequent court proceedings (see Chapters 8–10). However, if this trend is to continue in a reliable and evidence-based fashion, the fundamental principles of crime linkage must be supported by empirical research. The current chapter, therefore, reviews the research studies that have amassed over the past decade or so that have tested the principles of behavioral consistency and distinctiveness which underpin crime linkage. This research has used a broad range of methodologies and the findings span a number of law enforcement jurisdictions across Europe, North America, Canada, Japan, and South Africa. The extant research will be critically considered to identify the disparity between how crime linkage is currently tested and how it is used during real-life police investigations. This sets the stage for subsequent Chapters 12 through 14 of the book that will describe how researchers are actively seeking to overcome these limitations and, therefore, provide a more solid empirical basis for the practice of crime linkage.

Why Is It Important to Test the Principles of Crime Linkage?

The potential benefits of identifying linked crime series are well known. First, crime linkage allows the evidence collected across several investigations to be pooled, which can increase the chances of catching and prosecuting the person responsible (Grubin, Kelly, & Brunsdon, 2001). This may also have a knock-on effect on public confidence in the police. Second, crime linkage allows multiple crimes to be investigated together, rather than separately, which is a more streamlined way of using resources (Woodhams, Hollin, & Bull, 2007). This is particularly important at a time when law enforcement agencies are being forced to make considerable reductions in their operational costs without compromising the ability to prevent and detect crime. However, the benefits of crime linkage depend on its reliability and accuracy. If there are errors in the linkage process, this will lead to unhelpful lines of inquiry being pursued, which ultimately makes it more difficult to apprehend offenders (Grubin et al., 2001). Furthermore, incorrect crime linkage can cause unnecessary anxiety and fear of crime among the general public and can even result in individuals being falsely accused of crimes that they did not commit (Snook, Luther, House, Bennell, & Taylor, 2012). Thus, there is a fine balance between the potential benefits of crime linkage and the damaging consequences if it goes wrong.

These points have an added significance when one considers that crime linkage is becoming increasingly used during criminal investigations and court proceedings (see Chapters 8–10). For example, a number of specialist units and computer packages have been established around the world to support this procedure, including units/packages in Canada, Japan, South Africa, Australia, New Zealand, the United States, and various European countries, including the United Kingdom (Hazelwood & Warren, 2004; Labuschagne, 2012; Snook et al., 2012; Yokota, Fujita, Watanabe, Yoshimoto, & Wachi, 2007). Furthermore, crime linkage has been presented in court as similar fact evidence to support the prosecution of suspects in several countries (e.g., Charron & Woodhams, 2010; Hazelwood & Warren, 2004; Labuschagne, 2012). In short, unless the principles of crime linkage are tested and shown to be valid, there is a significant risk that criminal investigations and court proceedings will be misled.

The Principles of Crime Linkage: Behavioral Consistency and Distinctiveness

The principles of behavioral consistency and distinctiveness that underpin crime linkage have been described elsewhere in this book (see Chapters 1 and 2), so they will only be given limited consideration in this chapter. However, it is worth emphasizing that both principles are testable (i.e., research can either prove or disprove them), which means that the potential value of crime linkage is open to scientific scrutiny. This is crucial if crime linkage is to become an empirically based area of research and practice.

But, before one can test whether consistency and distinctiveness exist in offender behavior, one must decide how to define these concepts. As explained by Canter (2000), behavioral consistency and distinctiveness can be defined in several ways. At the broadest level (Level 1), one might examine whether individuals are consistent over time in their decision to offend (i.e., persistence vs. desistance in criminal behavior; Blumstein, Farrington, & Moitra, 1985; Laub & Sampson, 2001; Moffitt, 1993). At this level, consistency is manifested as an individual who either persistently chooses to break the law or persistently refuses to break it. At the next level (Level 2), consistency can be defined in terms of offender specialization versus versatility (e.g., Farrington, Snyder, & Finnegan, 1988). Consistency at this level is manifested by an offender who prefers one type of offense over another. At a finer level of analysis (Level 3), one can test whether individuals display similar patterns/themes in their offending behavior (e.g., Bennell & Canter, 2002; Santtila, Junkkila, & Sandnabba, 2005). For example, a sexual offender who repeatedly relates to his victims by being excessively violent would be considered consistent at this level. At the most refined level (Level 4), consistency can manifest as the offender repeatedly displaying a single isolated behavior from one crime to the next (e.g., Bateman & Salfati, 2007; Harbort & Mokros, 2001; Sjöstedt, Långström, Sturidsson, & Grann, 2004). This is distinct from Level 3, where groups of behaviors are displayed consistently. For example, an offender might always tie his victims up with hosiery.

Although all four levels of analysis are theoretically interesting, not all of them are necessarily relevant to the practice of crime linkage (at least not directly). As discussed by Woodhams, Hollin, et al. (2007), behavioral consistency and distinctiveness must be addressed at a level that achieves a correct balance between being sufficiently refined to allow the police to distinguish between individual offenders and not being so refined that noise in the data obscures meaningful patterns in offender behavior. For example, an offender might be highly consistent in the type of offense he commits (e.g., he only commits burglaries), but without more detailed information on when, where, and how he behaves when offending it is unlikely that the police will be able to distinguish his crimes from the many other burglaries committed in a jurisdiction. Consequently, research that functions at Levels 1 and 2 is arguably too general to provide workable methods for linking crimes.

Likewise, it is also possible for research to examine behavioral consistency and distinctiveness at a level that is too refined (e.g., at the level of individual behaviors, Level 4), for example, an offender might tie the victim up using rope in one offense, but handcuff the victim in a second offense. At the level of individual behaviors, these two crimes might be classified as behaviorally inconsistent because different methods of restraining the victim were used. But this may be inappropriate because some form of victim restraint was evident in both offenses, thereby demonstrating similarity in offender behavior. One should expect slight behavioral variation such as this across a series of crimes due to situational factors and the inevitable noise that will exist in police data. Consequently, researchers have tended to look for consistency/distinctiveness in clusters of individual offense behaviors rather than behaviors in isolation (i.e., Level 3) because this approach helps to counteract the influence of situational variation and low data quality (e.g., Bateman & Salfati, 2007). The remaining sections of this chapter will review and critique this work.

Empirical Tests of Behavioral Consistency and Distinctiveness

Three distinct bodies of research will be considered in this section, each of which is based on a different methodological approach to testing behavioral consistency, distinctiveness, and discrimination accuracy.* The first approach uses statistical procedures such as multidimensional scaling and cluster analysis to form groups of behavior that are thought to share a similar psychological meaning (referred to as the *thematic approach* hereafter). The second approach, developed by Bennell (2002, and referred to as the *Bennell approach* hereafter), creates clusters of offense behavior in an intuitive/nonstatistical manner by combining behaviors that either serve a similar function during the offense (e.g., they facilitate entry into the property during a burglary) or represent one "type" of offender behavior (e.g., spatial behavior) (Tonkin, Santtila, & Bull, 2012). The third approach has developed and tested automated crime linkage systems. The extent to which these systems are successful can be interpreted as evidence to support the existence of behavioral consistency and distinctiveness. The first body of research we will consider is the thematic approach to crime linkage.

The Thematic Approach to Crime Linkage

Grubin et al. (2001) were the first to explore a statistically based approach to identifying behavioral themes.† Within their sample of serial rapes, Grubin and colleagues identified four offense domains, each of which represented a different aspect of rape behavior (control, sex, escape, and style behaviors). Control behaviors were those directed toward gaining control of the victim so that the offense could be completed successfully (e.g., victim restraint and the way the victim was approached). Sex behaviors were those associated with the sexual component of the offense (e.g., anal penetration and fellatio). Escape behaviors were those associated with leaving the crime scene and/or avoiding detection (e.g., wearing a mask or gloves). Style behaviors were those that were not necessary for the offense to be successfully completed and, thus, may reflect the offender's personality or offense style (e.g., complimenting the victim). Within each of these four offense domains, Grubin

* However, it is worth highlighting to the reader the range of research that is not covered in any depth during this chapter. The following studies have adopted a miscellaneous range of approaches to behavioral consistency and/or distinctiveness, including multidimensional scalogram analysis (MSA; see Canter et al., 1991; Mokros, 1999, cited in Canter, 2000), Bayesian analysis (Salo et al., 2012), fuzzy logic (Austin, 1996, cited in Grubin et al., 2001), and other approaches that do not fit into a neat category (e.g., Bateman & Salfati, 2007; Beutler, Hinton, Crago, & Collier, 1995; Goodwill & Alison, 2006; Green, Booth, & Biderman, 1976; Guay, Proulx, Cusson, & Ouimet, 2001; Lundrigan, Czarnomski, & Wilson, 2010; Sjöstedt et al., 2004; Yokota-Sano & Watanabe, 1998).

† It should be noted that Grubin et al. (2001) actually used a combination of statistical and intuitive approaches to form the behavioral themes in their study, but this research is discussed under the current subheading because their methodology bears greater resemblance to the thematic approach than the Bennell approach.

and colleagues used cluster analysis to identify four behavioral themes, thus creating a total of 256 (4 × 4 × 4 × 4) domain type combinations that could be used to describe a given offense in their sample. This allowed Grubin et al. (2001) to examine both single-domain consistency in offense behavior (i.e., the extent to which an offender displayed the same domain type from one crime to the next, e.g., an offender who displayed control type 1 in all of his or her offenses) and multi domain consistency (i.e., the extent to which an offender displayed the same domain type combination from one offense to the next, e.g., an offender who displayed control type 1, sex type 2, escape type 4, and style type 3 in all of his or her offenses).

It was found that 83% of the serial rapists demonstrated single-domain consistency in at least one of the four domains throughout their series and 26% had at least two offenses within their series that matched across all four domains. This was significantly greater than chance, thereby demonstrating support for the assumption of behavioral consistency. Interestingly, offenders were most consistent in their control behaviors (e.g., weapon use and the method of approaching the victim) and least consistent in style behaviors (i.e., those behaviors that were not necessary for the crime to be completed successfully, such as asking the victim personal questions and complimenting them during the assault). These are important findings because they suggest that crime linkage will be more successful if law enforcement personnel focus selectively on certain types of offender behavior over others (this issue is discussed in greater depth below).

Having demonstrated statistically significant levels of behavioral consistency, Grubin et al. (2001) tested whether these findings could be translated into a statistical methodology to support crime linkage (thereby testing behavioral distinctiveness). For each offense in their sample, they identified the 10% of cases that were most similar to this index offense in terms of domain types (using a specially designed statistical algorithm). With the exception of two offense series, the number of correct cases within the top 10% was statistically larger than the number that would be expected through chance. Furthermore, Grubin and colleagues demonstrated that the relatively large false positive rate (where an unlinked crime was incorrectly included within the top 10%) could be reduced to some extent by applying geographical and temporal filters, which gave greater weight to those crimes that were committed close together in space and time. Nevertheless, Grubin et al. (2001) concluded that their linking algorithm was not robust enough to be used during routine screening of large national databases. They called for further research and refinement of their methodology.

Since this initial study, a number of subsequent studies have adopted a statistical approach to identifying behavioral themes. In particular, Santtila and colleagues have used a variety of statistical approaches for this purpose, including principal components analysis, multidimensional scaling, Mokken scaling, and discriminant function analysis (Santtila, Fritzon, & Tamelander, 2004; Santtila, Junkkila, & Sandnabba, 2005; Santtila, Korpela, & Häkkänen, 2004; Santtila et al., 2008). For example, Santtila et al. (2008) used Mokken scaling (a nonparametric method similar to factor analysis) to identify seven behavioral themes among a sample of 116 Italian homicides. These behavioral themes were subsequently entered into a discriminant function analysis to produce a number of probability values for each crime, which indicated the predicted likelihood that the crime belonged to each series in the sample. It was found that 62.9% of the crimes were assigned to the correct series (only 6.2% would have been expected through chance). Similar (albeit slightly less successful) findings have been observed with samples of serial arson, rape, and car theft (Santtila, Fritzon, et al., 2004; Santtila et al., 2005; Santtila, Korpela, et al., 2004).

Another approach has been pioneered by Salfati and colleagues, who use multidimensional scaling techniques to identify behavioral themes in offense behavior (e.g., Horning & Salfati, 2008; Magyar & Salfati, 2007; Sorochinski & Salfati, 2010). These studies have found statistically significant levels of behavioral consistency in samples of serial rape and homicide. For example, in their sample of 19 US homicide offenders, Sorochinski and Salfati (2010) found that the level of consistency observed in planning behaviors, wounding, and victim–offender interaction was between 1.5 and 26.5 times greater than the level expected through chance. Not only do these findings support the assumption of behavioral consistency, but they further suggest that certain types of offender behavior are more consistently displayed than others (Sorochinski & Salfati, 2010; e.g., behaviors indicative of the victim–offender interaction were the most consistent and forms of wounding were the least consistent).

The Bennell Approach to Crime Linkage

A frequently used approach to testing behavioral consistency and distinctiveness was proposed by Bennell (2002). Although slight variation exists in how Bennell's methodology has been applied, the general process is similar across studies (see Figure 6.1). This process begins by identifying all offenders who have committed more than one offense during a given time period (e.g., all offenders who have committed two or more residential burglaries in the past three years). Next, content analysis is used to identify relevant behavioral features for analysis. These features are clustered into domains that contain behaviors that either serve a similar function during the offense or represent one type of offender behavior (Tonkin, Santtila, et al., 2012). Each crime in the sample is then coded for the presence or absence of the identified behavioral features.

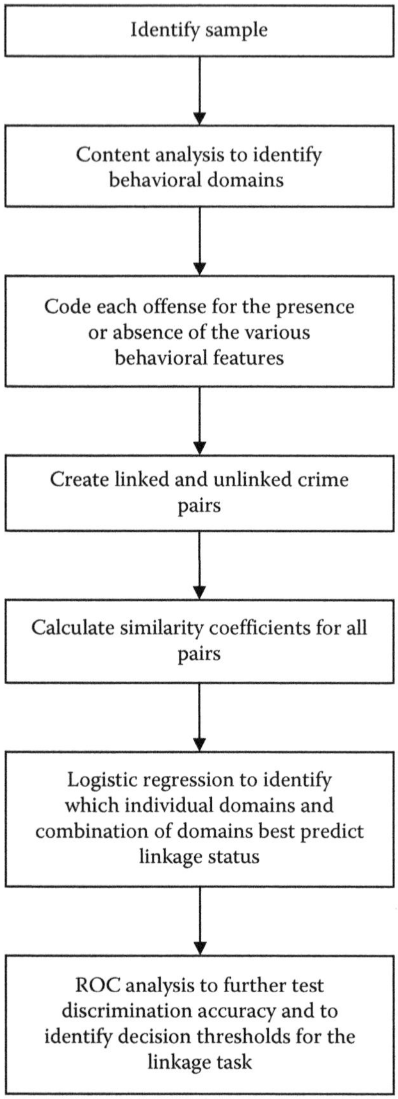

Figure 6.1 The Bennell approach to behavioral consistency, distinctiveness, and discrimination accuracy.

The sample is subsequently used to create linked crime pairs (containing two crimes committed by the same person) and unlinked crime pairs (containing two crimes committed by different people). Various similarity coefficients are then calculated, which indicate the degree of behavioral similarity and/or geographical/temporal proximity between the two crimes in each pair. In terms of geographical and temporal similarity, the number of kilometers and the number of days separating the two crimes in each pair are calculated (referred to as inter-crime distance and temporal proximity, respectively).

In terms of behavioral similarity, statistical coefficients are calculated to indicate the number of shared behavioral features in the two crimes, with coefficients produced that typically range from 0 (indicating no shared features) to 1 (indicating complete behavioral similarity). Traditionally, separate coefficients are calculated for each behavioral domain, but a combined coefficient that indicates the level of similarity across all behavioral features is often calculated as well, thus allowing researchers to examine both the combined and independent value of different types of offender behavior for the purposes of crime linkage.

These measures of behavioral, geographical, and temporal similarity are subsequently used to predict whether crime pairs are linked or unlinked (referred to as discrimination accuracy). Typically, direct logistic regression is used to indicate the potential value of each behavioral domain in isolation and stepwise regression is used to indicate the combination of domains that maximizes discrimination accuracy (Bennell & Canter, 2002). Statistically significant regression models are interpreted as evidence for behavioral consistency, distinctiveness, and discrimination accuracy.

Finally, receiver operating characteristic (ROC) analysis is used to further test discrimination accuracy. The metric that is produced by ROC analysis, the area under the curve (AUC), ranges from 0 to 1, with an AUC of 0.50 indicative of a chance level of discrimination accuracy* (see Chapter 14 for further information on ROC analysis). The AUC is used to examine which domains (and combinations thereof) have the greatest potential to support crime linkage. Statistically significant AUC values that indicate moderate to high levels of discrimination accuracy are interpreted as evidence for behavioral consistency, distinctiveness, and discrimination accuracy. Researchers have also used the output from ROC analysis to estimate decision thresholds that can be used to guide practitioners when they are conducting crime linkage in practice (e.g., Bennell, 2002; Tonkin, Grant, & Bond, 2008; Woodhams & Toye, 2007). These thresholds identify the point at which two crimes are sufficiently similar (on a given measure of behavioral, geographical, or temporal similarity) to conclude that they have been committed by the same person, thereby helping to maximize the number of correct linkage decisions (Bennell, 2002).

A number of studies have adopted Bennell's (2002) methodology since it was originally proposed (see Table 6.1 for a summary). These studies have found evidence to suggest that certain types of offender behavior demonstrate statistically significant levels of consistency and distinctiveness and that these behaviors can be used to facilitate moderate to high levels of

* Typically, AUCs between 0.50 and 0.70 are said to indicate low levels of accuracy, AUCs between 0.70 and 0.90 indicate moderate levels of accuracy, and AUCs between 0.90 and 1.00 indicate high levels of accuracy (Swets, 1988).

Table 6.1 A Summary of Research Evidence Using the Bennell Approach to Crime Linkage

Crime Type/Study	Country	Area under the Curve (AUC)
	Commercial Burglary	
Bennell and Canter (2002)		
Inter-crime distance	United Kingdom	0.80**
Target		0.68*
Entry		0.65*
Property		0.63*
Stepwise[a]		0.81**
Bennell and Jones (2005)[b]		
Inter-crime distance	United Kingdom	0.84**
Target		0.61*
Entry		0.57*
Property		0.55*
Stepwise		0.85**
	Residential Burglary	
Bennell and Jones (2005)[b]		
Inter-crime distance	United Kingdom	0.90**
Target		0.58*
Entry		0.59*
Property		0.59*
Stepwise		0.90**
Markson et al. (2010)		
Inter-crime distance	United Kingdom	0.90**
Temporal proximity		0.86**
All behaviors		0.61*
Target		0.54*
Entry		0.54*
Property		0.58*
Stepwise		0.95***
Melnyk et al. (2011)[c]		
All behaviors	United Kingdom	0.62*
Tonkin, Woodhams, et al. (2012)[d]		
Inter-crime distance	Finland	0.84**
Temporal proximity		0.82**
All behaviors		0.72**
Target		0.73**
Entry		0.66*
Internal		0.66*
Property		0.58*
Stepwise		0.86**
Tonkin, Santtila, et al. (2012)		
Inter-crime distance	Finland	0.83**
All behaviors		0.82**

(Continued)

Table 6.1 (Continued) A Summary of Research Evidence Using the Bennell Approach to Crime Linkage

Crime Type/Study	Country	Area under the Curve (AUC)
Target		0.77**
Entry		0.70*
Internal		0.78**
Property		0.66*
Stepwise		0.87**
Classification tree model		0.80**
	Commercial Robbery	
Woodhams and Toye (2007)		
Inter-crime distance	United Kingdom	0.89**
Target		0.79**
Planning		0.70*
Control		0.90**
Stepwise		0.95***
	Personal Robbery	
Burrell et al. (2012)[e]		
Inter-crime distance	United Kingdom	0.92***
Temporal proximity		0.83**
All behaviors		0.64*
Target selection		0.64*
Control		0.56*
Property		0.45*
Stepwise		0.90***
	Rape/Sexual Assault	
Bennell et al. (2009)		
All behaviors	United Kingdom	0.75**
Bennell et al. (2010)[c]		
All behaviors	United Kingdom	0.81**
Woodhams and Labuschagne (2012)		
All behaviors (two crimes per offender)	South Africa	0.77**
All behaviors (all crimes per offender)		0.88**
Winter et al. (2013)[f]		
All behaviors (dimensional)	United Kingdom	0.74**
All behaviors (multivariate)		0.84**
	Car Theft	
Tonkin et al. (2008)		
Inter-crime distance	United Kingdom	0.81**
Interdump distance		0.77**
Target selection		0.57*
Target acquisition		0.56*
Disposal behavior		0.56*

(Continued)

Table 6.1 (Continued) A Summary of Research Evidence Using the Bennell Approach to Crime Linkage

Crime Type/Study	Country	Area under the Curve (AUC)
Davies et al. (2012)		
Inter-crime distance	United Kingdom	0.91***
Interdump distance		0.88**
Temporal proximity		0.78**
Target selection (old)		0.62*
Target selection (new)		0.76**
Target acquisition		0.64*
Disposal behavior		0.64*
Age difference		0.62*
Value difference		0.56*
Stepwise		0.93***
Tonkin, Woodhams, et al. (2012)		
Inter-crime distance	United Kingdom	0.82**
All behaviors		0.56*
Target selection		0.54*
Target acquisition		0.54*
Disposal behavior		0.50*
	Homicide	
Melnyk et al. (2011)[c]		
All behaviors	United Stated	0.96***
	Arson	
Ellingwood et al. (2013)[g]		
All behaviors	United Kingdom	0.88**
Instrumental person		0.77**
Instrumental object		0.82**
Expressive person		0.72**
Expressive object		0.78**
Stepwise		0.87**

Note: This table is restricted to peer-reviewed studies that are either published or in press at the time of writing.

[a] Stepwise refers to the combination of behavioral domains identified through stepwise binary logistic regression analysis.

[b] Bennell and Jones present AUC statistics separately for several different police districts. For the purposes of clarity, the mean statistics are collapsed by district to provide average scores for each domain across all districts.

[c] Bennell et al. and Melnyk et al. present AUC statistics for two similarity coefficients over a range of experimental conditions. For the purposes of clarity, only the AUC statistic using Jaccard's coefficient with 100% of behaviors is presented, as this represents the variation of Bennell's methodology most commonly used in the literature.

[d] Tonkin et al. tested two different methodological approaches to crime linkage, but only those following Bennell's original methodology are presented here.

(*Continued*)

Table 6.1 (Continued) A Summary of Research Evidence Using the Bennell Approach to Crime Linkage

[e] Burrell et al. present AUC statistics derived using Bennell's original methodology and using an altered methodology. Only those findings using the original methodology are presented in this table.

[f] Winter et al. present AUC statistics based on serial data only and a combination of serial and nonserial rapes. Only those findings from the serial data are presented in this table because this reflects the methodology used in all previous research using Bennell's methodology. However, Winter et al.'s findings are discussed in greater depth below.

[g] Ellingwood et al. present AUC statistics for two similarity coefficients over a range of experimental conditions. For the purposes of clarity, only the AUC statistics using Jaccard's coefficient and the theoretical domains are presented.

* Low predictive accuracy (AUC = 0.50–0.70); ** moderate predictive accuracy (AUC = 0.70–0.90); *** high predictive accuracy (AUC = 0.90–1.00) (Swets, 1988).

discrimination accuracy when they are used to distinguish between linked and unlinked crime pairs. This evidence spans a variety of crime types, including residential and commercial burglary (e.g., Bennell & Jones, 2005), personal and commercial robbery (Burrell, Bull, & Bond, 2012; Woodhams & Toye, 2007), car theft (e.g., Tonkin et al., 2008), arson (Ellingwood, Mugford, Bennell, Melnyk, & Fritzon, 2013), sexual assault (e.g., Bennell, Jones, & Melnyk, 2009), and homicide (Melnyk, Bennell, Gauthier, & Gauthier, 2011).

Although these findings are promising, it is important to note the variation in linking results that exists in Table 6.1. First, there is variation in discrimination accuracy between different types of crime; for example, the combination of different types of *modus operandi* (MO) behavior is more successful at discriminating between linked and unlinked homicides than it is at discriminating between linked and unlinked burglaries, car thefts, and sexual offenses. These findings suggest that certain types of crime may be more suitable for crime linkage than others. However, considerable research is needed before definitive conclusions of this nature can be drawn.

Second, discrimination accuracy differs from one police jurisdiction to the next. For example, the AUC value obtained when using inter-crime distance to discriminate between linked and unlinked residential burglaries has varied from 0.76 in some jurisdictions up to 0.97 in other jurisdictions. Furthermore, when Tonkin, Santtila, et al. (2012) examined behavioral consistency, distinctiveness, and discrimination accuracy in a sample of Finnish residential burglaries, they found that the level of accuracy was greater than that observed in previous UK-based research. Notably, the AUC value for all MO behaviors in Finland was 0.72 (compared to an average AUC value in UK-based research of 0.65), the AUC value for the target domain was 0.73 (compared to a UK average of 0.60), and the AUCs for entry and internal behaviors were both 0.66 (compared to UK averages of 0.58 and 0.51, respectively). These findings demonstrate that the potential for crime linkage cannot be assumed to have a universal value across all police jurisdictions. There is clearly variation between different countries (Tonkin, Santtila, et al., 2012), there is also variation between different forces within the same country (Bennell, 2002), and there is even variation between different districts within a single police force (Bennell & Jones, 2005). There are a number of factors that might explain such variation, including data storage practices, the distribution of potential targets/victims, and even differences in behavioral consistency and distinctiveness between offenders (see Tonkin, Santtila, et al., 2012, for further discussion).

Third, Table 6.1 shows that there is variation from one behavioral domain to the next in terms of discrimination accuracy. For example, inter-crime distance and temporal proximity have consistently demonstrated larger AUC values than any other type of burglar behavior, including what type of property was targeted, how the property was entered, the behavior of the offender while inside the property (e.g., search behavior), and what property was stolen (Bennell & Canter, 2002; Bennell & Jones, 2005; Markson, Woodhams, & Bond, 2010; Tonkin, Santtila, et al., 2012, Tonkin, Woodhams, Bull, Bond, & Santtila, 2012). Similar findings have been observed with car theft (Davies, Tonkin, Bull, & Bond, 2012; Tonkin et al., 2008) and personal robbery (Burrell et al., 2012).

A number of explanations have been proposed for the finding that discrimination accuracy varies as a function of the behavioral domain under examination (see Bennell & Jones, 2005). One possibility is that certain types of behavior (such as spatial behavior) are coded more consistently and reliably than other types of behavior, which would increase the likelihood of finding consistent and distinctive behavioral patterns. Alternatively, some behaviors may be less dependent on the situation and more under the offender's control than others. For example, the choice of offending location is arguably a decision over which the offender has considerable control, whereas the items stolen during a burglary or robbery depend on what is available to steal, and the method of entry during a burglary or car theft depends to some extent on the behavior of the owner (e.g., if the owner left the property unlocked). This latter explanation is given some credence when one considers that it is consistent with findings from the thematic approach to crime linkage (Grubin et al., 2001; Sorochinski & Salfati, 2010). For example, Grubin and colleagues found that control behaviors (such as whether the offender used a weapon) were the most consistent. These are crime scene behaviors over which the offender has considerable control. A similar explanation has also been used in studies of noncriminal behavior, where behaviors that are less situation-dependent were found to be more consistent across situations (Funder & Colvin, 1991; Furr & Funder, 2004; Hettema & Hol, 1998; Hettema & van Bakel, 1997; Shoda, Mischel, & Wright, 1993).

Regardless of how the superiority of certain behaviors is explained, if law enforcement agencies are looking to reduce the number of offender behaviors used when linking crime, these findings provide guidance on which particular behaviors might be prioritized. These findings might, therefore, help analysts to avoid errors in the linkage task by focusing their attention on those behaviors that are most likely to demonstrate consistency and distinctiveness. They also provide law enforcement agencies with guidance on what types of evidential material they should routinely collect and store on force intelligence systems. The latter is particularly useful with volume crime, where the burden on the police to collect and store large quantities of information is considerable.

However, it is important to bear in mind that regardless of which behavioral feature is used to support crime linkage, one should always expect a degree of error. Indeed, none of the studies summarized in Table 6.1 reported AUC values of 1.00, which indicates that errors were made even when the most successful of domains were used. This should be an important consideration for practitioners of crime linkage.

Automated Crime Linkage Systems

A number of studies have developed and tested automated crime linkage systems. These systems interface with law enforcement databases to extract and analyze offense information, thus producing an output that identifies potentially linked crimes and gives an associated degree of confidence (often as a percentage score). The extent to which these systems are successful can be interpreted as evidence to support the existence of behavioral consistency and distinctiveness.

Yokota and colleagues have developed and tested the behavioral investigative support system (BISS) with samples of burglary and sexual assault from Japan (Yokota et al., 2007; Yokota & Watanabe, 2002). Oatley and colleagues have developed and tested a decision support system that has a range of mapping and predictive capabilities, including the ability to identify potentially linked crimes (Ewart, Oatley, & Burn, 2005; Oatley & Ewart, 2003). Adderley and colleagues have developed a crime linkage system that uses data mining techniques and neural networks (e.g., Adderley & Musgrove, 2003), whereas Wang and colleagues proposed a system based on Shannon information theory (e.g., Wang & Lin, 2010), and Canter et al. have developed a computerized system called the interactive offender profiling system (IOPS, Canter & Youngs, 2008).

Several studies have now demonstrated the potential practical value of these automated systems (e.g., Ewart et al., 2005; Yokota et al., 2007; Yokota & Watanabe, 2002). Ewart and colleagues, for example, found that an algorithm combining MO, geographical, and temporal behavior was able to successfully identify linked residential burglaries committed in the United Kingdom. Specifically, for 94% of their sample of 966 crimes, the top 50 prioritized crimes produced using the automated system contained a crime from the same series. Likewise, a crime from the same series was within the top 30 crimes for 77% of the sample and within the top 10 crimes for 59% of the sample. These findings suggest that automated crime linkage systems may be a fruitful way of screening large databases to identify potentially linked crimes that an analyst can then follow up manually. This may reduce the time that law enforcement personnel spend conducting crime linkage.

A Summary of the Evidence on Behavioral Consistency, Distinctiveness, and Discrimination Accuracy

Within this chapter, a range of empirical evidence relating to behavioral consistency, distinctiveness, and discrimination accuracy has been examined. Overall, there is evidence to suggest that many offenders demonstrate consistency and distinctiveness in their offending behavior and that these patterns can be used to distinguish between linked and unlinked crimes to a level that is statistically significant. However, it seems that certain types of offender behavior show greater consistency/distinctiveness and, therefore, greater potential to support the practice of crime linkage than others. These findings have important practical implications because they suggest that law enforcement agencies might prioritize the use of certain behavioral features during crime linkage (if they are looking to reduce the amount of behavioral information used when linking crime). Not only may this help to reduce the error rate associated with crime linkage (by helping analysts to avoid inappropriate linkage strategies), but it might save resources because law enforcement personnel could restrict the amount of behavioral evidence gathered/analyzed during crime linkage (Bennell & Canter, 2002). However, the literature is not yet sufficiently developed for recommendations of this nature to be made (see Section How Offending Behavior Is Operationalized).

However, it is important to note that some offenders do not behave in a consistent or distinctive manner when committing crime. Grubin et al. (2001), for example, reported that 17% of their sample was not consistent in any of the four sexual offense domains they examined. Furthermore, none of the studies using Bennell's methodology have reported AUC values that reach the theoretical maximum of 1.00. Also, automated crime linkage systems are associated with both false positive and false negative errors.*

* When two crimes that were committed by different people are incorrectly labeled "linked" this is described as a false positive error, and when two crimes that were committed by the same person are incorrectly labeled "unlinked" this is described as a false negative error.

One must, therefore, accept that there will always be a degree of error associated with crime linkage. The key question, though, is whether that degree of error is too large for it to be of practical use during a criminal investigation. The research reviewed in this chapter seems to suggest that crime linkage does have potential practical value. But there are a number of limitations associated with this research that must be addressed before practical recommendations can be made to law enforcement agencies. The next section will consider these limitations and the gaps that exist in the literature.

The Limitations of Crime Linkage Research

To provide structure to this section, the limitations of existing research will be mapped on to the various stages of Bennell's (2002) methodology (see Figure 6.2 for a summary). Bennell's methodology was chosen for this purpose because it is currently the most common approach to crime linkage research. But it should be noted that many of the limitations discussed below are also relevant to research conducted using other methodological approaches.

Stage 1: Identify Sample and Behaviors

The first stage for crime linkage research is to select a sample of crimes for analysis and to identify behavioral features that have the potential to demonstrate consistency and distinctiveness. This stage is crucial because, unless the sample selected reflects the types of offense for which crime linkage is typically used in practice and appropriate behaviors are selected for inclusion in the research, the findings produced may not be relevant or useful. Currently, however, there are several aspects of sample selection that lead us to question the validity of existing crime linkage research.

Over-Reliance on Solved Crime

The vast majority of crime linkage research has restricted its focus to samples of solved crime, which does not reflect the sorts of crimes that are often encountered by linkage analysts (i.e., unsolved offenses; Bennell & Canter, 2002; Woodhams, Hollin, et al. 2007). This is a limitation that spans the full range of methodologies discussed above, including the thematic approach (e.g., Santtila et al., 2005; Sorochinski & Salfati, 2010), Bennell's approach (e.g., Bennell & Canter, 2002; Tonkin et al., 2008; Woodhams & Toye, 2007), approaches that have tested automated crime linkage systems (e.g., Ewart et al., 2005; Yokota & Watanabe, 2002), and those that have adopted miscellaneous approaches to linkage research (e.g., Beutler et al.,

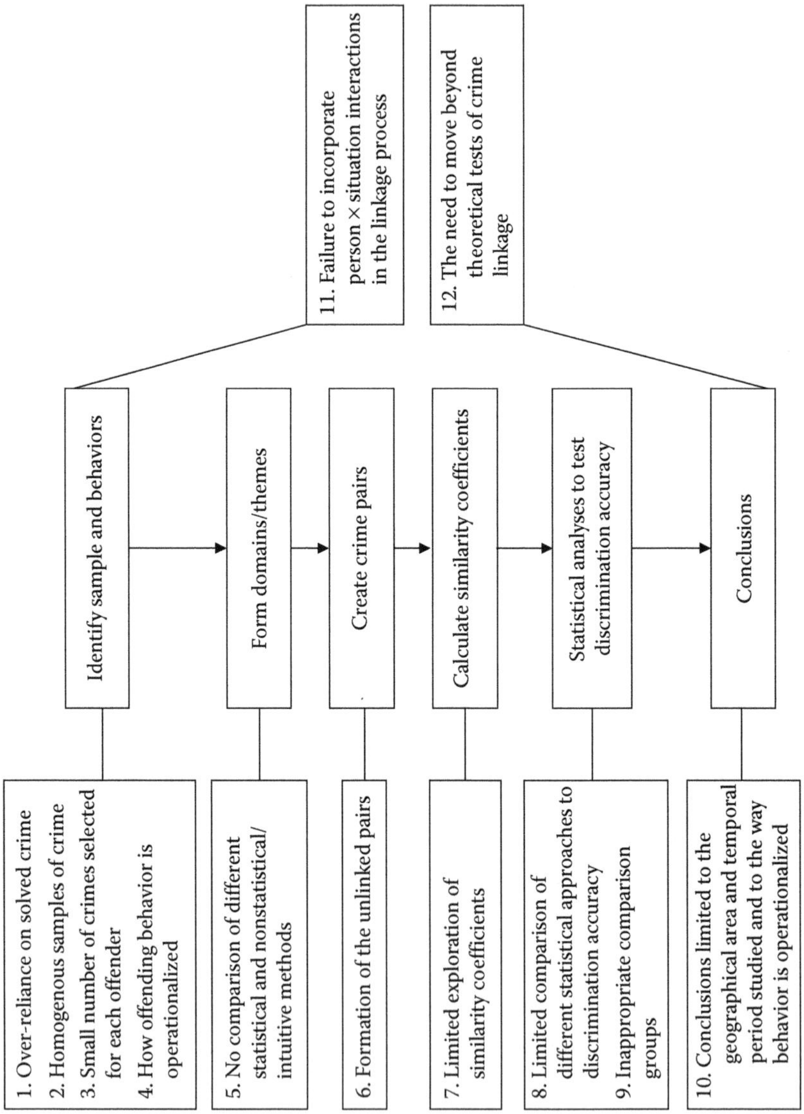

Figure 6.2 The generic process of crime linkage research and its associated limitations.

1995; Canter et al., 1991; Goodwill & Alison, 2006; Sjöstedt et al., 2004). The use of solved crime is problematic due to the fact that crimes may have been solved because they were committed in a highly consistent and/or distinctive manner (e.g., Bennell & Canter, 2002; Sorochinski & Salfati, 2010). Consequently, estimates of consistency, distinctiveness, and discrimination accuracy may be artificially inflated in samples of solved crime relative to what we might expect to see in the real world when unsolved offenses are analyzed (Bennell, 2002).

Fortunately, however, researchers have considered alternative methods of sample selection that might overcome this problem. For example, Woodhams, Bull, and Hollin (2007) have suggested that unsolved crimes can be included in crime linkage research by creating samples of crime that have been linked as a series using physical evidence, such as DNA. This methodology would allow the researcher to be confident of series membership (i.e., the researcher would know which crimes were linked to the same offender and which crimes were not), while also allowing discrimination accuracy to be examined using a more realistic sample of unsolved crime. Using this methodology, Woodhams and Labuschagne (2012) have recently demonstrated using a sample of serial sex offenses from South Africa that crime series identified through behavioral similarity are only marginally less consistent than those identified through physical evidence. These findings tentatively imply that findings from solved crime may generalize to samples of unsolved crime. However, these findings must be replicated with different crime types and using larger samples that allow more robust analyses to be conducted (Woodhams & Labuschagne, 2012). This work is crucial if crime linkage research is to have a lasting and valued impact on law enforcement practice.

Homogenous Samples of Crime

Until recently, all previous studies of crime linkage have examined consistency, distinctiveness, and discrimination accuracy with samples of crime that are homogenous in terms of crime type (i.e., they contain only one type of crime, e.g., residential burglaries). This is despite the fact that many offenders, particularly the most prolific, do not restrict themselves to committing just one type of offense (Farrington et al., 1988; Piquero, Farrington, & Blumstein, 2007). Existing research does not, therefore, provide guidance for conducting crime linkage with series that contain several different types of crime. This is particularly problematic given recent evidence to suggest that law enforcement personnel are already attempting so-called cross-crime linkage (Burrell & Bull, 2011). Fortunately, recent research has started to address this issue, but this work is still at a very preliminary stage and a number of questions remain unanswered (see Chapter 12 for a summary of this work).

Small Number of Crimes Selected for Each Offender

Researchers of crime linkage have often analyzed a constant number of offenses per offender to prevent highly prolific offenders, who may be unique in their levels of behavioral consistency and distinctiveness, from biasing the findings (Bennell, 2002). In some instances, this constant has been just two crimes per offender (e.g., Bennell & Canter, 2002; Tonkin et al., 2008; Woodhams & Toye, 2007), but sometimes as many as five (e.g., Bennell, 2002; Goodwill & Alison, 2006; Melnyk et al., 2011). However, Woodhams and Labuschagne (2012) have criticized this approach, arguing that it does not "reflect the reality of the linking task" (p. 88) because law enforcement databases will contain crime series that differ in length. Consequently, the methodology used to test crime linkage may not provide a true reflection of the real-life circumstances in which it is used. Furthermore, by focusing on such a limited snapshot of an offender's series, this does not give any insight into patterns of behavioral change over time, which might be just as useful as behavioral consistency in terms of identifying linked crime series (see Sorochinski & Salfati, 2010, for an examination of these issues).

To underscore this point, Woodhams and Labuschagne (2012) recently demonstrated the impact of including series of different length in crime linkage analyses. A combination of MO behaviors was able to achieve an AUC of 0.77 when the sample was restricted to two crimes per offender, but the AUC increased to 0.88 when each offender's entire series, as known to the police, was analyzed. Naturally, these findings must be replicated before conclusions can be drawn, but they illustrate the impact that methodological change can have on the findings of crime linkage research. Indeed, these are issues that must be explored before reliable practical recommendations can be made.

It is important to note, however, that this limitation does not apply to all crime linkage research, as some studies have included series of varying length in their analyses (see Ellingwood et al., 2013; Ewart et al., 2005; Grubin et al., 2001; Santtila, Fritzon, et al., 2004; Santtila et al., 2005, 2008; Yokota et al., 2007; Yokota & Watanabe, 2002).

How Offending Behavior Is Operationalized

The points raised thus far highlight some of the issues that plague sample selection in crime linkage research. A further issue is how to operationalize offender behavior for the purposes of analysis. Some research has coded the data exactly as it is recorded in law enforcement databases (e.g., Bennell, 2002; Tonkin et al., 2008), which has the benefit of being ecologically valid, of immediate practical relevance and simple. However, a full and complete psychological understanding of offenders is not the primary aim of law enforcement. Consequently, law enforcement agencies may not categorize behavior in the most psychologically appropriate way. For example, the police force studied by Tonkin et al. (2008) used a 12-category coding system to record the type of car stolen during a car theft (e.g., hatchback, saloon, estate, van). This system does not necessarily capture features such as engine size and anti-theft security measures, which may be more relevant to a car thief when he or she is deciding whether to steal a car or not. Consequently, discrimination accuracy might be improved if the data were operationalized in a more appropriate manner. Indeed, Davies et al. (2012) recently demonstrated this point in their study of serial car theft. They found that a new target selection domain—consisting of whether the car theft was a car key burglary,* whether the offender knew the victim, and whether an immobilizer was present—was able to achieve an AUC of 0.76, which was larger than that achieved using Tonkin et al.'s (2008) original target selection domain with the same data (AUC = 0.62). Furthermore, even when research has developed its own coding schemes for the purpose of crime linkage research (e.g., Woodhams, 2008), these studies have still only tested one way of coding data. Thus, all of the extant crime linkage literature can be criticized for not exploring alternative ways of operationalizing offender behavior for the purposes of crime linkage analysis. Unless this issue is given greater attention, it will be difficult to make recommendations to prioritize the use of certain offense behaviors over others. Furthermore, researchers may risk rejecting behavioral features that can actually be used to link crime.

Stage 2: Form Domains/Themes

The issues we have explored thus far were concerned with how research currently selects offenders, crimes, and behaviors for analysis. The next stage of the research process is to cluster these crime scene behaviors into themes/domains.

No Comparison of Different Statistical and Nonstatistical/Intuitive Methods

One of the main differences between Bennell's (2002) approach and the thematic approach to crime linkage research is the method by which the offense behaviors are clustered to form behavioral themes/domains. Bennell's (2002) methodology uses an intuitive, nonstatistical approach to domain formation, whereas the thematic approach uses statistical methods of clustering data (e.g., multidimensional scaling). Unfortunately, this creates a methodological divide in the literature that makes it difficult to compare the findings across studies. Unless this issue is addressed, the development of theoretical and

* Where the car keys are stolen during the course of a burglary and it appears that the primary purpose of breaking into the property was to obtain these keys, rather than to steal other property from the residence.

practical insights will be hindered. Future work must, therefore, endeavor to conduct a comprehensive comparison of these different methodological approaches. Fortunately, researchers are beginning to conduct such comparisons (see Winter et al., 2013).

Stage 3: Create Crime Pairs

Having identified behavioral domains/themes, the next stage of crime linkage research is the formation of linked and unlinked crime pairs. In the Bennell methodology, the unlinked pairs act as a control group to which the linked pairs are compared in order to test the assumptions of behavioral consistency and distinctiveness. Thus, any consistency and distinctiveness observed in the linked pairs that exceeds that in the unlinked pairs can be interpreted as evidence to support the underlying assumptions of crime linkage. The methodology used to form the unlinked pairs, therefore, has significant potential to influence the validity of crime linkage research.

Formation of the Unlinked Crime Pairs

Traditionally, research has formed the unlinked pairs by randomly pairing crimes from the linked subset that are known to have been committed by different offenders. But, as explained by Woodhams (2008), there are both practical and statistical problems associated with this approach. From a statistical perspective, this method violates the assumption of statistical independence that is necessary for binary logistic regression analysis. (However, it should be noted that ROC analysis overcomes this problem; Bennell, 2002). From a practical perspective, the current method of forming the unlinked pairs leads to a sample consisting solely of serial offenses (Bennell & Canter, 2002). This is problematic because in a real-life setting law enforcement personnel would have to identify potentially linked crimes from a backdrop of both serial and nonserial crimes, which means that Bennell's approach to crime linkage research is not as realistic as it might be (Bennell, 2002; Tonkin, Santtila, et al., 2012; Woodhams & Labuschagne, 2012). This limitation also applies to research using different methodologies, which has excluded nonserial offenses from the analysis (e.g., Bateman & Salfati, 2007; Beutler et al., 1995; Lundrigan, Czarnomski, & Wilson, 2010; Salfati & Bateman, 2005; Salo et al., 2012; Santtila, Fritzon, et al., 2004; Santtila et al., 2005, 2008).

However, a small number of studies have included nonserial crimes in their tests of behavioral consistency, distinctiveness, and discrimination accuracy (e.g., Grubin et al., 2001; Woodhams, 2008; Yokota et al., 2007). Furthermore, research is beginning to examine whether previous findings can be replicated using samples of serial and nonserial crime. Tonkin, Santtila, et al. (2012), for example, compared the findings produced using

Bennell's traditional methodology with those produced using a new methodology that formed the unlinked pairs from an independent sample of serial and nonserial burglaries. They found that similar findings were produced using these two methodologies, with the average difference in the AUC across the methodologies being 0.02 (the maximum difference was 0.06), which was not statistically significant ($p > .05$). These findings suggest that, although Bennell's original methodology may have practical and statistical limitations, these limitations may not have a significant real-world impact on the findings of crime linkage research. However, it should be noted that Winter et al. (2013) recently found that the inclusion of non-serial crimes did lead to a statistically significant increase in discrimination accuracy when compared to the accuracy achieved with a sample that contained only serial crimes. This highlights the need for further research on this issue.

Stage 4: Calculate Similarity Coefficients

The next stage of crime linkage research is to calculate similarity coefficients that can be used to discriminate between linked and unlinked crimes. Although this discussion is clearly of most relevance to research using Bennell's (2002) methodology, it should be noted that it is also relevant to research using multidimensional scaling because these analyses are based on the calculation of similarity coefficients (e.g., Santtila et al., 2005; Sorochinski & Salfati, 2010). These coefficients are crucial because they form the basis of subsequent analyses that test discrimination accuracy and they may also form the basis of decision support tools that can support crime linkage in practice. In short, the statistical coefficient used by researchers and practitioners has the potential to impact considerably on the outcome of crime linkage (Bennell, Gauthier, Gauthier, Melnyk, & Musolino, 2010).

Limited Exploration of Similarity Coefficients

Despite the importance of this issue, research has only recently begun to explore the variety of similarity coefficients that might be used to quantify behavioral consistency/distinctiveness (see Bennell, Gauthier et al., 2010; Ellingwood et al., 2013; Melnyk et al., 2011; Woodhams, Grant, & Price, 2007). Woodhams, Grant, et al. (2007), for example, compared the traditionally used Jaccard's coefficient with an alternative coefficient, the taxonomic similarity index (Delta S). They found that Delta S was more resistant to missing data than Jaccard's coefficient and better able to identify consistent and distinctive patterns in offender behavior with a sample of serial sex offenders. However, these initial findings have since been questioned by Melnyk and colleagues, who found that the superiority of Delta S did not replicate with larger samples of residential burglary, homicide, and sexual assault (Bennell, Gauthier et al., 2010; Melnyk et al., 2011). In a similar vein, Ellingwood et al. (2013) recently compared the degree of discrimination accuracy achieved using Jaccard's coefficient and the Simple Matching Index (S). It was found that S facilitated marginally larger AUC values than Jaccard's coefficient.

Research has, therefore, begun to explore the most appropriate way of quantifying behavioral similarity for the purposes of linking crime. However, this work is still at a very preliminary stage and there are a number of similarity coefficients yet to be explored (see Romesburg, 1984). This work should continue if we are to maximize the potential practical value of crime linkage research.

Stage 5: Statistical Analyses to Test Discrimination Accuracy

The calculation of similarity coefficients gives way to more complex statistical analyses that aim to test the ability of offender behavior to discriminate between linked and unlinked crimes. Again, however, research has only recently begun to explore the various statistical procedures that might be used at this stage of the research, and a considerable amount of work is still needed before conclusions can be drawn about the relative effectiveness of the procedures.

Limited Comparison of Different Statistical Approaches to Discrimination Accuracy

Traditionally, crime linkage research has used binary logistic regression analysis (or discriminant function analysis) to combine the various behavioral domains/themes for the purposes of linking crime. However, there are alternative statistical techniques that crime linkage research might explore. Bennell, Woodhams, Beauregard, and Mugford (in press), for example, have recently suggested that classification tree analysis might enable more accurate, sensitive, and usable predictive models to be developed than those that are produced using logistic regression analysis. They tested this hypothesis with samples of residential burglary, commercial robbery, and rape. It was found that classification tree analysis was able to discriminate between linked and unlinked offenses at a level that was comparable to that achieved when logistic regression was used. Bennell et al. (in press), therefore, suggested that classification tree analysis may be a useful alternative to logistic regression, as the models produced using tree-based methods are more simple and easy to implement in practice than regression-based models. However, Tonkin, Woodhams, et al. (2012) have recently questioned the superiority of classification tree analysis using samples of residential burglary and car theft. Tonkin and colleagues found that the classification tree models were unable to classify a large proportion of cases (20% of burglaries and 32% of car thefts) and the level of discrimination accuracy was not stable across the training and test samples.* These problems were not experienced by the logistic regression models.

Researchers have also started to explore the value of Bayesian analysis and neural network models for the purpose of crime linkage (Adderley & Musgrove, 2003; Salo et al., 2012; Winter et al., 2013). These studies are showing promising initial findings, with evidence that these approaches may be able to facilitate significant improvements in discrimination accuracy compared to previously used approaches (Salo et al., 2012; see also Chapter 14). Research such as this must continue if we are to build a robust body of evidence that can guide the use of crime linkage in practice.

Inappropriate Comparison Groups

A further issue at this stage of the research process is that the vast majority of research (including research from the Bennell and thematic approaches, as well as research on automated crime linkage systems) has used chance as the benchmark for judging whether a particular statistical model/algorithm has the potential to support crime linkage. These studies assume that, if discrimination accuracy exceeds chance (e.g., an AUC of 0.50), it can be concluded that there is the potential for this model to support the linking of crime in practice. Although this approach is justified from a statistical point of view, it is arguably more appropriate from a practical perspective to compare statistical models with the methods that are already available to law enforcement agencies (i.e., the discrimination accuracy achieved by law enforcement personnel who are responsible for conducting crime linkage in practice, such as crime analysts). Crime analysts often have considerable experience of crime, criminal behavior, and, specifically, crime linkage, so we might expect them to perform at a level that exceeds chance when linking crime. Thus, statistical models must be able to distinguish between linked and unlinked crimes at a level that is at least comparable to crime analysts if we are to conclude that they have practical value. Unfortunately, there is very little empirical research on this issue. Consequently, it is difficult to determine whether crime linkage research has the potential to improve existing law enforcement practice.

There are only two studies that have compared the performance of experts, nonexperts, and statistical models in mock crime linkage tasks (Bennell, Bloomfield, Snook, Taylor, & Barnes, 2010; Tonkin, Woodhams, Bull, & Bond, in press). Bennell, Bloomfield, et al. (2010) compared students,

* Some researchers of crime linkage have split their sample into training and test subsamples to determine whether a comparable level of discrimination accuracy can be achieved across different offenders/offences (e.g., Bennell & Canter, 2002). If a comparable level of accuracy is found, this suggests that the findings are robust and can be applied to future crimes within that jurisdiction.

police professionals, and a logistic regression model in terms of their ability to distinguish between linked and unlinked commercial burglaries. It was found that the regression model achieved a larger AUC value (AUC = 0.87) than trained and untrained students (AUCs = 0.79 and 0.70, respectively) and trained and untrained police professionals (AUCs = 0.71 and 0.64, respectively). These findings suggest that statistical models may have a valuable role to play when linking crimes in practice.

However, there were a number of limitations to the study conducted by Bennell, Bloomfield, et al. (2010). First, the police professionals in that study had "almost no linkage experience" (Bennell, personal communication, March 6, 2012), which raises questions about the observed superiority of the statistical model. Given a greater level of relevant linkage experience, the police participants in that study may have outperformed the regression model. Second, the crimes used by Bennell, Bloomfield, et al. (2010) were drawn from a geographical area that was unfamiliar to the participants (because the participants were drawn from several countries). As explained by Bennell, Bloomfield et al. (2010), this may have disadvantaged the participants if they were using locally derived linkage strategies that were inappropriate to the geographical location studied. It may also have created an unfair advantage in favor of the logistic regression model, which was developed on data from the same geographical area to that presented to the human participants. Third, Bennell, Bloomfield, et al. (2010) did not provide participants with temporal information about each offense. Over 50% of the police professionals in their study commented on this omission, suggesting that it is a behavioral feature that they would normally use when linking crime (as noted by Bennell, Bloomfield, et al., 2010). Arguably, the police professionals may have been more successful in the linkage task if they had been provided with temporal information.

Tonkin, Woodhams, Bull, and Bond (in press), therefore, conducted a replication of this study that was designed to overcome these limitations. First, their sample of police professionals had greater linkage experience than those sampled by Bennell, Bloomfield, et al. (2010) (approximately seven years experience compared to less than two). Also, the majority of analysts had experience with the specific crime type that they were asked to analyze in this study. Second, the participants were provided with temporal information about the offenses, as well as geographical and behavioral information. Third, two out of the three statistical models tested by Tonkin, Woodhams, Bull, and Bond (in press) were developed in a geographical area that was entirely different to that used to construct the questionnaires in this study. It was found that students, police professionals, and the logistic regression models achieved a comparable level of discrimination accuracy when distinguishing between linked and unlinked residential burglaries and linked and unlinked commercial robberies. Given the potential for statistical models to process large quantities of offense information in a quick, efficient, and standardized manner, these findings further support the notion that statistical decision support tools might be of value when linking crime in practice.

Although these initial studies are promising, future work is clearly needed to replicate these findings with other crime types and different samples. Furthermore, research must attempt to create more representative experimental designs, for example, by presenting participants with a database of crimes (rather than a set of crime pairs), by varying whether participants are told the number of linked crimes to search for (i.e., base rate information), and by presenting participants with a prose paragraph describing the circumstances of each crime, instead of a crime report that segregates the information into different types of offender behavior. Later, more ambitious studies might attempt to examine the accuracy of crime linkage during real-life police investigations.

Stage 6: Conclusions

The final stage in crime linkage research is to draw conclusions from the preceding analyses.

Conclusions Limited by Geography, Time, and Methodology

It should be abundantly clear from the discussion above that any conclusions drawn from crime linkage research are necessarily limited to the methodology used, the sample selected, and the behaviors used. Furthermore, any findings are inherently tied to the geographical area and temporal period from which the data were sampled. This highlights the final limitation of existing research: the generalizability of findings. Several types of crime, particularly sexual assault and burglary, have received a disproportionate amount of empirical attention compared to crimes such as robbery and arson. Furthermore, some crime types, such as the theft of metal, for example, from a church roof, have received no empirical attention whatsoever. Crime linkage research is also unevenly distributed around the world, with the majority of studies using samples from the United Kingdom. Although studies have been conducted in a variety of countries, there are some notable exceptions, such as Australia, where crime linkage research has never been conducted, despite the strong possibility that this procedure is being used during police investigations (Snook et al., 2012). Consequently, the generalizability of crime linkage research remains relatively untested in some countries and with some crime types. Significant replication work is, therefore, required before practical recommendations can be made to law enforcement agencies.

General Limitations

The limitations highlighted thus far are associated with particular stages of the research process, but there are two more general limitations that are not associated with any particular stage.

Person × Situation Interactions

This issue was originally raised by Woodhams, Hollin, and Bull (2007, 2008), who argued that discrimination accuracy might be improved if crime linkage research were able to capture aspects of the person, the situation, and how they interact when examining behavioral consistency and distinctiveness. Indeed, these interactions are considered by police crime analysts who conduct crime linkage in practice (Woodhams, Bull, et al., 2007). Woodhams et al. (2008) presented a potential methodology for doing this (a linguistic computational program called Wordsmith©; Scott, 2004–2007). This program allows the researcher to simultaneously incorporate both victim and offender behavior in the analyses (e.g., if the victim verbally seeks help, then the offender gags the victim). This is not possible in the previous crime linkage methodologies discussed above. However, due to the small sample size in this study, the analyses were restricted to descriptive statistics. Nonetheless, the fundamental approach presented by Woodhams and colleagues is potentially very significant, and future research that attempts to incorporate the interaction of person and situation variables in crime linkage analysis is certainly necessary (see Chapter 13 for a discussion of ongoing work in this area).

Moving Beyond Theoretical Tests of Crime Linkage

With the exception of the literature on crime linkage systems, the majority of research discussed in this chapter has primarily tested whether behavioral consistency and distinctiveness exist in offender behavior. Although this is clearly an important issue, research of this nature can only be said to test the *potential* for crime linkage, rather than whether this procedure will actually function successfully in practice. This is important because there are a multitude of factors beyond behavioral consistency and distinctiveness that will impact on whether crime linkage is able to function successfully in practice (e.g., the decision-making ability of law enforcement personnel, their motivation to use statistical tools and/or follow guidelines, the usability of such tools, the extent to which these tools are able to integrate with complex police databases, the resources that are available to law enforcement personnel). Although a small number of the studies discussed in this chapter can shed light on some of these issues, much of the research provides very little insight into whether these more practically oriented problems can be overcome. A focused research effort is, therefore, needed to determine if and how the extant crime linkage literature can be translated into usable methods for linking crime.

Conclusion

Within this chapter, a broad range of research has been reviewed that has tested the theoretical principles of behavioral consistency and distinctiveness that underpin the practice of crime linkage. Overall, there is evidence to suggest that many offenders demonstrate consistency and distinctiveness in their offending behavior and that these patterns can be used to distinguish between linked and unlinked crimes to a level that is statistically significant.

However, researchers of crime linkage are keenly aware of the limitations to their work. This is important because crime linkage is primarily an applied area of research, so consistency and distinctiveness must be tested in the most realistic way possible. Although the literature reviewed in this chapter has limitations, these limitations can be (and are being) addressed. Some of this work has been briefly highlighted in this chapter, and Chapters 12 through 14 of this book also highlight the novel and exciting ways in which research is striving to test the principles of crime linkage. This work will undoubtedly help to ensure that crime linkage research has a lasting and valued impact on law enforcement practice.

References

Adderley, R., & Musgrove, P. B. (2003). Modus operandi modelling of group offending: A data mining case study. *International Journal of Police Science & Management, 5,* 265–276.

Bateman, A. L., & Salfati, C. G. (2007). An examination of behavioral consistency using individual behaviors or groups of behaviors in serial homicide. *Behavioral Sciences & the Law, 25,* 527–544.

Bennell, C. (2002). *Behavioural consistency and discrimination in serial burglary* (Unpublished doctoral dissertation). University of Liverpool, Liverpool, England.

Bennell, C., Bloomfield, S., Snook, B., Taylor, P., & Barnes, C. (2010). Linkage analysis in cases of serial burglary: Comparing the performance of university students, police professionals, and a logistic regression model. *Psychology, Crime & Law, 16,* 507–524.

Bennell, C., & Canter, D. V. (2002). Linking commercial burglaries by *modus operandi*: Tests using regression and ROC analysis. *Science & Justice, 42,* 153–164.

Bennell, C., Gauthier, D., Gauthier, D., Melnyk, T., & Musolino, E. (2010). The impact of data degradation and sample size on the performance of two similarity coefficients used in behavioural linkage analysis. *Forensic Science International, 199,* 85–92.

Bennell, C., & Jones, N. J. (2005). Between a ROC and a hard place: A method for linking serial burglaries by modus operandi. *Journal of Investigative Psychology and Offender Profiling, 2,* 23–41.

Bennell, C., Jones, N. J., & Melnyk, T. (2009). Addressing problems with traditional crime linking methods using receiver operating characteristic analysis. *Legal and Criminological Psychology, 14,* 293–310.

Bennell, C., Woodhams, J., Beauregard, E., & Mugford, R. (in press). *Investigating individual differences in the expression of behavioural consistency in crime series using ICT analyses*. Manuscript in preparation.

Beutler, L. E., Hinton, R. M., Crago, M., & Collier, S. J. (1995). Evaluation of "fixed propensity" to commit sexual offenses: A preliminary report. *Criminal Justice and Behavior, 22,* 284–294.

Blumstein, A., Farrington, D. P., & Moitra, S. D. (1985). Delinquency careers: Innocents, desisters, and persisters. In M. Tonry & N. Morris (Eds.), *Crime and justice: An annual review of research* (Vol. 6, pp. 187–219). Chicago, IL: University of Chicago Press.

Burrell, A., & Bull, R. (2011). A preliminary examination of crime analysts' views and experiences of comparative case analysis. *International Journal of Police Science & Management, 13,* 2–15.

Burrell, A., Bull, R., & Bond, J. W. (2012). Linking personal robbery offences using offender behaviour. *Journal of Investigative Psychology and Offender Profiling, 9,* 201–222.

Canter, D. (2000). Offender profiling and criminal differentiation. *Legal and Criminological Psychology, 5,* 23–46.

Canter, D., Heritage, R., Wilson, M., Davies, A., Kirby, S., Holden, R., … Donald, I. (1991). *A facet approach to offender profiling*. London, England: Home Office.

Canter, D., & Youngs, D. (2008). Interactive offender profiling system (IOPS). In S. Chainey & L. Tompson (Eds.), *Crime mapping case studies: Practice and research* (pp. 153–160). Chichester, England: Wiley.

Charron, A., & Woodhams, J. (2010). A qualitative analysis of mock jurors' deliberations of linkage analysis evidence. *Journal of Investigative Psychology and Offender Profiling, 7,* 165–183.

Davies, K., Tonkin, M., Bull, R., & Bond, J. W. (2012). The course of case linkage never did run smooth: A new investigation to tackle the behavioural changes in serial car theft. *Journal of Investigative Psychology and Offender Profiling, 9,* 274–295.

Ellingwood, H., Mugford, R., Bennell, C., Melnyk, T., & Fritzon, K. (2013). Examining the role of similarity coefficients and the value of behavioural themes in attempts to link serial arson offences. *Journal of Investigative Psychology and Offender Profiling, 10,* 1–27.

Ewart, B. W., Oatley, G. C., & Burn, K. (2005). Matching crimes using burglars' modus operandi: A test of three models. *International Journal of Police Science & Management, 7,* 160–174.

Farrington, D. P., Snyder, H. N., & Finnegan, T. A. (1988). Specialization in juvenile court careers. *Criminology, 26,* 461–487.

Funder, D. C., & Colvin, C. R. (1991). Explorations in behavioral consistency: Properties of persons, situations, and behaviors. *Journal of Personality and Social Psychology, 60,* 773–794.

Furr, R. M., & Funder, D. C. (2004). Situational similarity and behavioral consistency: Subjective, objective, variable-centred, and person-centred approaches. *Journal of Research in Personality, 38,* 421–447.

Goodwill, A. M., & Alison, L. J. (2006). The development of a filter model for prioritizing suspects in burglary offences. *Psychology, Crime & Law, 12,* 395–416.

Green, E. J., Booth, C. E., & Biderman, M. D. (1976). Cluster analysis of burglary M/Os. *Journal of Police Science and Administration, 4,* 382–388.

Grubin, D., Kelly, P., & Brunsdon, C. (2001). *Linking serious sexual assaults through behavior. Home office research study 215.* London, England: Home Office Research, Development and Statistics Directorate.

Guay, J. P., Proulx, J., Cusson, M., & Ouimet, M. (2001). Victim-choice polymorphia among serious sex offenders. *Archives of Sexual Behavior, 30,* 521–533.

Harbort, S., & Mokros, A. (2001). Serial murderers in Germany from 1945 to 1995: A descriptive study. *Homicide Studies, 5,* 311–334.

Hazelwood, R. R., & Warren J. I. (2004). Linkage analysis: Modus operandi, ritual, and signature in serial sexual crime. *Aggression and Violent Behavior, 9,* 307–318.

Hettema, J., & Hol, D. P. (1998). Primary control and the consistency of interpersonal behaviour across different situations. *European Journal of Personality, 12,* 231–247.

Hettema, J., & van Bakel, A. P. (1997). Cross-situational consistency in a mastery condition. *Journal of Research in Personality, 31,* 222–239.

Horning, A. M., & Salfati, C. G. (2008, November). *South African serial homicide: Behavioral consistency and victim types.* Poster presented at the Annual American Society of Criminology Conference, St. Louis, MO. Abstract retrieved from http://www.allacademic.com/meta/p275824_index.html

Labuschagne, G. N. (2012). The use of a linkage analysis as an investigative tool and evidential material in serial offenses. In K. Borgeson & K. Kuehnle (Eds.), *Serial offenders: Theory and practice* (pp. 187–215). Sudbury, MA: Jones & Bartlett Learning.

Laub, J. H., & Sampson, R. J. (2001). Understanding desistance from crime. In M. Tonry (Ed.), *Crime and justice* (Vol. 28, pp. 1–69). Chicago, IL: University of Chicago Press.

Lundrigan, S., Czarnomski, S., & Wilson, M. (2010). Spatial and environmental consistency in serial sexual assault. *Journal of Investigative Psychology and Offender Profiling, 7,* 15–30.

Magyar, M., & Salfati, C. G. (2007, November). *Linking serial rape: An examination of behavioral consistency.* Paper presented at the Annual Meeting of the American Society of Criminology, Atlanta, GA.

Markson, L., Woodhams, J., & Bond, J. W. (2010). Linking serial residential burglary: Comparing the utility of *modus operandi* behaviours, geographical proximity, and temporal proximity. *Journal of Investigative Psychology and Offender Profiling, 7,* 91–107.

Melnyk, T., Bennell, C., Gauthier, D. J., & Gauthier, D. (2011). Another look at across-crime similarity coefficients for use in behavioural linkage analysis: An attempt to replicate Woodhams, Grant, and Price (2007). *Psychology, Crime & Law, 17,* 359–380.

Moffitt, T. E. (1993). Life-course persistent and adolescence-limited antisocial behavior: A developmental taxonomy. *Psychological Review, 100,* 674–701.

Oatley, G. C., & Ewart, B. W. (2003). Crimes analysis software: "Pins in maps," clustering and Bayes net prediction. *Expert Systems with Applications, 25,* 569–588.

Piquero, A. R., Farrington, D. P., & Blumstein, A. (2007). *Key issues in criminal career research: New analyses of the Cambridge study in delinquent development.* New York, NY: Cambridge University Press.

Romesburg, H. C. (1984). Resemblance coefficients for qualitative attributes. In H. C. Romesburg (Ed.), *Cluster analysis for researchers* (pp. 141–163). Belmont, CA: Lifetime Learning Publications.

Salfati, C. G., & Bateman, A. L. (2005). Serial homicide: An investigation of behavioural consistency. *Journal of Investigative Psychology and Offender Profiling, 2,* 121–144.

Salo, B., Sirén, J., Corander, J., Zappalà, A., Bosco, D., Mokros, A., & Santtila, P. (2012). Using Bayes' theorem in behavioural crime linking of serial homicide. *Legal and Criminological Psychology, 18,* 356–370.

Santtila, P., Fritzon, K., & Tamelander, A. L. (2004). Linking serial arson incidents on the basis of crime scene behavior. *Journal of Police and Criminal Psychology, 19,* 1–16.

Santtila, P., Junkkila, J., & Sandnabba, N. K. (2005). Behavioural linking of stranger rapes. *Journal of Investigative Psychology and Offender Profiling, 2,* 87–103.

Santtila, P., Korpela, S., & Häkkänen, H. (2004). Expertise and decision-making in the linking of car crime series. *Psychology, Crime & Law, 10,* 97–112.

Santtila, P., Pakkanen, T., Zappalá, A., Bosco, D., Valkama, M., & Mokros, A. (2008). Behavioural crime linking in serial homicide. *Psychology, Crime & Law, 14,* 245–265.

Shoda, Y., Mischel, W., & Wright, J. C. (1993). The role of situational demands and cognitive competencies in behavior organisation and personality coherence. *Journal of Personality and Social Psychology, 65,* 1023–1035.

Sjöstedt, G., Långström, N., Sturidsson, K., & Grann, M. (2004). Stability of modus operandi in sexual offending. *Criminal Justice and Behavior, 31,* 609–623.

Snook, B., Luther, K., House, J. C., Bennell, C., & Taylor, P. J. (2012). The violent crime linkage analysis system: A test of interrater reliability. *Criminal Justice and Behavior, 39,* 607–619.

Sorochinski, M., & Salfati, C. G. (2010). The consistency of inconsistency in serial homicide: Patterns of behavioural change across series. *Journal of Investigative Psychology and Offender Profiling, 7,* 109–136.

Swets, J. A. (1988). Measuring the accuracy of diagnostic systems. *Science, 240,* 1285–1293.

Tonkin, M., Grant, T., & Bond, J. W. (2008). To link or not to link: A test of the case linkage principles using serial car theft data. *Journal of Investigative Psychology and Offender Profiling, 5,* 59–77.

Tonkin, M., Santtila, P., & Bull, R. (2012). The linking of burglary crimes using offender behaviour: Testing research cross-nationally and in more realistic settings. *Legal and Criminological Psychology, 17,* 276–293.

Tonkin, M., Woodhams, J., Bull, R., & Bond, J. W. (in press). *Behavioral case linkage: The role of professional experience, training, and statistics.* Manuscript submitted for publication.

Tonkin, M., Woodhams, J., Bull, R., Bond, J. W., & Santtila, P. (2012). A comparison of logistic regression and classification tree analysis for behavioural case linkage. *Journal of Investigative Psychology and Offender Profiling, 9,* 235–258.

Wang, J. H., & Lin, C. L. (2010). An association model for implicit crime link analysis. *Lecture Notes in Computer Science, 6122/2010,* 15–21.

Winter, J. M., Lemeire, J., Meganck, S., Geboers, J., Rossi, G., & Mokros, A. (2013). Comparing the predictive accuracy of case linkage methods in serious sexual assaults. *Journal of Investigative Psychology and Offender Profiling, 10,* 28–56.

Woodhams, J. (2008). *Understanding juvenile sexual offending: An investigative perspective* (Unpublished doctoral dissertation). University of Leicester, Leicester, England.

Woodhams, J., Bull, R., & Hollin, C. R. (2007). Case linkage: Identifying crimes committed by the same offender. In R. N. Kocsis (Ed.), *Criminal profiling: International theory, research, and practice* (pp. 117–133). Totowa, NJ: Humana Press.

Woodhams, J., Grant, T. D., & Price, A. R. G. (2007). From marine ecology to crime analysis: Improving the detection of serial sexual offences using a taxonomic similarity measure. *Journal of Investigative Psychology and Offender Profiling, 4,* 17–27.

Woodhams, J., Hollin, C. R., & Bull, R. (2007). The psychology of linking crimes: A review of the evidence. *Legal and Criminological Psychology, 12,* 233–249.

Woodhams, J., Hollin, C., & Bull, R. (2008). Incorporating context in linking crimes: An exploratory study of situational similarity and if-then contingencies. *Journal of Investigative Psychology and Offender Profiling, 5,* 1–23.

Woodhams, J., & Labuschagne, G. (2012). A test of case linkage principles with solved and unsolved serial rapes. *Journal of Police and Criminal Psychology, 27,* 85–98.

Woodhams, J., & Toye, K. (2007). An empirical test of the assumptions of case linkage and offender profiling with serial commercial robberies. *Psychology, Public Policy, and Law, 13,* 59–85.

Yokota, K., Fujita, G., Watanabe, K., Yoshimoto, K., & Wachi, T. (2007). Application of the behavioral investigative support system for profiling perpetrators of serious sexual assaults. *Behavioral Sciences & the Law, 25,* 841–856.

Yokota, K., & Watanabe, S. (2002). Computer-based retrieval of suspects using similarity of *modus operandi. International Journal of Police Science & Management, 4,* 5–15.

Yokota-Sano, K., & Watanabe, S. (1998). An analysis on the repetition of criminal modus operandi. *Japanese Journal of Science and Technology for Identification, 3,* 49–55.

7 A Cross-National Comparison of Behavioral Consistency in Serial Homicide

C. GABRIELLE SALFATI

Contents

Introduction 142
General Issues of Consistency 143
Cultural Influences on Serial Homicide 144
Setting the Worldwide Context—Trends of Serial Homicide across Countries 146
Comparing Patterns of Serial Homicide Behavior across Countries 147
  US Trends 148
    Behaviors 148
    Victims 149
  Non-US Trends 149
    Transnational Comparisons 149
    Canada 152
    Australia 152
    Japan 153
    Summary 154
Behavioral Consistency Research to Date 154
  Consistency Studies on US Cases of Serial Homicide 155
    Individual Behaviors 156
    Themes 157
    Victims 160
  International Studies on Consistency in Serial Homicide 161
    Germany 161
    Italy 162
    Republic of South Africa 163
Conclusion 166
References 168

Introduction

In 2005, the Federal Bureau of Investigation's National Center for the Analysis of Violent Crime (NCAVC) invited 135 international experts in serial homicide to a dedicated symposium on the topic. Those invited included law enforcement personnel who had been involved in investigating cases of serial homicide, legal professionals including prosecutors and defense attorneys who had been part of the court process in serial homicide cases, members of the media and investigative journalists who had reported on these cases, clinicians who had been involved in the assessment of serial offenders, and academics who had written on the topic. The objective of the symposium was to create a reference manual for investigators of serial homicide covering issues such as how serial homicide should be defined, the offenders' characteristics, and the linking of homicide series. One of the major conclusions from this meeting was that there was a real lack of valid empirical research in the field that could be relied upon to inform serial homicide investigations (NCAVC, 2005). Most of what was known up to that point either came from investigative experience or was based on case studies. In addition, much of this work had, until that date, been focused primarily on the United States. During this meeting, representatives from numerous countries highlighted the very real need for an understanding of trends and patterns from different cultural and national viewpoints, as input from a US perspective may not provide a valid perspective on investigations in other countries.

Although the general issue of behavioral consistency has been given much attention in the social and personality psychology literature, and to some extent in the literature on violence, studies pertaining to how the principles underlying consistency apply to actual criminal behavior and how these issues may be understood within the field of serial homicide research have been less developed. Indeed, a review of the published literature to date indicates that only seven published empirical studies of crime linkage relate to serial homicide (Salfati, 2015). Only four of these seven studies have focused in detail on behavioral consistency and the analysis of *full* crime series as they progress over time (Bateman & Salfati, 2007; Salfati & Bateman, 2005; Salfati, Horning, Sorochinski, & Labuschagne, 2014a; Sorochinski & Salfati, 2010).*

As was noted above, much of the research on the consistency of criminal behavior has been conducted in Europe and North America and this also applies to the limited research on serial homicide. Therefore, although

* A distinction is being made here between an assessment of individual offender's consistency across their entire series compared with the measurements of consistency (similarity) being focused on individual pairs of offenses.

crime linkage practitioners in other countries may wish to draw on this research to inform their practice of crime linkage, one important question relates to whether findings from these studies will generalize (see Salfati, Labuschagne, Horning, Sorochinski, & De Wet, 2014b, for further discussion of this issue). This chapter provides an overview of the research on behavioral consistency and linking as it relates to serial homicide and also presents other international research regarding serial homicide to establish baselines and differences across countries. To achieve this, findings from the United States, Canada, Europe, Asia, and Republic of South Africa are drawn on.

General Issues of Consistency

The key research questions in the area of crime linkage analysis have been whether we can link crime scenes to *each other* and thereby identify an *individual crime series* while also distinguishing this series from crimes committed by other offenders. To do this successfully requires some recognition of *what* behaviors are the most consistently displayed by serial offenders, which in turn requires that we clearly define what is meant by *consistency* and understand how this consistency is *displayed* by offenders.

When researchers speak of consistency, they are generally referring to the idea that an offender will display similar behaviors across situations (i.e., different crime scenes), which provides the basis for linking a crime series together. However, when examining consistency across a series, there are a number of other issues that need to be considered, and this is particularly the case for interpersonal forms of crime, such as homicide.

Although offenders are known to be consistent in some ways, behavior is also impacted by context (Bateman & Salfati, 2007; Bennell & Canter, 2002; Woodhams, Hollin, & Bull, 2008; Woodhams & Toye, 2007). For example, one of the contextual factors relevant in interpersonal crimes, such as homicide, is the offender's interaction with the victim (Horning, Salfati, & Labuschagne, 2014; Keppel & Walters, 1999; Salfati, 2013; Salfati & Bateman, 2005). Victim–offender interactions may be planned out by the offender in advance or they may be more opportunistic, and they may change depending on the victim's reactions during the crime. In addition to situational factors, there may be an element of development and maturation over a crime series that impacts how offenders behave, as there is with any person as they move through time. This could include an element of experimentation that might appear to researchers or investigators as inconsistent behavioral patterns, but which are instead simply the offender experimenting with different things at each crime scene (Canter & Youngs, 2009). If we are examining consistency within a social psychological context, there may also be an element of learning that needs to be considered (Canter, 1994; Canter & Youngs, 2009); that is, as an offender develops and becomes more experienced, they may learn what works and what does not work, and they may change their behavior accordingly. The frequency of behaviors is also an important issue to consider. Although some behaviors may be consistently expressed by offenders over time, they might also be common to the offending of a large number of individuals. These consistent but high frequency behaviors may have little discriminatory power in the linking context (Salfati, 2003). In contrast, it may be possible to identify consistent but low-frequency variables referred to by some as *signatures* (Bateman & Salfati, 2007; Keppel, 1995).

In order to fully understand and analyze consistency, all these factors need to be accounted for in our analysis so it can be determined whether they do affect consistency, and if so, how. Indeed, the question often becomes: Are changes in criminal behavior a reflection of inconsistency, or do they reflect predictable (i.e., consistent) patterns of change within an offender's series (Salfati, 2008)? To answer these sorts of questions, we need to review the empirical studies that have looked into these issues and we need to determine whether there are differences in findings across countries.

Cultural Influences on Serial Homicide*

As noted at the start of this chapter, although practitioners may wish to draw on the findings of crime linkage studies of serial homicide from Europe and North America, we do not know yet how well these findings will generalize. Research from the fields of social psychology, anthropology, and criminology suggests there may be problems with generalizing such findings across countries.

According to Swidler (1986), culture can be seen as a "tool kit" of symbols, stories, rituals, and worldviews, which people use in varying configurations to solve different kinds of problems. This suggests that in the case of homicide, patterns of behavior may differ across countries that are known to have different cultural trends as behavior may, in part, be guided by "strategies of action" that are specific to that country (Salfati & Haratsis, 2001). For example, from an anthropological view, Leyton (1995) suggests that the immediate cause of homicide is the presence in the culture of specific messages teaching people about the

* Readers interested in a cross-cultural comparison of serial rape are referred to Woodhams and Labuschagne (2012).

appropriateness of violence. It follows that changes in culture (particularly messages regarding violence) would affect the manifestation of homicide. This could be observed in differences in offender–victim interactions, the physical context of homicide, weapon use, and/or variation in how serial homicide offending develops over time as offenders move through a learning process.

An interesting question that follows this line of thinking is whether aggressive strategies, and the cultural influence on these strategies, are encoded in scripts of actions that are adopted by individuals and hence retrieved and used in the appropriate situation or scenario (see Chapter 2 for a discussion of how scripts of actions interact with situational triggers to produce behavior). Social psychological theory would certainly suggest this to be the case. For example, Huesmann and Eron (1984) state that the manner in which an offender demonstrates aggression, as well as the intensity of that aggression, can be attributed to social learning. They specifically hypothesized that learned responses for social behavior in general, and for aggressive behavior in particular, are largely controlled by what they term *cognitive scripts*. These scripts are stored in a person's memory and used as guides for behavior and social problem solving, suggesting how one should respond to events and what the likely outcomes of these responses will be. In this way, cultural messages regarding violence and its use can influence crime scene behaviors through an individual offender's cognitive scripts. No research to date has actually examined these possibilities, however, through interviewing offenders, it may be possible to discern the behavioral scripts that offenders use in situations of aggression and ascertain the cultural availability and acceptance of these scripts.

Although there is an abundance of general writings based on case studies of serial homicides, as well as an abundance of research on national homicide trends which will briefly be examined below, there is currently a lack of comparative research looking at the expression of homicide, especially serial homicide, in different countries; in particular how this relates to issues of behavioral consistency. This shortcoming has prevented any reliable conclusions from being drawn about culturally based influences on serial homicide behavior (Jackson & Bekerian, 1997; Lafree, 1999; Salfati, 2001). As outlined, research from the fields of social psychology and criminology links directly to key issues from the field of anthropology regarding how patterns of interpersonal violence are exhibited within different cultural contexts (e.g., Swidler, 1986). Developing an understanding of these issues from an international comparative perspective will provide further depth to the understanding of consistency patterns in general and will ultimately lead to a better appreciation for the applicability of general models and results to specific cultural contexts.

Setting the Worldwide Context—Trends of Serial Homicide across Countries

A Western bias, which is common to much research, has limited a full appreciation and understanding of serial homicide (Gorby, 2000). In addition, popular myths that serial homicide is solely a US problem would wrongly suggest there is no merit in making international comparisons (Lester, 1995; Toufexis, 1994, cited in Gorby, 2000). Where comparisons are attempted there are challenges that must be overcome, including the use of differing definitions and reporting practices, access to different data sources ranging from police files to media accounts, and data samples that are often small, especially in cases where the data have been collected from police files. In addition, the focus of researchers (e.g., with respect to the variables they analyze) varies from study to study.

Despite these challenges, homicide is thought to offer some of the most valid and reliable data for cross-national comparisons because, compared to other crimes such as rape, homicides are more likely to be reported to the police, they are more likely to be recorded, and legal systems usually devote considerable resources to solving homicides (Archer & Gartner, 1984; Fox & Zawitz, 1999, cited in Gorby, 2000). However, there is also thought to be a *dark figure* of serial homicide due to issues such as *linkage blindness*, which refers to a lack of communication that exists across police forces in different jurisdictions that may prevent these forces from recognizing the existence of linked serial crimes (Egger, 1984; Quinet, 2007).

In 2012, Aamodt produced the Radford Serial Killer Database, which, although it does not as yet provide figures on consistency within series, provides some basic figures on the composition of serial homicide overall,* as well as basic comparative figures for serial homicides committed in different countries (see Table 7.1). This database includes 18 years of data, which is updated on a regular basis, and which at the time of writing contained 2756 serial homicide offenders, of which 1788 were from the United States and 968 were from other countries. A total of 7400 victims are also included in this dataset. Table 7.1 provides a summary of the number of serial homicide series included in Aamodt's database from each country based on a population ratio. Aamodt's table compares the United States with other countries in terms of serial homicide cases known from media accounts.† Contrary to

* Readers are referred to the Radford Serial Killer website for more information: http://maamodt.asp.radford.edu/serial killer information center/projectdescription.htm

† Although the figures from the United States are considered representative of what we know, the figures from other countries may be less well represented due to lack of access to data (Aamodt, 2012, personal communication).

Table 7.1 Incidences of Serial Homicide across Countries

Country	Percentage of World Population	Percentage of Serial Killers	Ratio
United States	4.47	64.9	14.51
Australia	0.33	1.7	5.15
Republic of South Africa	0.72	3.6	3.00
United Kingdom	0.94	4.1	4.36
Italy	0.87	3.7	4.25
Canada	0.50	2.1	4.20
Germany	1.17	2.6	2.22
France	0.94	1.7	1.81
Japan	1.82	3.0	1.65
Poland	0.55	0.4	0.73
Russia	2.04	1.3	0.64
Mexico	1.60	0.7	0.44
Brazil	2.75	0.5	0.13
India	17.28	1.1	0.06
China	19.24	1.0	0.05

Source: From Aamodt, M. A. *Incidences of serial homicide across countries.* 2012. Reproduced with permission.

the popular myth that serial homicide only occurs in the United States, it is clear that it is a problem in many different countries, although clearly the ratio for the United States is much higher than any other country included in Aamodt's database.

Comparing Patterns of Serial Homicide Behavior across Countries

Although most of the research conducted on serial homicide to date has been carried out on US cases, there are a number of other studies from other countries allowing us to draw some comparisons. The main focus of these studies have centered on: (1) descriptions of the characteristics of serial homicide and (2) attempts to understand behavioral consistency in serial homicide cases (and the effectiveness of behavioral patterns for differentiating crimes committed by different offenders). The descriptive studies have primarily been based on media accounts of serial homicide. However, a smaller number of more recent studies have used actual police files of serial cases.

US Trends

Hickey's (1991) study on US serial homicide trends was the first such study in the literature based on a large dataset,* and it is still the most comprehensive survey on general serial homicide trends. His research was based on media accounts of cases from 1800 to 1995, involving 337 offenders and a total of 2526–3860 victims, an average of 7–11 victims per offender.† This study indicated that, contrary to popular myths, the commission of serial murder is not limited to White males who are strangers to their victims. According to Hickey (2012), one in five offenders in the United States is Black, 17% are female, and as he states:

> To suggest, for example, that all victims of serial murder are strangers, that the killers operate primarily in pairs, or that they do not kill for financial gain is derived more from speculation than verifiable evidence, given the current state of serial murder research. (p. 32)

Although Hickey included data from a variety of sources, and from a large time span, he did not specifically look at consistency patterns in serial homicide behavior. That being said, the results outlined in Hickey's book provide a useful overview of some of the general trends in serial homicide. These trends provide a good starting point for elucidating what are common trends within this group of offenses and thus, what behaviors may be less useful when trying to distinguish one offender from another when carrying out crime linkage analysis. This research can therefore be a useful measure against which subsequent studies on consistency can compare their results. In this way, researchers responsible for smaller-scale studies of consistency in serial homicide can assess the representativeness of their sample.

Behaviors

Although Hickey's study did not focus in detail on serial homicide behaviors, some of the basic trends he identified highlight important differences between the offending behaviors of male and female serial homicide offenders. For example, he found clear behavioral differences between male and

* A number of other smaller studies exist that could be consulted, but these studies generally focus on samples defined as sexual serial homicides, and, as such, pertain to a very specific population (e.g., Pakhomou, 2004; Ressler, Burgess, & Douglas, 1988). There is still contentious debate concerning whether serial homicides should be defined as sexual in nature or whether they are a more diverse group that includes sexually motivated offenders as a subsample. For these reasons, these smaller studies are not included in this review.

† The latest 2012 edition of Hickey's book includes an updated sample of cases up to 2011, which totals approximately 500 series, nearly 650 serial offenders, and between 3500 and 5650 homicides. However, this chapter will draw comparisons using Hickey's original study because it is this study that has been replicated in other countries. The trends are similar overall, however, whether his original or updated study is used.

female serial killers with respect to weapon choice and the consistency of weapon use throughout a crime series when looking at overall trends across the sample from 1800–1995. On the one hand, most male offenders in this sample used a mix of weapons throughout their series, but when a pattern was observed, they most often used a firearm (19%), followed by stabbing (13%), strangulation/suffocation (11%), bludgeoning (9%), or poisoning (5%). On the other hand, 45% of female offenders used poison as their weapon, and 35% used it as their sole weapon.

Victims

Although offender–victim relationships were not explored as a factor related to consistency in Hickey's work, there were differences between male and female offenders. Eighty-four percent of offenders surveyed were male and most killed strangers. However, 16% killed one or more family members. Forty-three percent of female offenders, on the other hand, killed family members. Just over half of the male offenders showed consistent patterns throughout their series in terms of victim gender, with 35% targeting female victims only, and 22% targeting males only.* In terms of victim age, 43% of male offenders targeted adults only, whereas 32% of female offenders targeted adults only. Six percent of male offenders targeted children exclusively, whereas 19% of females consistently targeted children.

Non-US Trends

Transnational Comparisons

Gorby (2000) examined archival data on non-US serial homicide offenders across 43 countries between 1800 and 1995 using the same framework and methodology as Hickey (1991). Two hundred and forty-one homicides by 300 offenders were analyzed representing crimes committed against 2917 victims. The offenders were assigned to a primary country based on where most of their victims were killed. Almost half (49.4%, $N = 119$) of the media accounts of serial homicides were identified in just four countries: the United Kingdom (19.5%, $N = 47$), Germany (14.9%, $N = 35$), Republic of South Africa (7.9%, $N = 19$), and Australia (7.15%, $N = 17$). This is in line with the data provided by Aamodt (2012), which was presented above (see Table 7.1). European countries accounted for approximately half the cases (56.8%, $N = 137$) and Asian countries for 13.7% ($N = 33$). North American (excluding the United States) and African countries each accounted for 7.9% ($N = 19$) of cases. Only 5.8% of cases were found in South America

* Comparable figures are not quoted for female serial offenders, but Hickey (2012) provides a table that outlines the breakdown of age and gender for female offenders (p. 301).

($N = 8$), Central America ($N = 4$), and the Middle East ($N = 2$) combined.* Just under 10% of offenders were transnational (i.e., offenders who had killed victims in more than one country; 9.1%, $N = 22$).

When considering the consistency of behaviors across the series sampled by Gorby (2000), it is useful to know the average series length. Forty-five percent ($N = 108$) of offenders killed between 3 and 5 victims, 22.4% ($N = 54$) killed 6–10 victims, 19.1% ($N = 46$) killed 11–20 victims, and 13.6% ($N = 33$) killed more than 20 victims. Most offenders killed alone (67%, $N = 201$). The 99 offenders who killed in pairs were responsible for 13.3% ($N = 40$) of cases. Just over 75% of offenders were male ($N = 227$). Although males were most likely to kill alone (72.2%, $N = 164$), approximately half of the females killed in pairs (49.3%, $N = 36$).†

Behaviors Some consistency trends were observed in relation to behaviors in Gorby's (2000) study. Results indicated that 49.7% ($N = 97$) of offenders evidenced some sexual behavior during their crime series, but only 20.5% ($N = 40$) of male offenders exhibited sexual behavior at each of their crime scenes. Results from the survey also suggested that 37.9% ($N = 74$) of male offenders mutilated or tortured at least some of their victims, with 14.9% ($N = 29$) of offenders doing so in all of their crimes.

The majority of male offenders used a combination of killing methods, but the study showed some evidence of specialization, for example, some offenders engaged in strangulation/asphyxiation only (19.5%, $N = 38$), or stabbing/cutting only (12.3%, $N = 19$). Female offenders mostly used poison (73.9%, $N = 34$) and 60.9% ($N = 28$) were consistent in this across their crimes. Eight female offenders strangled/asphyxiated their victims and half of these (8.7%, $N = 4$) were consistent in this method of killing. No females stabbed or bludgeoned their victims.

In terms of theft, 35.9% ($N = 70$) of male offenders and 56.5% ($N = 26$) of female offenders took material gains away from at least some of their murders. There was, however, no information on how many offenders consistently stole from their victims or what the stolen items were.

Victims When looking at the type of victim targeted, solo offenders mostly killed nonfamily members (79.3%, $N = 191$), 20.8% ($N = 50$) killed one or more family members, and 5% ($N = 12$) killed only family members. On the one hand, 12% ($N = 23$) of male offenders killed one or more family members, showing that the killing of family members is not limited to

* As with all studies based on media accounts, it is important to keep in mind that these figures may reflect availability of information and reporting, rather than actual numbers. See Gorby (2000) for a further discussion of this.

† For more information on studies specifically looking at female serial murderers, see a review by Scott (2005).

female serial killers. On the other hand, over half of all the female offenders (58.7%, $N = 27$) killed at least one family member and 13% killed family members exclusively.

In terms of victim gender and age, just over one-third of offenders (38.6%, $N = 93$) restricted their murders to a particular group. Twenty-three percent ($N = 44$) of male offenders killed only adult female victims. In contrast, no female offenders exclusively targeted adult females, and the one female who targeted exclusively females killed only children. Almost a tenth (9.7%, $N = 19$) of male offenders killed male adults only, 5.1% ($N = 10$) killed male children only, and 4.6% ($N = 3.1$) killed female children only. Over half (56.7%, $N = 110$) killed at least one female or male child. In terms of older victims, 3.1% ($N = 6$) of offenders killed elderly people only (all female), and 21.5% ($N = 42$) killed at least one male or female elderly victim.*

Summary The trends Gorby (2000) highlighted provide some information about serial murders committed outside the United States. However, this study did not compare the different countries with each other, an important limitation of his work. As Gorby used the same methodology and categories as Hickey's (1991) work, comparisons can, however, be made. In both samples, there is a predominance of male offenders, although the proportion is higher in the United States (84%) than internationally (75%). Both samples also had a majority of stranger victims, and the proportions of victims who were family members were also similar between the United States and internationally (16% and 12%, respectively).

Where the information was reported, some similarities and differences in behavioral consistency patterns in victim targeting and actions at the crime scene could be seen. When comparing international figures to US figures, the proportion of female victims being consistently targeted by male offenders across the whole series was approximately one-quarter to one-third, with the larger proportion observed in the United States. A much more important difference was observed in the consistency of age of victim across series, with US male offenders showing a much higher proportion of offenders targeting only adult victims across their series (43% vs. 9.7%). The proportion of offenders targeting only children across their series was, however, comparable when comparing male offenders (6% and 5.1%). An important point to keep in mind before drawing conclusions from these figures is that data included for analysis spanned a very large number of years, which includes different reporting methods and societal trends. As such, these figures provide a basic indicator and a historical overview, but cannot be used more precisely to indicate current trends between the United States and other countries.

* No comparable figures were quoted for female offenders.

Canada

Mellor (2012) has researched the number of Canadian serial murderers reported in the media from 1926 to 2010. From Figure 7.1, it is apparent that the number of known serial murderers operating at any one time in Canada has increased since 1926. Mellor, however, did not examine the behavior of the serial homicide offenders included in his study in a systematic way, but instead took a case study approach (direct comparisons based on behaviors are difficult).

Australia

Mouzos and West (2007) reviewed 11 murder series, ranging from 3 to 12 crimes per series, that occurred between 1989 and 2006.* The crime series were committed by 13 offenders with 52 known victims. All but one of the offenders was male, and 33 (63%) of the victims were female. All cases were predominantly intra-racial. About half of the sample killed victims who were strangers to them and the other half knew their victim in some capacity. With regard to victim types, Mouzos and West reported that, in accord with the findings of previous international research, vulnerable groups such as the very young, the elderly, and disabled

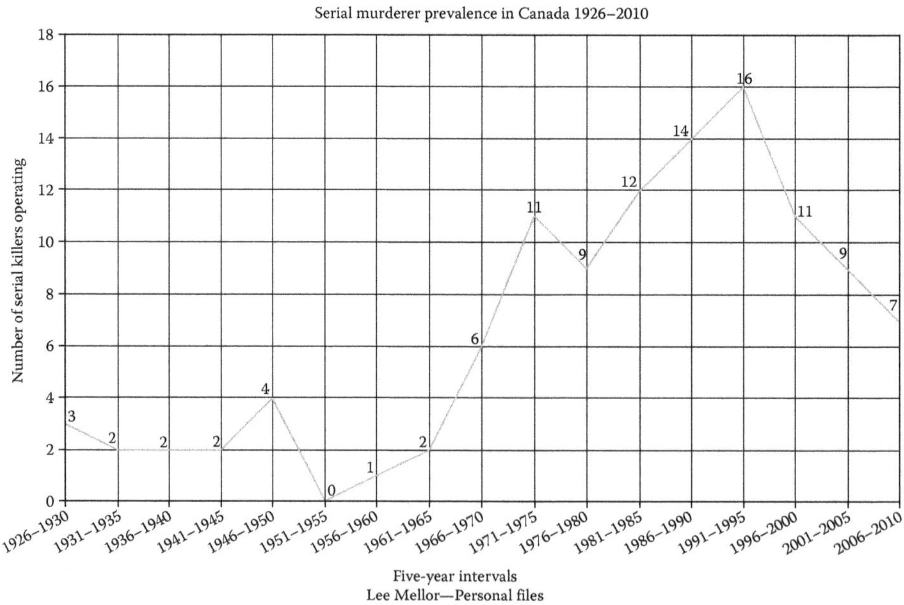

Figure 7.1 Incidences of serial homicide in Canada as reported in the media. (From Mellor, L. (2012). *Cold north killers: Canadian serial murder.* Toronto, Canada: Dundurn. Reproduced with permission.)

* See Pinto and Wilson (1990) and Kidd (2006, both cited in Mouzos & West, 2007) for numbers of serial homicide prior to 1989.

pensioners were targeted, as were persons who were easily accessible, such as hitchhikers.

Other general trends included the fact that in several series, the victims were abducted from an outdoor location and either killed at that location or taken elsewhere and killed. Victims who were killed in a residential location tended to know the offender. In most cases, the victims were killed with a knife and it was common to find that they had suffered multiple stab wounds. Three of the series involved predominantly elderly victims, and in these cases, the victims were strangled to death with a ligature. In two of the series, the offenders used a firearm or the pretence of a firearm to overpower their victims and demand obedience. Six out of the 11 series involved a sexual element; however, the authors' definition of this was broad. In all but one of these series, the offenders were strangers to the victim. Five of the 13 offenders had a previous history of sexual offending, but no figures were given on the relationship between prior offending and whether the series was sexual in nature.

Japan

There has been only one unpublished study to date that has examined serial homicide in Japan (Aki, 2003). As with Gorby (2000), this study was a comparative analysis to Hickey's (1991) work on US cases.* It therefore provides a good comparative framework on overall trends, which helps to provide baseline figures for behaviors that can be useful when considering the distinctiveness of behaviors in crime linkage. However, the study did not provide any figures on consistency. Sixty-four series were sampled that were committed by 82 offenders and were perpetrated against 496–588 victims between 1800 and 2002. These cases were compared with 342 US series committed by 402 offenders, mainly from Hickey's (1991) dataset. As with Hickey's US dataset, the Japanese cases were sourced from journals, books, newspapers, biographies, and the Internet.

The mean number of victims per series was six and 31.7% of the offenders (N = 26) killed an average of three victims across the series. Forty-two of the series lasted 1 year or less. In terms of demographics, 81.7% (N = 67) of offenders were male and 54.9% (N = 45) offended alone. Twenty nine of the offenders (36.7%) killed male victims predominantly and 20% killed adult females exclusively. Forty-three percent of the offenders (N = 32) killed strangers, 60% (N = 43) killed acquaintances, and 16.3% (N = 13) killed family members. Seventy-nine percent of the murders (N = 64) were motivated by money. Sixty percent of the offenders (N = 39) killed their victim by strangulation/asphyxiation, 24.3% (N = 18) used poison, 23.2% (N = 16) used stabbing/slashing/decapitation, and 7.2% (N = 5) shot their victim.

* This study was also outlined in Hickey (2013).

Summary

Although studies exist outside the United States that have investigated homicide trends over time and/or the characteristics of the offenders, victims, and the offenses themselves, very little of this research can tell us anything about the consistency of the offenders' behavior. The remainder of this chapter addresses this gap and compares the findings of studies conducted in various countries that have examined behavioral consistency in serial homicide.

Behavioral Consistency Research to Date

Only recently have empirical studies started to emerge that have focused specifically on behavioral consistency in serial homicide cases. This section will explore that research by focusing first on studies conducted in the United States and then by examining studies conducted outside the United States. As was described in Chapter 6, there are several dominant approaches used for assessing behavioral consistency and distinctiveness in crime linkage research. One involves comparing the behavioral similarity of linked and unlinked crime pairs and the other involves predicting, for a given crime in the dataset, to which series it belongs. A limitation of these approaches is that they do not take account of the order in which offenses were committed and in most cases, the entire crime series has not been included in the analysis. They also do not examine the consistency or inconsistency of individual offenders across their entire series.

To date, few studies have examined whether offenders remain consistent as they progress through their entire series, which would provide an important addition to our understanding of behavioral consistency and change. In terms of serial homicide, only four studies to date have taken this approach (Bateman & Salfati, 2007; Salfati & Bateman, 2005; Salfati, Horning, Sorochinski, & Labuschagne, 2014; Sorochinski & Salfati, 2010). Some of this recent literature has started to test some of the theoretical and anecdotal literature on consistency and identify the salient features upon which consistency analysis can be based. These include behaviors relating to victim selection, violence, control, and planning. These aspects of serial homicide have also been highlighted in previous literature as crucial to analyzing offenders' behaviors (outlined below) and, when taken together, cover the full set of behaviors exhibited in an act of homicide.

Behaviors related to offender cognition (e.g., degree of planning, level of control exhibited by the offender in the offense) have been highlighted as important when linking crimes since the first works on offender profiling and crime scene analysis (e.g., Holmes & Holmes, 1998; Keppel & Walter, 1999; Ressler, Burgess, Douglas, Hartman, & D'Agostino, 1986). More recent studies (outlined below) have assessed their potential contribution to crime linkage (in terms of assessing their consistency and distinctiveness; Bateman & Salfati,

2007; Salfati & Bateman, 2005; Sorochinski & Salfati, 2010). More recent follow-up studies have considered how offender cognition may help explain consistency patterns, notably in relation to planning and how this may relate to national differences in serial homicide demographics and consistency patterns (Salfati et al., 2014a; Sorochinski & Salfati, 2010; Sorochinski et al., 2014).

The other notable behaviors that have been examined relate to victim selection. Based on studies of rape, it has been argued that the way an offender interacts with his victim depends on the role the offender assigns to the victim (Canter, 2000). Three roles have been proposed: Victim as a Person, where the victim has some personal significance to the offender; Victim as a Vehicle, where the offender uses the victim as a vehicle for getting what the offender wants; and Victim as an Object, where the offender handles the victim as though the victim is an inanimate object, doing things to the victim rather than with the victim. This framework has been supported in studies of homicide (Salfati & Canter, 1999), attempted homicide (Fritzon & Ridgway, 2001), and serial homicide (Canter, Alison, Alison, & Wentink, 2004, re-reinterpreted by Canter & Youngs, 2012). More recent studies have looked at the role of the victim in terms of evaluating consistency patterns in serial homicide (e.g., Salfati et al., 2014a) and these will be discussed further below.

Consistency Studies on US Cases of Serial Homicide

Most published work in the area of linking serial homicide takes the form of theoretical and practice-led papers (for a review, see Salfati, 2015), which while providing the reader with a good basis for understanding behavior are not rigorous in terms of how linking and behavioral consistency were defined or examined. For example, authors have outlined the importance of "signatures"* in the linking process (Keppel, 1995). However, these claims have not typically been accompanied by empirical evidence to validate their consistency over a series, nor their reliability in linking cases (Bateman & Salfati, 2007). Although some authors have demonstrated consistency in signatures across series, evidence for this has been based on case studies (e.g., Keppel, Weis, Brown, & Welch, 2005).

Research published in the last decade has, however, started to address this gap in our understanding. This section outlines findings regarding behavioral consistency from US studies of serial homicide. Studies are divided into those that have examined the consistency of individual crime

* Douglas and Munn (1992) define signature as the "calling card" left by the offender that is unique to the offender's pattern of behavior throughout their offenses. For example, this signature may be related to ritualistic acts, committed by an offender to fulfil a specific fantasy. They explain that the signature aspect of the violent offense is a constant behavior performed by an offender during his offenses but that it may evolve and become more developed throughout the offense series.

scene behaviors and those that have grouped such behaviors into themes. These studies will later be used for evaluating the key similarities and differences that exist between the United States and other countries.

Individual Behaviors

In order to evaluate some of the theoretical literature on signatures and how they may be used to link cases of serial homicide, Bateman and Salfati (2007) conducted the first study to empirically examine the observable behaviors comprising signatures. Based on a review of the literature on signatures and serial homicide, they identified six behavioral categories (body disposal, planning/control, mutilation, sexual, theft, weapon). Each one of these categories contained a diverse number of individual behaviors. Bateman and Salfati collated a sample of 90 US serial homicide series, with five offenses in each series. To fully assess consistency patterns, three approaches were taken. First, the overall frequency of each behavior across all the homicides in the sample was calculated to assess if the behavior was common to most offenders or whether it was distinct enough to be used as a *discriminator* between offenders. Second, evidence for consistency was examined by determining, for those offenders who exhibited the *individual* behaviors in one or more of their homicides, whether they did so consistently across their series. A very stringent 80% consistency criterion was used, where an offender was only deemed consistent if they exhibited the individual behavior in at least four out of their five crime scenes. Third, frequency and consistency were calculated for each of the six behavioral categories; if an offender exhibited any of the behaviors in a category, they were deemed to have displayed that behavioral category and then the same consistency criterion (80%) was applied to the category types.

Results showed that some individual behaviors were exhibited consistently throughout the series, however, the analysis also showed that the majority of these individual behaviors were those that were also exhibited in most crimes included in the sample; as such, the behaviors possessed no discriminatory function but instead identified what was common to the sample as a whole. Overall, only five of the 35 behaviors analyzed were shown to occur consistently across the 90 series, while not occurring at a high frequency level. These were two behaviors representing planning and control (bringing a crime kit and destroying evidence), one theft behavior (stealing clothing), one weapon behavior (use of a ligature), and one sexual behavior (oral sex performed by the victim). In terms of consistent use of overall categories of behaviors, only two of the categories (planning/control and theft) showed high consistency rates. However, theft had an average frequency value higher than 50% and therefore was not deemed to have sufficient discriminatory function. This study therefore provided preliminary evidence that planning and control may be the most useful behaviors when linking homicides. This finding suggests that, although the *individual* behaviors of planning and controlling the victim may change over a series of homicides, the presence or absence of *any* planning and control throughout a series of homicides may be a more reliable indicator of whether or not the homicides in question are part of the same series.

Bateman and Salfati's (2007) initial findings suggest that despite claims in the earlier literature regarding the consistency of signatures or specific key behaviors (Douglas & Munn, 1992; Keppel & Walter, 1999), most individual behaviors could not be used to reliably identify homicide series. One of the suggested reasons for this is that behavioral expression is also influenced by situational characteristics (e.g., Bennell & Canter, 2002; Douglas & Munn, 1992; see Chapter 2).

Themes

As described in Chapter 6, other research has assessed the effectiveness of linking homicides using themes (or categories of behaviors). Using a thematic approach allows investigators and researchers to examine *pools* of offending behaviors that all encompass the same function or psychological meaning rather than simply examining the individual behaviors displayed throughout the course of the crime series (Canter, 1994; Salfati, 2000). This may be a more effective approach because offenders may use different behaviors during different crimes due to situational influence but these different behaviors may belong to the same theme or offending style. In this case, using the theme-based approach rather than a signature or individual behavior approach would help to alleviate the problem of finding inconsistency in behaviors due to their situational dependency.

Salfati and Bateman (2005) provided the first empirical study focusing on developing methodological benchmarks for the theme-based approach to assessing behavioral consistency with serial homicides. They sampled the first three crimes in the series of 23 serial homicide offenders, for a total of 69 US homicides. They tested whether the thematic classification of Expressive/Instrumental* produced from research with *single*† homicides (Salfati, 2000; Salfati & Canter, 1999) would apply to serial homicide (for a fuller discussion of this, see Salfati, 2015).

* As Salfati and Bateman (2005) highlight, one of the most notable models for crime scene classification, as it pertains to profiling, has drawn upon Instrumental and Expressive aggression as a thematic distinction between crime scene behaviors in single homicide offenses. The instrumental pole consists of behaviors relating to the offender attacking in order to gain something from the offense, such as money or sex. Here, the offender views the victim not as a person, but rather as a vehicle through which they can gratify some need. The primary goal of the expressive homicide offender is to harm the victim. This theme of aggression is often provoked through an emotional, interpersonal confrontation and is most likely to occur against someone the victim knows intimately. Here, the victim as the person is the target and the behaviors centre on an extreme physical attack against the individual.

† Apparent one-off homicides.

Having found the Expressive/Instrumental typology to replicate in serial homicide, Salfati and Bateman (2005) went on to test the consistency with which offenders displayed the same thematic style across their series. If all three crime scenes in a series displayed the same theme (i.e., all three were expressive, or all three were instrumental), it was classified as a consistent series.*

Only 13%–26% of series demonstrated consistency in theme dominance (i.e., where each of the three crime scenes showed not only a dominant theme, but the same dominant theme across the series). Results thus showed that although using themes based on psychological theory might be more useful for analyzing consistency than single behaviors or subgroups of behaviors, consistency levels were still not high. In addition, Salfati and Bateman (2005) showed that results varied depending on the stringency of method for classifying theme dominance. One of the additional issues the study highlighted was that future linking research will need to examine the individual behaviors that make up each theme to determine which are more susceptible to situational influence because these behaviors will be less reliable for linking purposes and thus, will need to be removed from the themes.

The issue of identifying a more restricted variable set for consistency analysis that enables both subtype differentiation and the use of behaviors that are not as influenced by situational factors was followed up by Sorochinski and Salfati (2010). They aimed to subject variables that were stated in early work as being important in establishing consistency (e.g., Bateman & Salfati, 2007; Canter et al., 2004; Grubin, Kelly, & Brunsdon, 2001; Hickey, 2006; Ressler et al., 1986; Salfati & Bateman, 2005) to empirical investigation. These related to behaviors hypothesized to display physical evidence of offender cognition. But rather than focusing on individual behaviors in isolation they examined behaviors using a thematic framework that would allow for variance due to contextual and situational factors. Three aspects of the crimes were focused upon, notably: (1) planning, (2) wounding, and (3) offender–victim interaction. Their study examined the consistency patterns across the first three crimes in the series of 19 homicide solo offenders who together were responsible for 104 victims, resulting in a final sample of 57 crime scenes (19 series with their first three crime scenes). Five of these crime scenes had multiple victims, thus resulting in a total of 65 victims in the sample.

Of the 19 offenders in the sample, eight (42.1%) were found to consistently exhibit behaviors from the same (pre or post) planning strategy theme across all three offenses. When change was observed, offenders were least consistent in their transition from the first to the second offense. This could suggest that the second offense is somewhat of a trial transition for most

* A crime scene's dominant sub-type (as assessed by the percent of behaviors present at one scene compared to the other) was assessed with varying degrees of stringency, and hence, the reports ranges for consistency

offenders and is consistent with the learning process hypothesis (Canter & Youngs, 2003; Showers & Cantor, 1985). However, as Sorochinski and Salfati (2010) highlighted, an examination of the full series would be necessary to determine whether offenders are more consistent in their planning strategies after the third offense.

Similar to previous studies (e.g., Salfati & Bateman, 2005), few offenders were consistent across their first three offenses in the way they killed the victim. Wounding was classified into two types of processes (related to method and end result). Complete thematic consistency was found in six (31.5%) of the 19 series. Again, most of the variation within this subgroup was seen between the first and second offenses. Change within this subgroup of behaviors was suggested to be related to the constant need to readjust the cognitive strategy in response to situational influences, such as the victim's resistance, thus suggesting that this subset of behaviors was linked to contextual influences. Results also suggested that offenders were more likely to decrease in their level control rather than increase, which is consistent with the theoretical literature on control (e.g., Hickey, 2006).

The strongest pattern of consistency was observed in the third category, relating to the possible psychological victim type (Victim as Person, Object, and Vehicle). These variables are related to behaviors that were not part of the actual murder, but reflect the way the offender views and interacts with the victim. As such, behaviors underlying this theme may represent evidence for the offender's own personal agenda. Overall consistency in this behavioral subgroup was found in 11 out of 19 (57.9%) of the series. Interestingly, offenders who displayed a Victim as Vehicle pattern in their first offense were less likely to change their pattern than those who displayed a Victim as Object style.

Finally, only 10.5% of ($N = 2$) offenders displayed consistency in all three subgroups of behavior (i.e., planning, wounding, and interaction with victim) and only 26.3% ($N = 5$) did so in two of the three subgroups. Forty-two percent of the offenders were consistent in only one aspect of their homicide behavior (i.e., planning, wounding, or interaction with the victim).

Using a sample of 79 male serial murderers from the United States who committed a total of 237 homicides, Melnyk, Bennell, Gauthier, and Gauthier (2011) also tested behavioral consistency by classifying offenses within a series into two overarching themes (the Disorganized/Organized classification as developed by the FBI; Ressler et al., 1986), which were further categorized into impulsive/planning, control, and ritualistic behaviors. At the same time, they tested the relative efficacy of various statistical coefficients, which were used to quantify behavioral similarity. How accurately linked crime pairs could be distinguished from unlinked crime pairs was assessed using receiver operating characteristic analysis, which produces a statistic called the area under the curve. The larger the area under the curve, the more accurately linked crime pairs can be distinguished from unlinked crime pairs.

They found that regardless of the statistical coefficient used, crimes committed by the same offender tended to be associated with significantly higher levels of behavioral similarity than crimes committed by different offenders. In addition, evidence was also found for behavioral distinctiveness since linked and unlinked crime pairs could be distinguished with a high level of accuracy (as evidenced by large and significant area under the curves).

Overall, in terms of understanding the salient behaviors or subtypes that may help in linking, while also providing an understanding of behavioral consistency across the full series, the literature has started to show some key trends of what may be fruitful avenues to explore, notably in relation to behaviors that may be indicators of levels of cognition by the offender. However, currently, the number of empirical studies on US samples remains small.

Victims

Vulnerable victims have been found to feature frequently in serial murders committed in the United States. For example, Egger (2003) found that nearly 78% of female victims of serial homicide offenders are prostitutes. Similarly, in a survey of US serial homicide from 1970 to 2009, Quinet (2011) found that, of cases from 2000 to 2009 involving female victims only, 69% involved prostitute victims. These findings confirm studies comparing serial with apparent "one-off" offenders, whereby when prostitutes are killed in the United States, a serial offender is responsible in at least 35% of the cases (Brewer et al., 2006). With regard to consistency and serial offending, Quinet found the series length for offenders that targeted prostitute victims to be longer than offenders that targeted other types of victim. These figures suggest a pattern of consistency that warrants closer inspection, particularly since what we know about consistency patterns in terms of victim selection is based on media accounts/case studies of prolific serial homicide offenders.

In a small pilot study aimed at establishing some baselines, Salfati (2007, 2013) looked at how consistent offenders were when their series included prostitute victims. Of the 19 series (19 offenders, and 106 victims) examined, eight (42%) were composed of prostitute victims only and 11 series (58%) contained both prostitute victims and nonprostitute victims, thus clearly showing that not all offenders specialize in terms of targeting prostitute victims specifically. That being said, it is still unclear what the difference is between offenders who target prostitute victims only and those that have a more varied style of victim selection (Salfati, 2015). Future research into the consistency of victim selection could also benefit from drawing on literature from criminology (e.g., Routine Activities Theory; Cohen & Felson, 1979). It may be that those offenders who target a mix of prostitutes and other victims are not showing inconsistency in their decision making but are rather showing consistency in their selection of vulnerable victims. Further research in this area would make an important contribution to what we know of serial homicide offenders' behavioral consistency.

International Studies on Consistency in Serial Homicide

Although there is not a large volume of research on serial homicide outside of the United States, there are a few studies from which we can draw some initial comparisons. Although the studies of Gorby (2000) and Mellor (2012) show that serial homicide offenders certainly operate within Canada and the United Kingdom, much of the research on linking offenses from the United Kingdom at least has focused on serial sex offenses or volume crime. Beyond case study analysis, there has been little work done in the rest of Europe on serial homicide. There are, however, a few notable exceptions.

Germany

Harbort and Mokros (2001) collected a sample from 1945 to 1995 of 61 German serial (sexual) homicide offenders who were identified from prosecution files. They provided a detailed outline of the offenders' characteristics, with reference to socio-demographics, family background, social integration, intellectual capability, and personality disorders. This information was sourced mainly from expert opinions given during trial proceedings or from mental health professionals who were treating the offenders. Additionally, unsolved cases were added from police files of cases presumed to be series, where either no suspect could be identified or the evidence did not suffice to prosecute. Additional data were also collected from the criminological and criminalistic literature and printed media.

In terms of behavioral consistency, their study focused on *modus operandi* (MO) and signature. From their results, they concluded that the majority of the offenders in their sample show marked differences in their actions from one homicide to the next, particularly from the first to the second offense in a series. The latter finding is similar to what Sorochinski and Salfati (2010) reported with their US sample. Across the sample, 59.1% of the individuals changed their MO during their series. This percentage was higher, at 72.7%, when considering those individuals in the sample who were *sexual* homicide offenders. Overall, Harbort and Mokros concluded that the sexual homicide offenders were markedly different from the rest of the sample. No support was found for the hypothesis that sexual homicide offenders would target one particular type of victim. Only three individuals in the sample (13.6%) showed a fixation on particular physical aspects of the victim (such as hair color and build). Harbort and Mokros did, however, find the offenders to show consistency in some elements of victim selection (i.e., victim age and gender). However, there was also evidence of crossover in victim selection with 18.2% of offenders killing victims of both genders and 22.7% killing both children and adults. They therefore caution against investigators taking their results to be any real evidence of consistency because they argue that MO may be influenced by learning and contextual factors. Any consistency, they suggest, is likely to be temporary because MO is subject to gradual developments or sudden changes from one homicide to the next.

As well as examining consistency in MO, Harbort and Mokros also looked at signatures. These were only found to be discernible in 22.7% of the offenders in the total sample (40.9% of the sexual murderers). However, unfortunately, as with many of the earlier studies in the field, the finer detail regarding how the offenders displayed consistency with respect to signatures was not specifically outlined in the study.

Italy

One study by Santtila et al. (2008) examined the behavioral consistency of Italian serial homicide offenders. They sampled the offenses of 23 serial homicide offenders from 1980 to 2001 who had killed a total of 116 victims. Information was extracted from court files for 15 of the cases and for the remaining 8 cases, criminological literature and newspaper articles were consulted for information about the crimes. The study aimed to develop subscales that captured the nature of serial homicide and then determine whether these scales could be used to match offenses to the correct series. Mokken scaling was used to produce seven scales, five that primarily measured variations in motivation and two scales that measured variations in level of planning. Discriminant function analysis was used to assess how accurately cases could be allocated to the correct series. Overall, they found a 62.9% accuracy rate in predicting series membership. Scales related to paraphilia, the sexual nature of the crime, and control were the most effective at attributing a case to the correct series. With regard to the former two, this is contrary to what was found by Bateman and Salfati (2007) suggesting that there may be differences between countries in terms of what behaviors are more effective when linking crimes. However, differences in statistical approaches would need to be compared to confirm this.

In 2012, Salo, Sirèn, Corander, Zappalà, Bosco, Mokros, and Santtila extended this study. Using the same sample, they applied a Bayesian model to 92 individual crime scene behaviors to see how accurately series membership could be predicted for each case in the dataset. In addition, they used this technique to assess the individual contribution of each behavior to the prediction of series membership, thereby identifying which behaviors were most useful for linking crimes in this dataset. Using all 92 behaviors, 84% of cases were attributed to the correct series, which represents a level much higher than you would get by chance alone (5.3%). All variables contributed to prediction, however, classification accuracy could be maintained at 84%

with just 15 variables in the model. These variables were reduced evidence, same encounter and murder scene, injuries to throat, body found at murder scene, body found in inner city, victim genitals exposed, injuries to several body parts, firearm used, victim forcibly moved while alive, injuries to just one body part, body found outside, body covered, victim manually strangled, killing occurred in association with rape, and vaginal penetration attempted or achieved. Within this list of behaviors are actions associated with sex, control, and potentially planning also. These findings therefore have some similarities with what was found in the original Santtila et al. (2008) study, as well as Bateman and Salfati's (2007) US study.

Republic of South Africa

Republic of South Africa has had an increase of almost 900% in the average annual incidence of serial homicide post-apartheid (1990–1996), making this specific type of homicide a key concern (Hodgskiss, 2004). Recent work on serial homicide in the Republic of South Africa has provided a great deal of comparative material and has identified key similarities and differences in consistency patterns, with respect to behaviors and victim targets. The results of these studies open up key questions about some of the issues surrounding the behavioral consistency debate that goes above and beyond simply comparing frequencies.

The studies reported below include a recent study that aimed to collect and code all available cases of solved serial homicide in the Republic of South Africa (Salfati et al., 2014b). All cases were coded using the same measurement instrument (the Homicide Profiling Index) as used in previous US studies (e.g., Sorochinski & Salfati, 2010). This is useful because it allows for a direct comparison between datasets. From 1953 until 2007, there were 53 known series of homicide reported to the police in Republic of South Africa, involving 77 offenders with approximately 557 victims. Of these, there were 30 solved serial homicide series from 1953 to 2007 with a total of 302 victims (254 crime scenes) available for analysis. Four of the series had only two crime scenes in total (eight victims). The remaining 26 series had a minimum of three crime scenes (275 victims). Twenty-two of the series had four or more crime scenes (263 victims). Also reported below is another study on South African serial homicide (Salfati et al., 2014a) that compared South African findings of behavioral consistency to those from the United States (Bateman & Salfati, 2007; Salfati & Bateman, 2005; Sorochinski & Salfati, 2010).

When comparing the pattern of pre- or post-planning behaviors between South African and US samples, pre-offense planning was evident in both countries; however, while US offenders often appeared to engage in post-offense planning, South African offenders seemed to do all their planning before the offense. The South African offenders could thus more reliably be differentiated into the subgroups of either *pre-offense planning* or *no planning* at all. When looking at the first three offenses in the series for the South African serial murderers, 36% of offenders were consistent in engaging in planning. When extending this to the first four crime scenes, results did not significantly differ (i.e., 37%). The number of offenders who consistently displayed a lack of any planning decreased gradually as the number of homicides per series that were analyzed increased (i.e., five offenders were consistently not displaying any planning across the first two offenses, three across the first three offenses, and only one across the first four offenses). This pattern suggests that a certain degree of prior planning is necessary for offenders to be able to continue their series for a longer period of time. In terms of change patterns, all of the offenders who were deemed inconsistent in their planning behaviors still displayed the same dominant planning theme in two (33%) or three (67%) of the four offenses analyzed. Overall, for the planning behavioral subgroup, these patterns may be regarded as evidence of the trial and error and/or learning process that takes place (Canter & Youngs, 2003). This is consistent with the conclusions drawn by Sorochinski and Salfati (2010) in their study of US serial homicides.

In terms of weapon use and the styles of wounding, consistency levels remained similar as the series developed over time, with 32% of offenders displaying consistency across their first three crime scenes. Of these, almost twice as many offenders displayed process-oriented wounding in comparison with goal-oriented wounding,* suggesting again an importance of the interaction of the victim. Whether offenders engaged in one type or another, consistency figures remained similar as series lengthened (37% were consistent across their first four crimes). For those cases that displayed inconsistency in their series of four crime scenes, the majority changed their wounding strategy between the first and second offenses. This variability between first and second offenses is similar to what has been found with US samples (Sorochinski & Salfati, 2010).

Overall, the vast majority of South African offenders (72%) exhibited thematic consistency in at least one subgroup of behaviors (either in how they approached planning their offense or in the way violence was exhibited).

* According to Sorochinski and Salfati (2010), "process-oriented" wounding included behaviors associated with a lengthy type of murder (e.g., multiple wounds, stabbing, strangulation, wounding to the neck, pelvic region). These behaviors are also commonly associated in the clinical literature with sexualized murder. "Goal-oriented" wounding included behaviors associated with a quick kill (e.g., shooting, bludgeoning, wounding to the head and face). These behaviors are also associated with more control of the scene by the offender (i.e., shooting someone with a gun is a much more controlled act with less possibility for unexpected events happening than stabbing someone multiple times).

Only 12% were consistent in both. Similarly in the US sample (Sorochinski & Salfati, 2010), it was found that while not many offenders were consistent across both wounding and planning behavioral subgroups,* 79% were consistent in at least one of the subgroups.

In terms of behavior, therefore, there were some similarities between the two samples. While it is important to take into account the cultural and environmental specifics, and although patterns themselves may differ, frameworks for studying offenders' behaviors appear generalizable across samples and provide a helpful baseline for comparison.

Based on consistent results across studies, which suggest that victimology may play a salient role in consistency analysis (for a review, see Salfati, 2014), the analysis of offender–victim interaction has also been expanded upon in the study of serial homicide in the Republic of South Africa (Salfati et al., 2014a). The aim of this study was to provide more insight into the thematic subgroups (e.g., Victim as Vehicle and Victim as Object†) as well as examining victim characteristics in more detail. In terms of consistency, across the first three crimes in the series, 50% (13 of 26 series) of offenders displayed absolute consistency in their thematic subgroup, decreasing to 45% (9 of 20 series) when examining the first four crime scenes. Fewer offenders treated their victim as an object; however, many of those that adopted this interaction style were consistent in it throughout their series. Conversely, offenders whose interaction represented the Victim as Vehicle theme became less consistent as the series progressed. These results may indicate that an offender's focus and involvement with the victim may influence consistency patterns. It may be that less inconsistency will be observed for those offenders who are less focused on interacting with the victim (falling into the subgroup of Victim as Object). This lends an additional level of complexity to the analysis of consistency (Salfati, 2008).

Additional analysis focused on individual victim characteristics, which included selecting male victims, couples, live victims,‡ and vulnerable victims (prostitutes, women looking for work, children, and the unidentified). Little consistency was found as series progressed for the individual behaviors of couples, live victims, and vulnerable victims despite these underpinning the thematic subgroups. However, offenders were more consistent when targeting male victims. It should be noted though that targeting males was not a common behavior. These results are similar to the original conclusions of Bateman and Salfati (2007) who concluded that consistency might be more

* As this study compared three separate subthemes, compared to only two subgroups in the Republic of South Africa study comparable figures are not available.

† The Victim as Person subtheme was not observed in South African serial homicides.

‡ Live victims usually indicate victims who were sexually assaulted or victims present at the scene but who were not the primary target.

apparent when one adopts a thematic approach to consistency (allowing for some situational influence) rather than seeking consistency at the level of individual behaviors.

Conclusion

This chapter aimed to provide an overview of international serial homicide research, specifically as it relates to similarities and differences in general demographics, behavioral consistency, and the implications of these findings for crime linkage. The role of culture in influencing behavior indicates the importance of conducting comparative research across countries because national country-level issues and cultural factors may influence consistency levels as well as the distinctiveness of behaviors.

As was highlighted at the beginning of the chapter, there is currently little detailed research on serial homicide outside studies conducted on US samples. Of the studies that have looked at serial homicide, most have focused on demographics and have drawn general conclusions about consistency, but without providing enough methodological detail to allow for meaningful comparisons across countries. However, some international comparisons are possible, for example, where researchers (e.g., Aki, 2003; Gorby, 2000) have intentionally collected samples that mirror Hickey's (1991) study of US homicide, and more recently, where the Homicide Profiling Index has been used to collect behavioral data in different countries (e.g., Salfati et al., 2014a; Sorochinski & Salfati, 2010).

In terms of similarities in the demographic characteristics of this type of offense, across several countries it is reported that most offenders are male. If the offender is male, it seems more likely that the victim will be a stranger to him, whereas if the offender is female, there is a higher proportion of victims from within the family. Several studies also suggest that prostitutes are a high-risk victim type. However, these conclusions are drawn very tentatively since variation in data sources, the time spans covered, and disparity in the information reported pose substantial challenges to drawing comparisons.

In terms of actual tests of behavioral consistency, some studies have examined individual behaviors while others have looked at thematic consistency. Across several studies, there were reports of the degree of consistency in victim selection. These were not particularly high indicating quite a lot of variation in victim targeting, at least for some serial homicide offenders. When combining all crime scene behaviors, Melnyk et al.'s (2011) test of the assumptions of behavioral consistency and distinctiveness with a US sample of serial homicide found good evidence for both assumptions. Similarly, for their Italian sample, Santtila et al. (2008) reported a predictive accuracy rate for series membership of 69% and this increased to 84% when

Salo et al. (2012) investigated the same sample using a different statistical method. Investigations of the efficacy of different types of individual crime scene behavior revealed that sexual behaviors in homicide were more effective for linking crimes in Italy (Salo et al., 2013; Santtila et al., 2008) compared to the United States (Bateman & Salfati, 2007). However, planning and control behaviors seem to be useful when linking homicides in both of these countries.

When adopting a thematic approach to assessing consistency, Salfati and Bateman (2005) found quite low rates of consistency (13%–26%) for the theme of Instrumentality and Expressiveness. Other studies have classified behaviors into the themes of planning, wounding, and victim–offender interaction. Using a sample of serial homicides from the United States, Sorochinski and Salfati (2010) found serial murderers to be most consistent in the way they interacted with their victim, followed by their use (or not) of planning, and then their method of wounding. Similarly, in their South African sample, Salfati et al. (2014a) found serial murderers to be more consistent in their planning behaviors than their wounding behaviors. Overall, 72%–79% of serial murderers in these latter two studies showed consistency in one of the themes across their series for South African and US serial murderers, respectively.

The value of examining behavioral themes becomes particularly apparent when considering the consistency of victim selection. In this case, seemingly inconsistent results across cultures can be seen to be thematically consistent. For example, in the United States, serial homicide offenders most often target victims working as prostitutes, yet in Republic of South Africa, almost no prostitutes are targeted as part of a crime series. We cannot therefore assume that specific crime scene behaviors will be consistently exhibited across cultures (and thus, the suitability of specific behaviors for linking purposes will not necessarily generalize across countries).* However, if one looks deeper at how the offender is targeting victims in each of the cultures, one can find similarities in behavior at the thematic level. In the case of US homicides, prostitutes can be considered vulnerable victims (they work on their own, in secluded areas; they do not necessarily know their clients; and they often travel to even more secluded areas with their clients). In Republic of South Africa, targets are rarely prostitutes, but the targets can nonetheless be viewed as vulnerable. In the South African context, the interaction often involves an offer of employment, which takes place informally as is common practice within the culture. Car ownership is uncommon in most of Republic of South Africa, and thus, the offer of employment often necessitates travel to a neighboring village or a secluded area, usually by public transport or by walking. Once in this secluded area, the offender attacks and kills the victim. Thus, despite

* For similar findings regarding serial rape, see Woodhams and Labuschagne (2012).

the fact that the observable behaviors vary somewhat across the United States and Republic of South Africa, the underlying psychology is the same—serial homicide offenders in both countries prey on vulnerable victims.

A final finding common to several international studies of serial homicide is that the time between the first and second offenses in a series seems particularly susceptible to behavioral change. This has been found for US, German, and South African samples (Harbort & Mokros, 2001; Salfati et al., 2014a; Sorochinski & Salfati, 2010). This consistent finding warrants further investigation to determine why behavioral change seems to occur at this stage compared to at other stages of a crime series.

In summary, it is apparent from the findings reported in this chapter that while serial homicide offenders might show greater levels of behavioral consistency than other types of offenders (e.g., serial rapists; Salo et al., 2013; Santtila et al., 2008), they do not show perfect consistency across their crimes. In addition, consistency rates may be influenced by how consistency is measured, and as such, basic measurement issues need to be standardized before solid results can be put forward regarding similarities and differences across countries and cultures. Steps are being taken to try and standardize the data collection process to facilitate such cross-cultural research. For example, the Homicide Profiling Index (Salfati, 2010) has now been used in several studies in order to allow for clearer cross-cultural comparisons. Such research is very important since variations in cultural attitudes and practices will likely affect not just the expression of behavioral consistency between countries but also behavioral distinctiveness. In turn, behavioral consistency and distinctiveness will influence the degree of accuracy that can be achieved when attempting to link homicides to the offender responsible.

References

Aamodt, M. A. (2012). *Incidences of serial homicide across countries.* Retrieved from http://maamodt.asp.radford.edu/Serial%20Killer%20Information%20Center/Project%20Description.htm.

Aki, K. (2003). *Serial killers: A cross-cultural study between Japan and the United States* (Unpublished graduate thesis), California State University, Fresno, CA.

Archer, D., & Gartner, R. (1984). *Violence and crime in cross-national perspective.* New Haven, CT: Yale University Press.

Bateman, A., & Salfati, G. (2007). An examination of behavioral consistency using individual behaviors or groups of behaviors in serial homicide. *Behavioral Sciences & the Law, 25,* 527–544.

Bennell, C., & Canter, D. (2002). Linking commercial burglaries by *modus operandi*: Tests using regression and ROC analysis. *Science & Justice, 42,* 153–164.

Brewer, D., Dudek, J., Potterat, J., Muth, S., Roberts, J., & Woodhouse, D. (2006). Extent, trends and perpetrators of prostitute-related homicide in the United States. *Journal of Forensic Sciences, 51,* 1101–1108.

Canter, D. V. (1994). Psychology of offender profiling. In R. Bull & D. Carson (Eds.), *Handbook of psychology in legal contexts* (pp. 343–355). Chichester, England: Wiley.

Canter, D. (2000). *Criminal shadows*. Irving, TX: Authorlink Press.

Canter, D. V., Alison, L. J., Alison, E., & Wentink, N. (2004). The organized/disorganized typology of serial murder: Myth or model? *Psychology, Public Policy, and Law, 10*, 293–320.

Canter, D., & Youngs, D. (2003). Beyond offender profiling: The need for an investigative psychology. In D. Carson & R. Bull (Eds.), *Handbook of psychology in legal contexts* (2nd ed., pp. 171–205). Chichester, England: Wiley.

Canter, D., & Youngs, D. (2009). *Investigative psychology: Offender profiling and the analysis of criminal action*. Chichester, England: Wiley.

Canter, D., & Youngs, D. (2012). Sexual and violent offenders' victim role assignments: A general model of offending style. *Journal of Forensic Psychiatry & Psychology, 23*, 297–326.

Cohen, L. E., & Felson, M. (1979). Social change and crime rate trends: A routine activity approach. *American Sociological Review, 44*, 588–608.

Douglas, J. E., & Munn, C. M. (1992). Modus operandi and the signature aspects of violent crime. In J. E. Douglas, A. W. Burgess, A. G. Burgess, & R. K. Ressler (Eds.), *Crime classification manual* (pp. 259–268). New York, NY: Lexington Books.

Egger, S. A. (1984). A working definition of serial murder and the reduction of linkage blindness. *Journal of Police Science and Administration, 12*, 348–357.

Egger, S. (2003). Methods of murder. In E. Hickey (Ed.), *Encyclopedia of murder and violent crime* (pp. 311–313). Thousand Oaks, CA: Sage.

Fox, J. A., & Zawitz, M. W. (1999). *Homicide trends in the United States*. Washington, DC: Bureau of Justice Statistics.

Fritzon, K., & Ridgway, J. (2001). Near-death experience: The role of victim reaction in attempted homicide. *Journal of Interpersonal Violence, 16*, 679–696.

Gorby, B. L. (2000). *Serial murder: A cross-national descriptive study* (Unpublished M.Sc. thesis). California State University, Fresno, CA.

Grubin, D., Kelly, P., & Brunsdon, C. (2001). *Linking serious sexual assaults through behaviour*. London, England: Home Office, Research, Development and Statistics Directorate.

Harbort, S., & Mokros, A. (2001). Serial murderers in Germany from 1945 to 1995: A descriptive study. *Homicide Studies, 5*, 311–334.

Hickey, E. W. (1991). *Serial murderers and their victims*. Pacific Grove, CA: Brooks/Cole Publishing Company.

Hickey, E. W. (2006). *Serial murderers and their victims* (4th ed.). Pacific Grove, CA: Sage.

Hickey, E. W. (2012). *Serial murderers and their victims* (6th ed.). Belmont, CA: Wadsworth.

Hodgskiss, B. (2004). Lessons from serial murder in South Africa. *Journal of Investigative Psychology and Offender Profiling, 1*, 67–94.

Holmes, R. M., & Holmes, S. T. (1998). *Serial murder* (2nd ed.). Thousand Oaks, CA: Sage.

Horning, A. M., Salfati, C. G., & Labuschagne, G. (2014). South African serial homicide: A victim focused behavioral typology. *Journal of Investigative Psychology and Offender Profiling*.

Huesmann, L. R., & Eron L. D. (1984). Cognitive processes and the persistence of aggressive behavior. *Aggressive Behavior, 10,* 243–251.

Jackson, J. L., & Bekerian, D. A. (Eds.). (1997). *Offender profiling: Theory, research, and practice.* Chichester, England: Wiley.

Keppel, R. D. (1995). Signature murders: A report of several related cases. *Journal of Forensic Sciences, 40,* 670–674.

Keppel, R. D., & Walter, R. (1999). Profiling killers: A revised classification model for understanding sexual murder. *International Journal of Offender Therapy and Comparative Criminology, 43,* 417–437.

Keppel, R. D., Wels, J. G., Brown, K. M., & Welch, K. (2005). The Jack the Ripper murders: A *modus operandi* and signature analysis of the 1888–1891 Whitechapel murders. *Journal of Investigative Psychology and Offender Profiling, 2,* 1–21.

LaFree, G. (1999). A summary and review of cross-national comparative studies of homicide. In M. D. Smith & M. A. Zahn (Eds.), *Homicide: A sourcebook of social research* (pp. 125–148). Thousand Oaks, CA: Sage.

Lester, D. (1995). *Serial killers: The insatiable passion.* Philadelphia, PA: The Charles Press.

Leyton, E. (1995). *Men of blood: Murder in modern England.* London, England: Constable.

Mellor, L. (2012). *Cold north killers: Canadian serial murder.* Toronto, Canada: Dundurn.

Melnyk, T., Bennell, C., Gauthier, D. J., & Gauthier, D. (2011). Another look at across-crime similarity coefficients for use in behavioral linkage analysis: An attempt to replicate Woodhams, Grant, and Price (2007). *Psychology, Crime & Law, 17,* 359–380.

Mouzos, J., & West, D. (2007). An examination of serial murder in Australia. *Trends & Issues in Crime and Criminal Justice, 346,* 1–6.

National Center for the Analysis of Violent Crime. (2005). *Serial murder: Multi-disciplinary perspectives for investigators.* San Antonio, TX: National Center for the Analysis of Violent Crime (NCAVC). Retrieved from http://www.fbi.gov/stats-services/publications/serial-murder.

Pakhomou, S. M. (2004). Serial killers: Offender's relationship to the victim and selected demographics. *International Journal of Police Science & Management, 6,* 219–233.

Quinet, K. (2007). The missing missing: Towards a quantification of serial murder victimization in the United States. *Homicide Studies, 11,* 319–339.

Quinet, K. (2011). Prostitutes as victims of serial homicide: Trends and case characteristics from 1970–2009. *Homicide Studies, 15,* 74–100.

Ressler, R. K., Burgess, A. W., & Douglas, J. E. (1988). *Sexual homicide: Patterns and motives.* New York, NY: Free Press.

Ressler, R. K., Burgess, A. W., Douglas, J. E., Hartman, C. R., & D'Agostino, R. B. (1986). Serial killers and their victims: Identifying patterns through crime scene analysis. *Journal of Interpersonal Violence, 1,* 288–308.

Salfati, C. G. (2000). The nature of expressiveness and instrumentality in homicide. *Homicide Studies, 4,* 265–293.

Salfati, C. G. (2001). A European perspective on the study of homicide. *Homicide Studies, 5,* 286–291.

Salfati, C. G. (2003). Offender interaction with victims in homicide: A multidimensional analysis of frequencies in crime scene behaviors. *Journal of Interpersonal Violence, 18,* 490–512.

Salfati, C. G. (2007, November). *Prostitutes: Vulnerable or sexual targets of serial homicide?* Presented at the Annual American Society of Criminology Conference, Atlanta, GA.
Salfati, C. G. (2008). Linking serial crimes. *Issues in Forensic Psychology, 8*, 68–81.
Salfati, C. G. (2013). Linkage analysis of serial murder cases involving prostitute victims. In J. B. Helfgott (Ed.), *Criminal psychology (Vols. 1–4)*. Westport, CT: Praeger.
Salfati, C. G. (2015). *Offender Profiling Series: Profiling homicide and linking serial homicide—A sourcebook*, Offender Profiling Series. Surrey, England: Ashgate.
Salfati, C. G., & Bateman, A. L. (2005). Serial homicide: An investigation of behavioural consistency. *Journal of Investigative Psychology and Offender Profiling, 2*, 121–144.
Salfati, C. G., & Canter, D. (1999). Differentiating stranger murders: Profiling offender characteristics from behavioral styles. *Behavioral Sciences & the Law, 17*, 391–406.
Salfati, C. G., & Haratsis, E. (2001). A behavioral examination of offender crime-scene actions. *Homicide Studies, 5*, 335–362.
Salfati, C. G., Horning, A. M., Sorochinski, M., & Labuschagne, G. N. (2014a). South African serial homicide: A victim focused behavioral typology. *Journal of Investigative Psychology and Offender Profiling.*
Salfati, C. G., Labuschagne, G. N., Horning, A. M., Sorochinski, M., & De Wet, J. (2014b). Demographics of all solved serial homicides in South Africa 1950–2007. *Journal of Investigative Psychology and Offender Profiling.*
Salo, B., Sirén, J., Corander, J., Zappalà, A., Bosco, D., Mokros, A., & Santtila, P. (2012). Using Bayes' theorem in behavioural crime linking of serial homicide. *Legal and Criminological Psychology, 18*, 356–370.
Santtila, P., Pakkanen, T., Zappalá, A., Bosco, D., Valkama, M., & Mokros, A. (2008). Behavioural crime linking in serial homicide. *Psychology, Crime & Law, 14*, 245–265.
Scott, H. (2005). *The female serial murderer: A sociological study of homicide and the "gentler sex."* Lewiston, NY: Edwin Mellen Press.
Showers, C., & Cantor, N. (1985). Social cognition: A look at motivated strategies. *Annual Review of Psychology, 36*, 275–305.
Sorochinski, M., & Salfati, C. G. (2010). The consistency of inconsistency in serial homicide: Patterns of behavioral change across series. *Journal of Investigative Psychology and Offender Profiling, 7*, 109–136.
Sorochinski, M., Salfati, C. G., & Labuschagne, G. N. (2014). Thematic classification of planning and violent behaviors in serial homicide: A cross-national comparison between South Africa and the US. *Journal of Investigative Psychology and Offender Profiling.*
Swidler, A. (1986). Culture in action. *American Sociological Review, 51*, 273–286.
Toufexis, A. (1994, April 4). Dances with werewolves. *Time, 143*, 64–66.
Woodhams, J., Hollin, C. R., & Bull, R. (2008). Incorporating context in linking crimes: An exploratory study of the relationship between behavioural consistency and situational similarity. *Journal of Investigative Psychology and Offender Profiling, 5*, 1–23.
Woodhams, J., & Labuschagne, G. N. (2012). South African serial rapists: The offenders, their victims and their offences. *Sexual Abuse: A Journal of Research and Treatment, 24*, 544–574.
Woodhams, J., & Toye, K. (2007). An empirical test of the assumptions of case linkage and offender profiling with serial commercial robberies. *Psychology, Public Policy, and Law, 13*, 59–85.

A Practitioner's Perspective
Theory, Practice, and Research

8

LEE RAINBOW

Contents

Introduction	173
Definitional Clarity	174
Behavioral Investigative Advice	175
Investigative Approach	176
Theoretical Considerations	176
Methodological Considerations	178
Practice	179
Report Extract Example	182
Further Considerations	187
Evidential Approach	188
Legal Context	188
Current Practice	189
Proposed Approach	190
Example	191
Further Considerations	192
Research Agenda	193
Conclusions	194
References	194

Introduction

Although crime linkage analysis (CLA) has received increasing attention by researchers in recent years, the focus of such activity remains largely an academic one, with little or no explicit reference to the practitioner community. This is most starkly reflected in the perceived holy grail of such endeavors, to reliably and accurately find linked crimes within a large dataset of similar offenses. This demonstrates a somewhat naïve confusion between comparative case analysis (CCA) and CLA and at present does little to assist practitioners in their endeavors to link crimes to a common perpetrator, from either an intelligence or evidential perspective.

It is highlighted that such commentary is not intended as a criticism of current research efforts, and indeed, it is acknowledged that some researchers have become more focused on such practical applications in recent times. Rather, the goal of this chapter is to illuminate the challenges faced by practitioners within the field of crime linkage and make explicit the gaps in knowledge and evidence-based practice which would benefit significantly from a refocused research agenda. It is acknowledged that much of the research within the field of CCA may, conceptually at least, be of benefit to the operational task of CLA, but as practitioners, such developments are currently either absent or inaccessible as explicit operational tools.

It should be further highlighted at the outset that the following experiences and working practices outlined below are UK specific and should not be generalized across different countries and policing jurisdictions. It is as naïve and simplistic to believe that all analysts and behavioral investigative advisers (BIAs) operate in the same way throughout the world as it is to believe that their police colleagues follow universally accepted processes and procedures, regardless of cultural, political, legislative, scientific, and experiential differences.

Definitional Clarity

The terms *crime linkage analysis* (CLA) and *comparative case analysis* (CCA) are often referred to as interchangeable terms describing the same process—the process which aims to identify offenses that have been committed by the same offender, based on behavioral similarities (e.g., Bennell & Canter, 2002; Hazelwood & Warren, 2003; Woodhams & Grant, 2006)—but should, from a practitioner perspective at least, be viewed as conceptually distinct. Although theoretically such congruence of meaning may be justified, within the operational context a clear distinction is required to differentiate between specific roles, aims, and objectives.

In contemporary UK operational practice, and in particular within a serious crime context, CCA refers to the proactive searching of large databases to find *similar* cases, which have the *potential* to be linked to the index case under consideration. This role is performed by crime analysts whose remit is to identify and highlight potentially similar cases for consideration by the officers investigating the index offense. No opinion regarding linkage—that is, whether the identified cases have been committed by the same offender—is intended or provided.

In contrast, CLA refers to the process of informing an investigation of whether two or more offenses are likely to have been committed by the same offender, that is, whether they are *linked*. In reality, such analysis is performed on a predetermined set of offenses provided by the investigating officer, who has reason to believe they may be linked. Such analysis does not involve the proactive searching of datasets for further offenses, but is restricted to the prescribed cases identified by the investigation. This role is performed by BIAs in the United Kingdom.

As such, it can be seen that in practice, two very different activities are being performed, with the focus of research activity almost exclusively directed toward CCA activity. It is imperative that researchers understand and acknowledge the clear distinction between CCA and CLA and focus on clear, unambiguous definitions that more accurately reflect the pragmatic applications of future research endeavors.

Behavioral Investigative Advice

As highlighted above, the task of CLA falls under the remit of BIAs in the United Kingdom. The underlying philosophy of behavioral investigative advice is the provision of an additional perspective and decision support throughout a serious crime investigation through the pragmatic application of behavioral science theory, research, and experience. Although debates continue regarding the scientific status of such activity, what behavioral investigative advice does (or certainly should) offer is methodologically rigorous, based upon observations of data, and situated within an understanding of the investigative and behavioral science contexts and limitations. Indeed, one of the underlying philosophies of such advice and support to major crime investigations is to enhance the scientific method of the investigative process through appropriate provision of hypotheses, evidence-based prioritization of the "most likely" (offender characteristics, sequence of events, motivation, etc.), and associated decision support strategies, grounded firmly in psychological principles and available empirical research findings (for a comprehensive review of contemporary BIA practice, see Rainbow & Gregory, 2011).

Although in an ideal world, the development of an accepted and standardized methodology for CLA would reflect the scientific approach of theory → research → practice, a fundamental discord exists between the immediate practical needs of the investigator and the ultimate goals of the researcher. As such, BIAs have developed an approach that attempts to satisfy their underlying philosophy through the less satisfactory route of theory → practice with aspirations that the missing link of relevant pragmatic research will soon follow. However, such current contributions are invaluable to an investigator, who is more concerned with intelligence and decision support than sample sizes and significance levels, and who, despite the prevailing view of many skeptics, can readily appreciate the difference between the two.

Investigative Approach

It should be highlighted that at present BIAs are engaged exclusively with the linking of offenses from an *intelligence* (rather than evidential) perspective. That is, in the absence of any physical evidence linking a number of crimes, a behavioral analysis is requested to support the investigative decision of whether two or more crimes have been committed by the same offender(s), referred to within this chapter as investigative CLA. It is made explicit within BIA reports that such opinions do not constitute expert evidence and should not be seen as the provision of a definitive answer to the questions of crime linkage that may exist. Rather the analysis should serve as a reference document that outlines the empirical and behavioral support (or otherwise) for two or more cases to be investigated as a linked series.

Successful crime linkage can assist the Police in several ways, from the efficient deployment of limited resources to increasing the amount of evidence against the offender(s) by combining information from different crime scenes and witnesses (Woodhams & Labuschagne, 2012). Additional pressure in the identification and investigation of serial sexual offenses in the United Kingdom has come from a recent report from Her Majesty's Inspectorate of Constabulary (HMIC) and Her Majesty's Inspectorate of the Crown Prosecution Service (HMICPS, 2012), which advocated both the improvement of the collection of intelligence, specifically with regard to serial rapists and the recommendation that investigators treat every stranger rape that is reported as part of a potential series. Given the cost of such a recommendation, in terms of both time and resources, the advantages of an evidence-based opinion to support crime linkage decision making are apparent.

As outlined above, in the absence of directly applicable research findings (or at least explicit operational tools) to guide this CLA process, the approach adopted by BIAs has been developed with reference to both pertinent theoretical and methodological considerations.

Theoretical Considerations

A review of the relevant research literature reveals that despite a variety of attempts to develop reliable and valid methodologies and systems (predominantly within the field of CCA), little attention appears to have been paid to the theoretical frameworks underpinning such endeavors. Where such theoretical considerations have been explicitly applied, it is within the field of personality theory where support for the concept of behavioral consistency, and hence the potential for crime linkage, is found.

Personality systems are believed to have an influence on the consistency of behaviors across offenses due to the activation of mental representations, goals, and expectations that are activated in response to situational triggers

(Mischel, Shoda, & Mendoza-Denton, 1992; see Chapter 2 for an in-depth discussion of personality systems and behavioral consistency/distinctiveness). During an offense, cognitive effects such as plans and strategies can be activated due to the interpretation of the situation by the offender. These behaviors are theorized to be relatively consistent throughout a series because the same plans and strategies are likely to be activated in situations similar to those previously encountered by the offender. Consistent behaviors can therefore emerge in a series of offenses, because the offender is reminded of the same behavioral strategy in any given (similar) situation.

Research has found that where there is a high degree of similarity between the current situation and a previous situation, a person (and theoretically offenders) may activate a common behavioral strategy that leads to consistent behaviors being produced (Meyer, 1990). Further support for this personality explanation of behavioral consistency is gained through suggestion that an offender will act out similar behaviors in similar situations simply because of the psychological meaning in each of the situations (Shoda, 1999) and that throughout a series an offender will be consistent in their behaviors because similar goals will trigger similar behavioral strategies (Greene, 1989). Therefore, behavioral consistency is considered to occur because an offender is more likely to produce the same behavior again if they know that the behavior has previously enabled them to fulfill their goal.

However, it should be highlighted that such research findings are restricted to more general population samples (i.e., law-abiding citizens), and as such, any generalization across offender samples remains less clear. Such stark recognition of the lack of a unified theory applicable to criminal behavioral consistency highlights the challenges faced by both researchers and those charged with making practical decisions in the field (i.e., practitioners).

Due to this relative sparseness of theoretical considerations of behavioral consistency within forensic settings, criticisms of such frameworks are virtually absent. However, reference to the analogous approach evident in much *offender profiling* (the conceptual and definitional precursor to behavioral investigative advice) activity is worthy of note, not least as the concept of offender consistency represents a major assumption supporting many of the original profiling methods and philosophies (Alison, Bennell, Mokros, & Ormerod, 2002).

Researchers posited that the assumptions underlying early profiling methods are similar to assumptions inherent in naïve trait theories of personality (Alison, 2005). In the naïve trait view, primary traits are seen as stable and general in that they determine a person's inclination to act consistently in a particular way across a variety of situations. As the notion of behavioral dispositions implies, traits are not directly observable but are inferred from behavior (Mischel, 1999). Traditional trait-based profiling tends to attribute behaviors to underlying, relatively context-free dispositional constructs.

Thus, both traditional trait-based profiling methods and traditional trait theories try to make general predictions about offenders; both make assumptions that all offenders are subject to the same set of processes that affect their behavior in predictable ways; and both assume behavior to be consistent in the face of environmental influences.

Although such concerns are justifiable in questioning the validity of inference generation *across different* offenders, such potential objections cannot be directed toward the personality approach to explaining consistency *within individual* offenders' behavior. The only exception to this would be the assumption of consistency across situational diversity. However, such an assumption has gained support within the personality research with findings that behaviors exhibited by individuals are consistent across situations, reflecting the individual's characteristics (Furr & Funder, 2003). Further discussion regarding how situational similarity could be construed for crime linkage purposes has provided further reassurances that such a theoretical standpoint may prove valid within the forensic arena (Woodhams, Hollin, & Bull, 2008).

Additionally, the validity of personality theory as an underlying theoretical approach to behavioral consistency relies upon the situations, or in this case the offenses having psychological meaning to the offender (Woodhams, Hollin, & Bull, 2007). The goal is not to predict the level of consistency in other offenses, but rather to support the assertion that if an identified series of offenses shows behavioral consistency, it can be presumed that the offender had a meaningful association with the crimes, which is consistent with the nature of the task in real-world behavioral crime linkage.

As such, although personality theory cannot definitively support or predict any prescribed level of consistency, it does provide an explanatory framework for the levels of consistency observed within the actions and offenses of individuals and suggests that theoretically at least, operational efforts at CLA represent a valid endeavor.

Methodological Considerations

There are differing schools of thought regarding both which behaviors should be analyzed and the specific method by which such analysis should be undertaken.

With regard to the specific behaviors of interest, researchers have debated whether *modus operandi* (MO) behaviors should be examined (Davies, 1992; Hazelwood & Warren, 2003). It has been argued that MO behaviors should not be considered when analyzing the behaviors of a suspected series because these can change from one offense to another due to situational factors altering the behaviors of the offender. As well as this, MO is subject to change throughout a series because of the new behaviors that an offender may learn from one offense to another (Davies, 1992). This view is supported with the argument that behavioral consistency between offenses in a suspected series should not rely too heavily on the MO, but instead should focus more closely on fantasy and ritual-based behaviors (Douglas & Munn, 1992).

Other researchers point out that the behavioral similarities and differences between one crime and another are not the only variables that need to be identified (Grubin, Kelly, & Brunsdon, 2001). When considering the similarities between crimes, consideration should also be given to whether these have occurred by simple coincidence. To achieve this, the similarities should be weighed against the frequency with which each similar behavior occurs in general across relevant populations of offenses (i.e., individual behaviors that occur frequently across the crime type may be expected to co-occur within a series simply by chance).

Other factors that have been identified as important considerations from a methodological perspective are the potential for development and change within the offender's behavior (Davies, 1992), the need to consider the antecedents for each behavior to better understand the context (Grubin et al., 2001), the timeframe across which the offenses are spread, and the distinctiveness of one offender's behavioral consistency to distinguish them from the actions of others (Woodhams et al., 2007).

In parallel to the earlier discussion focused on theoretical issues, most of the methodological considerations raised in the research literature are directed toward the problem of trying to identify potentially linked offenses from within a large dataset of other, unrelated offenses (i.e., false positives). Within the field of CLA (as opposed to CCA), however, such methodological considerations may be argued to have lesser impact. Although the issues of offender development, contextual and situational factors, MO behaviors, and the timeframe all provide explanations for why offender behavior may not be demonstrably consistent, where explicit behavioral consistency is found, such concerns are somewhat redundant.

As such, it may be argued that for the purposes of CLA, the two methodological considerations of greatest relevance are the need to address the areas of distinctiveness and coincidence, to demonstrate

- The offender is consistent in an individual way that is not similar to the consistent behaviors used by other offenders (distinctiveness).
- The offender is consistent in a way that has not occurred through chance (coincidence).

Practice

As outlined above, CLA is currently performed by BIAs who are tasked to provide an opinion regarding whether a prescribed set of offenses are likely to have been committed by the same offender(s). These offenses have been preselected by investigators who have reason to believe they may be linked to a common offender(s). The task is not to assign additional cases to the already identified previous offending of a known individual, but to consider a number of undetected cases which may or may not have a common offender(s).

It has been suggested by many that there are two distinct approaches to assessing crime linkage (e.g., Copson, 1995) and indeed to behavioral analysis of serious interpersonal crimes in general. These approaches are typically referred to as *clinical* and *statistical* approaches. In a purely statistical or empirical approach, offenses are broken down into variables by way of content analysis of relevant documentation, and these variables are compared against variables identified in other cases. In this way, it is proposed that cases that share significant numbers of behavioral variables are more likely to have been committed by the same offender than those that share little or none.

Furthermore, within this approach the analyst is usually able to determine exactly how rare or common particular combinations of behaviors are in offenses as a whole, provided that a relevant comparative database is available and suitable for this purpose. The limitations of a purely statistical approach are that by reducing each offense to a list of behavioral variables, it is not always possible to gain a complete understanding of the behavior exhibited in the offense, the way in which the offense has taken place, the interaction between the offender and the victim, potential motivations of the offender, contextual and situational factors, and so on. Put simply, the "behavioral richness" of offenses may not translate particularly well into simple data.

In the *clinical* approach, greater emphasis is placed on the consideration of every individual behavioral detail exhibited by the offender in the commission of his offending and the picture that emerges when these features are considered as a whole. The clinical approach therefore elicits a more complete understanding of what purpose the offense may be serving for the offender as well as allowing for more consideration to be given to any behavioral discrepancies between one offense and the next.

The limitations of the purely clinical approach, however, are that base rate frequencies of particular behaviors are often not considered and comparative datasets are often absent, incomplete, or simply drawn exclusively from the experiences of the practitioner. Therefore, predictions of what is and is not important for the purposes of behavioral linking have little or no scientific or empirical foundation.

However, the misconception that often prevails is that the two approaches outlined above are incompatible and indeed, mutually exclusive. This is not true. It is more sensible to think of the two approaches as complementary rather than conflicting. In truth, the *clinical* approach is greatly enhanced by drawing upon relevant empirical databases in the same way that the statistical approach is enriched through adopting a more clinical mind set in parallel with the empirical foundations.

Therefore, the methodology currently employed by BIAs draws heavily on both models outlined above. An objective, empirical foundation to the analysis is provided by utilizing relevant databases as a way of establishing the rarity or otherwise of salient behaviors and combinations of behavior seen in the offenses. A more subtle and thorough behavioral interpretation of the offenses drawing upon the BIA's own experiences of offender actions is also undertaken, allowing for a richer psychological understanding of the offense dynamic and the identification of the issues central to crime linkage.

Two separate strands of empirical analysis are carried out on cases submitted for analysis. It should be noted that at this stage, all analyses focus on the behavioral characteristics of the offenses, with no consideration given to the geographical locations, availability of suspects, and so on.

The first strand of analysis employed is a thematic analysis (since identified in the literature as *dimensional behavioral linking*; Winter et al., 2013). Research into the behavioral structure of sexual offenses within the Behavioral Science Section of Surrey Police led to the development of a model describing different styles of offense (see Canter & Heritage, 1990 as an illustrative example of this approach). Each of these styles is defined by a subset of behaviors that share the same underlying interpretation. For example, gagging the victim, threats of using a weapon, and being forensically aware are interpreted as *criminal* behaviors. Similarly, kissing, complimenting, and extending time with the victim are interpreted as *intimate*, with acts of violence, tearing of clothing, and demeaning behavior falling within an *aggressive* style.*

When considering an offender's behavior within an offense, it is often useful to examine the "style" of the offense from this broader thematic perspective, rather than expecting an offender to exactly replicate individual behaviors from the first offense to the last. Internal, unpublished research has demonstrated that although differences exist between the exact behaviors exhibited by offenders across a series of crimes, broader classifications of offending style remain highly consistent. By analyzing the relative contribution of each identified style within an offense, those crimes sharing a similar thematic distribution can be distinguished.

The second strand of analysis undertaken is the exact match searching of the individual behaviors present in the cases submitted for analysis (since identified in the literature as *multivariate behavioral linkage*; Winter et al., 2013). Relevant comparative databases are examined to identify how common these behaviors are, both individually and in combination, to assess their validity in linking the crimes.

* The listed behaviors are examples of those within each theme, not the exhaustive total.

By way of an illustrative example, the following is an anonymized extract from a real-life case report prepared almost a decade ago. The example has been deliberately chosen to represent a prototype, which highlights both the general approach and also provides insight into the type, quality, and quantity of behavioral information available in real-world scenarios. It serves to emphasize the gap that continues to exist between methodological ideologies and research findings and the realities faced in the real world. Perhaps, the best example of this is the fact that despite the practitioner's commitment to thematic analysis as a valid and useful tool in the linkage process, the circumstances of the case prevented such an approach.

By way of context, the report relates to five cases of sexual assault (A, B, C, D, and E) which had been reported in a 9-week period. The assaults were within relatively close proximity to a main road in a major UK city. Two of the victims (A and C) had been subject to digital penetration with a third (D) having her breasts and vagina groped and squeezed. One victim (E) suffered fondling to the breasts before the offender was disturbed and chased away by witnesses. The final victim (B) reported only that an unknown male approached her from behind and tried to pull her top down.

Report Extract Example

> It is important to highlight that the offence committed against B is not amenable to such analysis, due to the complete lack of behavioural detail in the absence of a victim account. As such, the offence committed against B will be excluded from behavioural analysis.
>
> Analysis of the remaining four offences under consideration is limited by the lack of overt behaviours recorded as having taken place during the offences. It should be noted however, that this low frequency of behaviour is not necessarily the result of lack of sexual activity (which is actually relatively high given that these offences represent indecent assaults) as might be expected. Investigation of the BADMAN database* reveals that the low levels of offender activity exhibited in these offences are found in approximately the same proportion of rapes where sexual acts were completed, as in attempted rapes and indecent assaults.

* The Behavioral Science section of Surrey Police developed a database (BADMAN) holding detailed information of sexual offences. Although this was a national database, it did not collect every sexual offence since its inception in 1995, and as such, it represents a sample of all sexual offences (dating as far back as 1973). It currently holds more than 900 cases. It should, however, be noted that more contemporary analyses into sexual or homicide offences would almost certainly be supported by reference to the Violent Crime Linkage Analysis System (ViCLAS) database, not BADMAN. ViCLAS is a national database maintained by the Serious Crime Analysis Section (SCAS) of the National Crime Agency (NCA). It holds detailed information on every rape, murder, and abduction (including attempts) committed within the United Kingdom since January 1, 1998 (providing notification has been received).

Given this low level of exhibited behaviours, the classification (thematic) analysis fails to reveal significant results. In fact, only the assault committed against C contains any recordable behaviour which contributes towards a thematic classification; that of a blitz attack* indicative of an "aggressive" theme. However, even this coding may be somewhat controversial, as the lack of a victim statement prevents greater interpretation of the precise circumstances surrounding the offender's initial encounter with the victim. The force used in the "rugby tackle" utilised to gain control over C may actually have been insufficient to incapacitate her, and as such may be more accurately coded as a "surprise"† attack.

Whilst the thematic classification analysis does not lend strong support to the potential of crime linkage, it must also be highlighted that this does not infer that support has been found against such linkage. Due to the lack of (thematically) significant behaviours being reported during these cases, the analysis regarding possible linkage from a thematic perspective is inconclusive.

A more detailed examination of some of the behaviours that are shared across a number of the offences may provide support for possible inclusions or exclusions from a potential series. The table below illustrates those behaviours that are present in each of the offences under consideration.

Reference to the below table reveals that the behaviour of assault site in open air is shared across all four offences. However sexual offences occur

Summary of Behaviors Reported in the Four Cases under Consideration

	A	C	D	E
Assault site in open air	√	√	√	√
Surprise attack	√		√	√
Blitz attack		√		
Offender sexual comment	√			
Digital penetration	√	√		
Fondled breasts/genitalia/buttocks	√	√	√	√
No speech		√	√	√

* A "Blitz" attack can be defined as the sudden and immediate use of violence, whether preceded by a confidence approach or not, which incapacitates the victim. Typically, this is the sudden blow that leaves the victim incapable to respond or react to the attack. The variable focuses on the extreme violence of the initial assault that leaves the victim incapable of reaction (Canter & Heritage, 1990).

† A "Surprise" attack can be defined as the immediate attack on the victim, whether preceded by a confidence approach or not, where force is used to obtain control of the victim. Force in respect of this variable includes threat with or without a weapon. Violence is used to gain physical control of the victim, that is, exercised against the victim in order to render her available to the offender but not the actions covered by blitz attack (Canter & Heritage, 1990).

outdoors in almost 70% of sexual offences and as such represents an invalid premise on which to base any crime linkage.*

With regard to the method of approach, it can be seen that this is inconsistent across the cases, varying between a "surprise" attack and a "blitz" attack. Analysis of the BADMAN database reveals that whilst the use of a surprise attack is extremely common, accounting for over 80% of sexual offences, the employment of the more aggressive "blitz" attack is relatively rare, accounting for less than 6% of all cases held on the database. As such, no decision support with regard to linkage can be made from the repeated presence of a surprise approach, although of potentially greater interest was analysis into the consistency with which serial offenders utilized one form of approach or attack. The results revealed that out of 86 serial offenders, all but 15 were consistent in their method of approach across their entire series. That is, 83% of recorded serial sexual offenders do not vary their attack style across their known linked offences, which may promote concerns regarding the likelihood of the variation seen in the cases under consideration being attributed to one individual.

However, the consistency analysis also revealed that only one offender across the entire database consistently used a blitz attack in all his offences. That is, whilst the use of a surprise attack is highly consistent, in those few cases where an offender does employ at least one blitz attack, further surprise attacks are also present within his series. Additionally, of those offenders who did employ the blitz attack in any of their offences, one third repeated such an attack style in further offences.

As such, it may be concluded that the style of initial attack cannot be relied upon in isolation for linkage analysis, due to both the frequency of surprise attack and the varying levels of consistency found within differing attack styles. It is emphasized that this does not infer that the cases are not linked, rather that the method of attack is not sufficiently discriminatory to support crime linkage. These considerations must also be viewed in tandem with earlier discussion concerning whether C was indeed the victim of a blitz attack at all, or whether greater knowledge surrounding the offence would result in the offender actions being viewed as the more common surprise approach.

The presence of fondling the victim's breasts, vagina or buttocks is common across all four offences under consideration and may thus appear to offer significant support with respect to crime linkage. Examination of a relevant national dataset however reveals that such activity is present in over 43% of all recorded cases. That is, one would expect to find such behaviour in almost every second offence of a sexual nature, which questions its discriminatory power in linkage determination. Similarly, as with previously stated concerns regarding interpretation, the exact nature of the fondling in the offence against A is difficult to determine. Whilst victim A describes the offender "messing around" once he had his hands under her knickers, there is

* For the purposes of this example, all base-rate frequencies are illustrative and should not be misinterpreted as true frequencies from any UK crime database.

no definitive statement regarding any deliberate fondling. This messing about may have been purely a reflection of trying to facilitate the intended digital penetration that followed.

Analysis of the other offences reveals that the focus of the fondling appears to be the victim's breasts, with only D also experiencing fondling of the genital region. As such, it may be the very absence of fondling, particularly with attention to the victim's breasts that distinguishes the A offence from the others. Whilst this may seem contrary to the statistical findings regarding the frequency of such behaviour, it may be viewed as significant that such lower level sexual activity is seen in offences following a more serious, concerted and successful act of digital penetration where such ancillary activity is absent.

It is however acknowledged that digital penetration took place in the offence against C and that the offences against D and E were interrupted by witnesses. However, again closer analysis reveals that whilst these two offences were interrupted, the offender would have almost certainly been aware of these witnesses prior to the assault and hence it may be inferred that he didn't intend to progress the sexual activity past such "low level" groping.

As discussed above, it is unrealistic to expect an offender to behave exactly the same across a series of offences however the purpose of such a detailed analysis is to demonstrate that in the current cases under consideration, these differences may be viewed as significant departures, which are only heightened when one considers the temporal sequence of the offences.

Finally, consideration should be given to the verbal behaviour exhibited by the offender. In three of the offences (C, D, and E) the offender did not speak throughout the assault. This lack of verbal behaviour is relatively rare, accounting for approximately 8% of recorded cases, and hence bolsters the similarity of these cases due to its discriminatory power. However, linkage analysis is best viewed from the perspective of behaviour presence, rather than behaviour absence and as such this feature alone should not attract undue weight in linkage considerations. Perhaps more significantly, is the presence of speech in the offence committed against A as support for this case not being part of any identified series.

The language exhibited against A can be characterised as demeaning and humiliating. Whilst the very nature of the other offences may be viewed in similar terms, with the exception of the offence committed against C where the offender laughs throughout the assault and in particular in response to victim (verbal) resistance, such themes are absent from the other offences. Such a use of language as expressed against A is likely to represent either a conscious or perhaps unconscious "script" for the offender, which could be inferred to be expected in any future offences. Its absence from the remaining cases under consideration then seriously questions the potential of the same individual being responsible.

The analyses conducted have attempted to demonstrate the significance of discriminatory behaviours when assessing behavioural similarity, to provide more evidence based support for potential linkage, and to guard against the danger in linking a series by picking individual commonalities between two offences and extending the process in this single variable manner until all the cases have been included. Similarly, attention has been paid to the realistic levels of consistency expected within an individual's series of offences, with resulting appropriate analyses and interpretations.

Due to the lack of sufficiently discriminatory offender behaviour reported by the victims, any definitive linkage opinion is difficult to support with conviction. However, whilst the reliability and validity of identified similarities may be questioned in support of linkage, the differences evident between the offence committed against A and the remaining offences are sufficient to recommend that it is unlikely that this offense was committed by the same individual responsible for any of the other offences.

The sightings provided by witnesses have been analysed from an eye-witness perspective in addition to the behavioural analysis. Whilst the majority of the features of offender description were within the expected range to account for normal processing and retrieval errors, there was insufficient discriminatory power in any of the variables for valid linkage support. Attention is however drawn to the inconsistencies in height and particularly age and the potential implications for assessing potential inclusions / exclusions into an inferred series with particular respect to C, A, and E.

From a more detailed behavioural analysis of the cases, again insufficient discriminatory behaviour was present to support valid linkage. Attention is however drawn to the potentially significant dissimilarities present in the offence committed against A to support its inclusion within any of the other offences as part of a potential series.

As a result of the above analyses, three tiers of linkage are recommended, with confidence in correct inclusion within a series decreasing with each tier. It must be highlighted that these confidence intervals are relative, and as such no cases have been excluded as definitely not being committed by the same individual.

As such, it is recommended that sufficient similarity (and lack of significant dissimilarity) exists between the offences committed against D and E for them to be considered as a potential series. Given the geographical and temporal proximity, there are stronger arguments to suggest that these two offences are the actions of one individual than different offenders. However, caution may be exercised when attempting to include the offence committed against C into this inferred series. Whilst many reasons could be forwarded to account for the demonstrated variance in behaviour (and description), from a purely objective behavioural perspective it is harder to argue conclusively that this offence is part of the inferred series outlined above.

Further caution is recommended when assessing the potential linkage of A into any inferred series. There is insufficient behavioural evidence to support such linkage, and from a purely behavioural standpoint the balance of probabilities would suggest its exclusion. However, it is acknowledged that given the geographic and temporal proximity, it is prudent not to discard this offence completely, rather to assign it lesser priority than the other offences highlighted above.

Finally, no opinion is possible with respect to the offence committed against B and as such no priority has been assigned to its potential inclusion or otherwise into any possible series.

The results of the linkage analysis can be summarised as three tiers of priority with respect to individual cases forming part of any potential series as follows:

Priority Linkage ONE

- D
- E

Priority linkage TWO

- C

Priority Linkage THREE

- A

Further Considerations

In addition to the above considerations regarding the current investigative CLA approach, a number of further issues are worthy of consideration. Before the inception of a nationally funded cadre of BIAs in the United Kingdom, such investigative CLA was often provided by the Behavioural Science Section of Surrey Police (which can be viewed as the predecessor to the current setup due to its employment of Association of Chief Police Officers Approved BIAs*), supported by statistics from the BADMAN database (as referred to above). It is interesting to note that despite this unit providing such services almost 15 years ago, additional statistical tools were available to assist in investigative CLA, which are no longer accessible to BIAs. The use of Jaccard's coefficients to generate a measure of behavioral similarity between crimes represented a routine aspect of the then investigative CLA approach (for an understanding of the use of Jaccard's coefficients in crime linkage see Woodhams & Labuschagne, 2012; also see Chapter 14). It is highly recommended that such an additional tool is reintroduced across the current contemporary datasets to support investigative CLA at the earliest opportunity.

Of perhaps greatest pertinence with respect to investigative CLA is recognition of the overriding objective and corresponding acceptable decision thresholds. The aim is not to prove beyond reasonable doubt that two or more crimes have been committed by the same offender(s), but rather to support

* In the United Kingdom, all provision of behavioral investigative advice is governed and regulated by the Association of Chief Police Officers and only those who hold formal approval from this governing body are authorized to provide such advice to UK investigators.

investigators in making pragmatic decisions regarding the likelihood of such scenarios. One must remember that the BIA has been approached with a set of cases precisely because the investigator has identified some similarity between them. It is the BIA's job to evaluate these perceived similarities, with reference to relevant psychological decision-making processes (for a comprehensive review of the role of the BIA with respect to investigative biases and heuristics, see Rainbow, Almond, & Alison, 2011), access to relevant base-rates, methodological rigor, and a greater understanding of the consistency and variability of offenders when committing a series of offenses. It is argued that this is likely to be sufficient for investigative CLA, but it is acknowledged that such practice falls fatally short as an evidential standard.

Evidential Approach

As already emphasized, the role of the BIA at present is focused exclusively within the investigative domain, and to date, no UK BIA has ever presented such CLA in a court of law. This is not a failing of BIAs, but rather recognition that current *investigative* practice is insufficiently relevant, unreliable, prejudicial, and unscientific for presentation at court, and attempts to do so would undermine the professionalism and integrity of the discipline.

Within the United Kingdom, although CCA is usually performed by crime analysts, and CLA by BIAs, the provision of *expert evidence* in linkage considerations falls back within the remit of crime analysts. The focus of such evidential contributions has been the presentation of statistics derived from large, relevant comparative databases to highlight the frequencies of the behaviors common across the inferred series. However, before discussing both current and proposed future approaches to evidential CLA, it is first necessary to provide an overview of the legal context against which such considerations must be viewed.

Legal Context

Although it is beyond the scope of this chapter to consider the legal technicalities of criminal justice in detail, it is perhaps pertinent to highlight the lack of specific UK laws of evidence regarding *similar fact* directly relevant to crime linkage. Sections 98–113 Criminal Justice Act 2003, which applies to all criminal proceedings begun on or after April 4, 2005, sets out the admissibility of *bad character* evidence, which is often confused with *similar fact* evidence. *Bad character* in criminal proceedings means "evidence of or a disposition toward misconduct" (Section 99 Criminal Justice Act 2003) and applies to conduct arising out of conviction, or conduct where there has been an acquittal and a person who has been charged with another offense, and a trial is pending (Crown Prosecution Service, 2012).

As such, in the absence of any specific legislative guidance relating to behavioral crime linkage, any attempt to support evidential CLA will be subject to the more general principles of admissibility of expert evidence, to establish how similar the offenses were and how peculiar they were. In some jurisdictions, a behavioral expert has testified to these issues, with respect to both consistency and distinctiveness (e.g., Labuschagne, 2006; *State v. Pennell,* 1991; *State v. Code,* 1999, cited by Ormerod & Sturman, 2005).

Where the jurors are asked to consider the likelihood that the offenses were all committed by the same person, an expert (e.g., BIA or analyst) might be in a position to shed light on that likelihood and assist the jury in their decision making regarding linkage. It is for the court to decide whether there is sufficient foundation for such expertise and is ultimately the judge's decision as to whether it passes the usual evidential standards for admissibility (see Ormerod & Sturman, 2005 for an informative review of the use of *behavioral* evidence in court; also see Chapters 9 and 10).

Current Practice

As it is not certain whether such evidence would be admissible within a UK court, the approach currently taken is the presentation of offense feature frequency statistics. This serves to contextualize the relative rarity of the behaviors shared across the potential series, particularly when viewed in combination, and is intended to assist the jury who are unlikely to possess such knowledge. As such, if behaviors A, B, and C are shared across two crimes, the court may be furnished with the frequency with which these behaviors are found across relevant comparable datasets, both individually (i.e., behavior A or B or C), and/or in combination (i.e., behaviors A and B and C).

Although it highlighted that such presentation explicitly avoids any conclusions regarding linkage per se, it may be argued that such testimony is at least an implicit indicator of distinctiveness or could be interpreted as such by the jury. Indeed, such issues may be conceptually linked to the jury observation fallacy (Fenton & Neil, 2000), where there is a basic misunderstanding about the belief in probability of guilt when a prior similar conviction by a defendant is revealed.

As such, although such a statistically based approach may be viewed as favorable to the reliance on individual experts' experience, which is quoted by international colleagues (Labuschagne, 2006; *State v. Pennell,* 1991; *State v. Code,* 1999, cited by Ormerod & Sturman, 2005), there remain significant weaknesses of this method, which are as follows:

- The offense features (i.e., behaviors) chosen are open to criticism for lacking transparency. The process of choosing the behaviors to be reported on appears at best subjective and may be subject to accusations of a prosecution bias. Although this may be deemed acceptable for investigative CLA (as outlined above, where the objective is to support investigative decision making), such cherry picking of the rarest behaviors lacks objective, methodological rigor. Basic statistical reasoning and previous experience suggest that virtually any two cases could be *linked* in this manner through such biased manipulation of the data.

- There is no attempt to quantify the similarity between the cases, for example, with a simple Jaccard's coefficient as outlined above.
- This method fails to account for any differences between the crimes under consideration, which may in fact be as significant as the identified similarities.
- Finally, and perhaps of greatest pertinence, with reference to the theoretical and methodological considerations highlighted above, is the exclusive focus on *distinctiveness*, with a lack of cognizance for the *coincidence* assumption.

If such contributions from the behavioral sciences are to be viewed as reliable, as well as relevant within court proceedings, it is proposed that an agreed analytical model needs to be developed that is capable of withstanding such judicial scrutiny.

Proposed Approach

The goal of supporting CLA conclusions from an empirical (rather than exclusively experiential or opinion) base requires an appropriate scientific and statistical framework for presenting and evaluating evidence of this kind. Although not universally accepted within the field of criminal evidence, one such method of evaluating probabilistic evidence is through *likelihood ratios* (LRs; see Fenton & Neil, 2011, for an informative overview). Such a framework addresses arguments that low joint frequencies of behaviors are not in themselves compelling evidence of similarity between cases and counters the fallacy of statistical reasoning often used in legal arguments (i.e., the prosecutor's fallacy, the defendant's fallacy, and the jury's fallacy; see Fenton & Neil, 2000).

In this context, an LR is not a measure of the likelihood that an individual has committed all the offenses under consideration, but rather a comparison of the probability of observing such behavioral consistency IF the offenses have been committed by the same person against the probability of observing such consistency IF they were committed by different individuals. It can therefore be seen to be a measure of the strength of evidence in favor of or against a hypothesis, not a statement of the probability of the hypothesis being true.

On the one hand, suppose you select a playing card at random from an ordinary pack of 52 cards. If you know nothing at all about the selected card, then the probability that it is a diamond is 1/4 (p = .25 or 25%). If on the other hand you see a flash of red as the card is drawn, then the probability that it is a diamond is 1/2 (p = .5 or 50%). The second probability is called a conditional probability; it is the probability that the card is a diamond GIVEN that it is a red card. The probability that the card is red given that it is a diamond is 1 (because all diamonds are red), which is NOT the same as the probability that the card is a diamond given that it is red. With respect to crime linkage, the probability of observing behavioral consistency if offenses have been committed by the same offender is NOT the same as the probability that they have been committed by the same person given the observed consistency.

When considering behavioral consistency as evidence for crime linkage, the strength of the evidence for a single offender can be formalized in the LR;

$$LR = \frac{\Pr\left[\text{behavioral consistency} \mid \text{common offender}\right]}{\Pr\left[\text{behavioral consistency} \mid \text{different offenders}\right]}$$

that is, a comparison of the probabilities of observing the evidence (behavioral consistency) under two hypotheses (common offender and different offenders). LR is defined as the ratio of two probabilities.

An LR of near 0 would represent a low strength of evidence in favor of a common offender and support the alternative hypothesis of different offenders. An LR of 1 would denote equal strength of evidence for both hypotheses (i.e., no preference). An LR larger than 1 would represent increasing strength of evidence in favor of a common offender and hence crime linkage. The impact of reframing current practice within this proposed framework can be demonstrated by way of an illustrative example.

Example

Let us suppose that the prosecution wish to convict an individual of two sexual offenses, but only has compelling forensic evidence incriminating the defendant in one of the cases. They wish to adduce CLA evidence to support the assertion that the defendant is indeed responsible for both offenses. Let us further suppose that an analyst has identified the shared behaviors across the offenses as weapon use, anal penetration, and apologetic language. Interrogation of a relevant comparative dataset reveals frequencies for these behaviors as 20%, 30%, and 5%, respectively. Further analytical activity reveals that the presence of these three behaviors in combination is rare, accounting for less than 0.01% of the entire database, and these statistics are presented to the court. Although such presentation may be intended to assist the jury in determining the potential distinctiveness of the offenses in question, they are subject to potential interpretation as compelling evidence for crime linkage.

If we now reconsider these results with additional consideration of the coincidence condition, the benefits of the LR framework are evident. Let us suppose that research endeavors have demonstrated that serial offenders demonstrate the following levels of consistency across the identified behaviors: weapon use 10%, anal penetration 90%, and apologetic language 5%. If we now calculate LRs for each individual behavior, the following results are obtained:

Weapon use: 0.1/0.2 = 0.5
Anal penetration: 0.9/0.3 = 3.0
Apologetic language: 0.05/0.05 = 1.0

It can thus be seen that even though apologetic behavior has a very low frequency across the relevant comparative database, its correspondingly low level of consistency in observed crime series' results in its presence having no effect on decisions regarding crime linkage—the evidence is neutral, in that it denotes equal strength of evidence for both a common and different offenders. Similarly, although anal penetration is actually one and a half times as common as weapon use across the relevant comparative dataset as a whole, its presence across these offenses provides greater strength of evidence for a common offender than weapon use, whose presence actually provides greater evidence for different offenders.

Given the assumption that weapon use, anal penetration, and apologetic language are all independent of one another, the overall or *composite* LR for these three behaviors in combination can be calculated by multiplying the respective LRs together. This would provide a composite LR in the above example of 1.5. This provides very marginal support for a common offender and crime linkage, although certainly well below the levels acceptable in court for related applications (e.g., DNA analysis, which is routinely reported as match probabilities in the millions). Comparison with the results obtained with current practice highlights the potential strengths and weaknesses of the respective methodological frameworks.

Further Considerations

It is readily acknowledged that the above provides a very simplistic presentation of a potential methodological approach to evidential CLA and that many further issues are in need of recognition, exploration, and integration if significant strides are to be achieved in this area.

First, the previously highlighted issue of cherry picking the variables to be analyzed must be addressed. It may be argued that the above methodology ultimately falls foul of previous criticisms regarding the subjective nature of the variables included within any analysis. However, consideration should be given to the mandatory inclusion of *all* variables available to the analyst. Comprehensive datasets exist within many policing jurisdictions (e.g., ViCLAS), which provide an objective and standardized list of variables across all collected comparable offenses. Although it is acknowledged that more detailed methodological issues will need to be addressed (such as mutual exclusivity and colinearity), it is proposed to adopt a top-down approach starting with all available data, rather than the traditional bottom-up approach of specifically selected variables. It is envisaged that such an approach would also allow for appropriate consideration of *absences* of behaviors, in addition to the current exclusive focus on presence.

Similarly, the proposed approach may remove the much debated issues surrounding predetermined thresholds of behavior frequency to be incorporated into any analytical model; that is, the choice of behaviors based solely on their underlying frequency across a relevant dataset. For example, only using behaviors exhibiting less than a maximum frequency and/or behaviors exhibiting more than a minimum frequency (e.g., see Grubin et al., 2001; Santtila, Fritzon, & Tamelander, 2004; Santtila, Junkkila, & Sandnabba, 2005). Although admittedly simplistic, it is hoped that such thresholds will be decided by statistical and/or admissibility principles or ultimately have no bearing other than on the final LR score, which is then within the realms of courts to judge regarding its significance.

However, one significant concern regarding the proposed approach is the removal of the expertise of the BIA/analyst. Although this may ultimately be viewed as desirable, practitioners may experience a degree of skepticism and resistance that such a data reductionist approach represents best practice. This remains to be seen, and indeed empirically tested, and may have further important implications for current investigative CLA practice, where at present a far greater qualitative contribution is evident.

Research Agenda

Although it is hoped the above reflects practitioners' aspirational goals to achieve the highest levels of methodological and scientific rigor in the field of crime linkage, it is imperative to note that on the whole they possess neither the methodological and statistical expertise nor the resources (particularly with respect to time) to achieve the intended outcomes of quality research. As such, the following pertinent issues and research areas have been summarized to make explicit the areas in which practitioners believe significant advancement could be made through constructive collaboration with their research colleagues. The issues and themes have been kept deliberately broad to encourage as broad and diverse a research agenda as possible, recognizing the potential across different disciplines, methodologies, approaches, and outcomes.

- Acknowledgment of the distinct practitioner activities of CCA and CLA
- The interpretation of *low joint co-occurrence* by lay persons/jurors on crime linkage decision making
- The development of a *likelihood ratio* approach to CLA
- The development of *consistency* measures across crime series
- The development of *distinctiveness* measures across crime series
- The development of *coincidence* measures across crime series
- Exploration of the effect of MO or more *ritualistic* behaviors on these measures and overall methodology
- The development of *intelligence CLA* (as opposed to CCA)
- The development of *evidential CLA*

Conclusions

As stated at the beginning of this chapter, the overriding aim of the chapter was to illuminate the challenges faced by contemporary practitioners within the field of crime linkage and make explicit the gaps in knowledge and evidence-based practice. Through consideration of current practice, a number of issues have been raised and discussed and a potential methodology proposed which, from a practitioner perspective at least, is believed to hold potential for future advancement within the field. It is sincerely hoped that if nothing else, this chapter will encourage debate and constructive collaboration between researchers, behavioral scientists, statisticians, and legal professionals to develop empirically based analytical tools capable of supporting both the investigative and evidential requirements within serious crime resolution.

Although significant research strides have been made within more *investigative* processes, and in particular in enhancing methods to find potential linked offenses within large crime databases, the need to set parallel agendas with respect to more reactive crime linkage and expert evidence should be recognized, and as practitioners we look forward to your call.

References

Alison, L. J. (2005). From trait-based profiling to psychological contributions to apprehension methods. In L. J. Alison (Ed.), *The forensic psychologist's casebook* (pp. 3–22). Devon, England: Willan Publishing.

Alison, L. J., Bennell, C., Mokros, A., & Ormerod, D. (2002). The personality paradox in offender profiling: A theoretical review of the processes involved in deriving background characteristics from crime scene actions. *Psychology, Public Policy, and Law, 8*, 115–135.

Bennell, C., & Canter, D. V. (2002). Linking commercial burglaries by *modus operandi*: Tests using regression and ROC analysis. *Science & Justice, 42*, 1–12.

Canter, D. V., & Heritage, R. (1990). A multivariate model of sexual offence behaviour: Developments in "offender profiling." *The Journal of Forensic Psychiatry, 1*, 185–212.

Copson, G. (1995). *PRG Special Interest Series: Coals to Newcastle? Part 1—A study of offender profiling (Paper 7)*. London, England: Home Office.

Criminal Justice Act 2003. London, England: The Stationary Office.

Crown Prosecution Service. (2012). *Bad character evidence*. Retrieved from http://www.cps.gov.uk/legal/a_to_c/bad_character_evidence

Davies, A. (1992). Rapists' behaviour: A three aspect model as a basis for analysis and identification of serial crime. *Forensic Science International, 55*, 173–194.

Douglas, J. E., & Munn, C. (1992). Violent crime scene analysis: Modus operandi, signature and staging. *FBI Law Enforcement Bulletin, 61*, 1–10.

Fenton, N. E., & Neil, M. (2000). The "jury observation fallacy" and the use of Bayesian networks to present probabilistic legal arguments. *Mathematics Today, 36*, 180–187.

Fenton, N. E., & Neil, M. (2011). Avoiding legal fallacies in practice using Bayesian networks. *Australian Journal of Legal Philosophy, 36*, 114–151.

Furr, R. M., & Funder, D. C. (2003). Situational similarity and behavioural consistency: Subjective, objective, variable-centred and person-centred approaches. *Journal of Research in Personality, 38*, 421–447.

Greene, J. O. (1989). The stability of nonverbal behaviour: An action-production approach to problems of cross-situational consistency and discriminativeness. *Journal of Language and Social Psychology, 8*, 193–220.

Grubin, D., Kelly, P., & Brunsdon, C. (2001). *Linking serious sexual assaults through behaviour*. London, England: Home Office.

Hazelwood, R. R., & Warren, J. I. (2003). Linkage analysis: Modus operandi, ritual and signature in serial sexual crime. *Aggression and Violent Behavior, 8*, 587–598.

Her Majesty's Inspectorate of Constabulary (HMIC) & Her Majesty's Inspectorate of the Crown Prosecution Service (HMICPS). (2012). *Forging the links: Rape investigation and prosecution*. Retrieved from http://www.hmic.gov.uk/media/forging-the-links-rape-investigation-and-prosecution-20120228.pdf

Labuschagne, G. (2006). The use of linkage analysis as evidence in the conviction of the Newcastle serial murderer, South Africa. *Journal of Investigative Psychology and Offender Profiling, 3*, 183–191.

Meyer, J. R. (1990). Cognitive processes underlying the retrieval of compliance-gaining strategies: An implicit rules model. In J. P. Dillard (Ed.), *Seeking compliance: The production of interpersonal influence messages* (pp. 57–74). Scottsdale, AZ: Gorsuch Scarisbrick.

Mischel, W. (1999). Personality coherence and dispositions in a cognitive-affective personality system (CAPS) approach. In D. Cervone & Y. Shoda (Eds.), *Social-cognitive bases of consistency, variability and organisation* (pp. 37–60). New York, NY: The Guildford Press.

Mischel, W., Shoda, Y., & Mendoza-Denton, R. (1992). Situation-behaviour profiles as a locus of consistency in personality. *Current Directions in Psychological Science, 11,* 50–54.

Ormerod, D., & Sturman, J. (2005). Working with the courts: Advice for expert witnesses. In L. J. Alison (Ed.), *The forensic psychologist's casebook: Psychological profiling and criminal investigation* (pp. 170–193). Devon, England: Willan.

Rainbow, L., Almond, L., & Alison, L. J. (2011). BIA support to investigative decision making. In L. J. Alison & L. Rainbow (Eds.), *Professionalizing offender profiling: Forensic and investigative psychology in practice* (pp. 35–50). Oxon, England: Routledge.

Rainbow, L., & Gregory, A. (2011). What behavioural investigative advisers actually do. In L. J. Alison & L. Rainbow (Eds.), *Professionalizing offender profiling: Forensic and investigative psychology in practice* (pp. 18–34). Oxfordshire, England: Routledge.

Santtila, P., Fritzon, K., & Tamelander, A. L. (2004). Linking arson incidents on the basis of crime scene behavior. *Journal of Police and Criminal Psychology, 19,* 1–16.

Santtila, P., Junkkila, J., & Sandnabba, N. K. (2005). Behavioural linking of stranger rapes. *Journal of Investigative Psychology and Offender Profiling, 2,* 87–103.

Shoda, Y. (1999). A unified framework for the study of behavioural consistency: Bridging person x situation interaction and the consistency paradox. *European Journal of Personality, 13,* 361–387.

Winter, J., Lemeire, J., Megank, S., Geboers, J., Rossi, G., & Mokros, A. (2013). Comparing the predictive accuracy of case linkage methods in serious sexual assaults. *Journal of Investigative Psychology and Offender Profiling, 10,* 28–56.

Woodhams, J., & Grant, T. (2006). Developing a categorisation system for rapists' speech. *Psychology, Crime & Law, 12,* 245–260.

Woodhams, J., Hollin, C., & Bull, R. (2007). The psychology of linking crimes: A review of the evidence. *Legal and Criminological Psychology, 12,* 233–249.

Woodhams, J., Hollin, C., & Bull, R. (2008). Incorporating context in linking crimes: An exploratory study of situational similarity and if-then contingencies. *Journal of Investigative Psychology and Offender Profiling, 4,* 17–27.

Woodhams, J., & Labuschagne, G. (2012). A test of case linkage principles with solved and unsolved serial rapes. *Journal of Police and Criminal Psychology, 27,* 85–98.

The Use of Linkage Analysis Evidence in Serial Offense Trials

9

GÉRARD LABUSCHAGNE

Contents

Introduction 198
The Uses of Linkage Analysis: Linkage Analysis Evidence in Court Cases 199
What Does the Research Say? Is Linking Possible? 201
  Behavioral and Thematic Similarity 201
  Behavioral Change and Evolution 203
Legal Principles under Which Linkage Evidence Is Admissible 205
  Legal Standards 205
  The Role of the Expert Witness 206
  Similar Fact Evidence and Other Crimes Evidence 207
  Legal Guidelines for the Use of Similar Fact Evidence 210
Cautionary Issues When Linking 211
  Using Linkage Analysis in Cases Involving Co-Offenders 211
  Using Linkage Analysis for Purposes Other than Establishing Behavioral Linkages 211
  Relying on Computerized Linkage Systems Exclusively 212
  Examining Isolated Behaviors without Taking into Account Context 213
  Missing Instances of Behavioral Similarity upon Initial Assessment 213
  Paying Attention to Dissimilarities 214
Case Example 1: *State v. D* 215
Case Example 2: The Sunday Serial Rapist 216
  The State's Evidence 216
  Linkage Analysis 217
    Approach Method 217
    Approach Location 217
    Sexual Acts 218
    Pseudo-Relationship Acts 218
    Description of the Offender 218
    Attempts to Cover the Victim's Head 218

Souvenirs 218
Conclusion 219
Trial 220
Comments on the Case Study 221
Conclusion 222
References 222

Introduction

Since the existence of modern law enforcement, investigators have been faced with the dilemma of trying to determine which crimes might be the work of one offender. Modern forensic sciences have simplified that task with the advent of deoxyribonucleic acid (DNA), the use of *touch* DNA, fingerprinting, ballistics, forensic odontology, and the like. However, despite the impressive development of the forensic sciences, and probably due to the proliferation of television programs relating to the forensic sciences, offenders are believed to be leaving less and less forensic evidence at crime scenes (House of Commons, 2005). It is an ongoing challenge for forensic science to improve in its ability to detect, collect, and process forensic evidence.

Parallel to the development of forensic sciences, albeit only in the past few decades, has been the development of behavioral sciences in relation to criminal behavior. It has been within the sphere of the behavioral sciences that emphasis has been increasingly placed on the analysis of human behavior during crimes, and more specifically the use of an offender's behavior to link crimes together during an investigation and during a criminal trial. This chapter focuses on the use of linkage analysis as an aid to secure convictions during criminal legal proceedings.

A linkage analysis, sometimes referred to as comparative case analysis (Bennell & Canter, 2002; Merry, 2000), can be useful during the investigation phase of a crime where it can assist investigators in deciding which crimes to include and which to exclude from an investigation into a series, or how to focus their search for other similar crimes previously committed in the area or committed in neighboring areas. In addition, linkage analysis evidence is increasingly being presented as evidence in court to convince the presiding officer/jury that a single offender is responsible for the commission of a number of crimes when hard forensic evidence may be lacking in some of those crimes.

In this chapter, the uses of linkage analysis will be briefly discussed, followed by linkage analysis as used in courts throughout the world. A review of some of the research pertaining to linkage analysis will thereafter be presented. Following this is a discussion of the legal principles under which linkage analysis is admissible and consideration of some legal guidelines. Cautionary issues relating to linkage analyses will be presented and the chapter will end with two case examples illustrating how similarities in serial crime trials can be used to secure convictions. The first case example does not have an expert testifying about linkage analysis and the second example included an expert testifying about linkage analysis during the trial.

The Uses of Linkage Analysis: Linkage Analysis Evidence in Court Cases

Linkage analysis can have various uses depending on at what stage of the criminal justice system it is being used. In initial phases, it can be used as a stand-alone report aimed at helping investigators sift through cases to determine if a series exists and which past and new cases should be allocated to a task team mandated to investigate the series. This can be based on similarities across a number of crimes or even an escalation of crime scene behavior across a series of crimes. Although this could be a stand-alone report, it is often, in Republic of South Africa, the first section of a broader offender profile (Labuschagne, 2003).

Second, linkage analysis can be used at the trial phase during the presentation of the prosecution's case, with the intention to give an opinion that certain crimes are the work of one individual. This may be because in some of the cases before the court there are no eyewitnesses, nor forensic evidence, linking the accused to the other cases for which he or she is on trial, but the manner in which the crimes were committed is strikingly similar and unique. The corollary to that is its use to convince the court that a particular crime was not the work of an offender, as would be the case if the analysis were being presented by the accused person's legal representative.

Linkage analysis reports have been presented as similar fact evidence in courts in Republic of South Africa (see *State v. Mogale*, 2012: Westonaria Serial Murderer; *State v. Nyauza*, 2007: Quarry Serial Murderer; *State v. Steyn*, 2012: Sunday Serial Rapist; *State v. Sukude*, 2006: Newcastle Serial Murderer; and *State v. van Rooyen*, 2007: Knysna Serial Murderer). In all of these South African cases, the linkage analysis evidence was accepted and the accused was found guilty of all of the crimes for which he was charged. In one case (*State v. Stander*, 2008: Port Elizabeth Prostitute Serial Murderer), the linkage analysis was provided to the defense before the author's testimony. Near the end of the trial, this led (in part) to the accused deciding to make formal admissions to the court that he had indeed murdered the two victims for which he was charged, with the proviso that the linkage analysis not be presented to the court as evidence. In this example, the physical evidence linked the accused to one murder but nothing linked him forensically to the other crimes.

The advantage of evidence presented in South African courts is that, although there is an adversarial system similar to those found in the United

States and the United Kingdom, there is no jury. Juries were abolished in 1969. At the end of a trial, the presiding officer summarizes all the witnesses' evidence, and gives his or her opinion of that particular evidence, and often indicates how persuasive he or she found that evidence. The advantage lies in that one can clearly see what role the linkage evidence played in influencing the presiding officer and for which particular cases it was used to secure a conviction.

Linkage evidence has also been presented in courts in other parts of the world. For example, Keppel (2000) refers to at least five instances in the United States where a signature analysis was admitted in murder trials, and their appeals, as evidence that certain cases were linked. He further states that signature analysis is "the only crime scene assessment technique that is accepted in court testimony and appellate decisions" (Keppel, Weis, Brown, & Welch, 2005, p. 14). Keppel and Birnes (2009) list the following cases where evidence was presented regarding the similarities of cases:

- *State of California v. Bogard* (1996). Evidence was offered that the same person was responsible for a series of six rapes.
- *State of New Jersey v. Fortin* (2000, 2007). Evidence was presented regarding the similarities across a series of offenses. However, this conviction was overturned on appeal, partly due to linkage evidence presented by a Federal Bureau of Investigation (FBI) agent.
- *State of South Dakota v. Anderson* (1998). A review of the signature aspects of two murders was offered at a hearing to determine if they would be joined for prosecution.

They also list a number of murder cases where linkage testimony was admitted at trial and upheld under appellate scrutiny in the United States:

- *State of Louisiana v. Code* (1994)
- *State of Delaware v. Pennell* (1989)
- *State of California v. Prince* (1992)
- *State of Washington v. Russell* (1994)
- *State of Washington v. Parker* (2002)

A more in-depth search reveals that linkage evidence, in one form or another (usually as *similar fact evidence* in UK-based legal systems, or *other crimes evidence* in the United States), has been presented in courts throughout the world. These cases include the following:

Australia:

- *R. v. Sutton* (1984)
- *Q v. Rich* (1997)
- *R. v. Hakeem* (2006)

Canada:
- *R. v. Arp* (1998)
- *R. v. Kembo* (2010)

New Zealand:
- *R. v. Holtz* (2002)

United Kingdom:
- *R. v. Straffen* (1952)
- *R. v. Toothill* (1998)

Although the term *signature* is often attributed to the field of offender profiling, Risinger and Loop (2002) state that

> in traditional evidence theory, the emphasis has always been on characteristics of the two crimes that were so unusual as to raise a strong inference of common perpetration, whether Douglas would classify those characteristics in his scheme as belonging to "MO" or to "signature". Indeed the term "signature" has been commonly used to refer to such a detail or combination of details since it was first applied in this context by Charles T. McCormick in the first edition of his *Handbook on Evidence* in 1954, and there are literally hundreds of examples of the usage in case law prior to Douglas' arrival on the scene. (p. 262)

This emphasizes that what we refer to today as linkage analysis has been in practice in courtrooms for decades. These cases listed above therefore represent only a few of the many cases where such evidence has been used.

What Does the Research Say? Is Linking Possible?

Activities or techniques that fall within the realm of behavioral analysis, such as offender profiling, often lack a solid foundation in research to support the assumptions underlying the techniques. Linkage analysis, however, seems to have a slowly growing body of empirical support for its claims. One field that has proven to be an asset in studying this process is that of personality psychology (Woodhams, Hollin, & Bull, 2007; see Chapters 2, 6, and 13). For many years, this field of psychology has been studying the consistency of people's behavior in nonforensic settings (Mischel, 1999). Researchers in this field have discovered that people often have stable but distinctive ways of reacting to situations. Personality psychologists have also shown that situational factors have an impact on people's behavior and can cause them to change their behavior over time.

Behavioral and Thematic Similarity

Much of the focus in linkage analysis has been on similarities in behavior across different cases in a series. As Grubin, Kelly, and Brunsdon (2001) state, if behavior is to provide a means for linking offenses committed by one offender, it must be assumed that at least some behaviors remain consistent across the series of offenses or evolve in a predictable way. This raises the following two questions: How much behavioral similarity is necessary to link crimes? On what level must there be similarity, *micro* or *macro*? Bateman and Salfati (2007) refer to two different types of consistency that correspond to these questions. According to them, consistency can be searched for at the micro-level of individual offense behaviors, or at a macro-level, by examining consistency in behavioral themes (see Chapters 6, 7, and 14).

When consistency is searched for at the level of individual behaviors, unique signature behaviors are often focused on, or one can focus on aspects of the offender's *modus operandi* (MO). Criticisms of the signature approach include the fact that much of the literature on signatures is anecdotal (i.e., not based on empirical studies). More empirical research has examined MO behaviors (e.g., see Chapters 6 and 14), but this research too is often criticized. Criticisms leveled against MO-based approaches to crime linkage focus on the fact that an offender's MO is known to change across their series. This could be because MO behaviors are often situationally dependent (Bennell & Canter, 2002), especially in contact crimes where the victim and offender interact (Salfati & Bateman, 2005), or because serial offenders learn from previous experiences (Grubin et al., 2001).

Using the thematic approach, investigators examine *pools* or groups of offender behaviors that all relate to the same psychological meaning (Bateman & Salfati, 2007). In this case, the same individual behaviors do not need to be exhibited across crimes for there to be evidence of consistency; the offender simply has to exhibit behaviors belonging to the same themes. For example, Grubin et al. (2001) examined consistency in serial sexual offenses. Using cluster analysis, he and his colleagues developed four offense domains of behaviors relating to (1) methods employed by the offender to control his victim, (2) sexual aspects of the offenses, (3) escape mechanisms used by the offender to avoid detection, and (4) the offender's offense style. Grubin et al. found that the control and escape domains proved to be more useful for linking purposes due to their consistency. Offenders did not necessarily exhibit the exact same control and escape behaviors across their crime series, but they did show relatively high levels of consistency at the thematic level. The advantage of this approach is that, even when situational factors prevent offenders from behaving in the same way across their crimes, it is still possible for them to behave in a consistent fashion. The following example illustrates the concept of thematic consistency.

A South African offender who eventually murdered an interior decorator (*State v. Da Silva*, 2004) in his home by means of multiple axe and hammer blows to the head, thereafter keeping her in his bath for a few days before finally leaving her almost completely naked body along a busy highway, first engaged in trial runs. His first potential victims, upon whom he inflicted no injury, were real-estate agents. He would make appointments with them at houses they had for sale, using a false name and a different cell phone number each time. He would meet with them, pretend to be interested in buying an expensive house, and enjoy the treatment he received from them. He would then leave without harming them and without them even realizing that they were in any danger. Just prior to the murder of the interior decorator, he met with his first interior decorator. She came to his house to give him a quote for work he wanted done to his house. She cut her consultation short after seeing a hammer in the bathroom, which made her feel uncomfortable. This was the same bathroom where the murder victim was finally attacked and murdered.

On the surface, there are many *changes* in behavior across these events. For example, at first the offender met real-estate agents at houses they were selling. Then, he moved onto interior decorators that would come to his house. The first few people he contacted were never hurt; only the final victim, the second interior decorator, was attacked and murdered in his house. However, the changes in this case relate to relatively superficial changes at a micro-level (moving from real-estate agents to interior decorators). The offender remained the same with respect to victimology (e.g., female victims) and his level of violence (he only harmed one individual, his final victim). The offender also showed other clear signs of thematic consistency, which could be observed despite changes in individual behaviors (e.g., the use of a con story to lure female victims who were employed in professions that required them to meet potential clients in isolation).

In another example of thematic consistency from the Republic of South Africa, there were two cases from a series of five murders where the offender made a small fire on the vagina of the victim. In another two cases within the series, the offender inserted objects into the victim's vagina, the first being a small bag of marijuana, and the second, the investigating officer's business card, which was rolled up and tied with a piece of the victim's hair. No insertion took place with the fifth victim. Across this series what the offender did to the vagina of the victim differed (fire vs. insertion) but the theme remained constant—tampering with the victim's genitals—and this was the offender's signature. Also in this particular series, the victims were from three different racial groups, but they were all sex workers, another part of the offender's signature. Keppel and Birnes (2009) note that in their experience, serial sex worker murderers tend to be racially indiscriminate in their victim selection.

Behavioral Change and Evolution

Although similarities are undoubtedly important in the crime linkage process and can perhaps be regarded as the *bread-and-butter* of linkage analysis, the author has experienced that changes in offender behavior across offenses can also be vital linkage factors. The importance of considering behavioral change in crime linkage analysis is echoed by Keppel and Birnes (2009) who regarded behaviors such as an "increasing number of death-producing wounds from the first case to the last case" (p. 11) and a "decreasing number of defensive wounds from the first case to the last case" (p. 11) as examples of linkage-relevant changes in crime scene behavior. Grubin et al. (2001) also found that behavioral evolution across a series occurred, especially in longer series, and that such evolution could provide valuable information about whether an offender was in the early, middle, or advanced stages of a series. They proposed that with further research this could be factored into a linking algorithm. Similarly, Wentink (2001), who analyzed the first three offenses of a sample of North American serial murderers, discovered that there was evolution across crime series in the form of thematic differentiation; in other words, offense behaviors became more thematically specific as a series progressed. Finally, in the Republic of South Africa, De Wet (2008) noted the importance of behavioral change with respect to the sexual behavior of South African serial rapists, and Hodgskiss' (2001) study of 13 South African serial murderers found that offense behaviors evolved as the series progressed, with MO developing over time and becoming more thematically distinct.

This evolution is often due to the progression of an offender's behavior across a series of offenses as more of their fantasy becomes enacted upon subsequent victims (see Chapter 3), or as the offender becomes more effective in committing his crimes due to experience and confidence. It is incorrect to describe this purely as *changes* in behavior, but rather as the acting out, or evolution of the offender's original intention as he "settles in" to his crime with each subsequent offense. Also, it is important to note that it is not necessarily in all aspects of behavior that change occurs. For example, victimology may remain the same, but specific behaviors may become embellished. These changes can be in the form of "trial runs" as an offender embarks upon his or her criminal career, which was clearly illustrated in the example above where the South African offender practiced certain aspects of his crimes on real estate agents before killing the interior decorator.

Another example of trial-runs in the early phases of a crime series involved events in the Free State Province town of Welkom, Republic of South Africa. A young couple lured an unsuspecting victim to a local graveyard under the pretenses of a blind-date between the female offender and the victim (*State v. van der Merwe*, 2012, and *State v. van Heerden*, 2011). Upon arrival, the victim was stabbed to death and his body dismembered. Some body parts were then taken home, whereas the remaining body parts were buried in a shallow grave at the graveyard. Among the body parts taken home was the head of the victim, which the female offender skinned the following day. Prior to this incident, the offenders had killed and skinned a cat on two separate occasions and had intended to move onto something bigger, such as a dog. Instead, they moved onto a human. Ironically, the reason for not inflicting a similar fate on a dog was that they could not face taking home a dog that was expecting to go to a loving home, only to then be killed.

In this particular case, the male offender had a fantasy to kill someone (*State v. van der Merwe*, 2012), whereas the female offender had a separate and distinct fantasy from a young age to skin a human being (*State v. Van Heerden*, 2011). The trials were separated due to the extensive examinations that had to be conducted on van der Merwe due to his pre-crime history of mental illness. So, although the killing of a cat and the murder of a human being are significantly different, both qualitatively and legally, there is a *logical* progression to their behavior, a continuum that the offenders were moving along over time. If one takes into account their pre-crime fascination with death and skinning as reflected in the collateral evidence, which was found in their home and on their computers, this logical progression becomes even more prominent.

Legal Principles under Which Linkage Evidence Is Admissible

Each country has its own legal system with its own rules for the admissibility of evidence and requirements for expert or opinion evidence. Even regions within the same country can have different rules (see Chapter 10). In the United States, for instance, some States use the *Daubert* standard (*Daubert v. Merrell Dow Pharmaceuticals, Inc.* 1993), whereas others use the *Frye* standard (*Frye v. United States*, 1923). Some states refer to *Kumho* (*Kumho Tire Company, Ltd. v. Carmichael*, 1999), and there are also the Federal Rules of Evidence (2000), which apply to federal cases in the United States.

Legal Standards

Under *Daubert*, unless the testimony rests on a reliable foundation and is based on scientifically valid principles, the judge may deem such testimony inadmissible. Under *Frye*, unless the testimony being offered reflects either a principle or discovery that has gained general acceptance in a particular field, it should be excluded by the judge (the *Frye* test is usually reserved for testimony involving new methods or new scientific principles from which conclusions are drawn). This was the test in *State of Delaware v. Pennell* (1989) and *State of Washington v. Russell* (1994), which were mentioned above. Under *Kumho*, so-called junk science may be excluded by the Judge as part of his or her gatekeeping function (i.e., it is up to the Judge to decide if the evidence being presented is true science or not). The Federal Rules of Evidence, specifically rule number 702, states:

> If scientific, technical, or other specialized knowledge will assist the trier of fact to understand the evidence or to determine a fact in issue, a witness qualified as an expert by knowledge, skill, experience, training, or education, may testify thereto in the form of an opinion or otherwise, if (1) the testimony is based upon sufficient facts or data, (2) the testimony is the product of reliable principles and methods, and (3) the witness has applied the principles and methods reliably to the facts of the case.

These different requirements should affect whether or not certain techniques, such as a linkage analysis, are deemed admissible. It is therefore essential to determine what the legal requirements are before applying any technique, or appearing as an expert, in a court of law.

The Role of the Expert Witness

An expert witness has primarily one role in the court: to provide the court with expertise, not typically within the knowledge framework of the court, or jury. If accepted, the court adopts the expert's opinion as its own, as the court may not delegate its responsibilities to another (i.e., the expert witness; van der Berg & van der Merwe, 2002). For this to happen, a person must be qualified as an expert by the court because, as a general rule, opinion evidence is not admissible except when the witness is in a better position than the court or jury to form an opinion. The opinion of an expert is admissible if it has evidential value and relevance. A person is qualified as an expert by the presiding officer based on knowledge and experience and ultimately the court decides whether or not to accept or reject the expert evidence, or in a jury system, to allow it to be used as evidence during the trial. It is imperative in the linkage analysis situation that the witness be not only an expert in the *process* of compiling linkage analyses and the supporting literature, but also an expert in the *type* of crime under investigation (e.g., serial murder or serial rape).

Invariably, for someone to be indicted on a crime (or for crimes), he or she must have been linked to the crimes in some manner, such as through DNA, fingerprints, confession, or any of the other traditional means by which an offender is identified. In democratic societies, police do not randomly arrest people for offenses. Similarly, without a prima facie case, a prosecutor will most likely withdraw the charges and instruct the police to conduct further investigations or decline to prosecute at all for a lack of evidence. A linkage analysis is typically presented by an expert witness at the end of the State's case (in adversarial systems), once all the evidence is before the court. In that sense, the linkage analysis presents the final, overarching, piece of evidence or the final *layer* of evidence. Ideally, the trial would proceed in the order that the offenses occurred, allowing the court to follow in the footsteps of the offender's series. To present linkage analysis too early might result in much of the information being regarded as hearsay evidence, as the expert witness would be testifying about facts that have not yet been presented to the court and were not personally experienced by the witness.

Similar Fact Evidence and Other Crimes Evidence

Another principle regarding the use of a linkage analysis in court is that of *similar fact* evidence or, as sometimes referred to, *other crimes* evidence. Other crime evidence was used in the cases *State of Louisiana v. Code* (1994), *State of Washington v. Russell* (1994), and *State of New Jersey v. Fortin* (2000) mentioned above, and similar fact evidence in *R. v. R.B.* (2003; a sexual assault trial) and *R. v. Burlingham* (1993; two murder cases) in Canada.

Generally, the courts will not admit similar fact evidence because the evidence is irrelevant to the facts at hand. An example of this is the use of previous convictions to try and convince the court that an accused is guilty of the current, similar charges, due to his or her character. This is regarded as irrelevant as it cannot prove or disprove the facts at hand for the current trial.* The underlying argument to this is that just because someone has committed a rape before does not mean he committed the rape for which he currently stands trial.

The exception to the rule is if the evidence can contribute to the facts in issue. For this to occur, there must be a logical link or nexus between the similar facts and the facts in issue. The greater the correspondence, and the closer the evidence and facts in issue are in time, place, manner, and nature, the easier it is to conclude that the required nexus exists (Schwikkard, 2002). The relevance of the similar fact evidence will also be determined by the strength of the other evidence available (Hoffmann & Zeffertt, 1988). Similar fact evidence is often used when an accused stands charged of numerous crimes of a similar nature that are unique in their MO (Petherick, Field, Lowe, & Fry, 2005), such as serial murder or serial rape, where there is strong evidence of guilt, such as DNA or an eyewitness identification, in some but not necessarily all of the instances. Based on these similarities, the court may conclude that the suspect was responsible for the other charges also, even without expert evidence regarding linkage having been given during the trial.

* Previous convictions may be enquired into if the defendant takes the witness stand to testify, as previous convictions are relevant to the defendant's credibility.

For other crimes evidence, evidence that the accused had committed a similar, unique, crime in the past can be introduced. In *State of Louisiana v. Code* (1994), the court stated the following:

> Several factors must be met for evidence to be considered as evidence of MO: (1) there must be clear and convincing evidence of the commission of the other crimes and the defendant's connection therewith; (2) the modus operandi employed by the defendant in both the charged and the uncharged offences must be so peculiarly distinctive that one must logically say they are the work of the same person; (3) the other crimes evidence must be substantially relevant for some other purpose than to show a probability that the defendant committed the crime on trial because he is a man of criminal character; (4) the other crimes evidence must tend to prove a material fact genuinely at issue; (5) the probative value of the extraneous crimes evidence must outweigh its prejudicial effect. (p. 11)

In the above, the emphasis is on a crime that the accused has committed previously that he is not currently on trial for, which is used to try and convince the court that the accused is guilty of the current offense for which he is on trial. Such a scenario has the potential to be highly prejudicial to the offender and can lead to an overturning of a conviction on appeal. The reason that this is prejudicial is that the trier of fact (a judge or jury) might be swayed to convict based on the fact that the accused has previously committed a crime of a similar nature, with similar unique characteristics. However, the fact that someone has previously committed *a* murder is not proof that a person has committed *the* murder that is before the court.

Similar fact evidence (or linkage analysis evidence more generally) has encountered frequent difficulties when used in certain situations. The following cases highlight some of the difficulties.

It appears particularly problematic to use this type of evidence when there is more than one perpetrator. For example, in the Australian case *R. v. Clune* (1993), three bank robberies were being considered, each involving a group of male offenders. Two of the robberies involved four offenders, while one involved three offenders. Although the similar fact evidence was accepted in the initial trial, on appeal the court held that similar fact evidence requires more than mere similarity, but also a unique feature that linked the offender in question. The Appeal Court ordered a retrial. This case also highlighted that mere similarity across crimes is not sufficient; the similarities must also be unique or distinctive (see *R. v. Clune*, 1993, and *Q v. Rich*, 1997, both from Australia). Similarly, in the Canadian case *R. v. Perrier* (2004), the Judges felt that similar fact evidence in a gang crime was insufficient when it came to establishing the identity of a single individual within the gang because membership and crime scene behaviors were said to have varied. Therefore, because the gang membership was not consistent, it could not be said with certainty if the same offenders were always present.

In the United States, the case of *State of New Jersey v. Fortin* (2000, 2007) is significant in understanding at least the use of linkage analysis evidence in the United States. Fortin had pleaded guilty to the sexual assault and strangulation of a State Trooper in Maine who survived his attack. Fortin had received a 20-year sentence for this crime. In *State of New Jersey v. Fortin* (2000), he was charged with the first-degree murder of Melissa Padilla. The State wished to introduce evidence of the previous crime against the State Trooper so as to establish an offender signature. The signature rested on five main behavioral similarities: bite marks to the left breast and chin, severe facial assault, manual strangulation from the front, and anal penetration.

Former FBI profiler Roy Hazelwood was called as an expert witness. Fortin appealed his conviction claiming that Hazelwood did not qualify as an expert witness, and the Supreme Court of New Jersey concurred, stating that the same admission requirements for scientific evidence were applicable when determining admissibility of linkage analysis evidence. The outcome of the various appeals was that behavioral linkage evidence must meet the following requirements:

- The testimony must concern a subject that is beyond the knowledge of the average juror.
- The tested field must be at a state of the art that such an expert's testimony could be sufficiently reliable.
- The witness must have sufficient expertise to offer the intended testimony.

So, although the expert evidence on linkage analysis was not allowed, the similar fact or other crimes evidence between the two crimes was allowed. However, the similar fact evidence could not be bolstered by the evidence of an expert. It would be up to the jury to decide if the similarities were unique enough to form a signature linking the two crimes, not an expert such as a *profiler*.

Fortin was retried in 2007 (*State of New Jersey v. Fortin*, 2007). The prosecution was allowed to present the bite mark evidence from the trial of the incident involving the State Trooper; however, the jury was instructed to decide for itself if the bite marks constituted a signature. The court instructed that other similarities, such as the brutality of the beating and the anal penetration, were common aspects of sexual assaults and were not to be considered as signature evidence. The court also felt that the Violent Criminal Apprehension Program (ViCAP) database,* which has been used

* ViCAP is a computerized database run by the FBI that is used to try and identify serial crimes.

to determine the uniqueness of the signature evidence, should not be used to bolster opinions as the State Trooper's case was added to the database for the sole purpose of litigation, thus creating bias. The court argued further that a match made by the ViCAP database did not necessarily establish a true signature match and that ViCAP was not accessible to the defense. As such, ViCAP was determined not to meet the standard of admissibility for the purposes of evidence to establish guilt or innocence. In essence, the court did not object to similarities and signature analysis to make linkages, but rather questioned the foundations for the opinions on similarity. Ultimately, Fortin was convicted a second time, during a retrial, of the murder of Padilla.

Legal Guidelines for the Use of Similar Fact Evidence

Canadian courts have set guidelines for the use of similar fact evidence. In *R. v. Arp* (1998), the use of similar fact evidence was upheld on appeal, with the court outlining certain suggestions for the admissibility of similar fact evidence, which include the following:

- A high degree of similarity is required where similar fact evidence is to be used to prove identity. This similarity between the acts may consist of a unique trademark or signature.
- The Judge should consider the manner in which the acts were committed and not the evidence as to the accused's involvement in each act.
- As a general rule if there is such a degree of similarity between the acts that it is likely that they were committed by the same person then the similar fact evidence will ordinarily have sufficient probative force to outweigh its prejudicial effect.

In another Canadian case, *R. v. Handy* (2002), further guidelines were set out by the court. In this case, Handy was convicted of sexual assault with intent to cause bodily harm. The conviction was appealed on the grounds that the similar fact evidence from the testimony of the accused's wife should not have been admitted. The behavioral similarities were that both the complainant and the wife's incidents involved initial consensual vaginal sex, with the accused later forcing anal sex. In this matter, similar fact evidence was rejected by the Supreme Court as there was a possibility of collusion by the witnesses, and the circumstances of the two cases were removed from time and place. The following guidelines were indicated to establish the degree of similarity needed in similar fact evidence:

- Proximity in time of the similar acts
- Extent to which the other acts are similar in detail
- Number of occurrences of the similar acts

- Circumstances surrounding or relating to the similar acts
- Any distinctive features unifying the incidents
- Intervening events
- Any other factor, which would tend to support or rebut the underlying unity of the similar acts

The guidelines set out in *R. v. Arp* (1998) and *R. v. Handy* (2002) were applied during a *voire dire* (a trial-within-a-trial used to determine the admissibility of certain evidence) in the Canadian case *R. v. Kembo* (2010), and the similar fact evidence was deemed admissible leading to the accused being found guilty of four murders. The court held that the pattern of behavior was strikingly similar, making it improbable that a different offender had committed each act.

Cautionary Issues When Linking

Based on court decisions and experience, there are certain instances where the use of linkage analysis evidence should at least be used with caution. Due to the multitude of potential scenarios and possibilities in serial offenses, it would be inappropriate to make a blanket list of scenarios where such evidence should never be used. What follows are some potentially problematic scenarios.

Using Linkage Analysis in Cases Involving Co-Offenders

Although there have been trials where similar fact evidence of behavioral similarity was accepted where there was more than one offender involved in the crimes, even more caution than usual should be exercised when attempting to use linkage analysis in such circumstances, if it is being used to prove identity. It might be best to attempt to conduct a linkage analysis on each individual offender and not the group per se. As highlighted above, in the Canadian case *R. v. Perrier* (2004), two offenders were convicted on several counts of breaking and entering, robbery, unlawful confinement, and possession of stolen property. In this case, the court felt that because gang membership varied over time, similar facts were not distinct and could not be used to establish the identity of an individual gang member for a particular incident in the series.

Using Linkage Analysis for Purposes Other than Establishing Behavioral Linkages

It must be remembered that the linkage analysis itself should not discuss nor mention other nonbehavioral evidence, such as fingerprint evidence and DNA evidence, which directly links an offender to a crime, nor attempt to say a particular person was responsible for the offenses. In essence, the linkage analysis report should stand irrespective of who is charged for the offenses, as it is based on crime scene behavior. It is the responsibility of the prosecutor to present other traditional forensic evidence. So, although the court uses linkage evidence to link individual crimes based on unique features, it is not up to the linkage expert to link a suspect to a crime; in other words, a linkage report should never mention an offender's name.

Relying on Computerized Linkage Systems Exclusively

Computer databases have been developed with the aim of linking serious and violent crimes such as murder and sexual assaults. In 1985, the FBI in the United States established ViCAP, which serves as the national repository for violent crimes (specifically homicides, sexual assaults, missing persons, and unidentified human remains). As discussed above, the intention of the program is to make linkages between cases that share similar features. A similar system, the Violent Crime Linkage Analysis System (ViCLAS), was developed by the Royal Canadian Mounted Police (RCMP) in Canada in the early 1990s. This is the most widely used computer database linkage system, with the following countries also making use of ViCLAS: Belgium, the Czech Republic, France, Germany, Ireland, the Netherlands, New Zealand, Switzerland, and the United Kingdom.

Although computer databases such as ViCAP and ViCLAS can undoubtedly be a valuable source of information about violent crimes, especially regarding the statistical occurrence of certain behaviors, and for linkage purposes, in *State of New Jersey v. Fortin* (2007) the Appeal Court was against the use of ViCAP. As highlighted above, the court's main argument was that ViCAP was not accessible to the defense counsel and is exempt from disclosure under the Freedom of Information Act (1966). The primary reason for the restricted access is that it contains detailed information about unsolved (and solved) cases and unrestricted access could damage those investigations, and result in the invasion of privacy of victims. In addition, the court stated that expert testimony regarding the ViCAP database did not establish that a crime match made by the database could confidently establish a true signature match and the court was concerned that adding Padilla's murder to the ViCAP system for the purpose of the trial resulted in potentially biased results.

This is a disappointing approach taken by this court as any database that can assist in determining the frequency of a particular behavior, or set of behaviors, would undoubtedly give weight to a linkage opinion. However, it is agreed that a linkage opinion should not be based solely on a statistical finding. For example, no matter how similar two events are, if they occurred simultaneously thousands of miles apart, it could never be the same offender.

Examining Isolated Behaviors without Taking into Account Context

Some judgments relating to similar fact evidence or linkage analysis evidence have gone against its use, or raised concerns relating to the level of uniqueness of a particular behavior (e.g., *R. v. Sutton*, 1984, and *R. v. Clune*, 1993, both in Australia, and *R. v. Boden*, 2011, in Canada). In other words, some courts have felt that a particular behavior is common in many crimes and therefore cannot be used for the purpose of establishing crime linkages. In *State of New Jersey v. Fortin* (2007), evidence of the brutality of the assaults and the anal penetration of both victims were regarded as common aspects of sexual assaults by the court and therefore could not to be considered as signature evidence, but bite mark evidence from both cases was admitted for the jury to decide upon.

However, there must be a caveat to such a statement. One should ideally not look at each crime scene behavior in isolation and make a determination if the individual behavior is common or generic. Behaviors should be seen in the context of other crime scene behavior and the circumstances of the crime. For example, an offender kissing his victim might not be deemed to be unique, nor an offender wearing a ski-mask to hide his identity, nor an offender gaining entrance via an open window. However, an offender who engages in all three of those behaviors increases the uniqueness, or signature value, compared to those behaviors occurring in isolation. Labuschagne (2010) argued that it is often a unique combination of common, individual crime scene behaviors that denotes a linkage. If this unique combination of behaviors is coupled with, for example, geographical proximity or proximity in time, then they grow in their evidential value.

Missing Instances of Behavioral Similarity upon Initial Assessment

At times similarities may not be so obvious upon initial assessment. In the South African case, *State v. Williams* (2009), Williams was charged with three murders that occurred over a 21 year time frame. The murder victims included an 8 year old girl in 1987, a 13 year old boy in 2004, and a 28 year old male in 2008. These cases were the focus of the case comparison report compiled by Labuschagne.*

Only the first murder was overtly sexual in nature. Labuschagne's key linkage factors related to three issues: despite apparent differences on the surface,

* There were other victims, acquaintances of the offender who had not been murdered, but merely assaulted by the offender. These cases were not part of the case comparison report.

all three victims were vulnerable in some fashion due to either age or physical health problems; in all three incidents there had been some form of post-mortem tampering with the body; and strangulation was used during all three incidents. The court deemed there to be enough similarities across the cases to use similar fact and circumstantial evidence to convict. In fact, the court went beyond the similarities highlighted in Labuschagne's case comparison report and commented on other similarities, such as the fact that the two other victims that made up the indictment, ex-girlfriends of the accused, had also experienced strangulation in their assaults, which the court felt was more than mere coincidence. Further, in two of the three murder incidents, items had been removed by the offender from the scene. Additionally, in all three murder incidents the accused was well known to the victim and had been seen with him or in the vicinity of their disappearance on the days in question. Finally, in two of the three murder incidents the accused had involved himself in some way in the investigation (facts that could not be included in the report as they would have the effect of linking a particular suspect to the offenses).

Although a linkage analysis does not take into account other factors of the identified offender (e.g., such as the fact, in the above example, that the offender was known to the victims; that he became involved in the various investigations, that he had attempted to place the blame on someone else, and that he used strangulation in the offenses against the assault victims), the court can take this information into account when considering similar fact evidence and use other similarities in its decision to convict. This relates to the earlier comments that a person compiling a linkage analysis should be cautious about commenting on the behavior of the identified offender (e.g., that he knew all the victims), but that the court can include broader similarities when making its verdict. What this illustrates is that similar fact evidence is something that goes beyond what is specifically testified about during linkage analysis evidence and that behavioral analysts' evidence is only part of the legal concept of similar fact evidence.

Paying Attention to Dissimilarities

Another criticism of linkage analysis evidence that has been heard in legal proceedings is that although there may be similarities across a series of offenses as identified by the expert, there may be significant dissimilarities (e.g., *R. v. Clune*, 1993; *R. v. Hakeem*, 2006; *R. v. R.B.*, 2003). It is best practice to give explicit attention to any dissimilarities in behavior within a linkage analysis report (e.g., see Hazelwood & Warren, 2004 as an illustration). Where there are dissimilarities, the linkage analysis practitioner should state whether or not these dissimilarities can be explained (e.g., by offender progression across a series of crimes) or why the dissimilarities should not hold significant weight in relation to the linkage opinion. For example, an offender may commit crimes at a later hour in the evening during summer because of a later sunset, compared to his crimes in winter, where sunset is earlier.

Case Example 1: *State v. D*

The following case relates to a serial rape trial in the Republic of South Africa. It illustrates that what behavioral experts currently testify about under the label of *linkage analysis* has been used by courts for over 20 years in Republic of South Africa, despite the absence of an expert testifying about these issues. It also illustrates that, although individual behaviors might not be persuasive in certain circumstances, combinations of behaviors can be persuasive.

In *State v. D* (1991), the accused had been convicted of multiple crimes including six counts of rape and one of robbery. He appealed some of the convictions, which related to one complainant. The complainant had been unable to identify the accused and the Trial Court had relied on circumstantial evidence to convict. The accused had made a confession to the other crimes but not to the counts for which he was appealing.

Evidence of the witness indicated that the offender who raped the victim in the disputed counts told her to "sleep down." These were the same words used by the accused in one of the other rape charges for which he did confess and was convicted. The Trial Court held that those words were so distinctive that their probative value was significant enough to establish the identity of the offender, in this case the accused.

The Appeal Court felt that these words on their own did not have sufficient weight to confirm identity, but if taken together with other similarities they did then achieve the required probative force. These other similarities included the fact that the rapes were all committed in a particular area within a 4-month period. The robbery and rape of the victim in the disputed counts occurred in the same area and in the middle of the series of the other crimes to which the accused had confessed. The conduct of the offender during the disputed counts was very similar to the conduct of the accused in the crimes for which he confessed. This included the fact that the crimes were committed during the morning or early afternoon and that the offender would enter the house silently and confront the victim, demand money, and thereafter rape the victim. When these facts were viewed together with the fact that the accused had been found in possession of the victims' keys, the Appeal Court maintained the view that the accused had been appropriately convicted.

It is interesting to note the court's reliance on concepts of serial offenders, which today are well known and researched (e.g., geographic profiling). For example, the court refers to the crimes occurring in the same geographical area, what is referred to in geographic profiling terms as a *comfort zone.*

Case Example 2: The Sunday Serial Rapist

This particular trial took place in 2012 in the South Gauteng High Court in the Republic of South Africa. The accused, Jaco Steyn, was on trial for numerous incidents relating to the kidnapping and sexual assault of young girls, spanning across at least two provinces, Gauteng and the North West Province.

Between November 2008 and October 2011, there were 10 incidents where 11 White females between the ages of 11 and 18 were either abducted or attempts were made to abduct them. In 2 of the 10 incidents, the victims managed to escape before being taken away by the offender. All were approached by an adult White male driving a vehicle. In most cases, the offender wore what appeared to the victims to be a wig and sunglasses. He would usually stop his vehicle next to the victim, or ahead of them in the direction they were walking, and once nearby he would point a firearm at them and pull them into his vehicle from the driver's side, over himself. He would force them into the footwell of the passenger's side and instruct them to stay down and not look at him. In some incidents, he used an item to cover their eyes. He would then drive them to a deserted area where he would sexually molest his victims. Once finished he would leave them in the same deserted area.

In one incident where he abducted two victims, one leapt from the moving vehicle and died as a result of her injuries. He was charged with murder for that particular victim's death (but ultimately found guilty of culpable homicide). The final victim was murdered by the offender and her body set on fire.

The State's Evidence

The victims were unable to identify the offender due to the use of a disguise, and hence, identity parades (lineups) were not held. Furthermore, there was no DNA evidence available to link the offender to the crimes and the crimes to each other, despite the victims having undergone a medicolegal examination. The offender made a confession to the final incident where he had murdered the victim and set her body on fire. In that confession, he made reference to the use of a wig and other items, which were relevant to the other cases. The offender was also placed nearby each crime scene at the time of the incident by means of his cell phone. Despite the confession made by the offender shortly after his arrest, he pleaded not guilty to all counts at the trial. The prosecution's evidence was grouped under the categories of circumstantial evidence, similar fact evidence, and the confession. The confession was dealt with during a "trial within a trial" or *voire dire*, when it was time for the State to present such evidence. The offender was found in possession of some of the items belonging to the final victim, who was murdered.

Linkage Analysis

As mentioned, this series consisted of 10 incidents, of which 2 were unsuccessful attempts to abduct a victim. The 10th incident involved the murder of the victim. As a result, these three incidents (the two unsuccessful attempts and the final case involving a murder) had less information about the offender's behavior during the post-abduction phase. In the 10th incident, the murdered victim was with a friend when she was abducted, and her friend was able to provide evidence of how the abduction took place and a description of the offender and his vehicle.

Brigadier Gérard Labuschagne, the head of the South African Police Service's Investigative Psychology Section, was approached by the prosecution to compile a linkage analysis report. The Investigative Psychology Section fulfills a role similar to that of the Behavioral Analysis Units of the FBI. Labuschagne reviewed the police case files and consulted with the investigating officer and the prosecutor to gather information about the manner in which the crimes were committed. No previous convictions were included in the linkage analysis, and they did not make part of the evidence presented by the prosecution, as was done in cases such as *State of New Jersey v. Fortin* (2000) above. In other words, the only cases upon which a linkage analysis was conducted were the cases that were on trial. The analysis rested on seven key similarities that are discussed below.

Approach Method

In four incidents, the offender approached two people (incidents 1, 6, 7, 10). In all 10 incidents, he used a vehicle, which was described as a *bakkie* (pick-up truck) and would stop next to the victim or slightly ahead of the victim in her path. As the victim approached, he would then point a firearm at her and pull the victim in through the driver's side of the vehicle over himself, to the passenger seat. Most serial rapists in the Republic of South Africa approach their victims on foot and lure unsuspecting victims to a secluded location by means of a con-story. The most frequently used con-story is that of an offer of employment. With an official unemployment rate of 25%, and an unofficial unemployment rate of 40%, many people are desperate for work. Furthermore, the use of a vehicle in such crimes is rare as most offenders are not stably employed and do not have access to vehicles. In fact, in the author's experience, the use of a vehicle in the commission of a rape series is almost exclusively found in White serial rape offenders or Black mini-bus taxi drivers. Finally, although not unheard of, most serial rape offenders, if using a weapon, will use a knife and not a firearm.

Approach Location

All victims were approached in a residential area and those successfully abducted were taken by vehicle to a secluded area where the sexual abuse occurred. They were then left in the secluded area. So, although the actual approach locations differed and occurred across two provinces, the type of area where the victims were approached was similar. In other serial rape cases, the actual geographical area where all victims were approached was the same. This relates back to the concept of consistency of individual behaviors (using the same geographical area) versus themes (approaching victims in residential areas, although geographically different).

Sexual Acts

In all of the successful abductions, the offender sexually abused the victim. It was not proven beyond a reasonable doubt that the final murder victim was sexually abused, although the offender was charged with rape for that particular victim. Most victims were penetrated either by a penis, digitally, or with an object described as a *vibrator*. Masturbation of the offender and fondling of the victims' breasts were also common.

Pseudo-Relationship Acts

In four incidents, the offender engaged in pseudo-relationship behaviors such as cunnilingus, asking sexual questions of the victim, asking the victim if she was enjoying the sexual acts, and attempting to kiss the victim. In three incidents, he also complimented the victim's physical appearance. In three incidents, he gave either alcohol or cigarettes to the victim. Pseudo-relationship behaviors are often seen as being linked to the offender's motive or inner fantasy, in which the victim is a willing participant to the incident. An offender motivated by a sadistic fantasy will not engage in pseudo-relationship actions.

Description of the Offender

In at least six incidents, the victim described the offender as wearing a wig; in six incidents, the offender wore sunglasses; and in four incidents, he wore a baseball cap. Disguises are extremely uncommon in rape series in the Republic of South Africa. All victims described the offender as being White. White serial rape offenders in the Republic of South Africa are not a common occurrence, primarily due to the fact that White people only make up approximately 8.9% of the population.

Attempts to Cover the Victim's Head

In all the successful abduction incidents where the victim was left alive, the offender pushed the victim down to the footwell of the passenger's side of the vehicle after forcing the victim into the vehicle. Additionally, for four of those six, he covered the victim's eyes with material of some nature.

Souvenirs

In all of the successful abduction incidents, the offender kept items belonging to the victims. These ranged from underwear (bra and/or panties), clothing (shoes, shirts), to hair accessories. As these items had no significant financial value, they were regarded as *souvenir* or *trophy* items.

Conclusion

Based only on an assessment of the crime scene behavior, and not taking into account any other evidence such as forensic evidence or admissions/confessions made by the accused, it was the opinion of Brigadier Labuschagne that the following offenses were *undoubtedly* the work of the same offender based on the unique similarities and combination of behaviors. He testified that there was enough consistency in the offender's behavior across the series of crimes and that there were enough unique features in this series that would differentiate it from other series:

- Counts 4–7 (Krugersdorp CAS 1022/10/2010)
- Counts 8–11 (Carletonville CAS 319/09/2010)
- Counts 12–16 (Erasmia CAS 100/09/2010)
- Counts 18–21 (Rustenburg CAS 423/03/2010)
- Counts 22–24 (Van der Bijl Park CAS 764/02/2010)
- Counts 25–29 (Potchefstroom CAS 49/11/2009)
- Counts 30–36 (Rustenburg CAS 1447/06/2009)

Labuschagne testified that the uniqueness of the behaviors and circumstances accompanying the crimes were indicative of one offender, and unlikely to be imitated by another offender in such a similar fashion, due to the psychological motivation of such offenders. To date, in the Republic of South Africa, he had not come across *copy-cat* offenders in the serial crime investigations that he has assisted on.

In relation to the two incidents where the attempts to kidnap a victim were unsuccessful, it was the opinion of Brigadier Labuschagne that the following two cases were *very likely* linked to the same offender responsible for the above-mentioned crimes due to the victimology, approach of two people by the offender in a residential area, wearing of headgear by the offender, the use of a vehicle and pointing of a firearm, victims forced into the vehicle via the driver's side, and in Count 17 the wearing of a wig:

- Count 37 (Rustenburg CAS 676/11/2008)
- Count 17 (Potchefstroom CAS 262/08/2010)

In relation to the final incident (Counts 1–3: Florida CAS 319/10/2011) where the victim was murdered. In this instance, it was also deemed *very likely* that the same offender was responsible for this incident due to the following: victimology, approach of two people by the offender in a residential area, the use of a vehicle and pointing of a firearm, sexual theme to the crime, victims forced into the vehicle via the driver's side, use of a plastic bag (as seen in Counts 22–24; Counts 4–7; Counts 1–3), and keeping of a souvenir (victim's school bag). It was noted that serial rapists often escalate in their crimes to murder as a series progresses or have a single murder at some point in their series. Many of Republic of South Africa's serial murderers first began as serial rapists.

Trial

The trial took place in the Jurisdiction of the South Gauteng High Court, sitting at Palm Ridge Court. The matter was heard by a Judge assisted by an assessor. Regarding the use of similar fact evidence, as presented in the form of a linkage analysis, the court stated the following:

> The issue is whether the State has proved beyond a reasonable doubt that the accused was the perpetrator of the offences relating to the remaining 9 incidents or whether on a conspectus of all the evidence the accused's denial of having been involved in the incidents, could reasonably possibly be true.
>
> The State relies on circumstantial and similar fact evidence to prove the Accused's involvement in all the incidents. This means that the State is asking the court to consider evidence admissible on one count to prove another count. This is of course permissible in certain circumstances. In *R. v. Simms* [1946] 1 ALL ER 697 the following was said: "[W]here there is an issue as to the identity of the Accused, we think that evidence is admissible of a series of similar acts done by him to other persons … evidence of other acts may tend to show the accused to be of bad disposition, but it also shows something more. The other acts have specific features connecting him with the crime charged and are on that account admissible."
>
> Admitting such evidence diminishes the possibility of coincidence. It will be remembered that the Accused was in respect of each of the 10 incidents, in the vicinity of the crime scenes as set out above. It may have been a coincidence for instance that the Accused was in the area of the abduction of Louise De Waal but it is unlikely to have been a coincidence that he was also in the vicinity of the area where her body was burnt which was removed in time and place and even less of a coincidence that he was in respect of the other 9 incidents, every time in the area of the abduction and where the abduction was successful, in the area where the complainants were sexually assaulted.
>
> So for instance was it held in *Jones v. S* 1970 2 PH H129 (A) that the admitted presence of the accused at various places where veld fires were started, diminished the coincidence between his presence and the occurrence of the fire.
>
> In *S v. M* 1963 (3) SA 183 on 186 F—188 A the court found that the manner in which one crime was committed or the modus operandi of the offender in one count could be used to prove the identity of the offender on other counts. This is exactly the exercise performed by Dr Labuschagne whose conclusions are based on modus operandi only.

> In addition, Warrant Officer du Toit determined that in all cases the complainants were molested on the way back to the Reef from where they had been abducted. The abduction of Louise De Waal was of course somewhat different although the Accused moved from Newlands to his own house.
>
> It was in our view proved beyond a reasonable doubt that the perpetrator of the abductions or attempted abductions referred to in counts 4, 8, 14, 17, 18, 22, 25 and 30 used a vehicle similar to a vehicle used by the Accused and that the perpetrator of count 37, in all probability also used a vehicle similar to a vehicle used by the Accused at the time.
>
> Having considered all of the above evidence we are of the view that the only reasonable inference that can be drawn from the proved facts is that the Accused was the perpetrator of the offences as found to have been proved supra and that on a conspectus of all the evidence the Accused's denial of involvement, cannot reasonably possibly true.

The accused was found to be the perpetrator in all 10 incidents. He was found guilty on 34 of 37 counts against him. He was found not guilty of rape for the final victim but he was convicted of the murder and kidnapping of that victim. For another victim, he was found not guilty of the sexual assault, but he was found guilty of the abduction and rape. In Republic of South Africa, the crimes of sexual assault and rape are two distinct crimes, best distinguished by the act of sexual penetration in rape cases and the absence of sexual penetration in sexual assault cases. For another victim, he was found not guilty of one count of sexual assault, but for the same victim he was found guilty of the remaining two counts of sexual assault, one count of kidnapping and one of rape.

Comments on the Case Study

In this case study, the person testifying was the head of the South African Police Service's Investigative Psychology Section. His evidence was admissible under the legal principle of similar fact evidence as discussed above. While not only highlighting similarities, he was allowed to give an opinion that the cases were committed by the same offender. Most likely in a trial where a jury is present (such as in the United States), the opinion about one offender having committed the crimes might not be allowed, similar to the final instructions in the *State of New Jersey v. Fortin* (2007) trial. Labuschagne testified as an expert witness and as a result had to first lay down a foundation for his expertise. This foundation rested upon extensive experience with serial crime investigations throughout the Republic of South Africa, having worked on over 200 rape series and 110 murder series, research of serial rape and serial murder in the Republic of South Africa, including specifically linkage issues, and finally, training in serial rape investigation.

The linkage report made use of examining individual behaviors, such as the wearing of a wig by the offender on certain occasions, and themes of behaviors, such as pseudo-relationship behaviors. What is also important to note is that it is not necessary that each individual behavior or theme be present in each and every incident. Also, two of the incidents involved unsuccessful attempts to obtain a victim, and one involved an abduction with a murder. The information available for these three last mentioned cases differed, and hence, the level of certainty for those cases differed from the majority of the cases.

Conclusion

Linkage analysis has proven to be not only a valuable tool for investigators of serial offenses but also a useful tool during a trial as evidence. A growing body of research is finding support for the hypotheses underlying linkage analysis. Although the concept of a linkage analysis has been understood and put into practice for investigative purposes for decades, its application to trial proceedings is relatively new. The rules of evidence will determine if such an analysis is admissible, along with the author of the analysis being qualified as an expert in court (depending on local legal requirements). In future, it might be more relevant for behavioral analysts to focus on presenting linkage analysis testimony as opposed to profile evidence in the courtroom.

References

Bateman, A. L., & Salfati, C. G. (2007). An examination of behavioural consistency using individual behaviours of groups of behaviours in serial homicide. *Behavioral Sciences & the Law, 25,* 527–544.

Bennell, C., & Canter, D. V. (2002). Linking commercial burglaries by *modus operandi*: Tests using regression and ROC analysis. *Science & Justice, 42,* 1–12.

Daubert v. Merrell Dow Pharmaceuticals, Inc., US., 125 L. Ed. 2d 469, 113 S. Ct. 2786 (1993).

De Wet, J. (2008). *An exploratory analysis of serial rape in South Africa* (Unpublished doctoral thesis). University of Pretoria, Pretoria, Republic of South Africa.

Federal Rules of Evidence 702. (2010). *Testimony by expert witnesses.* Retrieved March 11, 2013 from http://www.law.cornell.edu/rules/fre/rule_702

Frye v. United States, 293 F. 1013 (D.C. Cir 1923) United States.

Grubin, D., Kelly, P., & Brunsdon, C. (2001). *Linking serious sexual assaults through behaviour.* London, England: Home Office.

Hazelwood, R. R., & Warren, J. I. (2004). Linkage analysis: Modus operandi, ritual, and signature in serial sexual crime. *Aggression and Violent Behavior, 9,* 307–318.

Hodgskiss, B. (2001). *A multivariate model of the offence behaviours of South African serial murderers* (Unpublished master's thesis). Rhodes University, Grahamstown, Republic of South Africa.

Hoffmann, L. H., & Zeffertt, D. (1988). *The South African law of evidence* (4th ed.). Durban, Republic of South Africa: Butterworths.

House of Commons. (2005). *Forensic science on trial: Seventh report of session 2004–05.* London, England: Stationery Office.

Keppel, R. D. (2000). Signature murders: A report of the 1984 Cranbrook, British Colombia cases. *Journal of Forensic Sciences, 45,* 500–503.

Keppel, R. D., & Birnes, W. J. (2009). *Serial violence. Analysis of modus operandi and signature characteristics of killers.* Boca Raton, FL: CRC Press.

Keppel, R. D., Weis, J. G., Brown, K. M., & Welch, K. (2005). The Jack the Ripper murders: A modus operandi and signature analysis of the 1888–1891 Whitechapel murders. *Journal of Investigative Psychology and Offender Profiling, 2,* 1–21.

Kumho Tire Company, Ltd. v. Carmichael, 526, US 137 (1999).

Labuschagne, G. N. (2003). Offender profiling in South Africa: Its definition and context. *Acta Criminologica: Southern African Journal of Criminology, 16,* 67–74.

Labuschagne, G. N. (2010). The use of a linkage analysis as an investigative tool and evidential material in serial offences. In K. Borgeson & K. Kuenhle (Eds.), *Serial offenders: Theory and practice* (pp. 187–215). Sudbury, MA: Jones & Bartlett Learning.

Merry, S. (2000). Crime analysis: Principles for analysing everyday serial crime. In D. V. Canter & L. J. Alison (Eds.), *Profiling property crime* (pp. 297–318). Aldershot, England: Ashgate.

Mischel, W. (1999). Personality coherence and dispositions in a cognitive-affective personality system (CAPS) approach. In D. Cervone & Y. Shoda (Eds.), *The coherence of personality: Social-cognitive bases of consistency, variability and organisation* (pp. 37–60). London, England: Guilford Press.

Petherick, W., Field, D., Lowe, A., & Fry, E. (2005). Criminal profiling as expert evidence. In W. Petherick. (Ed.), *Serial crime: Theoretical and practical issues in behavioural profiling* (pp. 72–73). New York, NY: Elsevier.

Q v. Rich. (1997). Australia.

R. v. Arp. 3 SCR 339 (1998). Canada.

R. v. Boden. BCPC 366 (2011). Canada.

R. v. Burlingham. B.C.J.No. 1986 Vancouver Registry: CA006715 (1993).

R. v. Clune. (1993). Australia.

R. v. Hakeem. (2006). Australia.

R. v. Handy. SCC 56, 2 SCR 908 (2002). Canada.

R. v. Holtz. NZLR 667 (2002). New Zealand.

R. v. Kembo. BCSC 914 (2010). Canada.

R. v. Perrier. SCC 56 (2004) Australia.

R. v. R.B. No 4589 (2003). Canada.

R. v. Straffen. 2QB 911 66(1952). United Kingdom.

R. v. Toothill. Crim LR 876 (1998). United Kingdom.

Risinger, D. M., & Loop, J. L. (2002). Three card monte, monty hall, modus operandi and "offender profiling": Some lessons of modern cognitive science for the law of evidence. *Cardozo Law Review, 24,* 193–285.

Salfati, C. G., & Bateman, A. L. (2005). Serial homicide: An investigation of behavioural consistency. *Journal of Investigative Psychology and Offender Profiling, 2,* 121–144.

Schwikkard, P. J. (2002). Similar fact evidence. In P. J. Schwikkard & S. E. van der Merwe (Eds.), *Principles of evidence* (pp. 66–77). Lansdowne, India: JUTA.

State of California v. Bogard. (1996). California Supreme Court hearing in San Diego.
State of California v. Prince. (1992). 9 CAL.App.4th 1176, 10 CAL.Rptr.2D 855. United States.
State of Delaware v. Pennell. (1989). Del.Super., 584 A.2d 513. United States.
State of Louisiana v. Code. (1994). 627 So.2d 1373. United States.
State of New Jersey v. Fortin. 745 A.2d 509 N.J. (2000). United States.
State of New Jersey v. Fortin. 189 N.J. 579, 917 A.2d 746 (2007). United States.
State of South Dakota v. Anderson. (1998). McCook County Court Preliminary Hearing. United States.
State of Washington v. Parker. Wash. App. LEXIS 3160 (2002). United States.
State of Washington v. Russell. 125 Wash.2d 24, 882 P.2D 747 (1994). United States.
State v. D. 2 SACR 543 A (1991). South Africa.
State v. Da Silva. Case No CC76/2004. Pretoria High Court, Republic of South Africa.
State v. Mogale. Case No 36/2009 (2012). South Gauteng High Court, Republic of South Africa.
State v. Nyauza. Case No CC97/2007 (2007). Pretoria High Court, Republic of South Africa.
State v. Steyn. Case No 47/2012 (2012). South Gauteng High Court, Republic of South Africa.
State v. Sukude. Case No 34/2006 (2006). Pietermaritzburg High Court, Republic of South Africa.
State v. van der Merwe. Case No 38/2011 (2012). Free State High Court, Republic of South Africa.
State v. van Heerden. Case No 38/2011 (2011). Free State High Court, Republic of South Africa.
State v. van Rooyen. Case No SS 55/2007 (2007). Cape High Court, Republic of South Africa.
State v. Williams. KS 18/09 (2009). Republic of South Africa.
Sutton v. R. HCA 5 (1984). Australia.
van der Berg, E., & van der Merwe, S. E. (2002). Opinion evidence. In P. J. Schwikkard & S. E. van der Merwe (Eds.), *Principles of evidence* (pp. 79–99). Lansdowne, India: JUTA.
Wentink, N. (2001). *Serial sexual murder: Classification and development over a series of offences* (Unpublished master's thesis). University of Liverpool, Liverpool, England.
Woodhams, J., Hollin, C. R., & Bull, R. (2007). The psychology of linking crimes: A review of the evidence. *Legal and Criminological Psychology, 12,* 233–249.

Crime Linkage as Expert Evidence
Making a Case for the *Daubert* Standard

10

TOM PAKKANEN, PEKKA SANTTILA, AND DARIO BOSCO

Contents

Introduction	225
The *Daubert* Standard	226
Review of Court Opinions in Crime Linkage Cases	229
Case 1: *State v. Russell* (1994)	231
Case 2: *State v. Fortin* (2000)	233
Problems in Current Ways of Producing Crime Linkage Expert Opinions	237
Practical Considerations in Giving Expert Evidence on Crime Linkage	239
Behavioral Consistency	240
A Reliable Database	241
Frequency	243
Is It Feasible to Achieve the *Daubert* Standard with Crime Linkage Evidence?	245
Conclusion	245
References	246

Introduction

This chapter considers how the field of crime linkage stands up against legal criteria for the admission of expert evidence, as well as whether crime linkage can or should be used in the courtroom. There is some disagreement on whether crime linkage should be used as evidence in the courts at all. Some authors (e.g., Cooley, 2012; Turvey & Freeman, 2012) argue that it should not, stating that current crime linkage practices, in the United States, are too ambiguous to hold up to standards of admissibility. On the other hand, Labuschagne (2006, 2012, see Chapter 9) argues that crime linkage can be useful as evidence in court, giving examples of cases from South Africa where behavioral linkage evidence has been admitted by the court. In a recent review, Bosco, Zappalà, and Santtila (2010) concluded that court decisions on the admissibility of crime linkage suggested a growing trend by the courts to expect expert opinions on any issue, including crime linkage, to be based on scientifically reliable methods.

Internationally, expert evidence on crime linkage is being admitted by courts based on a varying set of admissibility standards (e.g., similar fact evidence,* opinion evidence†). The argument being made in this chapter is that expert testimony based on scientific evidence is more reliable than, for example, evidence based on the opinion of an experienced forensic investigator. Therefore, this chapter focuses on the *Daubert* (1993) standard because its criteria best describe scientific principles in legal terms. Although the *Daubert* standard would legally only apply in the United States, other countries have also adopted similar standards, as will be outlined. Because of this focus, most of the cases given close scrutiny in this chapter are from the US legal system.

Some methodological problems with the current practice of the police asking the expert "Are these two cases related?" will be discussed, along with suggestions regarding the direction in which crime linkage practice and research needs to go to fill in the gaps to make linkage evidence more likely to fulfill criteria for admissibility in the courtroom.

The *Daubert* Standard

The growing involvement of science in the courts has introduced a number of legal and scientific questions about how science can be helpful in a forensic context. In the United States, in particular, the famous Supreme Court opinions known as the *Daubert–Joiner–Kumho trilogy* have been important in defining the interrelationship between science and the law. The US Supreme Court has, with these opinions, set general standards for the use of scientific evidence in the courtroom, by identifying differences between reliable and unreliable science. The court also defined when the work of an expert witness in a scientific, technical, or other specialized area can be called reliable and be admissible in court. These rules can be found in the reformed Rule 702 of the Federal Rules of Evidence (2010) that dictate the grounds for assessing the reliability and admissibility of scientific expert testimony in the United States.

* Similar fact evidence refers to evidence of a prior offense of the accused, which is used to infer that the accused has committed the offense at issue (e.g., *R. v. Handy*, 2002).

† Opinion evidence commonly refers to evidence of what the witness thinks, believes, or infers in regard to facts. With this type of evidence, the opinion is typically evaluated through the experts' education and experience in the area (e.g., Labuschagne, 2012).

Before this trilogy, the standard for admissibility of scientific evidence in the United States was the *Frye* test. It derives from a 1923 case, in which the defendant offered the results of a lie detector test to demonstrate that he was telling the truth when he denied killing a victim (*Frye v. United States*, 1923). The court ruled that the evidence was inadmissible because the scientific principles upon which the procedure was based were not "sufficiently established to have gained general acceptance in the particular field in which it belongs." This became known as the *Frye* general acceptance test.

The *Frye* test was the standard for admissibility of scientific evidence up to the *Daubert* decision in 1993. The petitioners in this particular case were minor children born with serious birth defects; they and their parents alleged that the birth defects had been caused by the mothers' ingestion of Bendectin, an antinausea drug produced by the respondent (Merrell Dow). The petitioner's experts' conclusions were based upon *in vitro* and *in vivo* animal studies that found a link between Bendectin and malformations. The District Court and the Court of Appeals (9th circuit) did not admit the petitioner's expert to testify because "the principle upon which the expert work is based is not generally accepted as reliable in the relevant scientific community." The US Supreme Court revoked the two lower court opinions and defined the principles and the methodology that must be followed by a court when judging scientific evidence.

The most important new standards for admissibility in the *Daubert* decision were as follows:

1. *Reliability.* The *Daubert* test requires that the methods used and the theories referred to must be tested and reliable and that statements made by the expert are falsifiable.
2. *Peer review and scientific publication.* To verify reliability of theories that are offered by an expert witness these must have been previously published or submitted to the scientific community for review.
3. *Error rate.* The expert has to be able to offer to the court the potential error rate of the findings and methods.
4. *General acceptance.* The general acceptance from the scientific community, while important, should not be considered a precondition for the admissibility of scientific evidence.
5. *Standard.* It is important to identify the existence and respect of standards known and recognized for the procedure and the methods adopted in the expert opinion.
6. *Applicability to the concrete case (fit).* Finally, for the method or the theory to be scientifically reliable, it must fit to the concrete case at hand and must be logically linked to it.

After the *Daubert* opinion, the Supreme Court, in the cases *Joiner* (1997) and *Kumho* (1999) went on to specify if, how, and when the *Daubert* test can and must be applied to soft sciences, which would also include crime linkage, and to expert witnesses. The central point of the opinions clarifies that the courts, in their gatekeeping role regarding the admissibility of scientific opinions, should apply the principles of the *Daubert* test to all expert witnesses and all types of evidence presented by an expert. Consequently, the *Daubert* test became the standard of admissibility in the United States not only for hard sciences, but also for soft sciences as well as technical and other specialized knowledge.

The use of these principles to determine the admissibility of evidence, and to evaluate it, can be found from the mid-1990s in Canadian, British, Australian, New Zealand, and Italian court opinions considering crime linkage and offender profiling evidence as well. For example, the Canadian Supreme Court has expressly adopted the *Daubert* standard in some cases: *R. v. Mohan* (1994), *R. v. J.L.J.* (2000), and for profiling evidence in *R. v. Ranger* (2003). In the United Kingdom, the courts have applied the *Daubert* standard in several cases: *R. v. Robb* (1991), *R. v. Stagg* (1994), and *R. v. Guilfoyle* (2001). Additionally, in 2005, the House of Commons Science and Technology Committee in the United Kingdom recommended the creation of a Forensic Science Advisory Council to regulate forensic evidence in the United Kingdom and observed that

> [t]he absence of an agreed protocol for the validation of scientific techniques prior to their being admitted in court is entirely unsatisfactory. Judges are not well-placed to determine scientific validity without input from scientists. We recommend that one of the first tasks of the Forensic Science Advisory Council be to develop a "gate-keeping" test for expert evidence. This should be done in partnership with judges, scientists and other key players in the criminal justice system, and should build on the US *Daubert* test. (House of Commons Science and Technology Committee, 2005, p. 76)

Finally, The Law Commission of England and Wales (2011) has proposed to adopt a criterion like the *Daubert* standard to help reform the law of evidence in regard to the admissibility of scientific evidence.

In Australia, the criteria have been applied to criminal profiling evidence in *R. v. Hillier* (2004). In New Zealand, Section 25 of New Zealand's Evidence Act of 2006 does not include an explicit reliability test for expert evidence, but the New Zealand Law Commission envisages that the US *Daubert* guidelines will "continue to be important in the inquiry about reliability that is inherent in the substantial helpfulness test" currently governing the admissibility of expert evidence in New Zealand (The Law Commission of New Zealand, 1999, p. 59). In Italy, too, in the Supreme Court opinion on the Franzese case

(2002), the criterion given in the *Daubert* opinion is used as a standard for evaluating scientific evidence.

What this means for crime linkage as expert evidence in these jurisdictions is that there is no place anymore for expert witnesses who give *ipse dixit* statements (stating something is true, just because they say so). Anyone who intends to offer expert opinions on crime linkage in these jurisdictions would need to fulfill the principles of the *Daubert* test and prove that the methods used are reliable. Practical problems with the implementation of the *Daubert* standard in court are discussed later in the chapter. The scientific community (including academics and practitioners) that deals with crime linkage would also need to agree on what constitutes scientifically reliable methods for its forensic application. If these challenges are not met, it will be increasingly difficult for crime linkage evidence to be admitted in some jurisdictions and for these techniques to find useful applications in the field of forensic science.

Review of Court Opinions in Crime Linkage Cases

Crime linkage is one of the offender profiling techniques used in the forensic context (Labuschagne, 2012; Turvey & Freeman, 2012). In our review of legal cases, the crime linkage expert typically offered an opinion on whether the same person had committed two or more crimes, that is, if the cases were linked. If, for instance, a prosecutor has hard evidence (e.g., a DNA test) linking an accused to a particular offense, but only has circumstantial evidence linking the same suspect to another offense under investigation (e.g., evidence that would put the suspect close to the crime scene of the second offense), the prosecutor may decide to charge the suspect for both cases using crime linkage analysis. Such an analysis would be conducted by examining the cases, the crime scenes, the *modus operandi*, the characteristics of the victims, and signature* behaviors. The expert then considers the similarity and distinctiveness of the crimes, stating the likelihood (either in descriptive terms, such as *it is likely*, or in statistical terms) of the offender being the same in all of the offenses (see Chapter 8 for a discussion of this issue). For the purposes of demonstrating what crime linkage evidence might look like and how the courts have reacted to such evidence, we present two cases in detail and summarize a number of others (see Table 10.1).

* An offender's signature is the unique combination of behaviors exhibited by the offender during the crimes (Labuschagne, 2006).

Table 10.1 Summary of Central Cases That Used Crime Linkage as Evidence in the United States and the Courts' Opinions Regarding Admission of the Crime Linkage Evidence

Year	Case	Court	Type of Crime	Evidence Request	Knowledge of Expert	Type of Evidence	Decision
1991	*Pennell v. State*	Superior Court of Delaware	Serial homicides	Prosecutor	FBI (BSU)	Crime linkage (all the homicides were committed by the same offender)	Admitted. Pre-*Daubert*. (not scientific evidence, so a *Frye* hearing about reliability not needed)
1994	*State v. Russell*	Court of Appeal of Washington	Serial homicides	Prosecutor	FBI (BSU)	Crime linkage (all the homicides were committed by the same offender)	Admitted. Post-*Daubert*. (not scientific evidence or new methods of proof so a *Frye* hearing about reliability not needed)
1999	*State v. Dunn*	Court of Appeal of Oregon	Robbery and kidnapping	Prosecutor	Sergeant Police Department	Crime linkage (evidence of other crime to prove crime linkage between two crimes by analysis of *modus operandi*)	Excluded. Post-*Daubert*. (The similarities are not sufficiently great to make evidence of the first crime admissible in the trial of the second)
1999–2000	*State v. Fortin*	Superior Court of New Jersey	Two homicides	Prosecutor	Crime scene analysis expert, criminologist	Crime linkage (all the homicides were committed by the same offender)	Excluded. Post-*Daubert*. (scientific evidence, so a *Daubert* hearing about reliability is needed)
2007	*People v. Prince*	Superior Court of California	Serial homicides; serial rape; serial burglaries	Prosecutor	FBI (BSU)	Crime linkage (the homicide and attempted homicide were committed by the same offender)	Admitted. Post-*Daubert*. (not scientific evidence, so a *Daubert* hearing about reliability not needed)
2007	*State v. Yates*	Superior Court of Washington	Two homicides	Prosecutor	FBI (BSU)	Crime linkage (common scheme or plan in two homicides)	Admitted. Post-*Daubert*. (reliability not discussed because the State presented abundant evidence, independent of the expert's testimony, that the two murders were a product of the same criminal plan)

BSU, Behavioral Science Unit.

Case 1: *State v. Russell* (1994)

In 1994, the Court of Appeals of Washington State gave an opinion in the case *State v. Russell*. George W. Russell was convicted by a King County jury of the first-degree murder of Mary Ann Pohlreich and two aggravated first-degree murders of Carol Beethe and Andrea Levine. The fourth issue the defendant raised in his appeal was whether the trial court erred in admitting expert testimony regarding the rarity of posed murder victims. In her pretrial ruling, the judge limited the experts by allowing them to testify only that the criminal methods employed in each case were unique and rose to the level of signature evidence. The experts were precluded from testifying that they thought that the same person committed all three crimes.

During the course of the trial, the court modified this ruling when defense counsel, during cross examination of the State's expert Robert Keppel, asked whether he knew of any other cases exhibiting the same behaviors. When the defense pursued the issue of the similarities and differences among these three murders and others, the court allowed Keppel to testify on redirect that in his opinion all of the murders were committed by the same person. Keppel based his opinion on the posing of victims and on the facts that all the victims were nude, all were female, and all were killed within a short period of time of their contact with the offender. He also observed that each crime involved the sexual insertion of a foreign object and that the offender needed to display these victims and ensure their discovery. Russell did not raise an objection to this line of testimony.

Later, at the same trial, the State's other expert, John Douglas, also testified that all of the victims were posed and that all of the murder scenes exhibited the same signature. Douglas based his opinion regarding signature on the fact that all of the victims had been posed in degrading and humiliating positions and on the fact that the murders occurred within a 67-day period and within a small geographical area. Again, Russell raised no objection but instead, in cross examination, sought to emphasize the differences between Pohlreich's murder and the other two murders. Douglas agreed that there were differences between the crimes, but explained on redirect that the differences were insignificant compared to the similarities. He stated that the significant issue was the posing of the victims in a degrading manner.

At issue here are references made by John Douglas and Robert Keppel to the HITS (the Washington State Attorney General's Homicide Investigation Tracking System) and ViCAP (the Federal Bureau of Investigation's Violent Criminal Apprehension Program) databases, which they used to support their testimony regarding the rarity of posing. These programs generate statistics regarding behavioral rarity on the basis of forms filled out by a local law enforcement officer for each homicide in the database. These forms list the various characteristics of homicides in Washington and the whole country, respectively. The trial court found that the expert testimony referring to HITS and ViCAP did not involve novel scientific evidence and was, therefore, subject only to the requirements of the Federal Rules of Evidence 702 (2010). The Court of Appeal's opinion about the admission of the expert testimonies was the following:

> In the case at bar, the trial court ruled that both Keppel and Douglas were widely recognised as authorities in crime scene analysis. Both men have extensive experience in serial crime analysis and investigation. The court then found that their testimony would not involve the application of a new scientific technique and that a Frye hearing was unnecessary. We agree with the trial court that the Frye test clearly was inapplicable to the expert testimony regarding the HITS and ViCAP programs. These programs are nothing more than sophisticated record-keeping systems. The court correctly analyzed the admissibility of this testimony under F.R.E. 702 and we find no abuse of discretion in the admission of the experts' testimony. Russell also objects to this testimony on the ground that it was statistical. Neither expert expressed his opinion about the rarity of posing in precisely quantified terms, though Douglas testified as to the number of cases on ViCAP and Keppel testified as to the number of cases on HITS. Russell maintains, however, that by specifying the extent of these databases, Keppel and Douglas implicitly testified that Russell was guilty as a matter of mathematical probability. We first note that there is no prohibition against using well-founded statistics to establish some fact that will be useful to the trier of fact. Second, both experts relied on the databases primarily as support for the conclusion that posing is a rare occurrence and not for the conclusion that there was a statistical probability that Russell committed the murders and both expressed their opinions in non-quantifiable terms.

This judgment, in our opinion, is interesting for a number of reasons. It illustrates how for some years after the *Daubert* ruling, the courts continued to apply the *Frye* test, especially in the case of soft science experts. In this decision, prior to *Kumho* (1999), the court deemed *Frye* (and *Daubert*) as irrelevant because the databases were only used to support the experts' conclusions and because both experts relied more on case materials and personal expertise in drawing their conclusions. It is important to notice, however, that the court also specifically pointed out that "both experts relied on the databases as support for the conclusion that posing is a rare occurrence and not for the conclusion that there was a statistical probability that Russell committed the murders."

According to our review of cases, it was a common procedure used by the courts before 2000 (which is when the Federal Rules of Evidence, Rule 702 was amended to include the *Daubert* standard) to avoid a hearing under the *Frye* or *Daubert* tests and to admit an expert to testify only for his *ipse dixit* and experience in a professional field.

Case 2: *State v. Fortin* (2000)

The case of Steven Fortin represents various trials and appeals. The case was initially tried in the Middlesex County Superior Court, New Jersey. The first appeals were made to the Appellate Division of the Superior Court in New Jersey, and the second round of appeals was handled by the Supreme Court of New Jersey. We chose this case for inclusion in the chapter because it is the first case where a State Supreme Court gave an opinion on the admissibility of crime linkage evidence and gave specific consideration to the reliability of the technique of crime linkage.

The defendant, Steven Fortin, was charged with the capital murder of Melissa Padilla, which had taken place on August 1994 in New Jersey. In pretrial evidentiary rulings, the Superior Court held that evidence to the effect that the defendant had sexually assaulted and nonfatally strangled a female police officer (Gardner) in Maine could be admitted as "other crimes evidence," and that a proposed witness could testify as an expert on ritualistic and signature crimes. The State's proposed expert on *modus operandi* and ritualistic behavior was Robert Hazelwood, a former FBI agent with 35 years of experience as a law enforcement professional. Hazelwood determined that the *modus operandi* of the crimes involving Padilla and Gardner included 15 similarities (for further details, see Hazelwood & Warren, 2004). Hazelwood concluded that the crimes committed against both victims were anger motivated and that the offender demonstrated anger through the following *ritualistic* or *signature* behavior in both crimes: (1) bites to the lower chin; (2) bites to the lateral left breast; (3) injurious anal penetration; (4) brutal facial beating; and (5) manual frontal strangulation.

In determining that the same person committed the two attacks, Hazelwood concluded:

> In my 35 years of experience with a variety of violent crimes, I have never observed this combination of behaviours in a single crime of violence. The likelihood of different offenders committing two such extremely unique crimes is highly improbable. It is my opinion that the same person was responsible for the two crimes.

The original trial judge accepted the expert under N.J.R.E. 702, to be qualified to offer an opinion that the same offender committed both crimes. In contrast, the opinion of the Supreme Court of New Jersey, Appellate Division (1999) was supportive of the defendant's claim that

> the judge erred in qualifying the witness as an expert on modus operandi and ritualistic behaviour, to express his opinion that the same person who committed the Maine assault against Trooper Gardner is the same person who committed the Padilla murder.

They explained that although Hazelwood's evidence was

> not based on science in the technical sense, his linkage-analysis methodology is certainly founded in the area of behavioural science. We conclude that the same detailed analysis regarding admission of scientific evidence is applicable and necessary in determining whether linkage analysis expert testimony is admissible.

In other words, the Appellate Court's opinion indicates that the *Daubert* standard should have been used as a method of assessing admissibility.

The Appellate Court made particular reference to their concerns regarding the reliability of crime linkage:

> Where we differ with the judge is his conclusion that the expert's linking analysis is sufficiently reliable for admission in this capital murder prosecution. The State argues that expert linkage analysis testimony has been admitted in other jurisdictions as sufficiently reliable like in Pennell v. State, 602 A.2d 48 (Del.Supr.1991). However, those cases involved serial killers or rapists, with multiple crimes. Here, there is an attempt to link behaviour in two crimes, under circumstances where there are as many differences as there are similarities.

The Appellate Court also made a distinction between the use of crime linkage to advise police investigations versus its use in the court:

> The expert testified that modus operandi and ritualistic behaviour are the subject of articles and books, and that he teaches this criminal investigative technique to law enforcement personnel. We have no doubt that these methods are valid and have great value in performing the very difficult task of criminal investigation. We are not persuaded, however, that these techniques are sufficiently reliable for an expert in those fields to testify that the same person who committed one crime committed the other under the analysis of the facts and circumstances presented in this case.

After the Appellate Court's decision, the case reached the Supreme Court of New Jersey on appeal and cross appeal. The Supreme Court of New Jersey, O'Hern opinion (2000) was as follows: "we agree with the judgment of the Appellate Division that the proposed expert testimony concerning linkage analysis lacks sufficient scientific reliability to establish that the same perpetrator committed the Maine and New Jersey crimes." The Supreme Court also added the following observation: "The government expert's report fails to meet the standards for the admission of testimony that relates to scientific knowledge. The field of linkage analysis is not at a 'state of the art' such that his testimony could be sufficiently reliable."

Referring to their earlier decision regarding the admission of expert testimony in the case *State v. Kelly* (1983), the Supreme Court again focused on the scientific reliability of the evidence, adding that "linkage analysis is a field in which only the expert and a few of his close associates are involved. In this respect, there are no peers to test his theories and no way in which to duplicate his results." Here, the court acknowledges a central trait of the scientific principle and an important criterion in the *Daubert* standard: others should be able to replicate the expert's findings in order for them to be deemed reliable.

The court also went on to criticize the expert's conclusion: "We are not so certain that the *modus operandi* factors cited by the expert, such as that both victims were mature females and were attacked while alone and at night time, demonstrate an 'unusual pattern,' " stating that the testimony could have been helpful if, for example,

> the witness can from a reliable database offer evidence that a combination of bite marks on the breast, bite marks on the chin, and rectal tearing inflicted during a sexual attack is unique in his experience of investigating sexual assault crimes.

The opinion goes on to state that

> [s]uch expert testimony would help a court make an initial determination of whether to admit the other-crime evidence and would, if presented at trial, better enable a jury to understand whether the crimes were "unusual and distinctive so as to be like a signature." It's not in this case.

The Supreme Court concluded: "Stripped of its scientific mantra, the [expert's] testimony is nothing more than a description of the physical circumstances present"; it affirmed the judgment of the Appellate Division and reversed the conviction. Subsequently, a new trial was ordered in which both the prosecution and defense called in new experts to testify. New appeal and cross appeal followed, partly because the prosecutor's new expert used the ViCAP database for a new crime linkage analysis. This evidence was consequently deemed inadmissible because the 1995 Gardner sexual assault had been inserted into the database for the sole purpose of making the link after the crime linkage testimony had initially been given. However, outside the legal dispute regarding this case, in our opinion, the Supreme Court of New Jersey's decision was a turning point for the admissibility of expert evidence in the field of soft science, in general, and for crime linkage or crime analysis in particular.

On the basis of this opinion, the new standard for all scientific experts in the United States (including crime linkage experts) would be the *Daubert* test. Indeed, the Supreme Court of New Jersey in the *Fortin* case stated a *Daubert* hearing would always be needed when the expert witness' methodology, although not based on science in the technical sense, is founded in the area of science. Also in the field of crime linkage, or other crime analysis techniques, the US courts must decide on the scientific reliability of the expert witness' testimony using the *Daubert* standard. Thus, the *Fortin* opinion sets out the *Daubert* standard as the preferred standard for assessing crime linkage evidence, and it is our opinion that its adoption across different jurisdictions would improve the reliability of expert testimony on crime linkage.

The *Fortin* opinion that the *Daubert* standard should be used to assess crime linkage evidence is not, however, the only opinion on crime linkage-like evidence from the United States (Table 10.1). For example, in the *People v. Prince* (2007) opinion, the California Supreme Court stated:

> [O]ther courts extend the rule permitting experienced officers to testify concerning criminal *modus operandi* to the topic of expert opinion testimony on *modus operandi* admitted for the purpose of establishing linkage among crimes. The Delaware Supreme Court concluded that an FBI agent properly was permitted to testify as an expert regarding serial murders, and that he properly could opine that the three charged murders were committed by the same person. (*Pennell v. State*, 1991). The court determined that the expert had extensive and specialised experience with signature crimes and crime analysis. (Ibid.) It added that the expert's testimony could assist the jury in understanding behaviour "unknown to the general public."

The Supreme Court of California continued:

> In our view, [The Supreme Court of New Jersey, in the Fortin case], applied an incorrect standard in searching the "scientific community" for "peers to test the expert's theories" and "duplicate his results."* [In fact the testimony in the *People v. Prince* case] was based upon the expert's extensive experience, not theories that normally would be subject to peer review or that would be otherwise comparable to DNA testing. This testimony was not cloaked in scientific garb but was expressed as a matter of professional experience gained over a lengthy period of observation and the expert did not employ a mathematical formula to add a specious weight to his conclusion.

We disagree with the latter opinion, because the court accepts the expert's opinion based on his experience, rather than looking at the scientific reliability of his statement, and concur with the *Fortin* opinion. These opinions are

* Here the court is referring to the *Daubert* standard, specifically the falsifiability of scientifically reliable statements, and the fact that any expert should be able to reach the same conclusion (duplicate the results) from the facts of the case. Essentially, what they are saying is that the *Daubert* standard was, in their opinion, the wrong set of criteria to evaluate the admissibility of an expert's opinion.

in line with the *Daubert* trilogy opinions and also with the new Federal Rules of Evidence 702 (2010).* Most importantly, we agree with the Supreme Court of New Jersey's statement in the *Fortin* case, in that crime linking indeed is set in the behavioral sciences as its aim is to analyze and quantify behavior. Therefore, crime linkage should be based on scientific theory and methodology that strives to meet the general scientific principles put forth in the *Daubert* standard. This would enable the courts to evaluate the reliability of experts' crime linkage methodology and use this as a standard in assessing the admissibility of said experts' testimony. Next, the weaknesses in an opinion-based approach to crime linkage analysis, and how these weaknesses can be addressed with a scientifically founded approach, will be discussed.

Problems in Current Ways of Producing Crime Linkage Expert Opinions

The reason why *ipse dixit* arguments are problematic is because they are open to the risk of cognitive bias or errors in reasoning that can distort our decision making. Our own experience, as a basis for decision making, is not a reliable database. Finnilä-Tuohimaa (2009) showed this to be true in a forensic expert decision-making context, suggesting the most reliable way of providing expert evidence and minimizing the risk of cognitive bias, would be to adopt a scientific method (such as the one outlined in the *Daubert* standard). This way, the experts' reasoning and conclusions would be transparent and verifiable. Other researchers have also questioned the importance of experience in forensic expert decision making. In psychological profiling, for example, Kocsis, Irwin, Hayes, and Nunn (2000) showed that education and insight into human behavior might be more important in forming an accurate decision, than actual experience of forensic investigations. In another study, Kocsis and his colleagues reported results that suggested an ability for scientific reasoning that might be more important than investigative experience in generating an accurate offender profile (Kocsis, Hayes, & Irwin, 2002). Although the influence of cognitive bias would have to be empirically tested for crime linkage decisions specifically, the risk of bias distorting experts' decision making is certainly something we have to con-

* If scientific, technical, or other specialized knowledge will assist the trier of fact to understand the evidence or to determine a fact in issue, a witness qualified as an expert by knowledge, skill, experience, training, or education, may testify thereto in the form of an opinion or otherwise, if (1) the testimony is based upon sufficient facts or data, (2) the testimony is the product of reliable principles and methods, and (3) the witness has applied the principles and methods reliably to the facts of the case (Federal Rules of Evidence 702, 2010).

sider. Another issue that needs to be studied further is whether investigative experience influences crime linking accuracy.

As pointed out above (see Table 10.1 for examples), the expert on crime linkage is most commonly asked by the prosecutor or investigating police officer to state whether the behavior from two (or more) crime scenes is similar and distinct enough for the crimes to be considered to have been committed by the same offender (see Chapter 8). Often the expert then testifies to the fact that the offender is the same (although there are some cases where the expert has testified to the opposite, e.g., Turvey, 2009). This scenario presents another serious problem from a psychological decision-making perspective. For example, Pakkanen, Zappalà, Grönroos, and Santtila (2012) pointed out that the expectancy effect* may influence how two crime scenes are viewed. In a practical situation, where an expert is asked to evaluate the linkage of offenses, the fact that the investigating authority suspects the same offender of committing the crimes under scrutiny might influence the expert to overemphasize similarities in the offenses and consequently make the incorrect conclusion that the cases are linked. This general phenomenon is widely recognized and is known as confirmation bias, a tendency for people to favor information that confirms their beliefs or hypotheses (Nickerson, 1998). Confirmation bias has been shown to also be an influencing factor in criminal investigations in general (e.g., Ask & Granhag, 2005; O'Brien, 2009; Rassin, Eerland, & Kuijpers, 2010).

The effect might be considered especially accentuated in a situation where the expert is called in when a particular suspect is already accused for the crimes the expert is asked to evaluate. In the *Fortin* case (described earlier), the Supreme Court of New Jersey was not convinced by the expert's statement about an "unusual [behavioral] pattern," saying he was focusing on the similarities of the two offenses, rather than the many differences between them. The court further suggested that the expert could provide a scientific backing for his analysis (e.g., they refer to *a reliable database* to ground his conclusion that the behavioral pattern was indeed unusual). After the Supreme Court ruling, the State presented a search from ViCAP demonstrating the similarities between the two crimes for which *Fortin* was on trial. However, this search was deemed inadmissible because the 1995 Gardner sexual assault had been inserted into the database after the crime linkage testimony had initially been given. This was done for the sole purpose of making the link and this could have biased the coding (into the database) of particular behaviors. For obvious reasons, there is a risk of confirmation bias distorting the ViCAP search, which the court noted and took into consideration when declining the admission of it into evidence. It is also of critical importance to objectively

* According to the expectancy effect, the outcome of a study is influenced by the expectations of the observer (Rosenthal, 1966).

evaluate the case as a whole, looking at both similarities and dissimilarities (as pointed out by the court's opinion; Turvey & Freeman, 2012) and ideally provide a statistical measure of rarity for said similarities and dissimilarities, in order to minimize the risk of confirmation bias.

In their review of observer effects, expectation, and suggestion in forensic science, Risinger, Saks, Thompson, and Rosenthal (2002) proposed blind testing as the principal method of preventing distortions caused by expectation. This is also the recommended method to minimize the effects of expectation in behavioral science research in general (Wilkinson, 1999). To introduce a blind method of testing crime linkage, the authors would like to suggest a similar setup to the one used by police in lineup identifications (e.g., Wells et al., 1998).

In a police lineup, a witness is asked whether the person he or she saw at the crime scene is present in a group of people constructed by the police, including a suspect. Similarly, the crime linkage task could be set up so that rather than asking the crime linkage expert "Is offense A similar to offense B?" the question could be, "Which of the offenses B, C, D, E, F, and G is similar to offense A?" In this setup, the crime suspected by the prosecution or police to be linked to offense A would be inserted into a sample of unlinked crimes, or *filler offenses.* A key question that would need to be resolved before this procedure could be considered fair (and the ensuing evaluation be considered reliable) is how to pick out the filler offenses. As a minimum, the offenses should be of the same crime category as the suspected linked crime (e.g., rape, burglary, or homicide), have occurred in the same geographical area, and have been committed within the same time frame. The filler offenses should also be convicted crimes, so that there would be some degree of certainty that the offenders who committed those crimes are not the same as the current suspect or there should be physical forensic evidence that confirms they are not the work of the same offender. A more complicated issue would be what parameters to set for the *modus operandi* of the filler offenses, so that they would be credible fillers (i.e., how similar with respect to behavior they should be to the query crime), yet make crime linkage possible. This could be a possible area for future research. With such results unavailable at this time, the recommendation would be to pick the filler offenses randomly.

Practical Considerations in Giving Expert Evidence on Crime Linkage

The fundamental question facing an expert giving testimony on the probability of linkage of two (or more) crimes is, "When is the behavior in offense A and offense B similar and distinct enough for the two offenses to be considered linked?" If we want to move away from *ipse dixit* testimonies on crime linkage and move toward a more systematic and scientifically based argumentation, as required by the *Daubert* standard, we need to critically consider what factors influence the probability of cases being linked.

It is important to stress that the question, "Are offenses A and B linked?" is not a simple yes or no question, but rather an estimate of probability. In our opinion, the expert should be able to quantify this probability, which amounts to providing an error rate for their estimate (third article of the *Daubert* standard). Hence, from a scientific point of view, we need to consider what is required for any expert to be able to estimate the probability of two (or more) cases being linked or not. The central factors to consider when estimating the probability of linkage are (1) behavioral consistency of offenders from one offense to another in a particular crime type, (2) a reliable, comprehensive database of a particular crime type for a particular area, where salient behavioral (and other) variables have been reliably entered, and (3) the base-rate frequency of crime features (and combinations thereof) in a particular crime type.

Behavioral Consistency

Behavioral consistency is a prerequisite for crime linkage (Woodhams, Hollin, & Bull, 2007). There is a growing body of research evidence suggesting offenders' behavior is somewhat stable over a series of offenses (for a review of the evidence see, e.g., Woodhams et al., 2007). Other chapters of this book go into more detail on the topic (see Chapters 2 and 6), and there is much to be done in terms of developing research methodology to take into account, for example, situational factors in a crime (see Chapter 13). When considering consistency, one needs to also consider how the type of crime impacts on the probability estimate of linkage. For example, research is needed to determine whether murderers are more consistent in their behavior than rapists. These are important questions for researchers to investigate because they would inform how practitioners conduct crime linkage.

In terms of the *Daubert* standard, this means that the practitioner conducting the crime linkage would have to take into account how these variations in consistency (e.g., in different crime types or different situations from one offense to another) influence their probability estimate of a particular case. Thus, the practitioner is also faced with the everlasting problem of applying research findings to the field: how does the average consistency of behavior calculated in a research study from a large sample of offenses apply to a specific case and the behavioral consistency of a particular offender? It may be that there are particular behaviors or behavioral patterns that define subgroups of offenses that are committed by more (or less) consistent offenders, which is an important empirical question to resolve.

When the expert is deciding on which crime scene variables to consider for a reliable linkage analysis, a bottom-up approach might be in order, instead of the top-down approach seen in the reviewed court cases. A bottom-up approach, or an empirical approach, would be to look into the current research to determine which variables are most reliable in establishing linkage decisions and then to look at these particular variables in the offenses at hand. In contrast to this, a top-down approach, or an intuitive approach, would consist of trying to apply an empirically unverified theory to the offenses, defining the similarities in behavior between the cases as the critical ones to consider. The risk with the latter approach is human error in the form of confirmation bias; the tendency to seek evidence that support our initial conception of the case. The expert's initial conception might again be distorted by the expectancy effect, as explained earlier.

However, as the Supreme Court of New Jersey pointed out in the *Fortin* case, reporting an offender's behavioral pattern is not sufficient alone to prove a link between crimes, the behavioral pattern needs to be related to a sample (or a *reliable database*) in order to provide a statistical measure of its uniqueness.

A Reliable Database

A reliable database should include variables that are salient for crime linkage. Further research is needed to establish what these variables are. In addition, this research needs to be conducted locally, for specific countries, jurisdictions, and areas, where the linkage analysis is to be applied. A dialogue between practitioners and researchers is necessary, not only for the practitioners to populate the database with the right variables, but also for the researchers to investigate how crime linkage can be made more reliable (or indeed discredit methods used in the field that are not efficient). The former point was partly the problem in the *Fortin* case: the ViCAP database did not include all the variables (e.g., "bites to the chin") that the testifying expert was analyzing.

Where a database can be developed, it needs to be populated with suitable cases. For example, if crime distances are used in the linkage of burglaries in a rural community, a database populated with burglaries from an urban area will be unsuitable because the distances between the crimes are likely to be significantly larger in the rural community. In terms of size (number of cases) of the database, it is again worth adopting a scientific method and tasking researchers to determine what size of sample is needed for the current crime linkage methods to produce reliable predictions.

Where databases already exist, or where they can be developed, another issue to be considered is how reliably cases can be coded (by law enforcement personnel). Snook, Luther, House, Bennell, and Taylor (2012) investigated the inter-rater reliability of the Violent Crime Linkage Analysis System* coding and found the level of agreement between police officers filling in the details of the same case to be low. To minimize the risk of human error in the coding process, the definitions for variables in any coding scheme need to be clearly formulated and communicated. Additionally, lengthy and laborious coding schemes could be refined with appropriate research, by suggesting which variables are salient for crime linking and thus worth registering in the database.

In terms of the financial resources needed to establish, develop, and maintain a reliable database, it needs to be recognized that this task might be unachievable for smaller jurisdictions, those in less affluent countries, and for volume crimes (such as burglary, shoplifting, or bicycle thefts). Where crime linkage systems (such as the Violent Crime Linkage Analysis System) are not available for law enforcement officials and experts, research samples could be used to provide the necessary statistical backing to claims of uniqueness and distinctiveness of offenders' behavioral patterns. These samples would again have to be evaluated for reliability and relevance to the cases at hand in order to estimate their impact (potential error rate) on the conclusions of crime linkage decisions.

If researchers and practitioners are to work together to identify the best means of establishing and developing databases that allow for scientific and reliable means of crime linkage, researchers will need to pay increased attention to the ecological validity† of their research. The more valid the research is, the more usefully that research can inform database development. For example, most existing studies of crime linkage use samples of solved (or convicted) crimes. This approach has been criticized for the fact that solved crimes may differ in *modus operandi* from unsolved crimes, making models for crime linkage, and recommendations for practice developed from samples of solved crimes, potentially inapplicable where crime linkage is conducted on unsolved crimes (Bennell & Canter, 2002; see Chapter 6). A few studies (e.g., Tonkin, Woodhams, Bull, & Bond, 2012; Woodhams & Labuschagne, 2012) have tried to increase the ecological validity of their research samples by including crimes classified as unsolved, but which have physical forensic evidence linking the crimes together.

Another problem concerning ecological validity in crime linkage research is that most studies have been conducted using only serial offenses, rather than samples that include both serial and one-off offenses. In reality, there is a large amount of unsolved crimes, where only a portion (varying to

* The Violent Crime Linkage Analysis System is an automated crime linkage system developed by the Royal Canadian Mounted Police (RCMP). It is presently also used in Belgium, the Czech Republic, France, Germany, Ireland, the Netherlands, New Zealand, Switzerland, and the United Kingdom. Similar systems are also used elsewhere in the world, for example, the FBI's ViCAP in the United States (Royal Canadian Mounted Police, n.d.).

† Ecological validity of a study means that the methods, materials, and setting of the study approximate the real world that is being examined (Brewer, 2000).

some extent, depending on the type of crime) of them have been committed by serial offenders. In the future, researchers need to use samples containing both serial and one-off offenses. The actual proportion of serial to one-off offenses for different types of crimes is something we do not yet know and is, therefore, another important research question for us to investigate further.

When examining crime linkage analysis using only serial offenses, research might overestimate behavioral similarity and linkage efficiency. Although some studies (e.g., Harbort & Mokros, 2001; Kraemer, Lord, & Heilbrun, 2004; Park, Schlesinger, Pinizzotto, & Davis, 2008) have investigated differences between one-off and serial (homicide and rape) offenses, further research is needed to find out if a crime series can be identified from a mixed sample of serial and one-off offenses and how a mixed sample influences crime linkage efficiency. These research questions would have to be answered by studying solved (or convicted) one-off offenses to have some certainty that the one-off offenses are not actually parts of yet undiscovered series.

In conclusion, decisions from legal cases in the United States have required crime linkage evidence to be supported by a reliable database. Developing such databases poses a number of research questions that first need to be answered (e.g., What behaviors should be included in the database? What sample size is sufficient for reliable predictions? How can coding reliability be maximized?). Answering these questions will require collaboration between researchers and practitioners.

Frequency

It would seem that in the cases reviewed for this chapter, the experts' arguments for a link between two crimes is made by saying that it is the rarity of a specific combination of behaviors, a behavioral pattern shared by two offenses, that is the key to offering the opinion that they are the work of the same offender. However, when adopting a scientific approach to crime linkage, it is not sufficient to list the similarities (and differences) of the cases under scrutiny and form an opinion on which similarities and difference are critical to consider; the observations of similarity need to be quantified, by providing supporting statistics that demonstrate how unlikely the behavioral pattern is to arise by chance (i.e., the likelihood that such a pattern would emerge for two unlinked offenses; see Chapter 8).

According to Bayesian reasoning,* frequencies of behavior or their combinations are needed to determine probability (e.g., of crime linkage). Thus, the probability of crimes being linked is influenced by answering the question, "How frequent (or rare) is a particular set of behaviors?" This

* For an explanation on Bayesian reasoning see Bernardo and Smith (2007). For a discussion on Bayesian versus orthodox statistics see Dienes (2011).

means that the likelihood of two offenses being linked is higher if they share a rare, as opposed to a frequently seen, combination of behaviors. However, this is not enough. It is also of importance to understand the likelihood of the database containing a linked offense. That is, for some offense types, serial crime is more likely than for other offense types. This base rate probability of a database containing a linked offense should similarly be taken into consideration when determining the likelihood of linkage.

To illustrate, let us assume that in a database of 1000 offenses, only 10 offenses include a particular combination of behaviors. An expert, considering the linkage of two crimes displaying this combination of behaviors, could conclude that because only 1% of the offenses display this particular behavioral pattern, it could be considered *unusual*, thus making the probability high that the two offenses were committed by the same offender. If then only 2 of the 10 offenses in the database are serial offenses (while 8 are one-off offenses), the probability that the offenses under consideration are linked is significantly smaller compared to the probability that the offenses have been committed by different individuals.

One critical issue here is that in the real world, we will not likely know with any certainty which offenses in a database are one-off offenses and which are not. Seemingly one-off offenses might be committed by serial offenders who have not yet been caught. Even with solved, apparent one-off cases, the police might not know if the crimes form part of an unknown offense series. More research is thus needed to determine whether serial and one-off offenders vary in their behavior enough to reliably classify an offense as either a serial offense or a one-off offense.

In addition, as highlighted above, we do not yet know the actual ratio of one-off to serial offenses for different crime types (nor how this ratio may vary across jurisdictions). Although this is another important research question that needs further investigation, the proposed mathematical model for an estimate of probability (i.e., a Bayesian model) allows us to estimate the error rate of such gaps in empirical evidence on our prediction. For the example above, we could review research findings and databases to come up with a qualified estimate of the proportion of one-off to serial offenses, for example, 15%–30%. The probability estimate could then be calculated for these threshold values, giving us an estimate of probability with error margins.* By comparing the frequency of the behavior(s) for the linked crimes to the frequency of the same behaviors in offenses that are not linked, we could estimate the uniqueness of the behavior(s) for that particular offender. From this, we could estimate the probability and error rate of the cases being linked.

* For the values provided in this example, the estimate would state that there is a 15%–30% probability of the crimes being committed by the same offender (assuming perfect behavioral consistency).

Is It Feasible to Achieve the *Daubert* Standard with Crime Linkage Evidence?

Gatowski et al. (2001) surveyed 400 state court judges in the United States on their opinion and understanding of the *Daubert* standard. A vast majority (91%) of the judges supported the gatekeeping role as defined by *Daubert*, regardless of the admissibility standard followed in their state. The study did, however, find that many of the judges lacked the scientific literacy needed to apply the standard (the hardest concepts to operationalize were falsifiability and error rate). Further, Groscup, Penrod, Studebaker, Huss, and O'Neil (2002) found in an evaluation of appellate opinions in the United States that the importance of *Frye* and the general acceptance criterion decreased over time, whereas the importance of the *Daubert* standard had increased. However, another study by Dahir et al. (2005) found that *Daubert*'s impact on the admissibility of offender profiling evidence was negligible. The study noted that most of the judges neither understood, nor applied the more technical terms of *Daubert*, specifically error rate and falsifiability. Judges need, therefore, to be trained in the basic concepts of scientific reasoning in order to be able to fulfill their gatekeeping role. As gatekeepers become more proficient in evaluating the reliability of expert evidence, experts will have to ensure that their statements are empirically founded.

It is important to recognize that the *Daubert* standard represents a set of guidelines. The standard summarizes core scientific principles and the guidelines show the courts what to consider when evaluating scientific expert evidence. Empirical science itself is ever evolving, and in accordance with *Daubert*, we are guided to use the most reliable methods and best evidence *currently* available. In the authors' view, the *Daubert* standard, therefore, presents us with an ideal to strive for with regard to crime linkage when it is being used as expert evidence. Following this ideal, we believe that the methods used for crime linking can be made more transparent and open to scientific inquiry. At the same time, this means that if the current methods of crime linking are found to be unreliable, we have to accept the fact that crime linking opinions should not be presented as evidence in court.

Conclusion

This chapter chose to evaluate current and past crime linkage practices as provided to the courts as expert evidence against the *Daubert* standard. This standard was chosen because it represents the most accurate legal definitions of scientific principles. Because crime linkage evidence pertains to behavior, it is a psychological practice and therefore has its roots in behavioral science. The authors firmly believe that striving to make crime linkage analysis more scientific, and using *Daubert* as a guide in achieving this, is the way toward more reliable and valid expert evidence on crime linkage. With the reviewed cases in mind, this would mean that experts would have to back up their opinions on crime linking by providing empirical support (e.g., frequencies from reliable databases, estimates of error) for their arguments. If this standard was adopted in all jurisdictions, it would have implications for the way crime linkage is practiced.

In terms of giving expert evidence on crime linkage, and looking at the current state of crime linkage research, we need to consider where we are lacking with regard to the *Daubert* standard. We must ask what additional data does the expert need in order to give scientifically valid and reliable testimony on the linkage of crimes? More work certainly needs to be carried out to integrate the experience and knowledge of crime investigators with the scientific know-how of the research community, which also presents a resourcing challenge for the police.

One useful step in this direction is the Crime Linkage International Network, an international collaborative network of researchers and practitioners who specialize in crime linkage analysis. This network was formed in 2013 with the aim of furthering research in the field of crime linkage analysis and developing guidelines for practice. Whereas some experts (e.g., those providing testimony in the court cases reviewed in this chapter) might lack scientific rigor in their methods and empirical backing to their claims, researchers could do a number of things to increase the ecological validity of their research, thereby making it more relevant and applicable to the needs of practitioners. The experiences and ideas of investigators need to be tested scientifically in order for them to stand up to the *Daubert* test. One place to start would be to test whether it is possible to identify serial offenses from a pool of crimes comprising both one-off and serial offenses. Another crucial area for investigation are the elements of human error (or cognitive biases) potentially affecting crime linkage decisions, the expectancy effect and confirmation bias being two of them. We need to consider, for example, if and how crime linkage decisions made by an expert are influenced if they know the crimes they are consulting on are believed to be linked.

References

Ask, K., & Granhag, P. (2005). Motivational sources of confirmation bias in criminal investigations: The need for cognitive closure. *Journal of Investigative Psychology and Offender Profiling, 2,* 43–63.

Bennell, C., & Canter, D. V. (2002). Linking commercial burglaries by *modus operandi*: Tests using regression and ROC analysis. *Science & Justice, 42,* 1–12.

Bernardo, J., & Smith, A. (2007). *Bayesian theory*. Chichester, England: John Wiley & Sons.

Bosco, D., Zappalà, A., & Santtila, P. (2010). The admissibility of offender profiling in courtroom: A review of legal issues and court opinions. *International Journal of Law and Psychiatry, 33,* 184–191.

Brewer, M. (2000). Research design and issues of validity. In H. Reis & C. Judd (Eds.), *Handbook of research methods in social and personality psychology* (pp. 3–16). Cambridge, England: Cambridge University Press.

Cooley, C. (2012). Criminal profiling on trial: The admissibility of criminal profiling evidence. In B. Turvey (Ed.), *Criminal profiling. An introduction to behavioral evidence analysis* (pp. 627–652). San Diego, CA: Academic Press.

Dahir, V., Richardson, J., Ginsburg, G., Gatowski, S., Dobbin, S., & Merlino, M. (2005). Judicial application of *Daubert* to psychological syndrome and profile evidence: A research note. *Psychology, Public Policy, and Law, 11,* 62–82.

Daubert v. Merrell Dow Pharmaceuticals, Inc. U.S., 125 L. Ed. 2d 469, 113 S. Ct. 2786 (1993).

Dienes, Z. (2011). Bayesian versus orthodox statistics: Which side are you on? *Perspectives on Psychological Science, 6,* 274–290.

Federal Rules of Evidence 702. (2010). *Testimony by expert witnesses.* Retrieved March 11, 2013 from http://www.law.cornell.edu/rules/fre/rule_702

Finnilä-Tuohimaa, K. (2009). *Expertise and decision making among clinicians in investigations of alleged child sexual abuse* (Doctoral dissertation). Turun Yliopisto, Turku, Finland.

Frye v. United States. 293 F. 1013 (D.C., Cir 1923).

Gatowski, S., Dobbin, S., Richardson, J., Ginsburg, G., Merlino, M., & Dahir, V. (2001). Asking the gatekeepers: A national survey of judges on judging expert evidence in a post-*Daubert* world. *Law and Human Behavior, 25,* 433–458.

General Electric Co. v. Joiner. 522 U.S. 136 (1997).

Groscup, J., Penrod, S., Studebaker, C., Huss, M., & O'Neil, K. (2002). The effects of *Daubert* on the admissibility of expert testimony in state and federal criminal cases. *Psychology, Public Policy, and Law, 8,* 339–372.

Harbort, S., & Mokros, A. (2001). Serial murderers in Germany from 1945 to 1995. *Homicide Studies, 4,* 311–334.

Hazelwood, R., & Warren, J. (2004). Linkage analysis: Modus operandi, ritual, and signature in serial sexual crime. *Aggression and Violent Behavior, 9,* 307–318.

House of Commons Science and Technology Committee. (2005). *Forensic science on trial. Seventh report of session 2004–05.* Retrieved March 11, 2013 from http://www.publications.parliament.uk/pa/cm200405/cmselect/cmsctech/96/96i.pdf

Kocsis, R. N., Irwin, H. J., Hayes, A. F., & Nunn, R. (2000). Expertise in psychological profiling: A comparative assessment. *Journal of Interpersonal Violence, 15,* 311–331.

Kraemer, G., Lord, W., & Heilbrun, K. (2004). Comparing single and serial homicide offenses. *Behavioral Sciences & the Law, 22,* 325–343.

Kumho Tire Company, Ltd. v. Carmichael. 526, U.S.137 (1999).

Labuschagne, G. (2006). The use of a linkage analysis as evidence in the conviction of the Newcastle serial murderer, South Africa. *Journal of Investigative Psychology and Offender Profiling, 3,* 183–191.

Labuschagne, G. (2012). The use of a linkage analysis as an investigative tool and evidential material in serial offences. In K. Borgeson & K. Kuenhle (Eds.), *Serial offenders: Theory and practice* (pp. 187–216). Sudbury, MA: Jones & Bartlett Press.

The Law Commission of England and Wales. (2011). *Expert evidence in criminal proceedings in England and Wales*. Retrieved March 11, 2013 from http://lawcommission.justice.gov.uk/docs/lc325_Expert_Evidence_Report.pdf

The Law Commission of New Zealand. (2009). *Evidence. Report 55—Volume 2. Evidence code and commentary*. Retrieved March 11, 2013 from http://www.lawcom.govt.nz/sites/default/files/publications/1999/08/Publication_58_178_R55%20Vol%202.pdf

Nickerson, R. (1998). Confirmation bias: A ubiquitous phenomenon in many guises. *Review of General Psychology, 2*, 175–220.

O'Brien, B. (2009). Prime suspect: An examination of factors that aggravate and counteract confirmation bias in criminal investigations. *Psychology, Public Policy, and Law, 15*, 315–334.

Pakkanen, T., Zappalà, A., Grönroos, C., & Santtila, P. (2012). The effects of coding bias on estimates of behavioural similarity in crime linking research of homicides. *Journal of Investigative Psychology and Offender Profiling, 9*, 223–234.

Park, J., Schlesinger, L., Pinizzotto, A., & Davis, E. (2008). Serial and single-victim rapists: Differences in crime-scene violence, interpersonal involvement, and criminal sophistication. *Behavioral Sciences & the Law, 26*, 227–237.

R. v. Guilfoyle. 2 Cr. App. Rep. 57 (2001).

R. v. Handy. 164 CCC (3d) 481, 2 SCR 908 (2002).

R. v. Hillier. ACTSC 81 (2004).

R. v. Robb. 93 Cr App R 161 (1991).

R. v. Stagg. U.K. Central Criminal Court, 121 (1994).

Rassin, E., Eerland, A., & Kuijpers, I. (2010). Let's find the evidence: An analogue study of confirmation bias in criminal investigations. *Journal of Investigative Psychology and Offender Profiling, 7*, 231–246.

Risinger, M., Saks, M., Thompson, W., & Rosenthal, R. (2002). The *Daubert*/Kumho implications of observer effects in forensic science: Hidden problems of expectation and suggestion. *California Law Review, 90*, 1–56.

Rosenthal, R. (1966). *Experimenter effects in behavioral research*. New York, NY: Appleton-Century-Crofts.

Royal Canadian Mounted Police. (n.d.). *Violent crime linkage analysis system*. Retrieved March 26, 2013 from http://www.rcmp-grc.gc.ca/tops-opst/bs-sc/viclas-salvac-eng.htm

Snook, B., Luther, K., House, J., Bennell, C., & Taylor, P. (2012). The violent crime linkage analysis system: A test of interrater reliability. *Criminal Justice and Behavior, 39*, 607–619.

State v. Kelly. 97 N.J. at 197, 478 A.2d 364 (1983).

Tonkin, M., Woodhams, J., Bull, R., & Bond, J. (2012). Behavioural case linkage with solved and unsolved crimes. *Forensic Science International, 222*, 146–153.

Turvey, B. (2009). *Linkage analysis report* (*re Commonwealth of Massachusetts v. Timothy Imbriglio*, Case No. 9773CR0017). Presented via expert testimony given March 9, 2010.

Turvey, B., & Freeman, J. (2012). Case linkage: Offender modus operandi and signature. In B. Turvey (Ed.), *Criminal profiling: An introduction to behavioral evidence analysis* (pp. 331–360). San Diego, CA: Academic Press.

Wells, G., Small, M., Penrod, S., Malpass, R., Fulero, S., & Brimacombe, C. (1998). Eyewitness identification procedures: Recommendations for lineups and photospreads. *Law and Human Behavior, 22,* 603–647.
Wilkinson, L. (Task Force on Statistical Interference, Board of Scientific affairs, APA). (1999). Statistical methods in psychology journals: Guidelines and explanations. *American Psychologist, 54,* 594–604.
Woodhams, J., Hollin, C. R., & Bull, R. (2007). The psychology of linking crimes: A review of the evidence. *Legal and Criminological Psychology, 12,* 233–249.
Woodhams, J., & Labuschagne, G. (2012). A test of case linkage principles with solved and unsolved serial rapes. *Journal of Police and Criminal Psychology, 27,* 85–98.

11 The Ability of Human Judges to Link Crimes Using Behavioral Information

Current Knowledge and Unresolved Issues

REBECCA MUGFORD AND
MELISSA MARTINEAU

Contents

Introduction 251
Studies Examining Human Performance on the Linking Task 252
Canter et al. (1991) 253
Santtila et al. (2004) 255
Bennell et al. (2010) 257
Tonkin (2012) 260
Limitations of the Research on Linking and Human Judgments 262
The Stimuli Employed in the Study Task 262
Variations in Defining *Experience* 266
Measurement of the Decision-Making Process 267
Overemphasis on Actuarial Linking Models for Comparison Purposes 270
The Type of Linkage Task Examined 271
Minimizing the Divide between Research and Practice 272
References 273

Introduction

A large body of empirical research conducted to date has focused on the extent to which humans can make accurate decisions under ambiguous conditions (e.g., Dawes, Faust, & Meehl, 1989; Kahneman, Slovic, & Tversky, 1982; Kuipers, Moskowitz, & Kassirer, 1988), and whether prior experience in a given domain can improve decision making (e.g., Chan, 1982; Fisher & Fonteyn, 1995; Meehl, 1954). A criminal investigation is one such situation where complex decisions must be made under considerable amounts of ambiguity (Ask & Alison, 2010). For example, decisions regarding whether the same offender is responsible for multiple crimes are often difficult to make as the physical evidence (e.g., DNA) that would typically eliminate uncertainty in these situations is often unavailable (Grubin, Kelly, & Brunsdon, 2001). As such, behavioral information obtained from the crime scene must sometimes be relied upon to make connections between crimes (Hazelwood & Warren, 2004; Woodhams, Hollin, & Bull, 2007). Making decisions using this type of information may be difficult because the quality of the data may be poor, and there are often ample behavioral features to choose from yet only a select few may result in accurate linkage decisions.

Despite these potential problems, a number of studies have shown that it is statistically possible to link crimes using certain subsets of behavioral information (e.g., Bennell & Canter, 2002; Grubin et al., 2001; Santtila et al., 2008; Tonkin, Grant, & Bond, 2008; Woodhams & Labuschagne, 2012). However, such statistical approaches to linking have not been adopted into widespread practice; rather, linking decisions are often made using the behavioral clues that are deemed relevant by individual practitioners (see Chapter 8 for a discussion of these issues). Few studies have examined the extent to which human judgment can result in accurate linking decisions (Canter et al., 1991; Tonkin, 2012). The purpose of this chapter is to review the findings of the few studies that do exist, discuss some of their limitations, and propose strategies for conducting studies that may move this field of research forward.

More specifically, we argue that the apparent discord between linking research and practice may exist because, in linking research, an emphasis has been placed on purely statistical approaches to linking, without considering the extent to which it is possible to make linkage decisions based on an integration of statistical findings and human judgment (i.e., often called structured professional judgments (SPJs); Hart & Logan, 2011). In addition to addressing some other methodological concerns, we argue that perhaps the most logical first step toward repairing this divide is to shift the focus in linking research from a comparison of the performance of statistical models and human judges to a comparison between statistical models, human judges, and an integration of both. Until practitioners see value in the linking models developed through research and can easily implement the tools developed, the extent to which linking research informs practice will continue to be minimal.

Studies Examining Human Performance on the Linking Task

Generally speaking, the practical importance of behavioral crime linking research lies in whether the linking models developed through empirical research provide a viable alternative to linking methods currently used in practice (i.e., decisions made by humans). To evaluate the practical importance of these linking models, a number of research questions need to be adequately examined. These include the following:

1. How do humans compare to the models developed through research in their ability to make accurate behaviorally based crime linkages?
2. Does the experience (e.g., investigative, crime analytics, and linkage analysis) of the human improve decision accuracy?
3. How do humans make their linking decisions (i.e., what information do they rely upon) and how does the provision of empirically based decision support impact upon their decision process and decision accuracy?

Successfully answering these questions will set the groundwork for determining (1) whether there is value in constructing and implementing a decision support tool to help practitioners make linkage judgments, (2) what type of decision support tool is best, and ultimately, (3) whether the nature of the decision support tool employed should vary as a result of different factors (and what these factors might be).*

To our knowledge, four studies have been conducted to date with the primary goal of assessing various issues surrounding human performance on the linking task (Bennell, Bloomfield, Snook, Taylor, & Barnes, 2010; Canter et al., 1991; Santtila, Korpela, & Häkkänen, 2004; Tonkin, 2012). To determine whether the research conducted thus far on human decision making and the linking task has satisfactorily answered the above questions, a review of the findings is provided next, followed by a review of some of the methodological pitfalls that may impact the weight placed on the findings of this body of research as it currently stands.

Canter et al. (1991)

In the first study to examine the performance of human judges on the linking task, Canter et al. (1991) provided a sample of detectives ($N = 32$) from five police departments in the United Kingdom with information on 12 solved serial sexual assaults committed by four offenders (each offender having three crimes in their series). The study was conducted in two phases: an individual phase, where the detectives were asked to make their own

* For example, it is possible that different decision support tools may be needed to cater to the different types of linking scenarios that are encountered in the investigative setting. One type of linking scenario involves instances where behavioral features of a predefined set of crimes are examined to determine whether or not they are likely the work of the same offender. Alternatively, large databases of crimes may be searched proactively to determine whether any noticeable patterns exist that could suggest the existence of a serial offender (Alison & Rainbow, 2011; Woodhams, Bull, & Hollin, 2007; also see Chapter 8).

individual linkage decisions, and a group phase, where the detectives were assigned to groups and asked to come to a consensus on the links between crimes. Detectives were provided with modified victim statements for each crime, describing only the offender's behavior during the sexual assault. While reviewing the materials, the detectives were asked to identify the characteristics of the assaults that they deemed pertinent to making their linkage decisions and to explicitly indicate which assaults possessed each of these characteristics. At the end of the session, they were asked to indicate which crimes they believed were part of the same series. Officers were then assigned to one of seven groups (containing three to six persons) and asked to deliberate among themselves on the similarities and differences between the crimes. Following the group discussions, each group was asked to provide a decision as to which crimes were linked to a common offender, comprising a series.

In terms of individuals' linking accuracy, results revealed substantial variation among detectives in terms of their ability to link crimes, with many performing at or below chance level. For example, out of the 28 detectives who provided individual linking decisions, the largest proportion (10 or 35.71%) correctly identified links between 3 out of the 12 crime pairs (25% accuracy). In contrast, a small proportion of participants (3 or 10.71%) correctly identified all but one series (8 of 12 identified, or 66.66% correct). Although these results indicate that at least some of the detectives were relying on appropriate behaviors and strategies, it is clear that the bulk of participants either (1) were relying on inappropriate linking strategies (e.g., noninformative linking behaviors) or (2) could not adequately connect the important aspects of these crimes to make accurate decisions (Canter et al., 1991).

Multidimensional Scalogram Analysis (MSA) was then conducted to determine whether statistically modeling the relationship between the crimes in terms of the behaviors reportedly relied upon could improve the accuracy of linking decisions.* Each detective was asked to select the top three or four behaviors he or she believed to be most relevant to the linking task out of their respective *relevant behaviors* lists. Using these behaviors, data matrices were then formed for each group of detectives, where the cells of the matrix reflected whether each identified characteristic was present or absent across all 12 crimes. This resulted in the construction of seven different data matrices and corresponding MSA plots (one for each group) that

* As explained by Canter et al. (1991), MSA is a multivariate approach to analyzing the relationship between different variables across cases. The results are displayed pictorially so the user is able to visualize the relationship between the items (i.e., crimes) on the plot in terms of how similar and different they are to one another with respect to the information used to construct the plot (e.g., in this case, linking features/cues deemed important by the detectives in the study). As such, the closer two crimes are in space to one another, the more similar their behavioral profiles are in terms of the linking features they reflect.

displayed the relationship between each of the 12 crimes on the basis of the behavioral features that were identified as most pertinent by the members of each group.

For each group, Canter et al. (1991) then compared two versions of their respective MSA plots—one where the crimes were separated into four series of three crimes as a function of their location on the plot (i.e., each of the three crimes closest in space were considered a part of the same series) and one where the crimes were separated into different series as a function of each group's predictions after the group discussion phase of the study. Results revealed that, although the same behavioral information was used to form both the MSA plots and group decisions, the MSA representations were better able to correctly identify crimes belonging to the same series than the groups of detectives themselves.

Overall, Canter et al.'s (1991) results suggest that police detectives, who do not have any specialized linkage analysis experience or training, do not perform well on crime linkage tasks when they are not provided with decision support. That being said, a higher number of correct linkage decisions were made using the MSA representation, which was comprised of the information detectives themselves identified as important. In other words, although the detectives were able to identify the relevant crime features to use when making linkage decisions, the detectives performed worse when asked to make the decisions themselves without the organizational framework offered by the MSA support. As explained by Canter et al. (1991), this is likely due to the fact that humans as a group possess limited cognitive capacity for processing complex relationships between variables, such as the similarities and differences between multiple crimes that need to be processed simultaneously in order for correct linkage decisions to be made. Indeed, a large body of research supports the notion that humans possess a highly limited working memory and can only process a select amount of information at any given time (e.g., Baddeley, 1992; Groeger, 1997; Miller, 1956; Neath, 1998).

Santtila et al. (2004)

It is difficult to determine how well versed the detectives in Canter et al.'s (1991) sample were in sexual assault behavior and investigation, as no specific information was provided outlining their prior experience with this crime type (nor their experience with linkage analysis). It is possible that appropriate investigative experience could have helped participants offset the cognitive load inherent in the linking task, potentially improving their performance. Indeed, studies in the domain of learning have shown that, under optimal conditions, experts in a given domain perform better, and experience lower levels of cognitive load, than novices (see Kalyuga, 2007 for a review of some of this research).* Moreover, a number of other studies have demonstrated that experience can improve decision-making accuracy in a variety of contexts (e.g., Charlin, Tardif, & Boshuizen, 2000; Fisher & Fonteyn, 1995; Lamond & Farnell, 1998). At the same time, some research has contradicted these findings, demonstrating that experience in a given domain does not always lead to increased accuracy (e.g., see Grove, Zald, Lebow, Snitzet, & Nelson, 2000). Shanteau (1992) explains that the performance of experts seems to depend on the nature of the domain in which their expertise lies. For example, many of the domains where experts are found to underperform deal with areas of human behavior that make it difficult for experts to obtain feedback on the accuracy of their decision-making process (e.g., parole decision making, student admissions). In contrast, domains where experts perform well are more concrete and provide ample opportunity for immediate feedback concerning the correctness of the particular strategies used (e.g., mathematics, chess).

Recognizing this body of research, Santtila et al. (2004) sought to examine the role that investigative experience plays in the linking context by comparing the accuracy of vehicular crime linking decisions made by four groups of individuals varying in degrees of experience: (1) veteran investigators with directly relevant (i.e., vehicular crime) experience ($n = 9$), (2) veteran investigators with more general (i.e., other types of crime) experience ($n = 9$), (3) novice investigators with 6 months or less of general investigative experience ($n = 7$), and (4) laypersons (i.e., students and office workers) with no investigative experience ($n = 8$).†

Participants were provided with the original crime reports for 30 solved Finnish vehicular crimes committed by 10 offenders, each with three offenses in their respective series. In order to monitor their decision-making strategies, participants were asked to think aloud while reviewing the crime reports and were also interviewed after completing each study session.

With respect to the decision accuracy of each group, results indicated that investigators, as a whole, made significantly more correct linking decisions than laypersons; however, no significant differences in decision accuracy were found between investigators with varying degrees of experience (i.e., the

* In this context, *optimal conditions* generally refers to tailoring the amount of external support provided to the individual to their level of prior experience with the particular domain of interest. Generally speaking, experts should be provided with less support than novices in order to decrease cognitive load and as such, increase learning/performance.

† The percentage of investigative work allotted to vehicular crimes was measured across groups, with vehicular crime investigators reporting that approximately two-thirds (63.61%) of their investigative work focused on vehicular crimes, whereas only a small segment of the cases encountered by experienced general investigators and novice investigators involved vehicular crimes (4.12% and 4.43%, respectively).

vehicular crime, general crime, or novice investigator groups). It is important to note, however, that the mean accuracy scores did follow the expected pattern, with the vehicular crime investigators scoring highest (59% correct), followed by the general investigators (43% correct), novice investigators (41% correct), and laypersons (28% correct). It is certainly plausible that the lack of significant findings in this respect may be the result of a lack of statistical power given the small size of each subgroup. As such, these results reflect a possibility that relevant, crime type-specific experience may be more beneficial in the linking context than simply having general investigative experience.*

In terms of the decision-making process, the vehicular crime investigators used significantly fewer linking clues in the process of making a linkage decision than all other groups, suggesting that they were possibly relying on their prior knowledge when making decisions. Moreover, a significant relationship was found between the accuracy of linking decisions across all participants and the number of linking clues used, with those using fewer clues making more correct linking decisions than those using a greater number of linking clues.

Overall, these results indicate that there may be an element of experience that is important to the linking task, at least in the context of serial car thefts. Moreover, accurate linking decisions seem to be related to a particular subset of variables, although not all participants (even those with relevant experience) were able to select the most appropriate features for this task. It is also important to note that the most experienced group (experienced vehicular crime investigators) still achieved a level of accuracy that was far from optimal (correctly linking, on average, 59% of crimes).

Bennell et al. (2010)

Although the results of Santtila et al. (2004) suggest that investigative experience may enhance the accuracy of linking decisions, the small number of participants comprising these groups limits the amount of weight that can be placed upon the results. Similarly, they did not directly examine whether groups with more experience relied significantly more or less on specific linking clues than groups with less experience. This may have shed light on the mechanisms behind the enhanced performance of the more experienced participants relative to the completely naïve participants in their study. Equally important, the method used to measure decision accuracy (i.e., percentage correct) makes it difficult to determine whether the more experienced investigators were truly using a more accurate linking strategy

* Santtila et al. (2004) do, however, indicate that the lack of significance here may also truly reflect the fact that expertise in the linking of vehicular crimes may be related to general investigative experience rather than experience with vehicular crime specifically.

than the novice participants, or whether they simply adopted different decision thresholds to determine when the crimes were similar enough to be considered linked (Bennell, Jones, & Melnyk, 2009). Finally, Santtila et al.'s (2004) sample did not make a high number of accurate linking decisions (e.g., 59% correct decisions for experienced vehicular crime investigators), raising the question of whether a purely statistical approach to linking could provide further improvements to decision-making accuracy.

In an attempt to resolve these issues, Bennell et al. (2010) directly compared the accuracy of linking decisions made by individuals varying in policing experience to the predictions made by a logistic regression model. A group of students ($n = 40$) and police professionals (consisting of crime analysts, police officers, police psychologists; $n = 31$) were provided with information on 38 pairs of commercial burglaries committed in the United Kingdom. A select subset of information was provided for each crime: the location of each offense on a map, the straight-line distance in kilometers between each pair (inter-crime distance), entry methods, target selection characteristics, and the property stolen. Approximately half of the students and half of the police professionals (i.e., the *trained* groups) were advised that, according to research, the single most accurate linking feature for determining whether the same offender has committed a pair of commercial burglaries is the inter-crime distance (e.g., see Bennell & Jones, 2005). For comparison purposes, the logistic regression equation containing only inter-crime distance from Bennell and Canter's (2002) study on commercial burglaries was also applied to the same 38 crime pairs. On 10-point scales, participants were asked to indicate their linkage decisions for each crime pair (1 = not at all confident crime pair is linked, 10 = extremely confident crime pair is linked) and the extent to which they used each piece of offense information to inform their linkage decisions (1 = not at all, 10 = very much).

To control for the possibility that the apparent differences in accuracy between groups may solely be the product of different linking decision thresholds, Bennell et al. (2010) used receiver operating characteristic (ROC) analysis to evaluate linking performance across the different groups (see Bennell et al., 2009; Chapter 14 for a more detailed explanation of how ROC analysis overcomes the threshold issue). Results revealed that all groups (including the logistic regression model) performed significantly better than chance ($p < .001$). However, the linking decisions made by students [mean area under the curve (mean AUC) = 0.76]* were significantly more accurate than decisions made by police professionals (mean AUC = 0.67). Similarly,

* The AUC varies between 0 and 1.00 and can be interpreted in a similar way to effect sizes. The guidelines for interpretation provided by Swets (1988) are often followed, which state that AUCs below 0.50 are uninformative, AUCs between 0.50 and 0.70 are indicative of low levels of decision accuracy, AUCs between 0.70 and 0.90 are indicative of moderate levels of decision accuracy, and AUCs above 0.90 are indicative of high levels of decision accuracy.

the linking decisions of trained participants (mean AUC = 0.77) were significantly more accurate than the decisions of untrained participants (mean AUC = 0.67). Overall, however, the logistic regression model made significantly more accurate linking predictions (mean AUC = 0.87) than all other groups combined (mean AUC = 0.72).

Relative to all other linking features, participants relied significantly less on spatial information, despite the findings of previous research suggesting that such information leads to the most accurate linking decisions (e.g., Bennell & Canter, 2002; Bennell & Jones, 2005; Tonkin et al., 2008). Students reported using the maps to a significantly greater extent than the police participants; however, there were no significant differences in reliance as a function of training condition (although the means were in the expected direction, with the trained individuals reporting higher mean reliance scores for the maps and inter-crime distance information than the untrained individuals).

The results of this study suggest that, even when individuals have some amount of investigative experience and/or have been provided with some basic training about which cues to attend to when making linking decisions, adopting a statistical approach to linking could be a viable way to increase the accuracy of linking decisions. As explained by Bennell et al. (2010), this may simply be because statistical approaches only rely on information that is empirically related to the linking process, whereas decision makers are free to rely on any of the information available, regardless of its empirical standing.

Interestingly, Bennell et al.'s (2010) results surrounding the role of experience in linking performance directly contradicted those of Santtila et al.'s (2004). Bennell et al. (2010) offered a number of possible explanations for the poor performance of police professionals relative to the naïve participants in their sample. For example, Bennell et al. (2010) acknowledged that the crimes used in the linking task were from a geographic area in which many of the police professionals lacked familiarity, whereas the statistical model was based on data from the same location as these crimes. Indeed, over half of the police participants were employed in the United States and Canada although the crimes in the linking task were sampled from the United Kingdom.* Second, approximately half of Bennell et al.'s (2010) police sample, but none of the student sample, indicated that temporal information (which was not provided to participants) would have enabled them to come to better linkage decisions. Indeed, previous research has found that temporal information is useful in distinguishing between linked and unlinked crimes, even after offender spatial behavior is taken into account (e.g., Markson, Woodhams, & Bond, 2010; Tonkin, Santtila, & Bull, 2012).

* Although the inability to use local knowledge may have negatively impacted the performance of police professionals, it likely would not have influenced the performance of the student sample.

Tonkin (2012)

Recently, Tonkin (2012) also pointed to the fact that the police group in Bennell et al.'s (2010) study consisted of a wide range of professionals (e.g., police officers, crime analysts, and other police professionals, such as police psychologists) that likely vary considerably in their degree of linkage analysis experience. It is possible that the wide variation in experience (including a lack thereof) among the members of this police sample may have negatively impacted the performance of the group as a whole.* As such, Tonkin conducted a study addressing the limitations of Bennell et al.'s (2010) study across two types of crime—residential burglary and commercial robbery. Although the same general procedure was followed as Bennell et al. (2010), some methodological adjustments were made. Specifically, to provide a more balanced comparison between *experts* and *non-experts* in the linking domain, Tonkin (2012) selected crime analysts with at least some real-world crime linkage experience.† Moreover, he purposely included statistical linking models that were not constructed using crimes from the same jurisdiction as those used in the study linkage task, to ensure that both the analysts and the statistical models were disadvantaged with respect to jurisdictional familiarity. Finally, Tonkin (2012) included temporal information as part of the stimuli used in the linking task.

Students ($n = 100$) and crime analysts ($n = 37$) were separated into trained and untrained groups, with half of each group receiving the residential burglary task and half receiving the commercial robbery task.‡ Each task was comprised of 15 crime pairs (three linked and 12 unlinked). Participants were provided with a package containing the following information: a map displaying the location for each possible crime pair, the inter-crime distance between each pair, the number of days lapsed between each pair, target property features, and items stolen during the offense. In the case of residential burglary, information pertaining to the offender's entry behaviors and behaviors while inside the premises was also provided. In the case of commercial robbery, additional information reflecting the offender's planning and attempts to exert control over the victim was also provided. Similar to Bennell et al. (2010), participants were asked to rate how likely it was that each particular

* Bennell et al. (2010) stated that the professional group's lower performance seemed to be the result of the police officers, rather than the crime analysts and other police professionals (although significance tests examining this issue could not be conducted due to the small sample sizes). In comparison with crime analysts, police officers in general may have less experience with conducting linkage analysis, which could have lowered the mean accuracy scores for the police group in Bennell et al.'s study.

† The crime analysts had an average of 7.09 (SD = 4.31) years of experience conducting behavioral linkage analysis, and all but five had experience with the particular crime types under examination.

‡ The training was accomplished in a similar way to Bennell et al. (2010).

crime pair was linked and the extent to which they used the various linking features to form their decisions.

In terms of residential burglary, results indicated that the two regression models employed (one constructed on crimes from the same location as the study task crimes and the other constructed using different crimes) were significantly more accurate at the linking task than any of the groups. In contrast, for the commercial robbery task, crime analysts achieved statistically higher levels of decision accuracy relative to the logistic regression model and the students. The only significant effect of training was found in the residential burglary task, where the training was found to increase the accuracy of decisions made by students, but decrease decision accuracy of crime analysts.

Finally, in terms of reliance on the different linking features, participants completing the residential burglary task generally indicated that they relied on a number of potentially irrelevant linking features (e.g., property stolen) to a significantly greater degree than more empirically robust features, such as the inter-crime distance. In contrast, participants completing the commercial robbery task relied on a mix of relevant (e.g., control behaviors) and irrelevant (e.g., planning behaviors) features. The only significant effects of experience and training were found in the residential burglary task, where crime analysts reportedly relied on the maps and inter-crime distance features to a significantly greater extent than did the students. Trained participants reportedly used inter-crime distance measures to a significantly greater degree than untrained participants.

What is important about Tonkin's (2012) findings is that the effect of linkage experience on decision accuracy directly contradicts the results of Bennell et al.'s (2010) study. It may be the case that when groups are defined more narrowly in terms of their experience, higher linking accuracy is achieved. That being said, this was not necessarily the case in the residential burglary sample, where the logistic regression models performed best.* Tonkin (2012) explains that the discrepancy between the two crime types may be that higher quality information is available in commercial robberies given that victim statements contain information that does not need to be inferred from the crime scene. There are, however, other differences that may account for the discrepancy in results between these studies. For instance, compared to Bennell et al. (2010), Tonkin (2012) used a much smaller number of crime pairs in the linking task (38 crime pairs vs. 15 crime pairs, respectively), which arguably may call into question the reliability of the reported AUCs. Similarly, the fact that the average AUCs achieved by many groups in Tonkin's (2012) study were extremely high (e.g., AUC = 0.99 for untrained

* It is important to note, however, that the crime analysts receiving the residential burglary task still maintained a high level of linking accuracy according to Swets (1988) guidelines (e.g., AUC = 0.91 for untrained crime analysts).

police participants provided with the commercial robbery task) compared to the AUCs reported by Bennell et al. (2010) raises the question of whether the linking task was somehow more simplistic than that used in other research.

Limitations of the Research on Linking and Human Judgments

Although the studies reviewed above have raised some compelling questions, there are a number of limitations within this body of research, which impact the extent to which some of the results should be relied upon. Given that different and sometimes contradictory findings have surfaced across the existing studies, it is difficult to synthesize the results of this research. As such, the questions raised at the outset of this chapter have not been fully answered yet. This is not to say that researchers in this area are unaware of the limitations of the existing studies. In fact, they often identify the limitations and call for further research to address these shortcomings.

The purpose of this section is to discuss these various limitations and propose some possible strategies for moving forward. The limitations can be grouped into those relating to (1) the stimuli used in the studies, (2) variations in defining *experience*, (3) how the decision-making process is measured, (4) the overemphasis on actuarial approaches to linking for comparison purposes, and (5) the type of linking task examined. Ultimately, the approach moving forward should be to design studies that address the issues raised below in order to provide more complete answers to the human performance questions raised above and to ensure that practitioners and researchers alike see the value in the subsequent results of such studies.

The Stimuli Employed in the Study Task

A number of issues exist with the stimuli used in existing studies. These issues generally involve the crime type used in the studies, the type, format, and amount of information provided about the crimes, and the extent to which the jurisdiction from which the crimes are drawn from parallels the jurisdiction in which the police participants work.*

* Other issues concerning the stimuli used in the human performance studies exist and can extend to the research on crime linking more generally. For example, data used to develop empirically based linking models to date have overwhelmingly relied on solved serial crimes. Researchers in this area have raised these types of concerns countless times, and some strides have been made to address the ecological validity of the data used in these studies (e.g., Woodhams & Labuschagne, 2012). As such, these issues are not a focus of our discussion in this chapter (see Chapter 6 for a more complete discussion).

First, the crime type subject to analysis has varied across each study conducted thus far. This makes it difficult to draw general conclusions concerning the robustness of the results of these studies. Indeed, research conducted on linking more generally suggests that the performance of statistical models seems to vary as a function of the crime type under examination, with a tendency for interpersonal crime linking models to result in higher levels of predictive accuracy than property crime linking models (see Bennell, Mugford, Ellingwood, & Woodhams, 2014, for a review of some of this research). It is therefore likely that the ability of human judges to link crimes also varies as a function of crime type. Indeed, Tonkin's (2012) results suggest that this may in fact be the case. Tonkin (2012) explains that the higher accuracy of crime analysts relative to the statistical model in his commercial robbery sample may simply be the result of the fact that interpersonal crimes may provide a richer data source when making linkage decisions. Indeed, crimes involving the collection of victim statements can provide more detailed information for linkage purposes than crimes where behavioral information must be inferred from the crime scene itself (e.g., residential burglary). It is also possible that the fundamental value of human judgment in the linking context may lie in scenarios involving crimes of an interpersonal nature. For example, it is well known that crimes involving victim/offender interaction provide ample opportunities for the offender's behavior to change as a result of the crime dynamics (Keppel & Birnes, 2009). It may be that human judgment is needed to recognize when behavioral inconsistencies are the result of situational factors, something that the statistical linking models used in this research do not explicitly account for at this time (although some preliminary attempts to incorporate situational information into linking models have been made; e.g., see Woodhams, Hollin, et al., 2008).* Indeed, the "behavioral richness" of such interpersonal crimes may not be well reflected in the statistical approach to linking crimes. With that said, Canter et al.'s (1991) findings do indicate that detectives (albeit with an unknown amount of linkage analysis experience) do not perform well when linking serial sexual assaults.

Second, to improve the extent to which study conditions reflect reality (i.e., ecological validity), there remains some room for improvement in

* Related to the issue of crime type, none of the studies conducted thus far employ more than one crime type within a single linking task; however, research has demonstrated that most offenders are not specialists and instead tend to commit many crimes of different types (e.g., Leitner & Kent, 2009; see Chapter 12). There is also some evidence to suggest that, at least in the United Kingdom, linking across different crime types is being done (Burrell & Bull, 2011). Given that research has just begun to examine which factors are reliable for linking purposes across crime types (e.g., Tonkin, Woodhams, Bull, Bond, & Palmer, 2011), future research should also examine human performance (relative to statistical models) in this context.

terms of the type, format, and amount of crime information provided to participants. Although Tonkin (2012) improved upon Bennell et al.'s (2010) study by providing participants with temporal information, there are certainly a number of nonbehavioral features that crime analysts have indicated are useful for linkage analysis purposes that were excluded from these two studies. For instance, despite some potential problems with eyewitness information (see Wells & Olson, 2003 for an overview), witness accounts concerning offender descriptions or vehicle descriptions could prove useful in this context. Examining whether this additional information can improve (or not improve) linkage decisions made by both analysts and statistical models would be valuable. Indeed, Tonkin (2012) calls for the use of as much information that is available to crime analysts as possible in order to approximate the conditions under which analysts typically make these judgments.

Likewise, the format in which the behavioral information was provided to participants varied across studies. Both Canter et al. (1991) and Santtila et al. (2004) provided participants with relatively unaltered materials (e.g., victim statements, crime reports); however, Bennell et al. (2010) and Tonkin (2012) provided information pertaining to a select number of behavioral domains. The benefit of providing participants with information in the format they would encounter in practice is that the accuracy levels achieved are more likely to generalize to the real-world setting. However, it may be the case that the participants in the Bennell et al. (2010) and Tonkin (2012) studies either performed worse than they would in reality because the information was not organized in a manner that was familiar to them or performed better than they would in reality because the information was structured in a way that removed redundant and/or irrelevant information that was not useful to the linking process. Omitting extraneous information may have made the task cognitively easier for these participants in comparison with the participants in Canter et al. (1991) and Santtila et al. (2004). Indeed, Tonkin (2012) calls for research that further explores this issue to determine the extent to which performance may vary as a function of how the information is presented to the participants. Regardless, future studies should strive to provide a specified group of crime analysts with all of the information they are privy to in the real world, in a format they are familiar with. Ultimately, this would allow us to place more weight on the conclusions drawn concerning how statistical predictions compare to crime analysts' decisions under more realistic conditions.

Finally, Bennell et al. (2010) acknowledged the fact that the crimes used to construct their statistical model and the crimes used in the study task were from the same geographical region, whereas the police participants were from numerous locations, many from a different country than the crimes included in the study task. As such, results could have favored the statistical model given that the participants could have been applying localized linking strategies to stimuli that do not warrant this approach. Tonkin (2012) addressed this issue by including a statistical model where the crimes used to construct the model were from a different area than the crimes used in the study task. In effect, then, both the analysts and the statistical model were at a disadvantage with respect to this issue.

Tonkin's (2012) results suggest that a comparable level of highly accurate linking decisions could be made using the linking model based on the same location as the study task crimes (AUC = 1.00) and the linking model constructed using crimes from a different, dissimilar location to the study task crimes (AUC = 0.92). Although this suggests that the jurisdictional issue may not have been a problem in Bennell et al.'s (2010) study, linking research more generally suggests that the accuracy of linking models might vary across jurisdictions (Bennell et al., 2014).* Similarly, although Tonkin's approach provides a better comparison of the linking performance of the crime analysts relative to the statistical models than previous research, it does not necessarily provide the best estimate of the analysts' true linking ability. Arguably, if locally relevant knowledge is in fact found to be important and the crime analysts are unable to make use of this knowledge in these studies, then it is difficult to conclude that the decisions they make in the real world are subpar.†

If analysts do possess locally relevant knowledge that is important to the linking task, then perhaps determining a way to allow for crime analysts in these samples to use this knowledge would provide a better estimate of their true linkage ability. Such conditions would better reflect the crime analysts' ability to make linkage decisions within the context that they make them on a daily basis. Of course, allowing for the use of localized knowledge may create some other methodological concerns. For example, crime analysts cannot be familiar with the crimes included in the study task, as this would artificially increase their performance. As such, the crimes should not be from the exact jurisdiction in which the crime analysts work. It may therefore be best to ensure that the analysts, the crimes used in the study task, and the statistical models used for comparison purposes are all based on different locations, but matched across as many jurisdictionally relevant variables as possible. Exactly what characteristics the analysts, the crimes, and the statistical models should be matched on is an issue that requires a considerable amount of forethought; however, some possible characteristics include population density, crime rates, and land-use patterns (Bennell et al., 2010; Santtila et al., 2004). It is possible that allowing for the use of localized

* Some possible explanations for this may involve differences in road and/or land networks across regions, the availability of property targets or victims in a particular region, etc.

† It would first need to be established that analysts do possess locally relevant knowledge that improves their linking decisions.

knowledge could have improved the accuracy of Tonkin's (2012) crime analysts for *both* crime types, rather than solely the commercial robbery crime type; however, this question still remains to be answered.

Variations in Defining *Experience*

The studies conducted to date have engaged diverse participants (laypersons, students, general police officers, police investigators, crime analysts) with varying levels of crime analysis and linkage experience. The studies specifically examining the effect of experience have all adopted different definitions of the construct, and consequently, the *experienced* human judges comprising each sample vary widely. Again, this makes it difficult to compare the results of these studies and may also, at least in part, account for discrepancies in results as a function of experience level. With that said, results from two of the three studies examining the influence of experience suggest that some type of police experience may have a significant impact on the ability of the participant to succeed in the linking task (Santtila et al., 2004; Tonkin, 2012 vs. Bennell et al., 2010).

The use of different definitions of experience impacts to whom the results can be generalized in practice. For instance, Bennell et al. (2010) used the following general definition of experience for inclusion in their police sample: "[A]nyone having experience in crime analysis, police work, or a related field (e.g., police psychology)" (p. 15). Given this, the results of Bennell et al.'s (2010) study are not necessarily generalizable to those who have been formally trained in linkage analysis or to those who perform this task on a frequent basis. Likewise, the fact that Santtila et al. (2004) focused on police with experience in vehicular crime investigations, but not linkage analysis, hinders the extent to which their results can be generalized to those who may have more experience with linkage analysis in general or linkage analysis involving vehicular crime specifically.

This is not to say that crime analysts or those with experience and/or training are the only ones who engage in linkage analysis in the practical setting. Indeed, there are likely countless subsets of police professionals who conduct linkage analysis in the course of their duties. However, results of existing studies cannot be generalized to analysts who have been formally trained and/or have extensive crime analysis experience when the samples involved in these studies are comprised, at least in part, of general investigators and sometimes police psychologists with minimal formalized training and/or experience in this context.

The most task-relevant definition of experience was employed by Tonkin (2012), where he ensured that *all* crime analysts in his sample had some sort of previous experience with linkage analysis. Although Tonkin (2012) did ask participants to indicate the number of years of experience with linkage analysis, the frequency with which they conduct linkage analysis, and whether they had experience linking the crime types included in the study, no information was provided on whether these analysts were formally trained on linkage analysis. Consequently, it is unclear whether any estimates currently exist of either the absolute or relative (compared to statistical models) performance of a group of crime analysts who have been formally trained to conduct linkage analysis with a particular type of crime.

Perhaps designing an all-encompassing study that is applicable to the entire population of individuals who conduct linking in practice is neither possible nor desirable given the variation in training and linking strategies that likely exist on a global scale. Conducting multiple studies catered to the conditions faced by different groups of crime analysts, and then comparing results of these studies, may be the best way to determine the extent to which these subgroups of individuals can make accurate linkage decisions (and how they compare to empirically based decisions). Such studies may also indicate whether or not statistically based decision support tools would be valuable in each particular situation, and what form this support should take (e.g., fully actuarial, structured professional). Although this will inevitably involve more resources, studies such as these may be needed to clearly demonstrate to practitioners that a decision support tool may be of value to them if in fact they are found to perform at meaningfully lower levels than these support systems.

Measurement of the Decision-Making Process

Monitoring participants' decision processes is crucial, as these data can shed light on how certain individuals come to a particular linkage decision. Identifying the linkage strategies used can help inform why different groups of humans may be performing comparatively better, worse, or similar to statistical models. Likewise, if the particular decision strategies used are identified, their relative advantages and disadvantages can be weighed. This information may ultimately inform the development of novel decision support tools that are suitable for use in the investigative setting.

All of the studies reviewed above have attempted to monitor the decision-making process in some way. Canter et al. (1991) asked individuals to list the linking features that they used to make their decisions, select the features they believed to be most important, and then, using the features identified as important by each group, modeled the decision-making process at the group level (but not individually for each detective). Bennell et al. (2010) and Tonkin (2012) asked the participants to provide a numerical rating to indicate the extent to which they relied on each of the pieces of information made available to them (higher ratings being indicative of more reliance). In contrast, Santtila et al. (2004) adopted multiple methodologies for assessing the decision-making process, which included asking participants to think aloud while completing the study tasks and conducting a semi-structured interview with participants after each study session.

As acknowledged by these researchers, there are both benefits and downfalls to adopting each approach. For example, reliance scores (used by Bennell et al., 2010; Tonkin, 2012) have the benefit of being easy to obtain and analyze, and they also provide more objective answers than methodologies requiring interpretation of the participant's meaning (e.g., think aloud interviews). However, simply asking individuals to indicate how much they relied on a particular piece of information does not necessarily mean that the responses obtained will be valid and truly reflect the cognitive processes underlying their decision (Bennell et al., 2010). In fact, studies have shown that while some individuals may possess metacognitive awareness, or awareness of their own thought processes, this is not true of everyone (e.g., Flavell, 1979; Kelemen, Frost, & Weaver, 2000; Schraw & Dennison, 1994; Song et al., 2011). Indeed, the high accuracy of linkage decisions made by Tonkin's (2012) participants were not paralleled by high reliance scores for linking features that have been found to be empirically related to the decision task. Tonkin (2012) indicated that this discrepancy could simply be the result of the methodology selected for monitoring the decision-making process or the fact that participants were using irrelevant linking features in a different way from how they are represented in statistical models. Adopting more in-depth methodologies to assess the decision-making process could provide insight into why these results occurred.

The think aloud protocol used by Santtila et al. (2004) is one methodology that could provide researchers with more detailed information for review. With that said, collecting this information in real time can lead to disjointed verbalizations that are often difficult to interpret (Ericsson & Simon, 1993). Given this, it is important to ensure that inter-rater reliability is assessed when using these types of procedures.* Another drawback of the think aloud methodology concerns the fact that the mere instruction to think aloud may impact the content of participants' verbalizations (i.e., reactivity; Russo, Johnson, & Stephens, 1989). Having a control condition where participants are not asked to think aloud would help determine the effect that these instructions have on the decision process reported. Finally, in the case of experienced persons, some of their thought processes may be so automated as a result of their prior knowledge and/or training that they do not verbalize key aspects of their decision-making strategy (Santtila et al., 2004). Although using retrospective interviews with more direct questions

* Santtila et al. (2004) did not report any inter-rater reliability indices for the coding of the think aloud protocols, nor for the coding of the retrospective interviews.

(like Santtila et al., 2004) can help overcome some of the above difficulties, research has demonstrated that participants can fabricate details, and they often forget at least some of their decision process after they have completed the task (Russo et al., 1989).

Consequently, it may be valuable to explore other methodologies for assessing cognitive processes. For example, in other domains of decision making, eye movements have been monitored to obtain insight into the decision process (see Glaholt & Reingold, 2011 for a review) and this may be a useful way to track what people consider when carrying out linking tasks (linking tasks would obviously have to be devised in such a way that eye tracking was meaningful). Some common indices that are measured using this method include where and for how long the eye fixates and re-fixates, as well as the frequency and sequence of fixations (Russo, 2011). In comparison with the methods mentioned above, eye tracking has the benefit of recording what information is attended to in a nonreactive way (i.e., the methodology does not directly interfere with the process; Russo, 2011). Moreover, because eye movements are difficult to control voluntarily, tracking the eye movement of experts may help overcome the difficulties of simply using think aloud protocols mentioned above. Of course, eye tracking equipment is expensive and often not a part of a standard research laboratory. Another downfall is that although eye movements provide information concerning *what* information is attended to (and for how long), they do not necessarily provide insight into *how* this information is used (Russo, 2011).

Another technique that may be valuable is active information search (Huber, Huber, & Schulte-Mecklenbeck, 2011). In this method, participants are first provided with a very basic description of what the study task entails and are then permitted to ask for further information that presumably they believe will help them lead to a decision (Huber et al., 2011). Typically, the type, sequence, and frequency of information requests are recorded. Beyond controlling for reactivity, a central benefit of this approach is that how the information (e.g., its structure) is provided to participants does not influence the decision process (Huber et al., 2011).

As shown, there are benefits and limitations to each of the above noted approaches, and any future research should weigh the benefits/costs of adopting each approach. It may be that simultaneously using a mix of procedures (e.g., reliance scores, think aloud instructions, and eye movement indices) while continuing to recognize the limitations inherent in each technique is the best option for moving forward. Regardless of the exact techniques explored, using both objective (e.g., eye tracking) and subjective (e.g., think aloud protocols) methodologies to monitor the decision-making process, and examining the extent to which these methodologies lead to converging results, would increase confidence in those results.

Overemphasis on Actuarial Linking Models for Comparison Purposes

Another central issue in the research reviewed above concerns the fact that actuarial (or purely statistically based) linking models are overemphasized as the best empirically informed comparison to human judges (e.g., Bennell et al., 2010; Tonkin, 2012). In the linking research more generally, it has also been implicitly assumed that tackling the linking task from a purely statistical perspective is the best approach (e.g., Bennell & Canter, 2002; Markson et al., 2010). It is true that decades of research in numerous areas of decision making (e.g., offender risk assessment, medical diagnoses, etc.) have illustrated that actuarial decisions are often more accurate than clinical or experience-based decisions (e.g., Ægisdóttir et al., 2006; Dawes & Corrigan, 1974; Dawes et al., 1989; Grove & Meehl, 1996; Grove et al., 2000; Hanson & Morton-Bourgon, 2009; Meehl, 1954). For instance, in the often-cited meta-analysis conducted by Grove et al. (2000), statistical predictions surrounding human health- and behavior-related questions (e.g., criminal recidivism, medical diagnoses, academic outcomes, and job outcomes) outperformed clinical predictions in approximately 46% of the studies, while clinical predictions outperformed actuarial predictions in approximately 6% of the studies (no significant differences were found in the remaining studies). Thus, it is reasonable to believe that decisions should be based on actuarial assessments, and such arguments have been made in other areas of research as well (Garb, 2005; Grove & Meehl, 1996; Quinsey, Harris, Rice, & Cormier, 1998; Swets, Dawes, & Monahan, 2000).*

In contrast, others have argued that blending actuarial and experience-based decision making may be a more appropriate course of action in certain contexts (e.g., Hart & Logan, 2011). Such tools, often referred to as SPJ, provide the decision maker with an empirical foundation for their decision process while allowing for the introduction of discretion based upon professional experience (Douglas & Reeves, 2009; Hart & Logan, 2011). In the context of linking, both empirically relevant variables, such as inter-crime distance, and unique case details deemed important by the analyst can be integrated to form the ultimate decision. Beyond their flexibility, there are a number of other reasons why SPJ tools may be a more appropriate alternative to actuarial tools in certain contexts (Hart & Logan, 2011). First, allowing for this discretion/flexibility acknowledges that there may be some value to

* The arguments often posed for relying upon actuarial methods of decision making typically center around the finding that humans tend to rely on inappropriate heuristics (i.e., general rules-of-thumb) when forming decisions (Kahneman & Tversky, 1973). The use of certain heuristics can lead to information processing biases, such as confirmation bias, or false beliefs in relationships between variables when in fact they do not exist (Kahneman et al., 1982).

human judgment in linking decision making, and this may increase the likelihood that a tool will actually be used. Likewise, because the factors incorporated into SPJ tools are selected on the basis of a large body of empirical research, rather than solely on the basis of a large development sample (as is the case for many actuarial tools), SPJ tools often generalize better to other samples (Helmus & Bourgon, 2011). Given these possibilities, it seems that exploring both the accuracy and utility of SPJ decision aids in the linking context is warranted.

It is important to note, however, that some research in other domains suggests decision accuracy decreases as discretion increases (e.g., Hanson & Morton-Bourgon, 2009). As such, practitioners may need to accept this decrease in accuracy if they wish to incorporate discretion into the decision-making process. Indeed, it may be that the increase in usability outweighs the decrease in accuracy that arises when using a SPJ approach as opposed to an actuarial approach to linking.

The Type of Linkage Task Examined

A final issue concerns whether or not the empirical models that are compared to humans in these studies reflect the different types of linkage tasks faced by analysts in practical settings (this issue has also been raised in crime linking research more generally; e.g., see Chapter 8). Depending on the context, there are a number of ways in which the linking task can be tackled in practice (Alison & Rainbow, 2011; Canter, 2012; Woodhams, Bull, et al., 2007). On the one hand, two or more crimes may be brought forth by an investigating officer seeking a crime analyst's advice concerning whether or not the crimes are likely the work of a common offender. On the other hand, analysts may search a large database of crimes to determine whether any noticeable patterns exist that could suggest the existence of a serial offender.

The empirical linking models used in Bennell et al. (2010) and Tonkin (2012) generally reflect the latter approach to linking (i.e., where a large database is searched for similarities between crimes). Some have argued that these models may not be applicable to decisions made in practice that stray from this particular process (e.g., see Chapter 8). In order for practitioners to see value in the conclusions drawn from this research, they first need to believe that the empirically informed linking models that are being compared to them in these studies are applicable to the different linkage tasks they encounter in the real world. As mentioned by Bennell et al. (2014), these models may very well extend to various types of linking tasks, and studies are currently underway to determine if this is in fact the case. That being said, regardless of which approach to linking is taken (i.e., actuarial, structured professional, or clinical), research generally needs to determine if the current linking models developed through research extend to all types of linking and, ultimately, whether different types of decision support tools may be more appropriate for different types of linking tasks. Indeed, it may be the case that humans perform certain types of linking tasks well without the need for decision support; however, there may be certain tasks where the provision of decision support is crucial to making accurate linkage decisions.

Minimizing the Divide between Research and Practice

As evidenced in this review, although actuarial approaches to crime linkage have been studied for quite some time, virtually no research (with the possible exception of Canter et al., 1991) has examined how these approaches may be used to support the decisions of individuals tasked with linking crimes in naturalistic investigative settings. Likewise, with the exception of Canter et al. (1991), the performance of individuals has solely been compared to the performance of statistical methods, without consideration of the extent to which a combination of the two may provide a potentially viable alternative in practice. As explained above, practitioners may see value in a tool that allows them to use the robust findings of empirical research while simultaneously allowing them to adjust the decision by taking into account the idiographic features of a particular case.

Furthermore, it is difficult to conduct research that is generalizable to the vast number of jurisdictions and crime linkage strategies that are employed in the practical setting on a global scale. Perhaps the best place to start with future research in this area is to explore whether the current statistical models developed for linking purposes can extend to the different types of decisions that are made by linkage analysts in practice. If so, then continuing to compare their performance to appropriately defined groups of analysts may prove beneficial in moving the field forward. If not, then exploring other ways in which new tools can be developed (e.g., structured professional decision support tools), and comparing these tools to different groups of analysts, may be most appropriate. Statistical models could be used as the *base* prediction, and crime analysts could then decide whether the linkage predictions need to be altered on the basis of additional information they deem valid to making the correct decision in that particular context. Not only would this allow practitioners to take advantage of empirical relationships (between crime scene similarities and linkage status) while also providing them with some discretionary power, but it would also help them structure and organize information so they are better able to evaluate and interpret it. By first ensuring that practitioners see value in the tools being compared to their performance, perhaps they may be more willing to partake in research that evaluates, and potentially improves, their decision-making performance.

Regardless, future studies examining the extent to which humans can make linking judgments need to be more ecologically valid. Ideally, these studies will examine trained analysts (representing homogenous groups in terms of the conditions in which they work). These analysts will complete crime linkage tasks involving the same crime types that are typically the focus of their analytical work and under the same conditions in which they make their linkage decisions. Although this would limit the extent to which results could be generalized to other groups, it would at least allow researchers to determine whether certain types of individuals (i.e., those who have been properly trained in linking the particular crime type of question) can make decisions that are comparable to statistical tools (or hybrid tools involving statistical methods and human judgments). Of course, appropriately monitoring the decision-making process would also be beneficial to provide insight into how decisions in this context can be best supported. Replication of these studies using different groups of analysts, crime types, and conditions under which decisions are made could then be explored to help further refine the support tools that are needed.

Again, it is important to stress that these are all *ideal conditions* under which these questions should be answered. The extent to which these conditions can be realized for research purposes is yet to be determined. It is our hope that opening up a discourse between researchers and practitioners will allow for future research initiatives to be undertaken that both parties see as valuable to investigative practice.

References

Ægisdóttir, S., White, M. J., Spengler, P. M., Maugherman, A. S., Anderson, L. A., Cook, R. S., … Rush, J. D. (2006). The meta-analysis of clinical judgment project: Fifty-six years of accumulated research on clinical versus statistical prediction. *The Counselling Psychologist, 34*, 341–382.

Alison, L. J., & Rainbow, L. (Eds.). (2011). *Professionalising offender profiling: Forensic and investigative psychology in practice*. London, England: Routledge.

Ask, K., & Alison, L. J. (2010). Investigators' decision-making. In P. A. Granhag (Ed.), *Forensic psychology in context: Nordic and international approaches* (pp. 35–55). Devon, England: Willan Publishing.

Baddeley, A. (1992). Working memory. *Science, 255*, 556–559.

Bennell, C., Bloomfield, S., Snook, B., Taylor, P., & Barnes, C. (2010). Linkage analysis in cases of serial burglary: Comparing the performance of university students, police professionals, and a logistic regression model. *Psychology, Crime & Law, 18*, 507–524.

Bennell, C., & Canter, D. V. (2002). Linking commercial burglaries by *modus operandi*: Tests using regression and ROC analysis. *Science & Justice, 42*, 153–164.

Bennell, C., & Jones, N. J. (2005). Between a ROC and a hard place: A method for linking serial burglaries by modus operandi. *Journal of Investigative Psychology and Offender Profiling, 2*, 23–41.

Bennell, C., Jones, N. J., & Melnyk, T. (2009). Addressing problems with traditional crime linking methods using receiver operating characteristic analysis. *Legal and Criminological Psychology, 14*, 293–310.

Bennell, C., Mugford, R., Ellingwood, H., & Woodhams, J. (2014). Linking crimes using behavioural clues: Current levels of linking accuracy and strategies for moving forward. *Journal of Investigative Psychology and Offender Profiling, 11*, 29–56.

Burrell, A., & Bull, R. (2011). A preliminary examination of crime analysts' views and experiences of comparative case analysis. *International Journal of Police Science & Management, 13*, 2–15.

Canter, D. V. (2012). *An ideographic approach to case-linkage.* Paper presented at the 14th International Conference of Investigative Psychology, London, England.

Canter, D. V., Heritage, R., Wilson, M., Davies, A., Kirby, S., Holden, R., ... Donald, I. (1991). *A facet approach to offender profiling.* London, England: Home Office.

Chan, S. (1982). Expert judgments made under uncertainty: Some evidence and suggestions. *Social Science Quarterly, 63*, 428–444.

Charlin, B., Tardif, J., & Boshuizen, H. (2000). Scripts and medical diagnostic knowledge: Theory and applications for clinical reasoning. *Academic Medicine, 75*, 182–190.

Dawes, R. M., & Corrigan, B. (1974). Linear models in decision making. *Psychological Bulletin, 81*, 95–106.

Dawes, R. M., Faust, D., & Meehl, P. E. (1989). Clinical versus actuarial judgment. *Science, 243*, 1668–1674.

Douglas, K. S., & Reeves, K. (2009). Historical-Clinical-Risk Management-20 (HCR-20) violence risk assessment scheme: Rationale, application, and empirical overview. In R. Otto & K. S. Douglas (Eds.), *Handbook of violence risk assessment* (pp. 147–186). Oxford, England: Routledge/Taylor & Francis.

Ericsson, K., & Simon, H. (1993). *Protocol analysis: Verbal reports as data* (2nd ed.). Boston, MA: MIT Press.

Fisher, A., & Fonteyn, M. (1995). An exploration of an innovative methodological approach for examining nurses' heuristic use in clinical practice. *Scholarly Inquiry for Nursing Practice: An International Journal, 9*, 263–276.

Flavell, J. H. (1979). Metacognition and cognitive monitoring. A new area of cognitive-development inquiry. *American Psychologist, 34*, 906–911.

Garb, H. N. (2005). Clinical judgment and decision making. *Annual Review of Clinical Psychology, 1*, 67–89.

Glaholt, M. G., & Reingold, E. M. (2011). Eye movement monitoring as a process tracing methodology in decision making research. *Journal of Neuroscience, Psychology, and Economics, 4*, 125–146.

Groeger, J. A. (1997). *Memory and remembering: Everyday memory in context.* London, England: Longman.

Grove, W. M., & Meehl, P. E. (1996). Comparative efficiency of informal (subjective, impressionistic) and formal (mechanical, algorithmic) prediction procedures: The clinical-statistical controversy. *Psychology, Public Policy, and Law, 2*, 293–323.

Grove, W. M., Zald, D. H., Lebow, B. S., Snitz, B. E., & Nelson, C. (2000). Clinical versus mechanical prediction: A meta-analysis. *Psychological Assessment, 12*, 19–30.

Grubin, D., Kelly, P., & Brunsdon, C. (2001). *Linking serious sexual assaults through behaviour*. London, England: Home Office.

Hanson, R. K., & Morton-Bourgon, K. E. (2009). The accuracy of recidivism risk assessments for sex offenders: A meta-analysis of 118 prediction studies. *Psychological Assessment, 21*, 1–21.

Hart, S. D., & Logan, C. (2011). Formulation of violence risk using evidence-based assessments: The structured professional judgment approach. In P. Sturmey & M. McMurran (Eds.), *Forensic case formulation* (pp. 81–106). Chichester, England: Wiley-Blackwell.

Hazelwood, R. R., & Warren, J. I. (2004). Linkage analysis: Modus operandi, ritual, and signature in serial sexual crime. *Aggression and Violent Behavior, 8*, 587–598.

Helmus, L., & Bourgon, G. (2011). Taking stock of 15 years of research on the Spousal Assault Risk Assessment Guide (SARA): A critical review. *International Journal of Forensic Mental Health, 10*, 64–75.

Huber, O., Huber, O. W., & Schulte-Mecklenbeck, M. (2011). Determining the information that participants need: Methods of active information search. In M. Schulte-Mecklenbeck, A. Kühberger, & R. Ranyard (Eds.), *A handbook of process tracing methods for decision research: A critical review and user's guide* (pp. 65–86). New York, NY: Taylor & Francis.

Kahneman, D., Slovic, P., & Tversky, A. (1982). *Judgment under uncertainty: Heuristics and biases*. New York, NY: Cambridge University Press.

Kahneman, D., & Tversky, A. (1973). On the psychology of prediction. *Psychological Review, 80*, 237–251.

Kalyuga, S. (2007). Expertise reversal effect and its implications for learner-tailored instruction. *Educational Psychology Review, 19*, 509–539.

Kelemen, W. L., Frost, P. J., & Weaver, C. A. (2000). Individual differences in metacognition: Evidence against a general metacognitive ability. *Memory & Cognition, 28*, 92–107.

Keppel, R. D., & Birnes, W. J. (2009). *Serial violence: Analysis of modus operandi and signature characteristics of killers*. Boca Raton, FL: CRC Press.

Kuipers, B., Moskowitz, A. J., & Kassirer, J. P. (1988). Critical decision under uncertainty: Representation and structure. *Cognitive Science: A Multidisciplinary Journal, 12*, 177–210.

Lamond, D., & Farnell, S. (1998). The treatment of pressure sores: A comparison of novice and expert nurses' knowledge, information use and decision accuracy. *Journal of Advanced Nursing, 27*, 280–286.

Leitner, M., & Kent, J. (2009). Bayesian journey to crime modeling of single- and multiple crime type series in Baltimore County, MD. *Journal of Investigative Psychology and Offender Profiling, 6*, 213–236.

Markson, L., Woodhams, J., & Bond, J. W. (2010). Linking serial residential burglary: Comparing the utility of modus operandi behaviours, geographical proximity and temporal proximity. *Journal of Investigative Psychology and Offender Profiling, 7*, 91–107.

Meehl, P. E. (1954). *Clinical versus statistical prediction: A theoretical analysis and a review of the evidence*. Minneapolis, MN: University of Minnesota Press.
Miller, G. A. (1956). The magical number seven, plus or minus two: Some limits on our capacity for processing information. *Psychological Review, 63*, 81–97.
Neath, I. (1998). *Human memory: An introduction to research, data, and theory*. Pacific Grove, CA: Brooks/Cole.
Quinsey, V. L., Harris, G. T., Rice, M. E., & Cormier, C. A. (1998). *Violent offenders: Appraising and managing risk*. Washington, DC: American Psychological Association.
Russo, J. E. (2011). Eye fixations as a process trace. In M. Schulte-Mecklenbeck, A. Kühberger, & R. Ranyard (Eds.), *A handbook of process tracing methods for decision research: A critical review and user's guide* (pp. 43–64). New York, NY: Taylor & Francis.
Russo, J. E., Johnson, E. J., & Stephens, D. L. (1989). The validity of verbal protocols. *Memory & Cognition, 17*, 759–769.
Santtila, P., Korpela, S., & Häkkänen, H. (2004). Expertise and decision-making in the linking of car crime series. *Psychology, Crime & Law, 10*, 97–112.
Santtila, P., Pakkanen, T., Zappalà, A., Bosco, D., Valkama, M., & Mokros, A. (2008). Behavioural crime linking in serial homicide. *Psychology, Crime & Law, 14*, 245–265.
Schraw, G., & Dennison, R. S. (1994). Assessing metacognitive awareness. *Contemporary Educational Psychology, 19*, 460–475.
Shanteau, J. (1992). The psychology of experts: An alternative view. In G. Wright & F. Bolger (Eds.), *Expertise and decision support* (pp. 11–21). New York, NY: Plenum Press.
Song, C., Kanai, R., Fleming, S. M., Weil, R. S., Schwarzkopf, D. S., & Rees, G. (2011). Relating inter-individual differences in metacognitive performance on different perceptual tasks. *Consciousness and Cognition, 20*, 1787–1792.
Swets, J. A. (1988). Measuring the accuracy of diagnostic systems. *Science, 240*, 1285–1293.
Swets, J. A., Dawes, R. M., & Monahan, J. (2000). Psychological science can improve diagnostic decisions. *Psychological Science in the Public Interest, 1*, 1–26.
Tonkin, M. (2012). *Behavioural case linkage: Generalisability, ecological validity, and methodology* (Unpublished doctoral dissertation). University of Leicester, England.
Tonkin, M., Grant, T., & Bond, J. W. (2008). To link or not to link: A test of the case linkage principles using serial car theft data. *Journal of Investigative Psychology and Offender Profiling, 5*, 59–77.
Tonkin, M., Santtila, P., & Bull, R. (2012). The linking of burglary crimes using offender behaviour: Testing research cross-nationally and exploring methodology. *Legal and Criminological Psychology, 17*, 276–293.
Tonkin, M., Woodhams, J., Bull, R., Bond, J. W., & Palmer, E. J. (2011). Linking different types of crime using geographical and temporal proximity. *Criminal Justice and Behavior, 38*, 1069–1088.
Wells, G. L., & Olson, E. A. (2003). Eyewitness testimony. *Annual Review of Psychology, 54*, 277–295.
Woodhams, J., Bull, R., & Hollin, C. R. (2007). Case linkage: Identifying crimes committed by the same offender. In R. N. Kocsis (Ed.), *Criminal profiling: International theory, research and practice* (pp. 117–133). Totowa, NJ: The Humana Press.

Woodhams, J., Hollin, C. R., & Bull, R. (2007). The psychology of linking crimes: A review of the evidence. *Legal and Criminological Psychology, 12*, 233–249.
Woodhams, J., Hollin, C. R., & Bull, R. (2008). Incorporating context in linking crimes: An exploratory study of situational similarity and if-then contingencies. *Journal of Investigative Psychology and Offender Profiling, 5*, 1–23.
Woodhams, J., & Labuschagne, G. (2012). A test of case linkage principles with solved and unsolved serial rapes. *Journal of Police and Criminal Psychology, 27*, 85–98.

Extending Crime Linkage to Versatile Offenders

12

MATTHEW TONKIN

Contents

Introduction 279
Why Is Cross-Crime Linkage Necessary and Important? 280
Research on Cross-Crime Linkage: Study 1 (Tonkin, Woodhams, Bull, Bond, & Palmer, 2011) 281
Methodology, Sample, and Data 281
Findings 284
Conclusions and Implications 288
Limitations of Tonkin et al. (2011) 291
Research on Cross-Crime Linkage: Study 2 (Tonkin, Woodhams, Bull, & Bond, 2012) 292
Methodology, Sample, and Data 292
Findings 293
Conclusions and Implications 296
Limitations of Tonkin, Woodhams, et al. (2012) 296
Future Directions for Research on Cross-Crime Linkage 297
Conclusions 299
Acknowledgments 300
References 300

Introduction

This chapter considers whether it is possible to use offender crime scene behavior to identify linked crime series that contain several different types of offense. This builds on previous research, which has restricted itself to testing the principles of crime linkage with samples that are homogenous with respect to crime type (i.e., that only contain one type of crime, e.g., residential burglary). The chapter begins by considering why cross-crime linkage is necessary and important, before exploring the findings from two previously published studies that have tested the potential for cross-crime linkage using simple measures of geographical and temporal offender behavior. The chapter will conclude with a discussion of future research directions.

Why Is Cross-Crime Linkage Necessary and Important?

The issue of whether offenders tend to specialize in certain types of crime or whether they are generalists is an issue that has received considerable academic attention (e.g., Farrington, Snyder, & Finnegan, 1988). One of the clear conclusions from this work is that the vast majority of offenders do not restrict themselves to committing just one type of crime (Piquero, Farrington, & Blumstein, 2007). For example, Peterson and Braiker (1980) found that 49% of the 624 prison inmates that they interviewed reported engaging in four or more different types of offense during the 3-year period preceding their incarceration, and just 18% reported engaging in only one type of offense during this period. Also, Leitner and Kent (2009) reported that 72.8% of the 3484 crime series on the Baltimore County police database contained multiple crime types (e.g., two burglaries, three vehicle thefts, and an arson offense). Versatility in offending behavior is, therefore, a common finding, particularly among prolific offenders who are of most interest to law enforcement agencies. Consequently, the police are regularly faced with apprehending versatile serial offenders, which, in the absence of alternative evidence of linkage, necessitates a method for behaviorally identifying linked crime series that contain several different types of crime.

Furthermore, it is not uncommon for law enforcement personnel to be responsible for the investigation and analysis of several different types of crime. In the United Kingdom, for example, the term *serious acquisitive crime* has recently been coined to refer to a group of robbery, burglary, and vehicle-related offenses that currently have a high priority among police forces in England and Wales (Department for Communities and Local Government, 2008). It might be argued that this trend will continue as police forces around the world are forced to reduce their operational costs. There is even tentative evidence to suggest that some crime analysts may already be engaged in cross-crime linkage. In a recent survey of crime analysts, one analyst stated that "[w]e look at all crime types that each individual may have committed, for example due to the fact that sex offenders generally have some history of violence, we also take into account violent offenders when investigating rapes" (Burrell & Bull, 2011, p. 12). Although this is just one survey and by no means reflects the use of crime linkage across the United Kingdom or elsewhere, it does raise the possibility that cross-crime linkage is currently being used in practice without any evidence to suggest that it is a reliable procedure. It is, therefore, very important that research be conducted to determine whether there is the potential for cross-crime linkage to work as a reliable investigative procedure and how this might function. The subsequent sections of this chapter will describe and discuss the findings of two previously published studies that have addressed this issue.

Research on Cross-Crime Linkage: Study 1 (Tonkin, Woodhams, Bull, Bond, & Palmer, 2011)

Given the potential value of cross-crime linkage, a recent study investigated this issue with data collected from a police force in the United Kingdom (Tonkin et al., 2011). This section will describe the methodology, findings, and implications of this study, before considering its limitations.

Methodology, Sample, and Data

As this was the first study of its kind, several new methodological issues had to be resolved before the study could commence. The first major issue was that the offender behaviors previously included in studies of crime linkage do not necessarily occur in every crime type (e.g., sexual behaviors very rarely occur during car theft crimes). Consequently, it was difficult to design a uniform behavioral coding system that would apply to all crime types. But a solution to this problem was found by using the straight-line kilometer distance between offense locations and the number of days between offenses (referred to as inter-crime distance and temporal proximity, respectively), which are two measures of offender behavior that are applicable to a wide variety of crimes. That is, most crime is committed in a particular geographical location at a specific point in time, which allows these two measures of behavior to be calculated.

Furthermore, inter-crime distance and temporal proximity have high pragmatic value because they are easy to calculate and implement in practice. Moreover, these two features have received consistent empirical support for their ability to distinguish linked from unlinked crime pairs in the crime linkage literature across a wide variety of crime types, including burglary, robbery, and car theft (e.g., Bennell & Canter, 2002; Tonkin, Grant, & Bond, 2008; Woodhams & Toye, 2007). For these reasons, it was logical to begin testing the potential for cross-crime linkage with inter-crime distance and temporal proximity.

Having decided upon the behavioral features that would be tested in this study, the next issue was how to define cross-crime linkage. In England and Wales, there is a distinction between crime *types* (which refer to specific individual crimes, such as residential burglary) and crime *categories* (which refer to broader groups of crime that contain several individual types, for example, the crime category *robbery*, which contains two specific types of robbery—personal and commercial).* Consequently, cross-crime linkage can be defined in terms of either crime *types* or crime *categories*. In terms of *types*, cross-crime linkage is defined as any situation in which two crimes of different specific types are linked (e.g., an attempt is made to link a personal robbery with a commercial robbery). Alternatively, cross-crime linkage in terms of *categories* is defined as any situation where two crimes from different offense categories are linked (e.g., a residential burglary is linked with a rape). Tonkin et al. (2011), therefore, examined cross-crime discrimination accuracy at both the *type* and *category* levels, and this performance was compared to discrimination accuracy within crime types (i.e., the *traditional* way in which crime linkage research has tested behavioral consistency, distinctiveness, and discrimination accuracy, e.g., by pairing two residential burglaries).

To examine these issues, Tonkin et al. (2011) extracted location information (x, y coordinates to the nearest meter) and temporal information (the date the offense was recorded by the police) from the databases of Northamptonshire police, a rural force in the United Kingdom with an area of 2364 km^2. This information related to 1951 solved crimes committed during 2009 by 537 serial offenders. For 300 of these offenders, two crimes were randomly selected from the crimes that they had committed during the study period, and within these data, violent, sexual, burglary, robbery, theft/handling, and criminal damage offenses were represented.†

Based on Bennell's (2002) approach to crime linkage research (see Chapters 6 and 14), a methodology was designed to examine discrimination accuracy across crime categories, across crime types, and within crime types. Six crime pair subsets were created, each containing a set of 100 pairs with two crimes per pair that had been randomly selected from the series of each offender (see Table 12.1 for a summary).

* The Home Office (who are responsible for setting definitions of crime in England and Wales) record 156 individual crime types, which are split into nine crime categories: violent offences (containing 38 individual crime types), sexual offences (containing 31 crime types), burglary offences (containing seven crime types), drugs offences (containing four types), robbery (containing two types), theft/handling offences (containing 16 types), fraud/forgery offences (containing 16 types), criminal damage offences (containing 11 types), and other offences (containing 31 types).

† Crimes included under the Home Office categories of "drugs offences," "fraud/forgery offences," and "other offences" were excluded by Tonkin et al. (2011) because these crimes typically do not have definite offence locations and times, which makes it difficult to calculate meaningful inter-crime distance and temporal proximity values. Furthermore, a small number of crime types were removed from the other six crime categories for similar reasons (see Tonkin et al., 2011, for a full list of the crime types included in their study).

Table 12.1 A Summary of the Six Crime Pair Subsets Included in Tonkin et al., 2011

Crime Pair Type	Linkage Status	Description	Example
Cross-category	Linked	This subset contains pairs of crimes that contain two crimes from different Home Office crime categories that have been committed by the same offender	A personal robbery committed by offender 1 was paired with a burglary in a dwelling also committed by offender 1
	Unlinked	This subset contains pairs of crimes that contain two crimes from different Home Office categories that have been committed by different offenders	A burglary in a dwelling committed by offender 1 was paired with the theft of a motor vehicle committed by offender 2
Cross-type	Linked	This subset contains pairs of crimes that contain two crimes from the same Home Office crime category that are of different specific crime types. These two crimes have been committed by the same offender	A personal robbery committed by offender 1 was paired with a commercial robbery also committed by offender 1
	Unlinked	This subset contains pairs of crimes that contain two crimes from the same Home Office crime category that are of different specific crime types. These two crimes have been committed by different offenders	A shoplifting offense committed by offender 1 was paired with a theft from a vehicle committed by offender 2
Within-type	Linked	This subset contains pairs of crimes that contain two crimes committed by the same offender that are of the same specific crime type	Two personal robbery crimes committed by offender 1 were paired
	Unlinked	This subset contains pairs of crimes that contain two crimes committed by different offenders that are of the same specific crime type	Two burglaries in a dwelling committed by different offenders were paired

Source: Tonkin et al. (2011). *Criminal Justice and Behavior, 38*, 1069–1088.

Inter-crime distance and temporal proximity values were calculated for each crime pair, and these formed the basis of the subsequent analyses. The rationale was that, by comparing the linked subsets with their unlinked counterparts in terms of inter-crime distance and temporal proximity (e.g., the linked cross-category subset was compared with the unlinked cross-category subset), it would be possible to determine if linked and unlinked crimes can be discriminated from each other in an absolute sense. That is, is there the potential for discrimination accuracy to exceed chance across crime categories, across crime types, and within crime types? Furthermore, by comparing the effect size across all three levels of analysis, it would be possible to determine the relative level of discrimination accuracy across and within crimes (Tonkin et al., 2011).

Findings

First, the six crime pair subsets were compared statistically in terms of inter-crime distance and temporal proximity. Tonkin et al. (2011) found that all linked subsets contained shorter inter-crime distance and temporal proximity values than their unlinked counterparts ($p < .01$). These findings indicated that crimes committed by the same offender occurred closer together in time and space than crimes committed by different offenders, regardless of whether those crimes were from the same offense type, from different offense types, or from completely different offense categories. This provided support for the principles of behavioral consistency and distinctiveness that underpin crime linkage. Furthermore, the effect size was similar across all three levels of analysis when comparing linked and unlinked crime pairs in terms of inter-crime distance and temporal proximity (r ranged from 0.69 to 0.83 for inter-crime distance and from 0.40 to 0.48 for the temporal proximity). These findings suggested that behavioral consistency and distinctiveness were somewhat equivalent across crime categories, across crime types, and within crime types.

The next stage of the analysis was to determine whether inter-crime distance and temporal proximity could be used to predict whether crime pairs were linked or unlinked (i.e., discrimination accuracy). When testing discrimination accuracy, it is important to explore whether the findings can be cross-validated (as discussed in Chapters 6 and 14). Tonkin et al. (2011), therefore, split each of the six crime pair subsets in half to form a training sample (containing 50 crime pairs) and a test sample (containing the remaining 50 crime pairs). Binary logistic regression was conducted on the training samples to provide an initial test of discrimination accuracy, and the regression models were then applied to the test samples using a method described by Bennell and Canter (2002). This produced predicted probability values that were subsequently used to conduct receiver operating characteristic (ROC) analysis, which further tested discrimination accuracy.

ROC analysis produces a measure of discrimination accuracy referred to as the area under the curve (AUC), which can range from 0 (indicating perfect negative prediction) to 1.00 (indicating perfect positive prediction), with a value of 0.50 indicating a chance level of discrimination accuracy. The ROC analyses produced by Tonkin et al. (2011) are summarized in Table 12.2. All models were statistically significant ($p < .01$) and achieved moderate to high levels of discrimination accuracy according to published guidelines (Swets, 1988). These findings indicated that both inter-crime distance and temporal proximity could discriminate successfully between linked and unlinked crimes, regardless of whether the pairs contained crimes of the same type, of different types, or from completely different offense categories. Indeed, when the AUC values were compared statistically across the three levels of analysis, there was no difference in terms of discrimination accuracy for either inter-crime distance or temporal proximity ($p > .05$). These findings, therefore, provided support for the notion that inter-crime distance and temporal proximity have the potential to support cross-crime linkage and that this procedure can function at a level that is comparable to that which has been observed in previous studies of crime linkage using homogenous samples of crime (e.g., Bennell & Canter, 2002; Markson, Woodhams, & Bond, 2010; Tonkin et al., 2008; Woodhams & Toye, 2007). But inter-crime distance appears to demonstrate greater potential for linking crimes than temporal proximity, as indicated by the statistically larger AUC values achieved across crime categories, across crime types, and within crime types ($p < .01$).

Also reported in Table 12.2 are the AUC values that were obtained using the training sample in Tonkin et al. (2011). When these values were compared with those from the test sample, there were only minor differences in terms of the AUC (the maximum difference was 0.05), none of which reached statistical significance ($p > .05$). We can, therefore, conclude that Tonkin et al.'s (2011) findings were successfully cross-validated, which suggested that they are robust and able to apply to future crimes in Northamptonshire. This is important given that the ultimate aim of this research was to develop recommendations that can be used to guide future criminal investigations.

Overall, these findings suggest that there is the potential for simple aspects of offender behavior to be used to identify linked crime series that contain several different types of offense. However, the two measures of offender behavior tested in this study were continuous, which raises the question: at what point are two crimes close enough in space and time for an analyst to reliably say that they are committed by the same person (i.e., to classify those crimes as linked)? To address this question, researchers have discussed different methods for identifying decision thresholds that might be used to guide the linking of crimes in practice (see Bennell, 2002; Bennell & Jones, 2005). These thresholds are designed to identify the particular point on a continuous measure of offender behavior that maximizes

Table 12.2 Receiver Operating Characteristic Analysis Results for Cross-Crime Linkage with Solved Crimes

		Training Sample		Test Sample	
Level of Analysis	Crime Linkage Feature	AUC (*SE*)	95% Confidence Interval	AUC (*SE*)	95% Confidence Interval
Across crime categories	Inter-crime distance	0.85 (0.04)**	0.77–0.92	0.88 (0.03)**	0.82–0.95
	Temporal proximity	0.66 (0.06)*	0.55–0.76	0.67 (0.05)*	0.57–0.78
	Combined[a]	0.84 (0.04)**	0.77–0.92	0.88 (0.04)**	0.82–0.95
Across crime types	Inter-crime distance	0.94 (0.02)**	0.89–0.98	0.90 (0.03)**	0.84–0.97
	Temporal proximity	0.69 (0.05)*	0.59–0.79	0.74 (0.05)**	0.64–0.83
	Combined[b]	–	–	–	–
Within crime types	Inter-crime distance	0.86 (0.04)**	0.79–0.94	0.91 (0.03)**	0.84–0.97
	Temporal proximity	0.73 (0.05)**	0.63–0.83	0.74 (0.05)**	0.64–0.84
	Combined[b]	–	–	–	–

Source: Tonkin et al. (2011). *Criminal Justice and Behavior, 38*, 1069–1088.

Note: AUC values of 0.50–0.70 are considered low, values of 0.70–0.90 are considered moderate, and values of 0.90–1.00 are considered high (Swets, 1988).

[a] Combined refers to the stepwise logistic regression analyses that combined inter-crime distance and temporal proximity.

[b] A combined model was not reported across crime types or within crime types because the combination of inter-crime distance and temporal proximity did not lead to statistically improved discrimination accuracy when compared with the single-feature regression models.

*$p < .01$; **$p < .001$.

SE, standard error.

the number of correct linkage decisions, while minimizing the number of incorrect decisions (Bennell, 2002). Consistent with previous research, Tonkin et al. (2011) used Youden's Index to estimate these decision thresholds (e.g., Bennell & Jones, 2005). Youden's Index is calculated using the following equation: $J = pH + pCR - 1$, where J refers to the Youden's Index, pH to the probability of correctly identifying a linked pair (a hit), and pCR to the probability of correctly identifying an unlinked pair (a correct rejection). The aim is to identify the decision threshold that results in the highest J value, which maximizes the number of correct linkage decisions, while minimizing the number of incorrect decisions. A separate threshold was estimated for inter-crime distance and temporal proximity at each level of analysis, thereby yielding a total of six decision thresholds (see Table 12.3).

To apply these thresholds to individual cases, one simply needs to determine whether the inter-crime distance or temporal proximity value for a particular crime pair is above or below the given threshold. If it is above the threshold, then the analyst can conclude that the two crimes are more likely to have been committed by different offenders (unlinked), whereas if the geographical/temporal distance between offenses is below the threshold, then it can be concluded that it is more likely that they were committed by the same offender (linked). These thresholds also illustrate the relatively superior performance of inter-crime distance over temporal proximity when linking crimes. At the within crime type level, a crime analyst relying on inter-crime distance would correctly identify an additional 24 linked crime pairs per 100 compared to an analyst relying on the temporal proximity and would make eight fewer false alarms* per 100 unlinked crime pairs. An analyst relying on inter-crime distance to link across crime types would identify

Table 12.3 Potential Decision Thresholds for Crime Linkage and Their Associated Proportion of Hits and Correct Rejections (Solved Offenses Only)

Level of Analysis	Inter-Crime Distance	Temporal Proximity
Across crime categories	<1.88 km	<120.50 days
	$pH = 0.70$; $pCR = 0.96$	$pH = 0.80$; $pCR = 0.50$
Across crime types	<10.61 km	<132.00 days
	$pH = 0.96$; $pCR = 0.78$	$pH = 0.94$; $pCR = 0.42$
Within crime types	<2.19 km	<26.50 days
	$pH = 0.86$; $pCR = 0.90$	$pH = 0.62$; $pCR = 0.82$

Source: Tonkin et al. (2011). *Criminal Justice and Behavior, 38*, 1069–1088.

pH, probability of obtaining a hit at this decision threshold (i.e., correctly identifying a linked crime pair); pCR, probability of obtaining a correct rejection at this decision threshold (i.e., correctly identifying an unlinked crime pair).

* A false alarm occurs when an unlinked crime pair is incorrectly labeled as a linked crime pair.

an additional two linked crime pairs per 100 compared to an analyst relying on the temporal proximity and would make 36 fewer false alarms per 100. Finally, while an analyst relying on inter-crime distance to link across crime categories would identify 10 fewer linked crime pairs per 100 than an analyst using the temporal proximity, he or she would make 46 fewer false alarms per 100 unlinked crime pairs by relying on inter-crime distance. These are substantial differences that have real practical significance. However, it is important to note that Youden's Index is limited as a means of calculating decision thresholds, and Tonkin et al. (2011) do not recommend the use of these thresholds in practice. This issue is discussed in greater detail below.

Conclusions and Implications

Tonkin et al.'s (2011) findings demonstrated that moderate to high levels of discrimination accuracy can be achieved when discriminating between linked and unlinked crimes using inter-crime distance and temporal proximity (Swets, 1988). Furthermore, the level of discrimination accuracy that was achieved is equivalent regardless of whether the crimes are of the same offense type, different offense types, or whether they are from completely different offense categories. Ultimately, this suggests that cross-crime linkage may be a viable investigative procedure.

These findings might, therefore, be used to develop a statistical tool that can support crime linkage across crime categories, across crime types, and within crime types. This tool would contain the logistic regression models developed by Tonkin et al. (2011).* The tool might also contain logistic regression models from other crime linkage studies (such as those reviewed in Chapter 6), and also the tool would allow the user to specify their own model parameters. Such diversity would help to ensure that the tool had widespread value and appeal. Depending on the particular regression model used, the analyst would load the relevant geographical and/or temporal information into the tool and a probability value would be calculated. This value would indicate the predicted likelihood that the crimes were committed by the same person, ranging from 0 (very unlikely to be linked) to 1.00 (very likely to be linked). Such a tool could be used to scan large law enforcement databases for potentially linked crimes (proactive crime linkage; Woodhams, Bull, & Hollin, 2007). In such a situation, the tool would calculate a predicted probability value for every pairwise combination of crimes in the database (i.e., crime 1 paired with crime 2, crime 1 paired with crime 3, etc.). These values would subsequently be organized from highest to lowest value, thereby

* The tool would contain the beta and constant values reported by Tonkin et al. (2011), which are the core components of a logistic regression model in terms of producing linkage predictions.

providing the law enforcement agency with a prioritized list of potentially linked crimes for consideration. This might reduce the time that it takes to conduct crime linkage and help to avoid linkage blindness (where linked crimes are missed).

The decision thresholds developed by Tonkin et al. (2011) might also be incorporated into such a tool, which would allow the analyst to determine when two crimes are sufficiently close together in space and time to be labeled as linked. However, practitioners should be cautious when using these decision thresholds because there are important limitations to Youden's Index, which was used to develop these thresholds. As discussed by Bennell (2002), Youden's Index does not take into account the prior probability that crimes are linked/unlinked, nor does it take into account the various costs and benefits associated with correct/incorrect linkage decisions. These are both important issues that should guide the selection of an appropriate decision threshold in practice. Furthermore, there is a risk that decision thresholds will be applied in a rigid, *black-and-white* manner. This might lead to a situation where two crime pairs are given different linkage classifications (one is classed as linked and the other classed as unlinked) despite the fact that they only differ very slightly in terms of inter-crime distance/temporal proximity (Tonkin et al., 2011). Crime linkage is not at the stage (nor is it ever likely to be) where definitive predictive decisions can be made. Instead, it is more realistic to expect that crime linkage will work in terms of probability, and the best that research can hope for is to reduce the degree of uncertainty as much as possible (although it will never be completely eradicated). Consequently, it seems inappropriate to recommend the use of thresholds that promote a rigid and inflexible approach to linking crimes. Future research must, therefore, attempt to develop decision thresholds that are sensitive to the prior probability that crimes are linked/unlinked and that account for the various costs and benefits associated with correct/incorrect linkage decisions (although the latter may be very difficult to assess because it would be hard to quantify the financial and personal costs associated with incorrectly linking an offense and thereby misleading a police investigation).

In addition to the potential practical implications, there are also theoretical implications that can be drawn from the work of Tonkin et al. (2011). The success of inter-crime distance indicates that the offenders in their sample tended to return to the same (or similar) places to offend, regardless of the type of crime being committed. These findings are consistent with several seminal theories in environmental criminology, such as rational choice theory and crime pattern theory, which suggest that offenders will seek to minimize the efforts and risks involved in offending (e.g., Brantingham & Brantingham, 1981; Clarke & Felson, 1993). However, it must be emphasized that the geographical areas in which Tonkin and colleagues' offenders chose to offend were not completely nonoverlapping (otherwise the AUC values would have been 1.00), thus different offenders sometimes chose to offend in similar locations. These findings are unsurprising given that crime targets are not evenly distributed through the environment and that certain areas are more favorable for the commission of crime than others, for example, due to the lack of guardianship (Brantingham & Brantingham, 1995; Kinney, Brantingham, Wuschke, Kirk, & Brantingham, 2008).

Tonkin et al.'s (2011) findings are also relevant to the issue of situational similarity and behavioral consistency, which was originally discussed within the personality literature (e.g., Furr & Funder, 2004) and subsequently applied in relation to crime linkage (Woodhams, Hollin, & Bull, 2008). In terms of crime linkage, it has been hypothesized that an offender's behavior will be most consistent when the situations that he or she encounters from one offense to the next are similar. As discussed by Woodhams et al. (2008), situational similarity in the criminal context can be defined in many ways; one of which is in terms of the type of crime being committed. Using such a definition, it would be predicted that crimes of the same type would elicit more similar offender behavior than crimes of different types. Although Woodhams et al. (2008) considered such relationships with regard to *modus operandi* behaviors, it could also logically be applied to the locations and times chosen for offending. Based on this hypothesis, one would predict consistency in temporal and geographical behavior to be greatest at the within-type level of Tonkin et al.'s (2011) study, followed by the cross-type level, and then the least consistent behavior would have been observed at the cross-category level. But, Tonkin et al.'s findings did not support this hypothesis because consistency, distinctiveness, and discrimination accuracy in terms of temporal and geographical behavior were comparable across all three levels of investigation. These findings might, therefore, lead one to question the assumed relationship between situational similarity and behavioral consistency (at least in the criminal domain and in terms of temporal and geographical behavior). Indeed, similar questions were raised by Woodhams et al. (2008), who found little relationship between situational similarity and consistency in *modus operandi* behavior in their sample of serial juvenile sexual offenders.

However, it may be inappropriate to define situational similarity in terms of the legal framework set out by the Home Office to distinguish between crime types and categories. Indeed, the personality literature defines situations as similar when they activate the same cognitive/affective units of the personality system. Thus, situational similarity is defined in terms of the psychological meaning a situation has to an individual, rather than objective/physical characteristics of the situation (Shoda, 1999). Consequently, Tonkin et al.'s (2011) study may not provide an appropriate test of the hypothesized relationship between situational similarity and behavioral consistency. Alternative approaches to testing this relationship are discussed in the section Future Directions for Research on Cross-Crime Linkage.

Limitations of Tonkin et al. (2011)

Having considered the main findings and some of their implications, it is important to consider the limitations of Tonkin et al.'s (2011) study. First, Tonkin and colleagues only sampled data from one geographical location. It is, therefore, unclear whether their findings will generalize to other locations in the United Kingdom or elsewhere, which limits the practical value of this study.

Second, the analysis was restricted to two crimes per offender. Although this decision was necessary to prevent prolific offenders having an undue influence on the analyses (e.g., Woodhams & Toye, 2007), researchers have recently argued that this approach does not replicate real-life crime linkage because investigative databases will contain crime series that vary in length (Woodhams & Labuschagne, 2012). This raises doubts over the ecological validity of the findings.

Third, Tonkin et al. (2011) did not examine a wide range of offender behaviors. Although the decision to test inter-crime distance and temporal proximity was justified, it is unclear whether other behavioral approaches might be able to facilitate cross-crime linkage. This is problematic because geographical and temporal behavior are not always available to law enforcement agencies when investigating crime, so Tonkin et al. (2011) provide no guidance for conducting cross-crime linkage in these situations.

Fourth (and most importantly), Tonkin et al. (2011) can be criticized for relying on a sample of solved crime, which does not reflect the real-life scenario in which crime linkage takes place (Bennell & Canter, 2002). In reality, there are two scenarios in which crime linkage would be conducted (Woodhams et al., 2007). In the first, a practitioner would be presented with a specific crime (often a solved crime) and they would be asked to search among their databases for unsolved crimes that were linked to this particular index offense (reactive crime linkage). In this situation the practitioner would be required to link a solved crime with an unsolved crime (referred to as solved–unsolved links). In the second scenario the practitioner would not have a specific index offense, but would instead be asked to search proactively through the organization's databases to identify potential linkages (proactive crime linkage). Typically, this would involve linking an unsolved crime with another unsolved crime (unsolved–unsolved links). In these two scenarios there is no situation where a practitioner would be required to conduct crime linkage with two crimes that have already been solved (solved–solved links) because there would be little investigative benefit. Empirical research into crime linkage would, therefore, be more realistic if it sampled both solved and unsolved crimes and only tested discrimination accuracy with solved–unsolved links and unsolved–unsolved links (thereby excluding the solved–solved links that have traditionally been used in previous research). Furthermore, such an approach would reduce the risk of inflated AUC values that accompanies research using samples of solved crime (Bennell & Canter, 2002; Woodhams et al., 2007; see also Chapter 6).

The next section will describe the findings of a second study that aimed to replicate the work of Tonkin et al. (2011) using both solved and unsolved crimes. This work provided a more ecologically valid test of cross-crime linkage.

Research on Cross-Crime Linkage: Study 2 (Tonkin, Woodhams, Bull, & Bond, 2012)

Methodology, Sample, and Data

In studies of crime linkage the researcher must know which crimes have been committed by which offender; otherwise it is not possible to determine whether the crime pairs are linked or unlinked, thereby making it impossible to test discrimination accuracy. With a sample of solved crime it is easy to determine the linkage status of each crime pair, but with a sample containing unsolved offenses it is more difficult. To overcome this problem, Tonkin, Woodhams, et al. (2012) used a sample of solved and unsolved crimes that had been linked via DNA evidence.* Such a sample allowed Tonkin and colleagues to determine the linkage status of each crime pair with a degree of confidence, while also allowing discrimination accuracy to be tested using a sample that was more representative of the real-life scenario in which crime linkage takes place.

Tonkin, Woodhams, et al. (2012) identified 132 offenders who had committed two or more offenses between 2005 and 2009 within Northamptonshire police force boundaries. Two crimes per offender were selected for analysis, ensuring that at least one of these crimes was classed as unsolved. This methodology guaranteed that no solved–solved links were included in the sample when the linked and unlinked crime pairs were created, thereby producing a more realistic test of cross-crime linkage. Thus, the sample consisted of 264 offenses committed by 132 serial offenders, with 195 (74%) of these offenses classed as unsolved and 69 classed as solved (26%). The geographical location of each offense (stored as an *x*, *y* coordinate to the nearest meter) and the time and date that the offense was reported to the police were recorded for each offense.

In line with Tonkin et al.'s (2011) methodology, six crime pair subsets were created, inter-crime distance and temporal proximity values were

* In Tonkin et al.'s (2012) study, solved crimes were those classed as "detected" on Northamptonshire police databases, whereas unsolved crimes were those classed as "undetected." A crime is classed as detected when there is sufficient evidence for the case to be submitted to the Crown Prosecution Service (the CPS are the government department responsible for prosecuting criminal offences in England and Wales). It should be noted that CPS policy does not allow a DNA match between a suspect and a crime scene to be submitted as evidence of guilt without corroborating evidence. Thus, it was possible in this study for two crimes to be linked via DNA evidence (and, therefore, considered to be committed by the same person), but for one of these crimes to be classed as solved (i.e., detected) and the other to be classed as unsolved (i.e., undetected).

calculated, and statistical comparisons, binary logistic regression analysis, and ROC analysis were used to explore discrimination accuracy across crime categories, across crime types, and within crime types using the same methodology as Tonkin et al. (2011).

It is important to note, however, that the number of crime pairs in each subset was smaller in Tonkin, Woodhams, et al. (2012) than Tonkin et al. (2011), with 47 linked and 47 unlinked across crime category pairs, 32 linked and 32 unlinked across crime type pairs, and 53 linked and 53 unlinked within crime type pairs. Given the smaller sample, the split-half method of cross-validation used by Tonkin et al. (2011) was inappropriate for use with this sample because this method only splits the data once, which increases the likelihood of a good (or bad) fit occurring through chance, particularly when sample size is small (Cohen, 1990; Grann & Långström, 2007). Instead, the findings were cross-validated using the leave-one-out cross-validation (LOOCV) method, which performs multiple splits of the data. As explained by Woodhams and Labuschagne (2012), this method involves removing each crime pair from the sample one at a time and the remaining data are then used to develop a logistic regression model, which is subsequently applied to the extracted pair to produce a predicted probability value. This pair is then returned to the dataset and the procedure repeated with the next pair until a probability value has been calculated for all pairs. Consequently, the logistic regression models are developed and tested on different samples, which provides reassurance that the estimates of discrimination accuracy derived by Tonkin, Woodhams, et al. (2012) have a reasonable likelihood of generalizing to future crimes in their jurisdiction.*

Findings

Tonkin, Woodhams, et al. (2012) found that the linked crime pairs contained statistically shorter inter-crime distance and temporal proximity values than unlinked crime pairs at all three levels of analysis ($p < .01$, except for temporal proximity across crime types, where the difference between linked and unlinked crime pairs was nonsignificant). Furthermore, the effect size remained relatively stable for inter-crime distance (r ranged from 0.65 to 0.74). These findings were broadly consistent with those reported by Tonkin et al. (2011), which suggested that the potential value of cross-crime linkage had been replicated in a sample containing both solved and unsolved offenses.

* It should be noted that Tonkin, Woodhams, et al. (2012) re-ran the analyses using split-half validation as well, to test whether the two methods of cross-validation produced comparable results. There were only minor differences in the AUC statistics (maximum difference between the two methods = 0.04), none of which reached statistical significance ($p > .05$).

Table 12.4 ROC Analysis Results for Cross-Crime Linkage with Solved and Unsolved Crimes

Level of Analysis	Crime Linkage Feature	AUC (*SE*)	95% Confidence Interval
Across crime categories	Inter-crime distance	0.86 (0.04)**	0.78–0.93
	Temporal proximity	0.67 (0.06)*	0.56–0.78
	Combined[a]	0.88 (0.04)**	0.80–0.95
Across crime types	Inter-crime distance	0.79 (0.06)**	0.67–0.90
	Temporal proximity	0.53 (0.08)	0.39–0.68
	Combined[b]	–	–
Within crime types	Inter-crime distance	0.77 (0.05)**	0.68–0.86
	Temporal proximity	0.77 (0.05)**	0.68–0.86
	Combined	0.83 (0.04)**	0.75–0.91

Source: Tonkin, Woodhams, et al., 2012.

Note: AUC values of 0.50–0.70 are considered low, values of 0.70–0.90 are considered moderate, and values of 0.90–1.00 are considered high (Swets, 1988).

[a] Combined refers to the stepwise logistic regression analyses that combined the inter-crime distance and temporal proximity.

[b] A combined model was not reported across crime types because the combination of inter-crime distance and temporal proximity did not lead to statistically improved discrimination accuracy when compared with the single-feature regression models.

*$p < .01$; **$p < .001$.

The ROC analyses reported by Tonkin, Woodhams, et al. (2012) are summarized in Table 12.4. From this table we can see that, with the exception of temporal proximity across crime types, all models achieved a statistically significant level of discrimination accuracy ($p < .01$) and moderate to high levels of discrimination accuracy (Swets, 1988). Thus, the basic conclusions of Tonkin et al. (2011) were shown to replicate in a sample that was more representative of the real-life scenario in which crime linkage takes place (i.e., with datasets containing both solved and unsolved offenses).

However, there were statistically significant differences in the size of the AUC statistics observed across these two studies ($p < .05$). Specifically, inter-crime distance achieved a lower level of discrimination accuracy within crime types in Tonkin, Woodhams, et al. (2012) than it did in the original study conducted by Tonkin et al. (2011). In addition, the level of accuracy achieved using temporal proximity was lower across crime types in Tonkin, Woodhams, et al. (2012). But, the other estimates of discrimination accuracy were similar across the two studies ($p > .05$).

Although Tonkin, Woodhams, et al. (2012) did not report decision thresholds in their study, they are presented in this chapter for comparison

Table 12.5 Potential Decision Thresholds for Crime Linkage and Their Associated Proportion of Hits and Correct Rejections (Solved and Unsolved Offenses)

Level of Analysis	Inter-Crime Distance	Temporal Proximity
Across crime categories	<3.17 km	<461.50 days
	*p*H = 0.68; *p*CR = 0.89	*p*H = 0.83; *p*CR = 0.47
Across crime types	<7.36 km	<722[a] days
	*p*H = 0.69; *p*CR = 0.53	*p*H = 0.89; *p*CR = 0.33
Within crime types	<12.98[b] km	<228[c] days
	*p*H = 0.80; *p*CR = 0.63	*p*H = 0.61; *p*CR = 0.82

Source: Tonkin, Woodhams, et al., 2012.

*p*H, probability of obtaining a hit at this decision threshold (i.e., correctly identifying a linked crime pair); *p*CR, probability of obtaining a correct rejection at this decision threshold (i.e., correctly identifying an unlinked crime pair).

[a] Five separate Youden's indices were identified that maximized discrimination accuracy (540, 666, 738, 764.50, and 901 days), so an average was taken and reported in the above table.

[b] Four separate Youden's indices were identified that maximized discrimination accuracy (8.90, 10.20, 11.87, and 20.93 km), so an average was taken and reported in the above table.

[c] Two separate Youden's indices were identified that maximized discrimination accuracy (226.50 and 230 days), so an average was taken and reported in the above table.

purposes (see Table 12.5). When we compare the two sets of decision thresholds reported in Tables 12.3 and 12.5, there are substantial differences. In particular, the thresholds for temporal proximity are much larger in the study of solved and unsolved crime than they are in Tonkin et al.'s (2011) original study with solved crime only. These differences are probably due to the size of the study period, which was larger (5 years) in Tonkin, Woodhams, et al. (2012) than the 1-year study period in Tonkin et al. (2011). Furthermore, there is clear variation in inter-crime distance thresholds; for example, Tonkin et al. (2011) report a threshold of <2.19 km at the within crime types level, whereas Tonkin, Woodhams, et al. (2012) report a threshold of <12.98 km at the same level. Again, these findings may be due to the size of the study period. The distribution of targets may have changed more substantially over a long period or the offenders may be more likely to have moved residence, which would lead to larger inter-crime distances over long compared to short study periods. These comparisons, therefore, demonstrate the sensitivity of decision thresholds to issues of sample selection and methodology, which raises important concerns regarding generalizability. That is, if the decision thresholds vary widely as a function of research methodology, then there is little reason to expect that they will be robust enough to be applied in practice. These findings further underscore the limitations of Youden's Index as a method for calculating decision thresholds in the context of crime linkage.

Conclusions and Implications

The statistically significant levels of discrimination accuracy reported by Tonkin, Woodhams, et al. (2012) further support the notion that cross-crime linkage is a viable investigative procedure. Indeed, the fact that these findings were observed using a sample that was more representative of the real-life scenario in which linkage is expected to perform provides some confidence that these findings may be applicable to practice.

However, the diminished level of discrimination accuracy that was observed in some models by Tonkin, Woodhams, et al. (2012) suggests that previous studies may have overestimated the potential value of crime linkage using samples of solved crime. This partially validates the concerns expressed by researchers of crime linkage (e.g., Bennell & Canter, 2002; Woodhams et al., 2007) and suggests that the degree of linkage error may be larger than previously thought. However, it is important to note that discrimination accuracy remained stable in many of the models tested in these two studies. Furthermore, even when there were reductions in discrimination accuracy, the majority of these models remained highly statistically significant. We should, therefore, remain cautiously optimistic regarding the potential of cross-crime linkage.

Limitations of Tonkin, Woodhams, et al. (2012)

Despite the promising findings of Tonkin, Woodhams, et al. (2012), there are important limitations to this research (many of which also apply to Tonkin et al., 2011). As discussed in the section Limitations of Tonkin et al. (2011), Tonkin, Woodhams, et al. (2012) were also limited by the fact that they only studied two crimes per offender, which does not reflect the real-life scenario in which crime linkage is conducted. Furthermore, Tonkin, Woodhams, et al. (2012) only examined discrimination accuracy for inter-crime distance and temporal proximity. It, therefore, remains unclear whether a wider range of offender behavior has the potential to facilitate cross-crime linkage.

But, there are also limitations that are unique to Tonkin, Woodhams, et al. (2012). In particular, it is important to recognize the potential biases that arise from using a sample of DNA-linked crimes. This methodology naturally meant that Tonkin and colleagues' sample consisted solely of offenders who had left DNA evidence at the scenes of their crimes. Arguably, these offenders may differ from those who do not leave physical evidence, which raises doubts about the generalizability of these findings to the wider offender population. One might argue, for example, that offenders who leave DNA are more impulsive and opportunistic and engage in less pre-offense planning than offenders who do not leave DNA. These are characteristics that might be associated with behavioral consistency and distinctiveness, and, therefore, may impact on discrimination accuracy.

In addition, Tonkin, Woodhams, et al. (2012) used scene-to-scene DNA matches as the basis for determining whether crime pairs were linked or unlinked. This is in contrast to previous research, which has used detection status to make these decisions (e.g., Bennell & Canter, 2002; Markson et al., 2010; Tonkin et al., 2011). This is potentially a limitation if the offender's DNA was found at a crime scene for some reason other than that he or she committed the crime. For example, maybe a suspect's DNA was left at the victim's house because he or she is a friend of the victim, rather than the perpetrator. In a situation such as this, a crime pair classed as linked by Tonkin, Woodhams, et al. (2012) would in fact be unlinked, thereby introducing noise into the analyses. However, the pattern of findings observed by Tonkin and colleagues does not suggest that noise was systematically introduced as a result of the methodology. If this were the case, one would have expected to see a significant reduction in discrimination accuracy across *all* statistical models when compared with Tonkin et al.'s (2011) findings. In reality, the majority of statistical models were comparable across the two studies in terms of discrimination accuracy.

Finally, although the sample size in Tonkin, Woodhams, et al. (2012) compares favorably to some previous crime linkage research (e.g., Markson et al., 2010; Tonkin, Santtila, & Bull, 2011; Woodhams & Toye, 2007), the sample should still be considered relatively small. Furthermore, certain types of crime were underrepresented in Tonkin, Woodhams, et al.'s (2012) sample (violent, sexual, and robbery offenses in particular). This places limits on the genaralizability of these findings. The limitations on sample size and diversity arose primarily due to the low recovery rate of DNA at the scenes of certain crimes, which precluded the inclusion of many unsolved offenses in the study. This demonstrates a limitation of the methodology used by Tonkin, Woodhams, et al. (2012) because, despite sampling data across the whole of Northamptonshire's electronic crime records, only 132 offenders were identified for analysis.

Future Directions for Research on Cross-Crime Linkage

Having described the preliminary research on cross-crime linkage, the chapter will conclude with a discussion of how future work might progress in this new area of crime linkage research. First, research must explore whether these findings can be replicated in different geographical areas. This is particularly important since the two studies described in this chapter have both sampled data from the same police force, and there is clear evidence to suggest that behavioral consistency, distinctiveness, and discrimination accuracy vary as a function of location (e.g., Bennell, 2002; Bennell & Jones, 2005; Tonkin, Santtila, & Bull, 2012). Without research such as this, it will be difficult to make reliable practical recommendations regarding cross-crime linkage.

Second, future research should explore whether the findings reported in this chapter replicate when all of the crimes committed by each offender are included in the analyses (rather than a constant of two offenses per offender). This may provide a more realistic test of cross-crime linkage.

Third, it has been emphasized throughout this chapter that research must attempt to include a wider range of offender behavior in studies of cross-crime linkage. This may, however, require a slightly different methodology to that used by Tonkin and colleagues. For example, researchers might focus on certain types of crime that share particular behavioral features, such as robbery, rape, and murder, which all contain elements of victim–offender interaction, control, and escape behaviors (e.g., the use of a weapon, methods of victim restraint, and attempts to conceal one's identity from the victim). Indeed, a research study investigating the potential to link across rapes and robberies using such behavior is already underway at the University of Birmingham, United Kingdom. This may help to overcome the obvious difficulty posed by studying a diverse range of crimes that contain often very different types of offender behavior. Alternatively, future work might consider developing behavioral themes from offender crime scene behavior that would subsequently be used to examine discrimination accuracy across crime categories/types. These themes could be developed statistically using techniques such as multidimensional scaling and cluster analysis (e.g., Bateman & Salfati, 2007; Santtila et al., 2008), or researchers might consider using theoretical models that are designed to apply to a wide variety of crime types, such as the Narrative Action System (NAS) model (Canter & Youngs, 2009; Youngs & Canter, 2009). Regardless of the approach used, research such as this is important because investigators will otherwise have no guidance in situations where geographical and temporal behavior is either unreliable or absent (e.g., where a victim has been drugged or knocked unconscious and is unable to recall where and when the offense took place).

Fourth, the limitations of using a DNA-linked sample of crimes to explore behavioral consistency, distinctiveness, and discrimination accuracy were discussed in the section Limitations of Tonkin, Woodhams, et al. (2012). One of these limitations was that it can be difficult to obtain a sample that is of sufficient size to facilitate reliable statistical analysis. Thus, future research using this methodology may have to consider sampling from larger, more urbanized, forces and/or combining datasets from several forces to facilitate reliable analyses. However, the latter may artificially inflate the discrimination accuracy of inter-crime distance relative to real life (Woodhams, 2008).

Fifth, Tonkin and colleagues used the Home Office framework as the basis for defining cross-crime linkage, which draws a distinction between crime types and crime categories. But, legal frameworks are not primarily designed to capture psychological similarities between offenses (Tonkin et al., 2011). Future research might, therefore attempt to develop a psychologically based classification system that can replace the Home Office framework used in these studies. Existing typologies such as those proposed by investigative psychologists (e.g., Youngs, 2006) and criminal career researchers (e.g., Cohen, 1986) might be used for this purpose. Alternatively, a new classification system might be developed using techniques such as multidimensional scaling, or even by asking serial offenders themselves to identify groups of *psychologically similar* offences (e.g., using card-sorting tasks; Woodhams et al., 2008). For example, offences that are primarily acquisitive in nature might be deemed psychologically distinct from those that have an expressive/violent nature. Alternatively, group offenses might be perceived to be similar when the composition of the group remains stable compared with when new members join the group (Magnusson, Gerzen, & Nyman, 1968). Research such as this would provide a different perspective on whether offenders behave in a relatively consistent and distinctive manner across diverse offending situations.

Sixth, it is clearly important (as discussed throughout this chapter) for future research to explore more appropriate methods of calculating decision thresholds in crime linkage research. The limitations of Youden's Index have been recognized for some time (e.g., Bennell, 2002) and the current chapter has further highlighted the fragility of this method for calculating decision thresholds. Future work must, therefore, develop decision thresholds that (1) account for the prior probability of linked crimes, and (2) quantify the various costs and benefits associated with correct/incorrect linkage decisions.

Seventh, researchers should begin to develop and test statistical decision-making tools (such as the one described in the section Conclusions and Implications). As discussed in Chapter 6, there are many factors beyond behavioral consistency and distinctiveness that will determine whether crime linkage findings can be successfully applied in practice, so it is important to explore whether the initial findings of Tonkin and colleagues can be translated into a usable method of linking across crime categories, across crime types, and within crime types.

Conclusions

Previous crime linkage research has restricted its focus to samples of crime that are homogenous in terms of crime type (i.e., they only contain one type of crime, such as residential burglary). Consequently, these studies provide no guidance for identifying crime series that contain several different types of offense. This is problematic because many offenders (particularly the most prolific) are versatile in their offending behavior (e.g., Farrington et al., 1988; Piquero et al., 2007), so the police are regularly faced with identifying such series. In this chapter two studies have been described that were the first to examine whether offender behavior can be used to facilitate crime linkage across crime categories and crime types. It was found that moderate to high levels of discrimination accuracy can be achieved using simple measures of spatial and temporal behavior, even when more realistic samples containing both solved and unsolved offenses are analyzed. These findings, therefore, provide tentative support for the notion that cross-crime linkage is a viable investigative procedure. But, a considerable amount of work is required before the potential value of cross-crime linkage is realized.

Acknowledgments

The author acknowledges that the work described in this chapter has been published by *Criminal Justice and Behavior* © Sage Publications Ltd (2011) and *Forensic Science International* © Elsevier (2012).

References

Bateman, A. L., & Salfati, C. G. (2007). An examination of behavioral consistency using individual behaviors or groups of behaviors in serial homicide. *Behavioral Sciences & the Law, 25*, 527–544.

Bennell, C. (2002). *Behavioural consistency and discrimination in serial burglary* (Unpublished doctoral dissertation). University of Liverpool, Liverpool, England.

Bennell, C., & Canter, D. V. (2002). Linking commercial burglaries by modus operandi: Tests using regression and ROC analysis. *Science & Justice, 42*, 153–164.

Bennell, C., & Jones, N. J. (2005). Between a ROC and a hard place: A method for linking serial burglaries by modus operandi. *Journal of Investigative Psychology and Offender Profiling, 2*, 23–41.

Brantingham, P. J., & Brantingham, P. L. (1981). *Environmental criminology*. Beverly Hills, CA: Sage.

Brantingham, P. J., & Brantingham, P. L. (1995). Criminality of place: Crime generators and crime attractors. *European Journal on Criminal Policy and Research, 3*, 5–26.

Burrell, A., & Bull, R. (2011). A preliminary examination of crime analysts' views and experiences of comparative case analysis. *International Journal of Police Science & Management, 13*, 2–15.

Canter, D. V., & Youngs, D. (2009). *Investigative psychology: Offender profiling and the analysis of criminal action*. Chichester, England: Wiley.

Clarke, R. V., & Felson, M. (1993). *Routine activity and rational choice*. New Brunswick, NJ: Transaction.

Cohen, J. (1986). Research on criminal careers: Individual frequency rates and offense seriousness. In A. Blumstein, J. Cohen, J. Roth, & C. A. Visher (Eds.), *Criminal careers and "career criminals"* (pp. 292–418). Washington, DC: National Academy Press.

Cohen, J. (1990). Things I have learned (so far). *American Psychologist, 45*, 1304–1312.

Department for Communities and Local Government. (2008). *National indicators for local authorities and local authority partnerships: Handbook of definitions*. Wetherby, England: Communities and Local Government Publications.

Farrington, D. P., Snyder, H. N., & Finnegan, T. A. (1988). Specialization in juvenile court careers. *Criminology, 26*, 461–487.

Furr, R. M., & Funder, D. C. (2004). Situational similarity and behavioral consistency: Subjective, objective, variable-centred, and person-centred approaches. *Journal of Research in Personality, 38*, 421–447.

Grann, M., & Långström, N. (2007). Actuarial assessment of violence risk: To weigh or not to weigh? *Criminal Justice and Behavior, 34*, 22–36.

Kinney, J. B., Brantingham, P. L., Wuschke, K., Kirk, M. G., & Brantingham, P. J. (2008). Crime attractors, generators and detractors: Land use and urban crime opportunities. *Built Environment, 34*, 62–74.

Leitner, M., & Kent, J. (2009). Bayesian journey-to-crime modelling of single and multiple crime-type series in Baltimore County, MD. *Journal of Investigative Psychology and Offender Profiling, 6*, 213–236.

Magnusson, D., Gerzen, M., & Nyman, B. (1968). The generality of behavioral data 1: Generalizations from observations on one occasion. *Multivariate Behavioral Research, 3*, 295–320.

Markson, L., Woodhams, J., & Bond, J. W. (2010). Linking serial residential burglary: Comparing the utility of *modus operandi* behaviours, geographical proximity, and temporal proximity. *Journal of Investigative Psychology and Offender Profiling, 7*, 91–107.

Peterson, M. A., & Braiker, H. B. (1980). *Doing crime: A survey of California prison inmates*. Santa Monica, CA: Rand Corporation.

Piquero, A. R., Farrington, D. P., & Blumstein, A. (2007). *Key issues in criminal career research: New analyses of the Cambridge study in delinquent development*. New York, NY: Cambridge University Press.

Santtila, P., Pakkanen, T., Zappalà, A., Bosco, D., Valkama, M., & Mokros, A. (2008). Behavioural crime linking in serial homicide. *Psychology, Crime & Law, 14*, 245–265.

Shoda, Y. (1999). A unified framework for the study of behavioral consistency: Bridging person × situation interaction and the consistency paradox. *European Journal of Personality, 13*, 361–387.

Swets, J. A. (1988). Measuring the accuracy of diagnostic systems. *Science, 240*, 1285–1293.

Tonkin, M., Grant, T., & Bond, J. W. (2008). To link or not to link: A test of the case linkage principles using serial car theft data. *Journal of Investigative Psychology and Offender Profiling, 5*, 59–77.

Tonkin, M., Santtila, P., & Bull, R. (2012). The linking of burglary crimes using offender behaviour: Testing research cross-nationally and in more realistic settings. *Legal and Criminological Psychology, 17*, 276–293.

Tonkin, M., Woodhams, J., Bull, R., & Bond, J. W. (2012). Linking solved and unsolved crimes using offender behaviour. Behavioural case linkage with solved and unsolved crimes. *Forensic Science International, 222*, 146–153.

Tonkin, M., Woodhams, J., Bull, R., Bond, J. W., & Palmer, E. J. (2011). Linking different types of crime using geographical and temporal proximity. *Criminal Justice and Behavior, 38*, 1069–1088.

Woodhams, J. (2008). *Understanding juvenile sexual offending: An investigative perspective* (Unpublished doctoral dissertation). University of Leicester, Leicester, England.

Woodhams, J., Bull, R., & Hollin, C. R. (2007). Case linkage: Identifying crimes committed by the same offender. In R. N. Kocsis (Ed.), *Criminal profiling: International theory, research, and practice* (pp. 117–133). Totowa, NJ: Humana Press.

Woodhams, J., Hollin, C. R., & Bull, R. (2008). Incorporating context in linking crimes: An exploratory study of situational similarity and if-then contingencies. *Journal of Investigative Psychology and Offender Profiling, 5*, 1–23.

Woodhams, J., & Labuschagne, G. (2012). A test of case linkage principles with solved and unsolved serial rapes. *Journal of Police and Criminal Psychology, 27*, 85–98.

Woodhams, J., & Toye, K. (2007). An empirical test of the assumptions of case linkage and offender profiling with serial commercial robberies. *Psychology, Public Policy, and Law, 13*, 59–85.

Youngs, D. (2006). How does crime pay? The differentiation of criminal specialisms by fundamental incentive. *Journal of Investigative Psychology and Offender Profiling, 3*, 1–19.

Youngs, D., & Canter, D. V. (2009). An emerging research agenda for investigative interviewing: Hypotheses from the narrative action system. *Journal of Investigative Psychology and Offender Profiling, 6*, 91–99.

Exploring If (Situation) ... Then (Behavior) Contingencies in Interpersonal Crimes

13

JAN M. WINTER

Contents

Introduction	304
A Critical Review of Crime Linkage Research to Date	306
The Cognitive–Affective Personality System as a Possible Framework for Crime Linkage Research	308
The Influence of Situations on Behavioral Distinctiveness	310
The Importance of the Offender–Victim Situation Interaction in Sexual Assaults	312
Cognitive and Affective Determinants of Offender Decision Making	312
Environmental Constraints in Serial Offender Decision Making	314
The Influence of Victim Resistance on Offense Outcome	315
Investigating If ... Then Contingencies in Serial Sexual Assaults	316
Integrating Time through Sequence Analysis of Interpersonal Crimes	317
The Use of Lag Sequential Analysis	318
If ... Then Contingencies Based on Proximity Coefficients	320
Applying True Sequence Analysis in Crime Linkage: A Primer	321
Sample Description	322
Data Coding	322
Statistical Analysis	323
Exploratory Results	326
Potential Issues in Sequence Analysis	327
Conclusion	329
References	329

Introduction

Probably one of the most pertinent questions in crime linkage research relates to what degree situational and contextual factors affect offending behavior and possibly *distort* a serial offender's *modus operandi*. Consider the following example.

A couple of years ago, a young woman in her early twenties walked home after a night out with her friends in a Western European town at 3 a.m. on a late autumn morning. She took a shortcut through a small and sparsely lit park in the city center. Near the end of the park, and close to her home, she was suddenly approached from behind by a hooded figure who threatened her with a gun-shaped object and dragged her during the ensuing struggle into the nearest bushes. After hitting her with the object, he forced her to fellate him and partially undressed her. His attempt for rear vaginal intercourse was thwarted when she started to scream. Her sudden verbal resistance apparently startled the offender. He made a threatening gesture but calmly walked away.

Two weeks later in the same town, a teenage girl left her friends—also after a night out in the city center—and strolled down an arterial road in the direction of her home. She too was suddenly attacked from behind but on this occasion the offender used violence immediately. Blocking her sight with the hood of her own top, he repeatedly punched her in the head. Taken by surprise and feeling paralyzed by the terrifying situation, the girl ceased her attempts to resist. The offender took her along the empty road on foot and forced her to fellate him several times during their journey. He also attempted to vaginally penetrate her from behind. Despite her compliant behavior, the offender repeatedly punched her in the head and dragged her further along in what appeared to be a specific direction. Only through the intervention of passersby's several minutes later, did he let her go and take flight.

During the subsequent police investigation and months to come, it turned out that both offenses were preceded and ensued by other sexual assaults and rapes in the same area. Behavioral Investigative Advisers (hereafter BIAs, see Chapter 8) were asked by detectives to assist them by developing an offender profile and circumscribing a geographical search area for the suspect. The *modus operandi* of the offender revealed a pattern of stalking, sexually assaulting, and occasionally robbing predominantly young women who were cycling or walking home after clubbing or socializing with friends in the heart of the town. Sometimes the women were attacked en route, sometimes while or shortly after entering their home residence. Because usable deoxyribonucleic acid (DNA) evidence was scarce and took time to process, one of the challenging questions during the crime linkage analysis was whether the above-described second offense could be attributed to the same offender. Although the case shared similar victim characteristics and routine activities, geospatial, temporal, and some sexual aspects, the offender in the second offense deviated in his interaction with the victim, specifically in his use of expressive violence. This was in stark contrast to all other offenses in this potential series, which were almost devoid of any expressive aggression, and where even instrumental violence was relatively moderate.

This apparent outlier could be hypothetically explained by situational factors such as heightened aggression being a result of pre-offense alcohol or drug use,* or frustration over earlier failed attempts, or unknown sources of severe irritation. It turned out that a viable suspect, who's DNA would be later linked to at least two of the attacks, lived in the vicinity of the crime scene(s) of the second offense. Because the offender appeared to be moving the victim in the direction of his house, it is possible that he was contemplating an abduction of the victim. Obviously, the inclusion of this offense in the series had consequences for the investigative focus, especially with regard to suspect prioritization.

This brief and very limited account is one of many examples of *real-world* incidents of violent offending that can challenge investigators, crime analysts, and BIAs to varying degrees with regard to whether "to link or not to link" (Tonkin, Grant, & Bond, 2008). It is presented here as an illustration of a fundamental challenge in crime linkage practice and research alike; that is, how to deal with offender–victim interactions and situational influences and interferences. Although some practitioners—as it will be explained later—have developed strategies to incorporate the dynamic aspects of an offense in their crime linkage analysis, research attempts in this regard have been few and limited. This chapter therefore seeks to offer a novel perspective on crime linkage research and begins by critically reviewing crime linkage research findings to date. The relevant theoretical framework is explained and possible explanations for situational differences are discussed. This is followed by a review of the various strands of empirical evidence for the particular dynamic interplay between offender, victim, and situation/environment. The chapter then explains how *if ... then* contingencies and behavioral similarity has been researched thus far and stresses the importance of taking the temporal sequence of actions in an offense into account. The chapter ends by giving an example of a new methodology—proximity coefficients—that does just this. This approach allows us to examine the whole interpersonal offense dynamic, rather than treating offense behaviors as a "black box," with the results possibly providing a more refined *if ... then* signature of serial offenders that in turn might allow for more realistic linking research than previously endeavored.

* Brecklin and Ullman (2010) found that victim injury was three times as likely when the offender had been under the influence of substances. However, the relationship between specific drugs and increased violence in general appears to be ambiguous (e.g., for methamphetamine and violence see Tyner & Fremouw, 2008).

A Critical Review of Crime Linkage Research to Date

This book, and a recent double issue in a peer-reviewed journal dedicated to crime linkage, is testament to advances in this field, especially in the last decade (Bennell & Woodhams, 2012). Crime linkage research has come a long way in the last two decades since early linking studies (e.g., Canter et al., 1990; see Chapters 2 and 6). The studies conducted in this period have provided some evidence for the assumptions underpinning crime linkage (behavioral consistency and distinctiveness) with a variety of different crime types, and research has demonstrated that predictions about linkage status can be made that are significantly better than chance (e.g., Bennell & Canter, 2002; Bennell & Jones, 2005; Burrell, Bull, & Bond, 2012; Davies, Tonkin, Bull, & Bond, 2012; Ellingwood, Mugford, Bennell, Melnyk, & Fritzon, 2013; Salo et al., 2012; Santtila, Junkkila, & Sandnabba, 2005; Santtila et al., 2008; Tonkin, Santtila, & Bull, 2011; Tonkin, Woodhams, Bull, Bond, & Palmer, 2011; Woodhams & Labuschagne, 2012; Woodhams & Toye, 2007). However, a thorough qualitative review of 19 published studies by Bennell, Mugford, Ellingwood, and Woodhams (2014) revealed a moderate range of crime linkage accuracy for different types of offending. In addition, there are several limitations with regard to crime linkage studies that make this enterprise for researchers and practitioners alike less straightforward than it might seem. For example:

- For most studies, it is unknown how the series being examined were first identified and yet offenses first linked by DNA have been shown to be less similar with respect to crime scene behavior than offenses first linked based on similar *modus operandi* (Woodhams & Labuschagne, 2012). We do not know how this might have impacted research findings to date.
- Distances related to crime locations and the time span between offenses appear to be much more accurate predictors of crime linkages than actual *modus operandi* behavior, at least for some crime types, particularly volume crime (e.g., Bennell & Jones, 2005; Goodwill & Alison, 2006; Markson, Woodhams, & Bond, 2010; Tonkin, Santtila, & Bull, 2011; see Chapters 2 and 5). This raises the question of whether it is necessary to code for a large number of behaviors in police databases for the purpose of carrying out crime linkage analysis instead of relying on a smaller, but more reliable number of offense characteristics (Grubin, Kelly, & Brunsdon, 2001; Santtila et al., 2008).*

* However, it should be noted, as Bennell et al. (2014) pointed out, that researchers have mostly focused on behavioral information and have tended to neglect other available nonbehavioral features (such as ethnicity, distinctive physical features, type of clothing, vehicle characteristics, and weapon description) that could potentially play a pivotal role in real-life crime linkage and that are stored in such databases.

- Some linkage studies have excluded from their analyses very common and also infrequent, or rare behaviors (e.g., Grubin et al., 2001; Sorochinski & Salfati, 2010; Woodhams, Hollin, & Bull, 2008; Woodhams & Toye, 2007).* However, in practice, an atypical behavior could be crucial in linking a series together, if that behavior was exhibited in a consistent fashion by an offender.
- At least some serial offenders appear to behave less consistently than others (e.g., Bootsma & Eshof, 2006; Deslauriers-Varin & Beauregard, 2010; Grubin et al., 2001; Harbers, Deslauriers-Varin, Beauregard, & van der Kemp, 2012; Sorochinski & Salfati, 2010). This presents a problem for practitioners who, at present, have no evidence-based means of determining whether the series with which they are concerned is the work of a consistent or inconsistent offender.
- Some crime scene behaviors seem more effective for linking crimes than others (e.g., Woodhams & Toye, 2007), and those that are associated with the victim–offender interaction (e.g., demeaning or complimenting the victim) seem to fare worse than those that relate to pre-crime decisions (e.g., prowling, vehicle use, type of approach location; see Grubin et al., 2001; Winter et al., 2013). Such findings suggest that there may be merit in giving greater weight to (or only including in an analysis) behaviors that precede the victim–offender interaction. Alternatively, one could have greater confidence in linking decisions in cases where the offender immediately immobilizes the victim (e.g., a blitz rape; Santtila et al., 2008), thereby allowing him to behave how he wishes without interference.

In summary, these bullet points indicate that there are still a number of unanswered questions in the field of crime linkage research, which need to be tackled from a theoretical and methodological perspective. All of these points share a common denominator: the concept (and therefore operationalization) of behavioral consistency remains somewhat elusive in this area of research and practice. Crime linkage still relies heavily on the assumption that people's behavior is consistent irrespective of context. Or, to put it less bluntly, the central idea of crime linkage reflects an underestimation of the power of the situation. However, contemporary personality psychology (e.g., Cervone & Shoda, 1999; Donnellan, Lucas, & Fleeson, 2009), as well as recent

* Obviously, "consistent but extremely uncommon behaviours" (Grubin et al., 2001, p.11) are the reason why databases like the Violent Crime Linkage Analysis System (ViCLAS) or the Violent Criminal Apprehension Program (ViCAP) contain so many categories and variables in order to capture the unique behavioral signature of a serial offender. Nevertheless, such idiosyncratic characteristics are likely the exception rather than the rule and can hardly be implemented in routine linkage filters or research designs (Grubin et al., 2001), leaving novel Bayesian analytical methods aside (Salo et al., 2012).

studies (e.g., Deslauriers-Varin & Beauregard, 2010), point toward the fact that an offender's level of consistency across a series of crimes must be, and is, significantly influenced by situational and contextual factors.

This is not a new statement. Others have already acknowledged that a more contemporary perspective, which incorporates patterns of individual *if ... then* contingencies across situations (e.g., Fleeson & Noftle, 2009), would be more appropriate for conceptualizing crime linkage research (Alison, Bennell, Mokros, & Ormerod, 2002; Woodhams, Hollin, & Bull, 2007; Woodhams et al. 2008). This chapter considers whether or not crime linkage can take a step forward by embracing this modern interactionist model of behavioral consistency.

The Cognitive–Affective Personality System as a Possible Framework for Crime Linkage Research

Crime linkage depends on an offender acting in a way that can be distinguished from the actions of other offenders. This postulation actually comprises two assumptions. The first is that an offender will act in a way that is predictable or identifiable as a nonrandom pattern of behavior (*behavioral stability assumption*; Bennell, Jones, & Melnyk, 2009). This is usually instantiated as an assumption that offenders need to act consistently (Canter, 1994), but, at a conceptual level, consistency is in reality a simplification of the necessary condition that they need only exhibit behaviors that represent a discernible pattern (e.g., Bennell et al., 2009; Sjöstedt, Långström, Sturidsson, & Grann, 2004). For example, an offender who alternates his killings between female prostitutes and underage childbearing mothers may be showing variation in target choice, but the remainder of his behavioral pattern might be sufficient to allow his offenses to be identified. The second assumption is that such patterns must be sufficiently different across offenders to enable one offender to be differentiated from another (*behavioral distinctiveness assumption*; Bennell et al., 2009). That is, linking requires not only a set of behaviors that are consistent enough for an offender to be identified, but those behaviors must also be distinct enough to allow the offender to be differentiated from his or her contemporaries.

Of these two assumptions, the first takes logical precedence, because if it is not possible to identify a pattern that links an offender to his or her crimes then it will not be possible to use offending behavior to differentiate between the crimes committed by different offenders. The question of behavioral consistency is one that has long been considered within the psychological literature (e.g., Mischel, 2009). Given this, it is useful to consider how a contemporary personality psychology framework—the cognitive–affective personality system (CAPS; e.g., Mischel & Shoda, 1995; Shoda & Mischel, 1998; see Chapter 2)—may relate to behavioral consistency and distinctiveness within the investigative context.

As Woodhams, Hollin, et al. (2007, 2008) have repeatedly pointed out, the CAPS offers a useful theoretical and contemporary framework for testing hypotheses in the area of crime linkage research. The CAPS would imply that offenders have distinct *if … then* profiles (Mischel & Shoda, 2008). Mischel and Shoda have proposed and demonstrated that despite our susceptibility to situational factors, human behavior is characterized by relatively stable and distinctive patterns of behavioral adaptations to various situations. The *if* of a situation, which is characterized by individually perceived external features, interacts with internally triggered and interconnected cognitions and affects that in turn activate the appropriate behavioral *then* response. In other words, the way we see and experience a specific circumstance influences directly how we feel and think, and therefore (re-)act, in that instance. The more we experience a situation as similar to an earlier experience, the more we tend to behave in the same manner. The key concept in the CAPS is that our personality structure remains the same, but situational cues influence our behavioral repertoire. As an example, if anyone in need asks you very politely and respectfully for your help, then you might tend to consistently reciprocate in a kind manner. This might be because the friendly demeanor is key to how you think and feel about that situation regardless of the sort of help that is requested, plus helping other people makes you feel good about yourself. Mischel and Shoda (2008) suggested that our internal catalogue of *if … then* contingencies is permeable to change, but sufficiently stable (at least in adulthood). Therefore, each individual should be identifiable by his or her situational *signature*.

In terms of how this model relates to crime linkage, we need to return to the example at the beginning of the chapter. In the first offense that was described, the offender may have perceived the opportunity of an available, but actively resistant victim who demanded him to exercise a necessary amount of control over her while trying to pursue his primary goal of sexual intercourse. If he perceived that his competency to master the situation was sufficiently challenged, he would choose to flee instead of trying to reestablish control. However, in situations like the second offense, the offender might have encountered a victim that, based on his perception at least, offered a much less demanding form of resistance. In this case, the offender succeeded rapidly in dominating her completely. The offender possibly felt elated by his "success," especially after a fruitless search for a suitable victim. Now that he sees himself as being fully in control, he might have recognized the opportunity to pursue two goals simultaneously: sexual intercourse and violent domination. He therefore exerted his *power* over the victim by forcing her into sexual acts and beating her throughout the offense. Only the emergence of a third party prompted him to release his victim and flee to safety. In the end, the offender's distinct behavioral signature could be characterized as controlling and sexually opportunistic with actively resistant victims, but violently dominating with victims that appear easier to subdue.

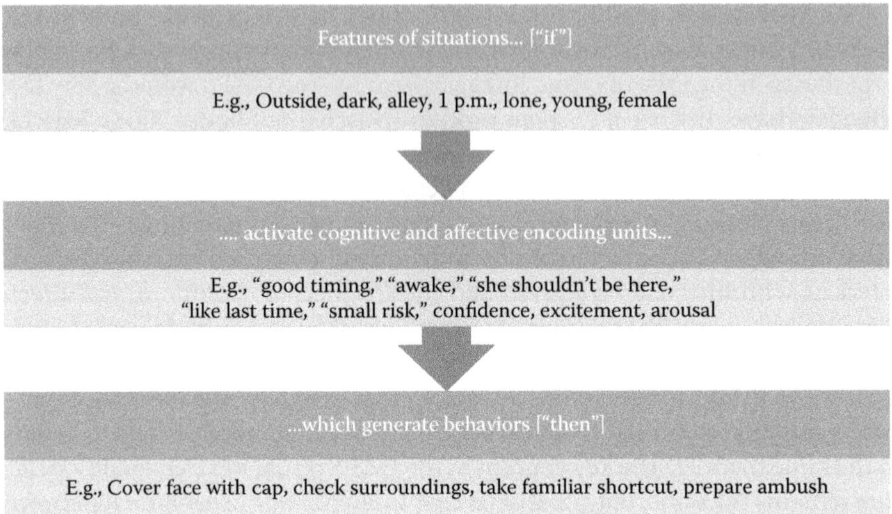

Figure 13.1 Illustration of Mischel and Shoda's (1995) CAPS. The figure shows how features of a specific situation (*if*) activate thoughts and feelings in a serial sex offender. The cognitive and affective units interact with each other, whereas other units remain deactivated or unaffected. The result is certain behaviors (*then*) that are specific for this offender in that situation. Depending on the outcome of the situation, the same behaviors might be activated again in a future event with a high degree of situational similarity. The result is a situational signature or *if ... then* profile. (From Mischel, W., & Shoda, Y. *Psychological Review, 102*, 246–268, 1995.)

Mischel and Shoda (2008) elucidated that the interaction between situational features, personal memories and expectancies, affective responses, valence of a situation, desired outcomes, and (perceived) competencies forge an individual's signature across situations, implying consistency and distinctiveness. This person–situation interaction appears to matter within the context of offending as well (see Figure 13.1). The question is whether this interaction can (1) be properly investigated in crime linkage studies and (2) whether its inclusion actually yields higher linkage accuracy than has been found previously (Woodhams et al., 2008).

The Influence of Situations on Behavioral Distinctiveness

The challenge is therefore to demonstrate whether true behavioral distinctiveness does exist and to what degree it is influenced by situational and contextual factors. One possibility is that certain offense behaviors are so consistent and distinctive that they remain impervious to variations in context. Therefore, they could reflect more stable dispositions of an offender or be less situation dependent (Woodhams, Hollin, et al., 2007). For crime linkage purposes, such behaviors should be consistent but not too common, as they need to enable accurate inter-offender differentiation. This possibility is the assumption that underpins the majority of existing linkage research, and there is a fair amount of evidence suggesting that spatial-, contextual-, and/or control-related behaviors (e.g., manner of approach/attack) offer sufficient discriminatory power to accurately link crimes. However, the predictors identified as being useful discriminators are not equally robust (e.g., Bennell & Canter, 2002; Markson et al., 2010; Tonkin et al., 2008; Tonkin, Santtila, et al., 2011; Tonkin et al., 2011) and even for those behaviors that are reasonably consistent, they are not perfectly consistent. For example, Grubin et al. (2001) reported that 68% of serial sex offenders from their UK sample displayed the same sort of control behaviors in two consecutive offenses. This implies that a nonnegligible amount of the offenders acted inconsistently with regard to the most stable linking domain in that study.

A second possibility is that offending behavior remains constant due to a stable homogeneous context, that is, offending situations for a particular crime type are more or less similar, thereby enabling the offender to rely on a consistent behavioral repertoire. This would also imply that crime linkage might be possible for some types of crime but not others. This has been scarcely addressed by researchers. Some studies tentatively suggest that certain crime categories yield higher levels of consistency (e.g., serial homicide; Salo et al., 2012; Santtila et al., 2008) than others (e.g., serial sexual assault; Santtila et al., 2005; Winter et al., 2013). This could be due to the greater amount of interaction in (serial) sexual offending, where a living/surviving victim potentially has more impact on an offender's behavior (Salo et al., 2012). It is certainly undeniable that sexual offending is a highly dynamic crime type, and a growing body of evidence underlines the volatility of a sexual offense and its outcome (e.g., Balemba & Beauregard, 2012; Beauregard, Proulx, Rossmo, Leclerc, & Allaire, 2007; Lawrence, Fossi, & Clarke, 2010; Polaschek & Hudson, 2004).

Even within a crime type such as rape, there appear to be different levels of consistency depending on the situation (Grubin et al., 2001). Grubin et al. distinguished between different types of serial sexual assaulters. Their data showed that one type appeared to carry out planned attacks inside a dwelling, using a surprise approach, a weapon, and exhibiting forensic awareness. In CAPS terms, they evidenced a specific selection of a situation. In contrast, the other three types of rapists identified by Grubin et al. seemed much more opportunistic: they were less likely to offend indoors and they displayed varying degrees of concern with escaping unidentified. In other words, the majority of Grubin et al.'s (2001) offenders did not have a clear preference for an offense situation, which could possibly account for the lower degree of consistency that is sometimes found for serial rapists in comparison with serial murderers (e.g., Santtila et al., 2005, 2008). Consistent with this, Polaschek, Hudson, Ward, and Siegert (2001) showed that committing a sexual offense is often not an explicit goal from the outset of the offense for many serial rapists. Rapists who are more impulsive and experience other self-regulation problems (e.g., Hanson & Morton-Bourgon, 2005; Knight & Guay, 2006) are unlikely to be as consistent as rapists (or other offenders) who plan their crimes, thereby decreasing the possibility of situational interference through the situations they create.

In sum, it can be assumed that variations in situations or situational features will elicit individual responses within the context of serial crime. Interpersonal crimes, in particular, reflect a context where an active, continuous interaction between offender, victim, and other situational features occurs. This dynamic interaction could affect behavioral consistency and distinctiveness. Therefore, it is worthwhile to consider the empirical evidence for the various situational interactions during sexual assaults and their influence on offender decision making.

The Importance of the Offender–Victim Situation Interaction in Sexual Assaults

The central idea of this chapter—that the features of an offense situation have a significant impact on the offender's behavior and outcome of a situation—has been researched in different but related efforts to reveal the underlying processes at work. All these efforts exemplify the possible amount of variation in a (serial) offense. The results in three different research areas regarding the volatility of a criminal event will be discussed in the following sections: (1) cognitive and affective factors affecting offender decision making, (2) the influence of environmental characteristics on offender decision making, and (3) victim resistance as a situational influence on the outcome of an offense.

Cognitive and Affective Determinants of Offender Decision Making

A CAPS perspective on serial offending stresses the important influence of situational features on offenders' thoughts and feelings and therefore on their responses. Polaschek and colleagues (Polaschek & Hudson, 2004; Polaschek et al., 2001) developed an insightful model of the situational impact on offenders' goal formation and decision making. They analyzed their in-depth interviews with incarcerated sex offenders ($N = 24$), drawing on principles of Grounded Theory (Strauss & Corbin, 1990). The offenders' narratives resulted in the descriptive Rape Model (RM) of the rapists' offense processes unfolding in time, including behavioral, cognitive, affective, and volitional elements of offender decision making. Six phases (from background factors to post-offense behavior) and 17 categories illustrate the complexity of an unfolding rape sequence where at least three different pathways were outlined. Contingent on their background factors, their general coping strategy, and their mood at the onset of the pathway, offenders would strive toward an established goal, which would change their current situation. Such a goal could be the enhancement of a positive distal mood by seeking sexual gratification or escape from a negative distal mood either by seeking sexual gratification or by redressing harm to oneself. The ensuing pathways highlight differences, such as how an offender would approach the victim, the degree of preparation, the use (or not) of degrading sexual behavior, as well as gratuitous physical violence (partially dependent on the victim's response during the assault), a positive or negative offense evaluation (e.g., valence in CAPS terms), post-offense situation management (e.g., adopting normalizing behavior or overtly controlling the risk of apprehension), an evaluation of the broader situation, an affective response (e.g., positive/neutral, angry, negative), and a behavioral response (e.g., the use of arrest-evading strategies).

The complexity of the RM highlights a variety of decision-making moments that could alter the course of the subsequent pathway. As postulated in the CAPS model, the interaction with the environment (i.e., situational features) repeatedly influences how an offender thinks (i.e., cognitive units) and feels (i.e., affective units) and consequently acts during the offending process (i.e., behavioral response). Therefore, the RM clearly underlines that temporal stability in offending goals (i.e., redressing harm, sexual gratification for augmenting a positive or escaping a negative mood) should not be expected. For example, Polaschek and colleagues found that some rapists changed their initial aim from sexual gratification to avenging a perceived wrong during the same offense due to victim behavior. Most notably, the RM showed that the offender–victim interaction shapes the course of the offense during almost every stage of the model. Still, the small sample size used in this study and the underrepresentation of stranger rapists in the sample warrant independent replication, as it is with these types of offenders that crime linkage would most likely be practiced. For example, research is needed to examine whether known offense goals vary to the same degree in stranger serial rapists. In addition, a quantitative sequence analysis of the interrelation of the RM offense stages would have been informative.

Notwithstanding these issues, the studies by Polaschek and her colleagues suggest that many offenders will evaluate the offenses they commit as they unfold (on many different levels) and they will act accordingly. Given this, crime linkage research (and practice) should pay greater attention to these dynamic interactions, which will to some degree influence an offender's behavioral consistency and distinctiveness.

Environmental Constraints in Serial Offender Decision Making

Theories from contemporary environmental criminology (Wortley & Mazerolle, 2008) can also shed light on the situational dynamics of (serial) criminal events. Like the RM, the rational choice perspective (Cornish & Clarke, 2008) treats offending behavior as purposeful and also to some degree goal oriented. Beauregard and colleagues (Beauregard & Leclerc, 2007; Beauregard, Proulx, et al., 2007; Beauregard, Rossmo, & Proulx, 2007) have investigated this theory by combining quantitative and qualitative methods in their investigation of the hunting strategies of serial sexual offenders against women and children.

Beauregard, Rossmo, et al. (2007) distinguished nine sequential phases with regard to the commission of serial sexual offenses: offender and victim routine activities, choice of hunting field, victim selection, method of approach, attack location choice, method to bring the victim to the crime site, crime location choice, method to commit crime, and victim release location choice. Like the RM, each phase offers the offender different choices depending on the environment, victim characteristics, and their behavior. For example, 42% of the sample examined by Beauregard and his colleagues (2007) prowled extensively for victims (i.e., actively searched for a preferred situation and a suitable target), whereas 17% of the serial offenders took advantage of an opportunity that arose during a commute as part of their routine activities. This indicates that environmental and situational features like time, place (victim availability), and victim type (e.g., perceived victim vulnerability, victim's reaction, etc.) can affect where, when, and how an offense is committed, which is reflected by the fact that 36% of the serial offenders in Beauregard, Rossmo, et al.'s sample switched between different methods of approach during their series, rapidly adapting to the situation. Obviously, an offender's behavioral consistency (*then*) partially depends on how suitable/risky he perceives a new offense situation to be (*if*).

Subsequent analyses of the same sample (Beauregard, Proulx, et al., 2007) revealed that environmental features such as the type of offense location (outdoor vs. indoor) and the familiarity with a location had a critical impact on offenders' decision making. Beauregard, Proulx, et al. identified three different crime scripts (similar to pathways) that encompassed the whole offender decision-making process before, during, and after the commission of a serial sexual offense (coercive, manipulative, and nonpersuasive script). Essentially, each script was associated with a distinct manner of searching for victims, attacking victims, and choosing a hunting field. In other words, the offenders behaved differently according to the constraints and possibilities of the respective environment. In an extension to Beauregard, Proulx, et al.'s research, Harbers et al. (2012) found that the degree of situational influence could vary depending on the type of offense location. They found that serial sex offenders behaved less consistently in commercial areas and outdoor crime locations than residential areas and inside crime locations.

The Influence of Victim Resistance on Offense Outcome

Not only can the environment or victim characteristics cause variation in serial offending behavior, but victim behavior can as well. As Beauregard and Leclerc (2007) stated, "to fully understand the offending behaviours of the offender, the victim's behaviour needs to be investigated as well" (pp. 128–129). In particular, studies of victims' resistance strategies indicate that this is not a one-way street but a complex interaction involving both the victim and the offender (Ullman, 1997, 2007). From a CAPS perspective, it becomes evident that the offender's behavior (*if*) influences the victim's response (*then*), which in turn (*if*) will affect the offender (*then*) to some degree. Obviously, the cyclical nature of such an interactive process is very relevant in crime linkage and should therefore be of vital importance for crime linkage research.

Studies indicate that *if* a victim uses active or forceful physical resistance (such as biting, kicking, and weapon use) *then* an offender has less chance to complete his sexual offense (Bart & O'Brien, 1985; Burgheim & Friese, 2008; Clay-Warner, 2002; Guerette & Santana, 2010; Marchbanks, Lui, & Mercy, 1990; Tark & Kleck, 2004; Ullman & Knight, 1992). The same holds for active verbal resistance (e.g., screaming, yelling; Clay-Warner, 2002; Quinsey, & Upfold, 1985; Ullman, 1998), in contrast to less active victim reactions such as freezing, crying, or reasoning (e.g., Clay-Warner, 2002; Galliano, Noble, Puechl, & Travis, 1993; Ullman & Knight, 1992).

Other situational *if* factors also influence victims' *then* resistance strategies. For example, weapon use, nighttime rapes, multiple assailants, and former intimates provoke less physical resistance (Clay-Warner, 2003; Ullman, 1999; Ullman & Siegel, 1993; in contrast to Burgheim & Friese, 2008). Likewise, alcohol intoxication by the offender and victim is associated with an increased chance of completed rape, impaired resistance, and less control/more violence by the offender and injuries inflicted on the victim (Beauregard, Lussier, & Proulx, 2007; Burgheim & Friese, 2008; Ullman, 2007). Furthermore, successful rape avoidance is more likely outdoors than indoors (Ullman & Knight, 1993), where it makes sense that environmental interventions (bystanders/third parties) can save the victim from further harm (Bart & O'Brien, 1985; Clay-Warner, 2002; Ullman & Knight, 1991).

Clearly, a variety of situational factors can influence a victim's resistance strategy, which in turn can impact the outcome of a serious sexual offense. In addition, victims have a potentially broad range of different strategies at their disposal (e.g., Woodhams, Hollin, Bull, & Cooke, 2012) and often use them alone or in combination with others during the different stages of an offense (Winter, Rossi, Serruys, & Ivaldi, 2011; Woodhams et al., 2012).

Resistance can also increase the risk of injury (Bachman, Saltzman, Thompson, & Carmody, 2002; Fossi, Clarke, & Lawrence, 2005), although some studies argue that this is more often the case in offenses where the offender is determined to hurt the victim from the outset (Balemba & Beauregard, 2012; Quinsey & Upfold, 1985; Tark & Kleck, 2004; Ullman, 1998; Ullman & Knight, 1992). Indeed, research shows that sex offenders exhibit variation in the way they react to victim resistance (e.g., Balemba & Beauregard, 2012; Fossi et al., 2005). However, research that has tried to classify sex offenders into types that differ in their reactions to victim resistance has produced mixed results (Prentky, Burgess, & Carter, 1986 vs. Ullman & Knight, 1995). This implies for crime linkage practice and research that a serial offender's consistency depends at least partially on his victim's resistance strategies.

In summary, the aforementioned studies plainly demonstrate that a variety of situational and contextual factors do play an important role in the course of sexually violent offenses and influence the offenders' and victims' decision making. This can be regarded as mounting evidence that an *if … then* perspective would be the appropriate lens through which to investigate crime linkage research questions, at least for interpersonal offenses.

Investigating If … Then Contingencies in Serial Sexual Assaults

To the knowledge of the author, Woodhams and colleagues (2008) were the first researchers to actually apply the CAPS interactionist approach in the crime linkage arena. They operationalized situational similarity as similarity in salient victim behaviors. Having subjected an array of victim behaviors to a combination of framework analysis and hierarchical cluster analysis, they constructed eight different situational profiles or themes (e.g., active resistance and face-saving noncompliance). Each profile hypothetically reflected a cluster of victim behaviors of the same valence (i.e., whether the offender assessed a situation as positive or negative), same demands (i.e., whether the offender's competency was challenged on a physical, social, or self-regulatory level), and same task type (i.e., whether the victim acted in a competitive, cooperative, or unstructured way). Therefore, each offense could reflect several distinct psychological meanings, such as whether the offender met active resistance, victim compliance, or manipulative behavior.

Woodhams and her colleagues then tested the effect of situational similarity on behavioral consistency with a sample of 78 stranger sex offenses (50% were committed by serial juvenile offenders). Despite hypothesizing that a higher degree of situational similarity (as measured from victim behavior) would be associated with a higher degree of behavioral consistency across offenders' crime series, this was not found to be the case. Woodhams et al. (2008) offered several reasons for these findings, predominantly relating to the difficulty of operationalizing situational similarity in an appropriate fashion. Obviously, this might be the biggest challenge in applying a CAPS perspective to naturally noisy and incomplete (serial) crime data, which must be collected outside an experimental setting: to what extent can we infer the psychological meaning of a situation for an offender without having him tell us directly? One possible solution to this problem will be offered in the subsequent paragraphs.

Woodhams et al. (2008) also investigated contingencies of direct victim–offender interactions. Using three different victim (*if*) behaviors, representing the three most common victim behaviors in their sample, they inspected the distribution of various immediate offender (*then*) responses across each series. However, no consistent patterns at this individual level emerged either.

Woodhams and her colleagues (2008) propose a number of reasons why they got the results they did. First, the available linkage research could have already accommodated for situational similarity by individual studies investigating behavioral consistency and distinctiveness within the same crime types (e.g., within a sample of stranger rapes or within a sample of commercial robberies). Second, it could simply be that police data might lack sufficient detail for the incorporation of a CAPS perspective. Third, the number of different *if ... then* contingencies that were available for examination in this study might have been insufficient. Fourth, the nature of the *if ... then* contingencies that Woodhams et al. were able to model may have been inadequate (e.g., they only investigated the behavior immediately preceding that of the offender). Finally, it is possible that the operationalization of situational similarity in itself was perfectly adequate, but that the degree of intensity of each theme should have been taken into account. For example, as Woodhams et al. suggested, the repeated occurrence of a specific theme throughout one offense could have had a stronger influence on situational similarity, but this was not taken into account in the study.

Despite the limitations of this study, Woodhams et al.'s (2008) approach was innovative and demonstrated that in order to capture true situational interaction in the crime linkage context, and any subsequent behavioral consistency that emerges, researchers need to adopt a more comprehensive approach to investigating victim–offender interactions.

Integrating Time through Sequence Analysis of Interpersonal Crimes

At the heart of a criminal investigation of a violent crime lies the sequential process of crime scene reconstruction: "In event analysis, recall that the overall crime or occurrence is the incident. The incident encompasses all actions related to the occurrence" (Bevel & Gardner, 2002, p. 45). Time is reflected in the chronology of the offense, which has, not only from an *if... then* CAPS perspective, a meaningful order. This means that offenders' decisions translate into actions that unfold over time and have short- and long-term consequences. For example, a successful blitz approach could enable an offender to take full control of the victim by bypassing further victim resistance, thereby enabling him to more easily start sexual manipulations (Woodhams et al., 2008). Also, the immediate use of overpowering violence might have a more lasting and intimidating effect on the victim than a con approach. As the earlier RM and rational choice perspectives suggest, there is a reason why one behavior or decision precedes another.

Dern, Dern, Horn, and Horn (2009) stressed this point when they explained the German methodological approach toward behavioral case analysis, which is also used for analyzing individual offenses for crime linkage purposes. They stated: "Only on the basis of the highly complex reconstruction of offender behaviour is it possible to reach conclusions or make predictions that can be termed professional and reliable" (p. 1087). Furthermore, in conducting their analysis, it seems that the approach adopted by German Violent Crime Linkage Analysis System (ViCLAS) analysts follows the principles of the *if... then* CAPS perspective; they conduct a detailed analysis of the sequence of events and how much competence (*then*) a rapist shows when dealing with the demands (*if*) of each phase of the offense (e.g., approach, establishing control, maintaining control, sexual acts, departure of the crime scene). Only after establishing the offender's competence per sequence is it considered whether idiosyncratic characteristics of the offense reflect consistent behavior inherent to the offender (and therefore indicative of a series) or situational influences (Stewen, personal communication, August 13, 2013). That a sequential approach to crime linkage is being adopted in practice further underscores the worthwhile nature of taking a sequential approach to crime linkage research.

As has been described, there have been few analyses in the field of crime linkage that have taken time into account and there are reasons for this. For example, Roe (2008) and Taylor et al. (2008) hypothesized that time has been neglected in general applied research because of the lack of an adequate methodology. Fortunately, there are some indications that this might be changing.

The Use of Lag Sequential Analysis

Fossi et al. (2005) and Lawrence et al. (2010) examined offender–victim interactions during sexual assaults using lag sequential analysis, a methodology that had already proven useful in the analysis of traffic accidents (e.g., Clarke, Forsyth, & Wright, 1999). They analyzed rape victim statements with regard to the various physical and verbal interactions that took place during different stages of the assault (e.g., events leading up to the victim being alerted and events between alert and first physical contact). Fossi et al. distinguished two sorts of offense styles within the specific situation of victims being raped in their bedroom by a stranger: (1) protracted multiple/compound assaults, where the offender seemed to enact a specific fantasy by establishing a pseudo-intimate relationship with the victim and (2) shorter single/direct assaults, with the sexual satisfaction of the offender being the sole objective. The style of the offender had an influence on victim resistance strategies. For example, in the shorter single/direct assaults, physical attempts to control the resisting victim by the offender were successful, resulting in victim compliance. This contrasted with the protracted multiple/compound assaults. In turn, offenders with different offending styles reacted differently to victims' resistance. For example, in protracted multiple/compound assaults, increasing victim resistance had no effect on perpetrator behavior, whereas the offender in single/direct assaults would respond with a heightened effort to physically control the victim. For crime linkage, this implies that even in a relatively confined situation (e.g., a "bedroom rape"), different *if ... then* contingencies can emerge, which might impact behavioral consistency.

Lawrence et al. (2010) developed this research further by extending the analysis to other offense locations (e.g., elsewhere in the victim's home and outside the home). They found evidence that variation in the type of location (e.g., indoors vs. outdoors) affected the behavior of one rapist type (i.e., perpetrators of multiple/compound assaults) more than the other (single/direct assault). There was greater variation in multiple/compound rapists' verbal strategies in outdoor locations, whereas offenders with a single/direct assault style behaved relatively similar across different locations, evidencing a more aggressive and controlled speech pattern. These findings add evidence that the *if ... then* contingencies between offenders and victims may vary across situations and across offender styles, which in turn might find some reflection in serial offenders' consistency across their crimes, but probably more in some offenders than in others.

Despite the valuable contributions made by these studies, there are several limitations. These limitations include the small sample sizes that were used ($N = 14$ and $N = 45$, respectively). In addition, assumptions made about the offenders' underlying motivations for the offenses were speculative without having any access to confirmatory data (Fossi et al., 2005). Moreover, lag-sequential analysis quantifies only the immediate relation between two adjacent behaviors at a time (similar to Woodhams et al., 2008) and not relationships between whole sequences of variables (Taylor, 2006). Finally, the a priori conceptualization of distinct phases of sexual assault may have distorted relationships between behaviors that were separated by stages (Taylor, 2006). Regardless of these limitations, the in-depth analyses presented in these studies signified an important step toward a more comprehensive approach of capturing the situation–behavior interaction in sexual crimes.

If ... Then Contingencies Based on Proximity Coefficients

The intricacies of the (mostly) dyadic offender–victim dynamics within violent offenses might be better dissected with a novel methodology that has been proposed by Taylor (2006) and Taylor and Donald (2007): the proximity coefficient (*P*) reflects the degree of association between preceding cues and following responses. Taylor proposed the coefficient to circumvent shortcomings of the sort of sequence analysis techniques discussed above, and he applied it successfully in the field of hostage negotiation.

The rationale underlying the use of *P* is that behaviors or actions that follow each other in short temporal succession have more in common than those separated by a longer time span (an elementary premise in social interactions; Taylor, 2006). In other words, a previous cue is more likely to trigger an immediate versus a delayed response, and the latter will affect the next action that follows, and so on. The key point is that unlike other approaches, such as the aforementioned lag sequential analysis, this approach can accommodate a delayed reaction. It also enables researchers to scrutinize a whole chain of events. This is because proximity coefficients reflect the varying relationships between every possible cue–response combination, making a priori (and potentially artificial) distinctions of offenses phases unnecessary (as was done by Fossi et al., 2005).

The value of *P* between two variables declines steadily as more behaviors occur in between the variables. However, this decrease of *P* is independent from the length of a sequence. Like other association coefficients, *P* can vary between 0 (a certain cue and response appear only at the beginning and end of a sequence) and 1 (a certain cue is always followed immediately by a specific response).

The proximity coefficient has been successfully applied to distinguish cultural differences in hostage negotiations (Giebels & Taylor, 2009) and investigative police interviews (Beune, Giebels, & Taylor, 2010). In addition, a preliminary study of a small sample of rape victim offense accounts ($N = 47$) revealed that rapists' behavioral themes identified in existing studies (e.g., Canter, Bennell, Alison, & Reddy, 2003; Häkkänen, Lindlöf, & Santtila, 2004) could not be replicated when the offender–victim interaction was taken into account (Winter & Taylor, 2006). According to the results, the *if... then* contingencies of rape offenses shared some underlying similarities that could not be explained by behavioral themes. In other words, the majority of offenses that shared a similar sequence of interactions did not necessarily share the same theme. However, similarities in terms of interaction could be much better explained by considering the time and location of the offense—both variables that have proven very important in offender decision making (e.g., Beauregard, Proulx, et al., 2007). More specifically, offenses that occurred in a similar location (indoors) during a similar time period (nighttime) shared more similar *if ... then* contingencies than if two offenses with differing locations and times were compared.

A further sequence analysis study of attempted and completed rapes from Belgium ($n = 121$ and $n = 82$, respectively; Winter et al., 2011) revealed that offender–victim interactions also significantly and meaningfully differed according to location and time. For example, (death-)threats by the offender were more quickly followed by active verbal resistance at an outdoor crime scene ($P = 0.92$) than when the offense took place indoors ($P = 0.70$). It is logical for a victim to more quickly adopt such a strategy outdoors where the chances of a third party intervention are greater. It also appeared that the offense dynamics were idiosyncratic across offense types. Like in the studies of Fossi et al. (2005) and Lawrence et al. (2010), offenders appeared to react differently to victims' responses across different environments. This variation in individual interactions could be an indication that such sequences are sufficiently distinctive from each other, which is obviously important for using this method for crime linkage purposes. The next question is whether such distinctiveness also captures situational similarity in serial sexual assaults. In other words, are *if ... then* sequences of offender–victim interactions also consistent throughout time.

Applying True Sequence Analysis in Crime Linkage: A Primer

To illustrate the capacity of the proximity coefficient to develop our understanding of crime linkage and its assumptions, the analysis of a new dataset of serial sexual assaults from the United Kingdom is presented here. This subsample ($n = 90$) had been used in another study (Winter et al., 2013) in order to compare two different statistical approaches for linkage analysis, neither of which were sequential in nature (i.e., a dimensional behavioral approach through Mokken scale analysis and discriminant function analysis; a multivariate behavioral approach developed by means of a naïve Bayesian classifier). Both statistical methods achieved significant but moderate levels of linkage accuracy that demonstrated that the crimes of the 30 serial offenders could be differentiated from the other one-off sexual assaulters ($n = 50$) and rapists ($n = 79$). Interestingly, this analysis found the behavioral dimensions of selected offense location(s) (indoors vs. outdoors) and controlling behavior by the offender to be the most useful aspects of behavior for accurate linkage. For the study adopting the new sequential approach, no hypotheses were formulated because it represented a purely exploratory investigation into the usefulness of the proximity coefficient for crime linkage.

Sample Description

Data related to the offenses under investigation were obtained from the British ViCLAS database, which is held and maintained by the Serious Crime Analysis Section of the National Crime Agency (UK). The Serious Crime Analysis Section database holds information on serious sexual, murder, and abduction offenses from across the United Kingdom. For this chapter, the offense accounts from 90 serial sexual assault and rape victims (committed by 30 offenders) were analyzed and sequentially coded. The 30 serial offenders were on average 28.9 years old ($SD = 7.6$), and the known, mean age for 84 victims of the serial offenders was 25.4 years ($SD = 11.99$). The average length of the rape series was three offenses ($SD = 1.2$), which was the case for 83.3% of the series. Only two offenders committed a detected maximum of six serial offenses. Not more than 20% ($n = 12$) of the offenses occurred inside a building, and the majority of the offenses were committed at night ($n = 66$).

Data Coding

For the purpose of sequential analysis, data were coded as follows: First, the author reviewed every offense account after which all (inter-)actions by the offender, victim, and third parties were broken down into separate *thought units*. A thought unit was defined as a meaningful behavior or a verbal utterance(s), which can be expressed in individual words, sentences, or paragraphs. The following extract from a victim statement serves as an example, where the symbol # indicates the end of a thought unit:

002 I was frightened and confused, and I started to scream as loud as I could.#
003 The man punched me to the left of my face at least twice.#
004 And started punching me in my body to the left and right of my ribs. It seemed as though he was trying to knock me out, the punches being so hard.#
005 He said, "Stop screaming,"#
006 And then he put his fist to my neck and kept pressing.#

In order to cover all possibly relevant actions, a coding dictionary was created, based on several previous studies of serial rape and sexual assault (Alison & Stein, 2001; Bootsma & Eshof, 2006; Canter et al., 2003; Dale, Davies, & Wei, 1997; Davies, 1992; Goodwill & Alison, 2007; Grubin, Kelly, & Ayis, 1997; Häkkänen et al., 2004; Lundrigan, Czarnomski, & Wilson, 2010; Park,

Table 13.1 Example of Sequential Coding of a Sexual Assault

Sequential Coding	Summary Sequence
Blitz	The victim was hit on the head from behind by an unknown object and fell to the ground
Physiccontrol	She is then dragged along the ground
Nonforceresist	But manages to slip her jacket off, kick off her remaining shoe
Nonforceresist	And runs
Physicviol	As she runs, she is hit again with an unknown object on the head
Location	The offender then leads the victim to scene nearby
Directive	And orders her to strip
Position	And to kneel down
Fellatio	And perform oral sex
Comply	Which she does
Digpen	He uses his fingers to open the victim's vagina
Vagpen	He then rapes her vaginally

Schlesinger, Pinizzotto, & Davis, 2008; Santtila et al., 2005; Scott, Lambie, Henwood, & Lamb, 2006; Woodhams, Grant, & Price, 2007; Woodhams et al., 2008). Initially, the coding dictionary comprised 70 offender- and victim-related behaviors within the following four broad categories: approach-related behaviors, verbal behaviors, physical behaviors, and sexual behaviors.

Each offense was therefore coded in a single sequence of chronologically succeeding variables that are representative of the interaction between victim and offender. In other words, each thought unit was assigned one single variable from the dictionary (see Table 13.1). Therefore, each offense was represented in a column of codes that reflected the offender–victim interaction throughout an offense. All but the last variable in the list reflected an *if* situation, and all but the first variable could be considered a *then* behavior. A random sample of 10% of the cases was drawn and coded by a second, independent rater. The inter-rater reliability was acceptable ($K = 0.76$; Shrout, 1998).

Statistical Analysis

P-coefficients for all *if* ... *then* contingencies within each offense were calculated, as well as the average *P*-coefficients for each behavior–behavior contingency across all 90 cases. These computations were carried out using the Proximity Coefficient Calculator (ProxCalc) 1.3 (Taylor, 2007). The state transition diagrams, which depict repeatedly occurring behavior contingencies, were drawn with ProxCalc 2010, version 1.1 (see Figure 13.2; Menacere & Taylor, 2010).

For the comparison of all serial cases in terms of their idiosyncratic *if* ... *then* signature, a proximity matrix was constructed, based on all possible contingencies. The matrix contained 6300 comparisons (90 cases × 70 variables).

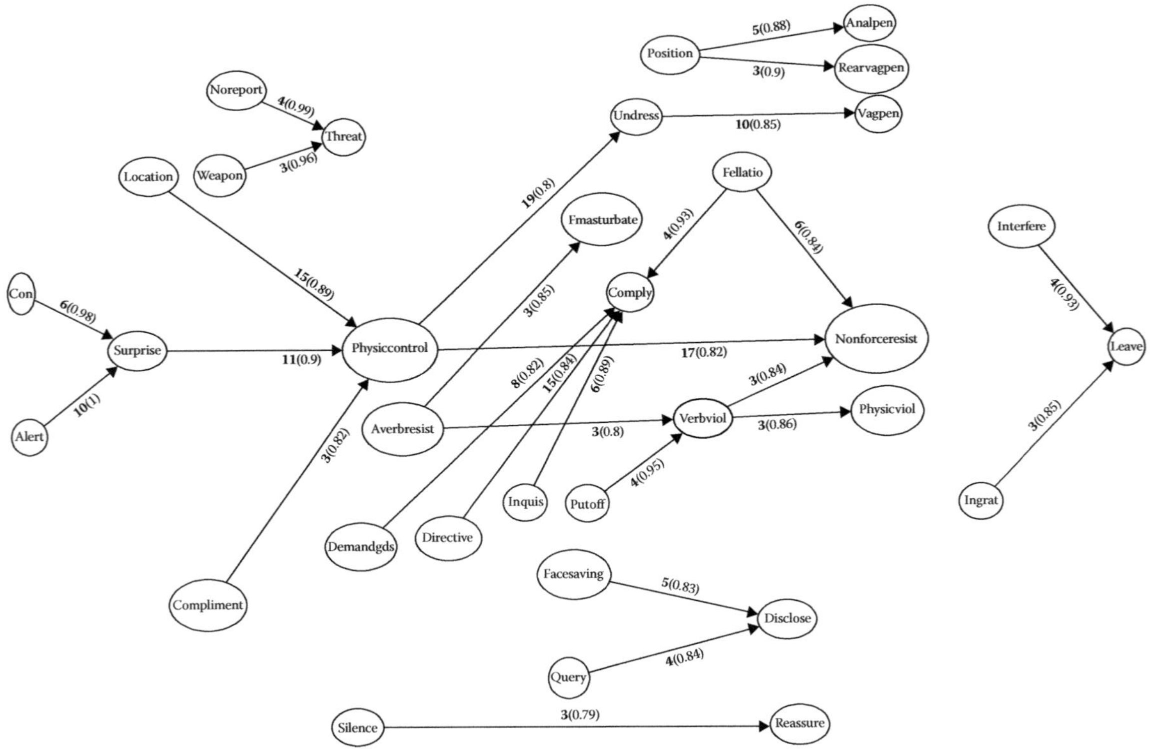

Figure 13.2 State transition diagram of sequential offender–victim interactions in indoor sexual assaults ($n = 63$) during the night. The diagram depicts behavioral contingencies that occurred more than twice in this subsample. It also shows only contingencies that occurred close in time, therefore with a *P*-coefficient >0.79. The diagram is read from left to right. For example, a *surprise approach* by the offender is typically followed by a further *physical control* attempt by the offender ($P = 0.90$). This occurred in 11 offenses in this sample. The length of the drawn arrows does not proportionally correspond with the value of the *P*-coefficient.

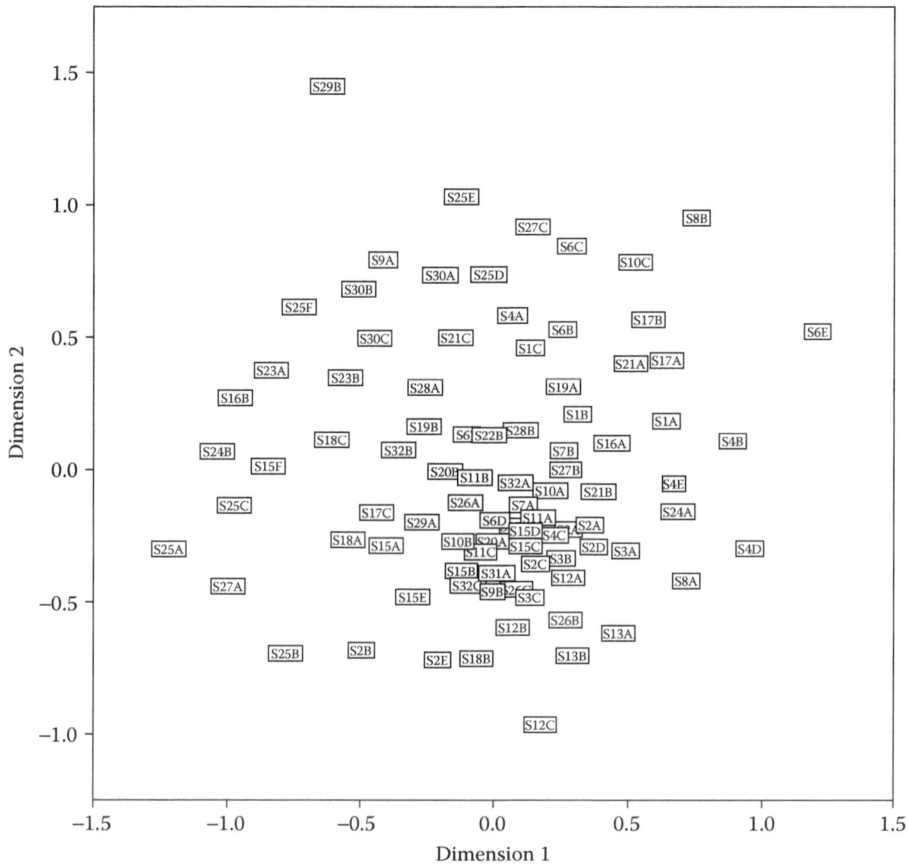

Figure 13.3 MDS plot of 90 serial sexual assaults from the United Kingdom based on their offender–victim interaction. Offenses with a similar offender–victim interaction appear closer in the two-dimensional space of the graph. Assaults with a strikingly dissimilar sequence are further away from each other. The numbers indicate the specific series; the capital letters denote the temporal sequence of the offenses within the series (e.g., *S25C* refers to the third detected offense of offender 25).

To test linkage effectiveness, this matrix was subjected to a multidimensional scaling (MDS) analysis using the PROXSCAL program in Statistical Package for the Social Sciences (SPSS) (v22). An MDS analysis is usually used to analyze the similarity or dissimilarity of a set of objects (Borg & Groenen, 2005). It models data as distances in Euclidean space, whereby the distance between two points reflects the similarity (correlation) of the variables. In this study, the resulting plot represented the 90 rape offenses in terms of their similarity according to their sequences of offender–victim interactions (see Figure 13.3). The closer two offenses are on the plot, the more similar they are in terms of their *if… then* signature.

Exploratory Results

In order to see whether the coded sequences would reveal effects known from the above cited victim resistance literature, the relevant average *P*-coefficients were inspected across all offenses. Table 13.2 shows the temporal relationship between victim resistance strategies and the respective physical reactions by the offenders. Forceful physical resistance by the victim was generally met with some form of physical violence by the offender and less immediately with physical control strategies. Active verbal resistance by the victim resulted less often in a physically violent reaction by the offender but rather in physical control. A compliant victim was more likely to be physically controlled by the offender than be reacted to with physical violence. These results provide some evidence for reciprocity in the actions of offenders and victims, which has been proposed within the more general literature about interpersonal transactions (Kiesler, 1983, cited in Alison & Stein, 2001). However, as can be seen from the state transition diagram (Figure 13.2*), the patterns of *if… then* contingencies were more complex than this.

In terms of crime linkage, the two-dimensional MDS plot (see Figure 13.3) shows several interesting properties. At first glance, *P*-coefficient-based *if… then* contingencies appear to offer some potential for linkage analysis. For example, in some instances, two offenses by the same offender can be found

Table 13.2 Example of Average Proximity Coefficients in $N = 90$ Serial Sexual Assaults

Victim	Offender: Physical Violence — Physical Violence	Offender: Physical Violence — Strangle	Offender: Physical Control
Physical Resistance Strategies			
Forceful resistance	0.82	0.85	0.75
Nonforceful resistance	0.78	0.48	0.80
Verbal Resistance Strategies			
Active verbal resistance	0.59	0.42	0.73
Face saving	0.46	0.24	0.52
Put-off	0.65	–	0.62
Passive verbal resistance	0.47	0.38	0.72
Compliance	0.29	0.26	0.70

Note: The table shows the temporal relationship between victim resistance strategies and the respective physical reactions by the offenders.

* For the sake of simplicity, Figure 13.2 only shows repeatedly occurring contingencies with a *P*-coefficient larger than 0.80. After all, every single behavior is connected to all the others, but only those that have strong and stable interconnections (i.e., that follow each other up faster than everything else) are shown here.

in close proximity of each other (e.g., S13A & S13B, S17A & S17B). However, the center of the plot is very crowded. Despite the occurrence of a few related offenses in close proximity of each other (e.g., S2A, S2C, S2D), the offenses in the center of the plot are apparently not that different from each other in terms of their *if… then* interactions. This suggests that there might be some difficulties in distinguishing between different serial offenders using these *if… then* contingencies.

There also appears to be some evidence for evolution in a series within the plot. Consider, for example, offender 25. His first (S25A) and third offense (S25C) are more similar to one another in behavior than his second offense (S25B). In addition, the remainder of his series appears to have evolved into a different interaction with little situational similarity shared between offenses (see S25D, S25E, S25F). Obviously, such a series would present quite a challenge to a practitioner trying to link the offenses together using this framework. However, it might still be possible to link a subset of his offenses.

Whether the patterns within the MDS plot were a result of any external common denominators was also explored (e.g., indoor vs. outdoor offenses). However, there were no clear groupings of cases that occurred only by day or only inside. This suggests that similar *if… then* contingencies by the same offender may share features of situational similarity that go beyond relatively objective offense characteristics, such as time and place.

Future studies need to take a closer look at the use of MDS plots, which have been derived on *P*-based *if… then* contingencies. The issues discussed above (e.g., the evolution of *if… then* contingencies across a crime series and the grouping of *if… then* contingencies based on external factors) need to be explored in more depth. In addition, future studies need to examine the degree to which this approach can be used to accurately link crimes, which is something that was not done in the current study.*

Potential Issues in Sequence Analysis

Although this exploratory analysis provides initial insights that can be taken forward in future developments in this area, it also results in new questions that need to be answered. First, the level of data coding that is required is

* The degree of similarity between any two offenses in such an MDS plot is expressed as a value per crime pair (the so-called transformed proximities). A logical way of establishing the level of linking accuracy that can be achieved with this analysis is to test whether offences from the same series share larger transformed proximities than crimes from different series. This can be explored using the ranked list approach. Alternatively, the same proximities could form the input data for a logistic regression analysis to assess how accurately linked and unlinked crime pairs can be differentiated. See Chapters 6 and 14 for more details of these various approaches.

very detailed and produces a large list of contingencies. This can affect the power of an analysis. For example, a large number of variables in an MDS analysis can distort the outcome of a two- or three-dimensional plot.* This tradeoff between ensuring appropriate statistical analyses and the desire to model offender–victim interactions as they happened will remain as long as all *if… then* contingencies are deemed equally useful and discriminative for the purpose of crime linkage. Second, and in relation to the previous point, a sequential perspective on crime linkage can only have an operational impact if the same type of information is recorded in police databases in equivalent detail. Future studies could investigate this issue by assessing the effectiveness of proximity coefficient-based linkage under conditions of decreasing information, much like Bennell, Gauthier, Gauthier, Melnyk, and Musolino (2010) did. Third, the microcoding of an offense sequence is time-consuming, which potentially makes the process more vulnerable to coding errors by analysts (Bennell, Snook, Macdonald, House, & Taylor, 2012). This also begs the question of whether such detailed coding is feasible in practice if it cannot be automated.

Aside from these important, practical challenges, other theoretical problems need to be resolved. It could be questioned whether situational similarity is sufficiently captured by simply comparing sequences of discrete behaviors. In reality, a struggle between two people is usually a messy and on-going process where behaviors can occur simultaneously. There is not only the resulting uncertainty regarding which behavior occurred first, but also how long a behavior lasts, which might reflect its intensity (another issue that might need to be captured). Consider, for example, a continuously sobbing victim. The sobbing would start at some point in the interaction but could go on unceasingly for some amount of time and therefore reflect a stronger *if* than a brief sob that occurs at some point during the offense. The same could be applied to a number of other behaviors exhibited by both victims and offenders (e.g., screaming and sexual penetration). The proximity coefficient method of sequence analysis (and other methods as well) creates a more abstract version of an event, where all behaviors have the same duration, or intensity. Obviously, this can be manipulated by coding the same variable successively for a set number of times, but this resembles a rather crude estimation of intensity. This issue could be tackled by inventing new codes, for example, "multiple blows with the fist/hand" instead of repeatedly coding "hit," "hit," "hit" when an offender beat the victim several times. But this would also increase the number of coding categories, which is potentially not desirable. Although such problems can be partially addressed from

* This would be reflected in relatively high stress scores (a statistic produced by an MDS analysis to indicate how well the plot represents the original associations that are being modeled).

a computational viewpoint by using variants of the proximity coefficient (Taylor & Donald, 2007), the main problem lies in the nature of the data: post hoc recollections by victims or bystanders of a dynamic event. If such an event is not captured on camera, there will be always a degree of uncertainty of what happened and when (Woodhams et al., 2008). Only empirical studies that elucidate the predictive accuracy of proximity coefficient-based linkage analysis can shed light on whether such uncertainty poses a significant threat to this potential approach to crime linkage.

A further question in need of research attention is whether purely focusing on the behavioral and verbal interaction between two actors, here the victim and the offender, can capture personal valence. This could be explored through interviews with offenders. By examining how serial offenders describe, and therefore evaluate events within an offense (e.g., see Chapter 4), researchers could develop a deeper understanding of what really matters for the offender throughout similar situations. If the sequential analyses of the serial offenders' perspective reveal higher situational similarity than victim-based analyses, new insights could emerge regarding the operationalizing of situational valence.

Conclusion

In terms of contemporary personality psychology, a CAPS-inspired *if ... then* perspective on serial violent crime deserves more concentrated research efforts. This chapter attempted to outline how such a perspective can assist our understanding of criminal events that are highly dynamic in nature. Although several practical and theoretical challenges remain to be solved, the explorative analyses in this chapter present a first step toward the incorporation of a sequential methodology for crime linkage purposes. Whether linkage accuracy will significantly improve by taking offense sequences into account in comparison with more traditional linkage methods remains to be tested. The methods outlined in this chapter provide one means of achieving this.

References

Alison, L. J., Bennell, C., Mokros, A., & Ormerod, D. (2002). The personality paradox in offender profiling: A theoretical review of the processes involved in deriving background characteristics from crime scene actions. *Psychology, Public Policy, and Law, 8*, 115–135.

Alison, L. J., & Stein, K. L. (2001). Vicious circles: Accounts of stranger sexual assault reflect abusive variants of conventional interactions. *The Journal of Forensic Psychiatry, 12*, 515–538.

Bachman, R., Saltzman, L., Thompson, M., & Carmody, D. (2002). Disentangling the effects of self-protective behaviours on the risk of injury in assaults against women. *Journal of Quantitative Criminology, 18,* 135–157.

Balemba, S., & Beauregard, E. (2012). Reactions to resistance: The role of contextual factors in sex offending. *Violence and Victims, 27,* 148–166.

Bart, P., & O'Brien, P. (1985). *Stopping rape: Successful survival strategies.* Elmsford, NY: Pergamon.

Beauregard, E., & Leclerc, B. (2007). An application of the rational choice approach to the offending process of sex offenders: A closer look at decision-making. *Sexual Abuse: A Journal of Research and Treatment, 19,* 115–133.

Beauregard, E., Lussier, P., & Proulx, J. (2007). Criminal propensity and criminal opportunity: An investigation of crime scene behaviours of sexual aggressors of women. In R. Kocsis (Ed.), *Criminal profiling: International theory, research, and practice* (pp. 89–112). Totowa, NJ: Humana Press.

Beauregard, E., Proulx, J., Rossmo, D., Leclerc, B., & Allaire, J. F. (2007). Script analysis of the hunting process of serial sex offenders. *Criminal Justice and Behavior, 34,* 1069–1084.

Beauregard, E., Rossmo, D., & Proulx, J. (2007). A descriptive model of the hunting process of serial sex offenders: A rational choice perspective. *Journal of Family Violence, 22,* 449–463.

Bennell, C., & Canter, D. (2002). Linking commercial burglaries by *modus operandi*: Tests using regression and ROC analysis. *Science & Justice, 42,* 153–164.

Bennell, C., Gauthier, D., Gauthier, D., Melnyk, T., & Musolino, E. (2010). The impact of data degradation *and* sample size on the performance of two similarity coefficients used in behavioural linkage analysis. *Forensic Science International, 199,* 85–92.

Bennell, C., & Jones, N. J. (2005). Between a ROC and a hard place: A method for linking serial burglaries by modus operandi. *Journal of Investigative Psychology and Offender Profiling, 2,* 23–41.

Bennell, C., Jones, N. J., & Melnyk, T. (2009). Addressing problems with traditional crime linking methods using receiver operating characteristic analysis. *Legal and Criminological Psychology, 14,* 293–310.

Bennell, C., Mugford, R., Ellingwood, H., & Woodhams, J. (2014). Linking crimes using behavioural clues: Current levels of linking accuracy and strategies for moving forward. *Journal of Investigative Psychology and Offender Profiling, 11,* 29–56. doi:10.1002/jip.1395.

Bennell, C., Snook, B., Macdonald, S., House, J. C., & Taylor, P. J. (2012). Computerized crime linkage systems: A critical review and research agenda. *Criminal Justice and Behavior, 39,* 620–634.

Bennell, C., & Woodhams, J. (2012). Behavioural linking of crimes. *Journal of Investigative Psychology and Offender Profiling, 9,* 199, 200.

Beune, K., Giebels, E., & Taylor, P. J. (2010). Interaction patterns in police interviews: The role of cultural dependency. *Criminal Justice and Behavior, 37,* 904–925.

Bevel, T., & Gardner, R. M. (2002). *Bloodstain pattern analysis* (2nd ed.). Boca Raton, FL: CRC Press.

Bootsma, L., & Eshof, P. van den (2006). *The use of behavioural themes in identifying serial rapists.* Paper presented at the 16th Annual Conference of the European Association of Psychology and Law, Liverpool, England.

Borg I., & Groenen, P. J. F. (2005). *Modern multidimensional scaling* (2nd ed.). Heidelberg, Germany: Springer.

Brecklin, L. R., & Ullman, S. E. (2010). The roles of victim and offender substance use in sexual assault outcomes. *Journal of Interpersonal Violence, 25,* 1503–1522.
Burgheim, J., & Friese, H. (2008). Täter-Opfer-Interaktionen bei Sexualdelikten [Offender-victim interaction in sexual offences]. *Kriminalistik, 62,* 486–492.
Burrell, A., Bull, R., & Bond, J. (2012). Linking personal robbery offences using offender behaviour. *Journal of Investigative Psychology and Offender Profiling, 9,* 201–222.
Canter, D. V. (1994). *Criminal shadows—Inside the mind of the serial killer.* London, England: HarperCollins.
Canter, D. V., Bennell, C., Alison, L. J., & Reddy, S. (2003). Differentiating sex offences: A behaviourally based thematic classification of stranger rapes. *Behavioral Sciences & the Law, 21,* 157–174.
Canter, D., Heritage, R., Davies, A., Holden, R., Kirby, S., Hancock, C., … McGinley, J. (1990). *Developments in offender profiling: Final report to the Home Office.* Guilford, England: University of Surrey, Department of Psychology.
Cervone, D., & Shoda, Y. (Eds.). (1999). *The coherence of personality: Social-cognitive bases of consistency, variability and organization.* New York, NY: Guilford Press.
Clarke, D. D., Forsyth, R., & Wright, R. (1999). Junction road accidents during cross-flow turns: A sequence analysis of police case files. *Accident Analysis & Prevention, 31,* 31–43.
Clay-Warner, J. (2002). Avoiding rape: The effects of protective actions and situational factors on rape outcome. *Violence and Victims, 17,* 691–705.
Clay-Warner, J. (2003). The context of sexual violence: Situational predictors of self-protective actions. *Violence and Victims, 18,* 543–556.
Cornish, D. B., & Clarke, R. V. (2008). The rational choice perspective. In R. Wortley & L. Mazerolle (Eds.), *Environmental criminology and crime analysis* (pp. 21–47). New York, NY: Routledge.
Dale, A., Davies, A., & Wei, L. (1997). Developing a typology of rapists' speech. *Journal of Pragmatics, 27,* 653–669.
Davies, A. (1992). Rapists' behaviour: A three aspect model as a basis for analysis and identification of serial crime. *Forensic Science International, 55,* 173–194.
Davies, K., Tonkin, M., Bull, R., & Bond, J. W. (2012). The course of case linkage never did run smooth: A new investigation to tackle the behavioural changes in serial car theft. *Journal of Investigative Psychology and Offender Profiling, 9,* 274–295.
Dern, H., Dern, C., Horn, A., & Horn, U. (2009). The fire behind the smoke: A reply to Snook and colleagues. *Criminal Justice and Behavior, 36,* 1085–1090.
Deslauriers-Varin, N., & Beauregard, E. (2010). Victims' routine activities and sex offenders' target selection scripts: A latent class analysis. *Sexual Abuse: A Journal of Research and Treatment, 22,* 315–342.
Donnellan, M. B., Lucas, R. E., & Fleeson, W. (2009). Introduction to personality and assessment at age 40: Reflections on the legacy of the person-situation debate and the future of person-situation integration. *Journal of Research in Personality, 43,* 117–119.
Ellingwood, H., Mugford, R., Bennell, C., Melnyk, T., & Fritzon, K. (2013). Examining the role of similarity coefficients and the value of behavioural themes in attempts to link serial arson offences. *Journal of Investigative Psychology and Offender Profiling, 10,* 1–27.

Fleeson, W., & Noftle, E. E. (2009). In favor of the synthetic resolution to the person—Situation debate. *Journal of Research in Personality, 43,* 150–154.

Fossi, J. J., Clarke, D. D., & Lawrence, C. (2005). Bedroom rape: Sequences of sexual behaviour in stranger assaults. *Journal of Interpersonal Violence, 20,* 1444–1466.

Galliano, G., Noble, L., Puechl, C., & Travis, L. (1993). Victim reactions during rape/sexual assault: A preliminary study of the immobility response and its correlates. *Journal of Interpersonal Violence, 8,* 109–118.

Giebels, E., & Taylor, P. J. (2009). Interaction patterns in crisis negotiations: Persuasive arguments and cultural differences. *Journal of Applied Psychology, 94,* 5–19.

Goodwill, A. M., & Alison, L. J. (2006). The development of a filter model for prioritizing suspects in burglary offences. *Psychology, Crime & Law, 12,* 395–416.

Goodwill, A. M., & Alison, L. J. (2007). When is profiling possible? Offense planning and aggression as moderators in predicting offender age from victim age in stranger rape. *Behavioral Sciences & the Law, 25,* 823–840.

Grubin, D., Kelly, P., & Ayis, S. (1997). *Linking serious sexual assaults.* London, England: Home Office.

Grubin, D., Kelly, P., & Brunsdon, C. (2001). *Linking serious sexual assaults through behaviour.* London, England: Home Office.

Guerette, R., & Santana, S. (2010). Explaining victim self-protective behaviour effects on crime incident outcomes: A test of opportunity theory. *Crime & Delinquency, 56,* 198–226.

Häkkänen, H., Lindlöf, P., & Santtila, P. (2004). Crime scene actions and offender characteristics in a sample of Finnish stranger rapes. *Journal of Investigative Psychology and Offender Profiling, 1,* 17–32.

Hanson, R. K., & Morton-Bourgon, K. E. (2005). The characteristics of persistent sexual offenders: A meta-analysis of recidivism studies. *Journal of Consulting and Clinical Psychology, 73,* 1154–1163.

Harbers, E., Deslauriers-Varin, N., Beauregard, E., & Kemp, J. J. van der. (2012). Testing the behavioural and environmental consistency of serial sex offenders: A signature approach. *Journal of Investigative Psychology and Offender Profiling, 9,* 259–273.

Knight, R. A., & Guay, J. P. (2006). The role of psychopathy in sexual coercion. In C. J. Patrick (Ed.), *Handbook of psychopathy* (pp. 512–532). New York, NY: The Guilford Press.

Lawrence, C., Fossi, J. J., & Clarke, D. D. (2010). A sequential examination of offenders' verbal strategies during stranger rapes: The influence of location. *Psychology, Crime & Law, 16,* 381–400.

Lundrigan, S., Czarnomski, S., & Wilson, M. (2010). Spatial and environmental consistency in serial sexual assault. *Journal of Investigative Psychology and Offender Profiling, 7,* 15–30.

Marchbanks, P., Lui, K. J., & Mercy, J. (1990). Risk of injury from resisting rape. *American Journal of Epidemiology, 132,* 540–549.

Markson, L., Woodhams, J., & Bond, J. W. (2010). Linking serial residential burglary: Comparing the utility of modus operandi behaviours, geographical proximity, and temporal proximity. *Journal of Investigative Psychology and Offender Profiling, 7,* 91–107.

Menacere, T., & Taylor P. J. (2010). *ProxCalc 2010: Proximity coefficient calculator software 1.1.* Lancaster, England: Lancaster University.

Mischel, W. (2009). From personality and assessment (1968) to personality science, 2009. *Journal of Research in Personality, 43,* 282–290.
Mischel, W., & Shoda, Y. (1995). A cognitive-affective system theory of personality: Reconceptualizing situations, dispositions, dynamics, and invariance in personality structure. *Psychological Review, 102,* 246–268.
Mischel, W., & Shoda, Y. (2008). Toward a unified theory of personality. In O. P. John, R. W. Robins, & L. A. Pervin (Eds.), *Handbook of personality: Theory and research* (pp. 208–241). New York, NY: The Guilford Press.
Park, J., Schlesinger, L. B., Pinizzotto, A. J., & Davis, E. F. (2008). Serial and single-victim rapists: Differences in crime-scene violence, interpersonal involvement, and criminal sophistication. *Behavioral Sciences & the Law, 26,* 227–237.
Polaschek, D., & Hudson, S. (2004). Pathways to rape: Preliminary examination of patterns in the offence processes of rapists and their rehabilitation implications. *Journal of Sexual Aggression, 10,* 7–20.
Polaschek, D., Hudson, S., Ward, T., & Siegert, R. (2001). Rapists' offence processes. A preliminary descriptive model. *Journal of Interpersonal Violence, 16*(6), 523–544.
Prentky, R., Burgess, A., & Carter, D. (1986). Victim response by rapist type—An empirical and clinical analysis. *Journal of Interpersonal Violence, 1,* 73–98.
Quinsey, V., & Upfold, D. (1985). Rape completion and victim injury as a function of female resistance strategy. *Canadian Journal of Behavioral Science, 17,* 40–50.
Roe, R. A. (2008). Time in applied psychology: The study of "what happens" rather than "what is." *European Psychologist, 13,* 37–52.
Salo, B., Sirén, J., Corander, J., Zappalà, A. Bosco, D., Mokros, A., & Santtila, P. (2012). Using Bayes' theorem in behavioural crime linking of serial homicide. *Legal and Criminological Psychology, 18,* 356–370.
Santtila, P., Junkkila, J., & Sandnabba, N. (2005). Behavioural linking of stranger rapes. *Journal of Investigative Psychology and Offender Profiling, 2,* 87–103.
Santtila, P., Pakkanen, T., Zappala, A., Bosco, D., Valkama, M., & Mokros, A. (2008). Behavioural crime linking in serial homicide. *Psychology, Crime & Law, 14,* 245–265.
Scott, D., Lambie, I., Henwood, D., & Lamb, R. (2006). Profiling stranger rapists: Linking offence behaviour to previous criminal histories using a regression model. *Journal of Sexual Aggression, 12,* 265–275.
Shoda, Y., & Mischel, W. (1998). Personality as a stable cognitive-affective activation network: Characteristic patterns of behaviour variation emerge from a stable personality structure. In S. J. Read & L. C. Miller (Eds.), *Connectionist models of social reasoning and social behaviour* (pp. 175–208). Mahwah, NJ: Erlbaum.
Shrout, P. E. (1998). Measurement in reliability and agreement in psychiatry. *Statistical Methods in Medical Research, 7,* 301–317.
Sjöstedt, G., Långström, N., Sturidsson, K., & Grann, M. (2004). Stability of modus operandi in sexual offending. *Criminal Justice and Behavior, 31,* 609–623.
Sorochinski, M., & Salfati, C. G. (2010). The consistency of inconsistency in serial homicide: Patterns of behavioural change across series. *Journal of Investigative Psychology and Offender Profiling, 7,* 109–136.
Strauss, A., & Corbin, J. (1990). *Basics of qualitative research: Grounded theory procedures and techniques.* Newbury Park, CA: Sage.
Tark, J., & Kleck, G. (2004). Resisting crime: The effects of victim action on the outcomes of crimes. *Criminology, 42,* 861–910.

Taylor, P. J. (2006). Proximity coefficients as a measure of interrelationships in sequences of behaviour. *Behavioural Research Methods, 38,* 42–50.
Taylor, P. J. (2007). *ProxCalc—A (very brief) user's guide.* Lancaster, England: Lancaster University.
Taylor, P. J., & Donald, I. J. (2007). Testing the relationship between local cue-response patterns and global dimensions of communication behaviour. *British Journal of Social Psychology, 46,* 273–298.
Taylor, P. J., Jacques, K., Giebels, E., Levine, M., Best, R., Winter, J., & Rossi, G. (2008). Analyzing forensic processes: Taking time into account. *Issues in Forensic Psychology, 8,* 45–57.
Tonkin, M., Grant, T. D., & Bond, J. W. (2008). To link or not to link: A test of the case linkage principles using serial car theft data. *Journal of Investigative Psychology and Offender Profiling, 5,* 59–77.
Tonkin, M., Santtila, P., & Bull, R. (2011). The linking of burglary crimes using offender behaviour: Testing research cross-nationally and in more realistic settings. *Legal and Criminological Psychology, 17,* 276–293. doi:10.1111/j.2044-8333.2010.02007.x.
Tonkin, M., Woodhams, J., Bull, R., & Bond, J. W. (2012). A comparison of logistic regression and classification tree analysis for behavioural case linkage. *Journal of Investigative Psychology and Offender Profiling, 9*(3), 235–258.
Tonkin, M., Woodhams, J., Bull, R., Bond, J. W., & Palmer, E. J. (2011). Linking different types of crime using geographical and temporal proximity. *Criminal Justice and Behavior, 38,* 1069–1088.
Tyner, E. A., & Fremouw, W. J. (2008). The relation of methamphetamine use and violence: A critical review. *Aggression and Violent Behavior, 13,* 285–297.
Ullman, S. E. (1997). Review and critique of empirical studies of rape avoidance. *Criminal Justice and Behavior, 24*(2), 177–204. doi:10.1177/009385489702400 2003.
Ullman, S. E. (1998). Does offender violence escalate when rape victims fight back? *Journal of Interpersonal Violence, 13,* 179–192.
Ullman, S. E. (1999). A comparison of gang and individual rape incidents. *Violence and Victims, 14,* 123–133.
Ullman, S. E. (2007). A 10 year-update of "review and critique of empirical studies of rape avoidance." *Criminal Justice and Behavior, 34,* 411–429.
Ullman, S. E., & Knight, R. A. (1991). A multivariate model for predicting rape and physical injury outcomes during sexual assaults. *Journal of Consulting and Clinical Psychology, 59,* 724–731.
Ullman, S. E., & Knight, R. A. (1992). Fighting back—Women's resistance to rape. *Journal of Interpersonal Violence, 7,* 31–43.
Ullman, S. E., & Knight, R. A. (1993). The efficacy of women's resistance strategies in rape situations. *Psychology of Women Quarterly, 17,* 23–38.
Ullman, S. E., & Knight, R. A. (1995). Women's resistance strategies to different rapist types. *Criminal Justice and Behavior, 22,* 263–283.
Ullman, S. E., & Siegel, J. (1993). Victim-offender relationship and sexual assault. *Violence and Victims, 8,* 121–134.
Winter, J., Lemeire, J., Meganck, S., Geboers, J., Rossi, G., & Mokros, A. (2013). Comparing the predictive accuracy of case linkage methods in serious sexual assaults. *Journal of Investigative Psychology and Offender Profiling, 56,* 28–56.

Winter, J., Rossi, G., Serruys, O., & Ivaldi, J. (2011, March 3). *Does the offender-victim interaction matter? Examining local cue-response contingencies in stranger rapes.* Paper presented at the Fourth International Congress on Psychology and Law, Miami, FL.

Winter, J., & Taylor, P. J. (2006, July 13). *The importance of the offender-victim interaction in rape.* Paper presented at the Second Summer Conference of Research in Forensic Psychology, Regensburg, Germany.

Woodhams, J., Grant, T., & Price, A. (2007). From marine ecology to crime analysis: Improving the detection of serial sexual offences using a taxonomic similarity measure. *Journal of Investigative Psychology and Offender Profiling, 4,* 17–27.

Woodhams, J., Hollin, C. R., & Bull, R. (2007). The psychology of linking crimes: A review of the evidence. *Legal and Criminological Psychology, 12,* 233–249.

Woodhams, J., Hollin, C. R., & Bull, R. (2008). Incorporating context in linking crimes: An exploratory study of situational similarity and if-then contingencies. *Journal of Investigative Psychology and Offender Profiling, 5,* 1–23.

Woodhams, J., Hollin, C. R., Bull, R., & Cooke, C. (2012). Behaviour displayed by female victims during rapes committed by lone and multiple perpetrators. *Psychology, Public Policy, and Law, 18,* 415–452.

Woodhams, J., & Labuschagne, G. (2012). A test of case linkage principles with solved and unsolved serial rapes. *Journal of Police and Criminal Psychology, 27,* 85–98.

Woodhams, J., & Toye, K. (2007). An empirical test of the assumptions of case linkage and offender profiling with serial commercial robberies. *Psychology, Public Policy, and Law, 13,* 59–85.

Wortley, R., & Mazerolle, L. (Eds.). (2008). *Environmental criminology and crime analysis.* Cullompton, England: Willan Publishing.

Informing Practice
Research Methods in Crime Linkage Analysis

14

CRAIG BENNELL,
ALASDAIR M. GOODWILL, AND
ANNIE CHINNECK

Contents

Introduction	338
Modus Operandi Behaviors, Psychological Themes, and Functional Domains	339
Methods for Examining MO Behaviors	340
MO-Based Clustering Procedures	341
Similarity Coefficients	342
General Algorithmic Approaches	343
Bayesian Modeling	345
Methods for Examining Functional Domains	346
Logistic Regression Analysis	347
Classification Trees	348
Methods for Examining Psychological Themes	350
Multidimensional Scaling	350
Principal Component Analysis	352
Cluster Analysis	352
Issues to Consider	353
Data Reliability	353
Ecological Validity	354
Cross-Validation	355
Decision Thresholds	357
Using ROC Analysis to Produce Valid Measures of Linking Accuracy	358
Pragmatism	361
Complexity versus Parsimony	361
Accuracy versus Precision	361

Nomothetic versus Idiographic 362
Automated versus Practitioner Oriented 363
Conclusion 364
References 365

Introduction

As made clear in previous chapters, the goal when carrying out crime linkage analysis is to identify patterns of offending behavior that meet two criteria: behavioral *similarity* and behavioral *distinctiveness*. Behavioral similarity exists when offenders behave in the same or similar way across crimes they have committed. Behavioral distinctiveness exists when the behaviors exhibited by different serial offenders differ from one another. When offenders behave in a relatively similar and distinct fashion, it should be possible to link offenders to the crimes they have committed and to differentiate between crimes committed by different offenders with some degree of accuracy. To accomplish this, a threshold must usually be set to determine when crimes are similar enough to warrant a linkage decision being made.

Much of the research conducted on crime linkage analysis to date has tested these principles or assumptions (see Chapter 6). Indeed, over the last decade, the number of publications examining these issues has increased significantly (Bennell, Mugford, Ellingwood, & Woodhams, 2014). Despite these advances, however, there are still many unanswered questions, including a pretty fundamental one: What method(s) should we use to study these assumptions? The purpose of this chapter is to review the various methods that researchers have adopted. We first provide a framework within which to discuss this issue, we then describe the main methods that have been used by researchers to date, and, finally, we present a variety of issues that researchers may wish to consider when setting out to study issues related to crime linkage analysis.

Some of the issues we discuss may lead researchers to choose certain methods of analysis over other methods. However, throughout this chapter we have purposefully resisted the temptation to provide a list of pros and cons that might end up becoming associated with the methods we describe. We are of the view that each method may have value for exploring specific issues of relevance to crime linkage analysis, and thus, the choice of what method to use often depends on the task at hand. In practical terms as well, a particular method may be useful for accomplishing one type of linking task, but not another type of linking task (see Chapter 8 for a discussion of various linking tasks). Therefore, it is difficult to present broad statements about the overall utility (or not) of the methods we discuss; their value is likely to be largely context (e.g., task) dependent.

Two other issues are important to clarify at the outset of this chapter. First, when reviewing the methods that have been used by researchers we have not attempted to describe every available study in the crime linkage field. To do so would exceed the space available for this chapter. Instead, our goal was to describe a selection of studies that represent the range of methods that have been used to study crime linkage assumptions to date.* Second, we decided to focus our discussion in a relatively narrow fashion by only reviewing studies that have explicitly examined the potential feasibility of conducting crime linkage analysis. Studies that examined a specific crime linkage assumption (e.g., behavioral similarity, or consistency; Bateman & Salfati, 2007), but have not gone so far as to address the potential feasibility of crime linkage per se (e.g., by examining both behavioral similarity and distinctiveness), are not reviewed in this chapter (see Chapter 6 for discussion of these studies). This is not to suggest that these studies do not contribute to our understanding of crime linkage analysis; they obviously do.

Modus Operandi Behaviors, Psychological Themes, and Functional Domains

Given the wide range of methods that have been used by researchers to study issues related to crime linkage analysis, it may be useful to provide a framework for categorizing the various methods. Adopting a similar approach to Tonkin (Chapter 6), we examine methods that focus on three different levels of analysis—using (1) *modus operandi* (MO) behaviors, (2) psychological themes, or (3) functional domains. The level of analysis that the researcher decides to adopt has implications for the sorts of methods that can be used to study the problem (i.e., some methods are more compatible with certain levels of analysis). Given this, we use this framework to structure our discussion of the methods we review. But first, we will briefly describe the framework.

Historically, crime linkage analysis has been examined at the level of MO behaviors. In Gross's (1906) classic book, *Criminal Investigation*, he highlighted the potential value in using MO to link serial crimes, and linkage systems developed by the police around this time were designed to categorize and compare MO behaviors exhibited at different crime scenes (Fosdick, 1915). The developers of these systems assumed that MO was highly stable. Although thinking around this issue eventually gave way to the view that MO may change over

* There is an important distinction between research that examines the principles of crime linkage analysis and research that examines crime linkage analysis in practice. In this chapter, we are primarily discussing the former issue, not the latter. Thus, the results of the studies we discuss in this chapter do not necessarily provide an indication of crime linkage accuracy per se because the studies do not necessarily reflect how crime linkage analysis is conducted in practice. Instead, the results from the studies we review provide an indication of the validity of crime linkage assumptions and perhaps the *potential* for crime linkage analysis under certain conditions (e.g., where linking tasks bear resemblance to the tasks examined within these studies).

time due to learning, maturation, and situational factors (Douglas & Munn, 1992), studies are still often conducted at this level of analysis. As described below, many of these studies suggest that certain aspects of an offender's MO may in fact be useful for linking the crimes they have committed; the trick is in determining which aspects of an offender's MO are useful for this purpose.

Because MO can change over time and across situations, linking researchers have examined whether linkage decisions can be made more accurately by relying on *psychological themes.* Some sort of clustering procedure (e.g., multidimensional scaling [MDS]) is usually used to identify behaviors that group together, in statistical terms, and the researcher then attempts to determine if the clustered behaviors reflect some higher-order (e.g., latent) theme. For example, a subset of rape behaviors may be found to co-occur within crimes at a high rate and be characterized by an overarching theme of overt hostility toward the victim (Santtila, Junkkila, & Sandnabba, 2005). As discussed in Chapter 6, the perceived value of relying on psychological themes for linking purposes is that themes may be more impervious to behavioral variation due to learning, maturation, and/or situational factors. For example, an offender may exhibit disparate MO behaviors across two separate crimes due to situational factors, yet if the behaviors exhibited are equally hostile (i.e., represent a theme of hostility), across-crime similarities may still be observed at the thematic level (Bateman & Salfati, 2007). A growing number of studies are examining whether behavioral similarity and distinctiveness exist at this thematic level of analysis.

Finally, there is an approach for studying crime linkage issues that arguably falls somewhere between these two extremes—the *functional domain* approach. Using this approach, MO behaviors are examined, but they are grouped into functional domains. Unlike the thematic approach, these domains are not determined statistically using clustering procedures, nor are the domains determined by reference to psychologically meaningful themes. Instead, behaviors are grouped based solely on their function. In the case of serial burglary, for example, domains may be constructed to represent characteristics of the targeted dwellings, methods of gaining entry to the property, and items that are stolen (Bennell & Canter, 2002). Also, unlike the thematic approach, the rationale behind this approach is purely pragmatic; the use of functional domains is simply a convenient way to determine whether certain subsets of behavior are exhibited in a more stable and distinct fashion compared to others (Goodwill & Alison, 2006). Increasingly, studies have used this approach to examine the utility of using certain groups of MO behaviors over others for crime linkage purposes.

Methods for Examining MO Behaviors

A variety of methods have been used to examine whether MO behaviors can be used to accurately identify linked crimes. These methods include the use of clustering procedures, similarity coefficients, general algorithmic approaches, and Bayesian modeling. Each of these methods will now be briefly discussed.

MO-Based Clustering Procedures

Although clustering procedures can be used to identify psychological themes (see below), they have also been used to determine whether crime linkage could be possible using MO behaviors. When these procedures are used for this purpose, the input for the analysis is usually comprised of dichotomous data indicating the behaviors that were present (or absent) in a predetermined sample of solved crimes. Although the algorithms for doing so vary depending on the specific procedure used, clustering procedures portray the level of behavioral similarity between crimes in visual form. For example, with some clustering procedures (e.g., MDS) a plot is produced, which consists of crimes represented as points in space, with the distance between the crimes being inversely related to their behavioral similarity (i.e., the closer together two crimes are on the visual plot the more similar the crimes are with respect to the behavioral data). The proximities between crimes on the plot are then used to determine whether crimes are likely to have been committed by the same offender, with offense clusters signaling that the crimes may form a crime series.

One of the first empirical studies to examine crime linkage assumptions relied on this method. Green, Booth, and Biderman (1976) set out to demonstrate how statistical analysis could objectify the bases of linkage decisions. In a number of different analyses, they demonstrated how cluster analysis could be used to visualize the behavioral similarities (and differences) between crimes and potentially identify different crime series. In one analysis, Green et al. examined behavioral data related to 15 solved burglaries, which were committed by three different offenders. They calculated across-crime similarity scores for each offence pair (similarity was defined by the number of identical features exhibited across the crimes) and submitted these similarity scores to their clustering procedure. The three distinct clusters derived from the computer analysis were relatively accurate. Indeed, the correspondence between the actual crime series and the computer-derived clusters was 93%.

Some years later, a similar method was examined by Canter et al. (1991; see Chapter 11 for more details of this study). They presented police officers with victim statements from a set of 12 solved rapes, which had been committed by four different offenders (three crimes each). The victim statements had been edited so that they only included behavioral information. Based on the victim statements, the officers were asked to link the three offenses committed by each of the four rapists and indicate which behavioral clues they felt were important for the linking task. The officers were then reorganized into groups who had to make final linkage decisions. Some groups received feedback to assist with the task, whereas other groups did not. Feedback came in the form of a Multidimensional Scalogram Analysis (MSA). Like other clustering procedures, MSA takes as input dichotomous behavioral data related to each of the crimes in question (in this case, the behavioral information the officers indicated was important when making their linking decisions). MSA provides visual output in the form of a plot in which crimes are positioned based on their level of similarity; those crimes that are more similar appear closer together on the plot. Using this information to make crime linkage decisions, the groups receiving feedback were able to achieve a significantly higher level of linking accuracy compared to the groups that received no feedback.

Similarity Coefficients

A number of other studies have, in a very direct way, based their examination of crime linkage assumptions on MO behaviors. Rather than using a statistical method to represent across-crime similarity scores in some sort of visual form, these studies have worked with the similarity coefficients themselves to examine how much behavioral similarity and distinctiveness is present in a sample of crimes (and thus, the degree of linking that can be accomplished in theory).

Perhaps the earliest, and clearest, example of this method is a study conducted by Canter et al. in the United Kingdom (1991; described in Bennell, 2013). Canter et al. calculated Jaccard (*J*) coefficients* for pairs of crimes that were committed either by the same offender or by different offenders. The calculations were based on dichotomous data indicating the presence or absence of behaviors across 12 crimes (four different crime series consisting of three crimes each). Behavioral similarity in this case was reflected by large coefficients being associated with crimes committed by the same offender, and behavioral distinctiveness was reflected by small coefficients being associated with crimes committed by different offenders. The degree to

* Jaccard's coefficient (Jaccard, 1908) is commonly used in crime linkage research to summarize the degree of behavioral similarity that exists across two crimes, with values ranging from 0 (no similarity) to 1 (complete similarity). Similarity in this case can be captured in a two by two table, where cell *a* indicates the frequency of joint behavioral occurrences (1,1), cells *b* and *c* indicate the frequency of behaviors occurring in one crime but not the other (1,0 and 0,1), and cell *d* indicates the frequency of joint nonoccurrences (0,0). Jaccard's coefficient is calculated using the formula, $a/(a + b + c)$, and thus, it does not incorporate joint nonoccurrences of behaviors into its calculation of similarity (i.e., across-crime similarity does not increase or decrease as a function of joint nonoccurrences). Researchers have argued that this omission is beneficial because the absence of a crime scene behavior in a dataset does not necessarily mean that the behavior was not exhibited at the crime (e.g., victims may forget what an offender did, they may be too embarrassed or traumatized to talk about the behavior, or the police may fail to record the behavior when it is talked about; Alison, Snook, & Stein, 2001).

which it was possible to differentiate between crimes committed by different offenders was examined by selecting a specific threshold of similarity, which was used to decide when a crime pair was similar enough to warrant being linked. When Canter and his colleagues applied a threshold of $J \geq 0.30$ to their data, they were able to correctly classify 7 out of the 12 (58.3%) crime pairs that were committed by the same offender and 49 out of the 54 (90.7%) crime pairs that were committed by different offenders. This represents an overall level of linking accuracy of 84.8%.

Adopting a more sophisticated approach, Goodwill and Alison (2006) sampled five convicted offenses from each of 43 residential burglars in the United Kingdom to develop a filter model for prioritizing the type of information that should be considered in crime linkage analysis. More specifically, the model used four filters based on geospatial, temporal, MO, and target information. Given the different sources of information, different metrics were used to quantify across-crime similarity, but Jaccard coefficients were used for both behavioral and target information. The results demonstrated that the most discriminatory features related to geospatial and temporal information and the least discriminatory features related to MO and target characteristics. The authors posited that these differences were not due to differences in methodology (e.g., different similarity metrics being used), but resulted from the fact that MO and target characteristics are more strongly influenced by contextual factors. Using various combinations of filters, Goodwill and Alison were able to make reasonably accurate linkage decisions within the context of their study, though they observed a trade-off between accuracy and precision. On the one hand, when using all filters together (e.g., geospatial, temporal, MO, and target information), relatively few linkages could be made, but all were made accurately. On the other hand, the use of a smaller number of relatively robust filters (e.g., geospatial and temporal information) resulted in a higher number of errors, but many more correct linkages.

General Algorithmic Approaches

At the same time that these previous studies were being conducted, various computer-based methods for identifying linked series were also being developed. These methods rely on different algorithmic approaches.

Over the past 10 years, much of this research has been undertaken by researchers at the Japanese National Research Institute of Police Science. In one early paper, Yokota and Watanabe (2002) described the development and evaluation of an MO-based suspect retrieval system. Their database consisted of MO information for 107,233 burglaries from Japan, which had been committed by 12,468 burglars between 1993 and 1998. For offenders that had committed more than one crime, their offenses were ordered chronologically in the database. To test the system for crime linkage purposes, the most recent offense for each of these serial offenders was removed from the database and treated as a target offense. This resulted in 7558 target offenses committed by 7558 offenders. Each of these 7558 offenders existed among the 12,468 burglars residing within the database because all the target offenses were extracted from serial burglars in the database. Based on the set of MO behaviors captured in the database, the retrieval system calculated a similarity score between each offense and the target offenses using a random choice probability method.* These similarity scores were then used to assign ranks to each offense (offender) in the database, which ranged from 1 (the highest degree of MO similarity with the target offense) to 12,468 (the lowest degree of MO similarity with the target offense). Given that higher ranked offenders were considered more likely to have committed the target offense, the system could be evaluated, for each of the 7558 trials, by considering the rank assigned to the actual offender responsible for the target offense. When this evaluation was conducted, the researchers deemed the system a success. They found that 1524 offenders of the actual offenders were assigned a rank of 1, reflecting that they were the top suspect. This represents an overall hit rate of 20.2%. The median rank score for offenders who were actually responsible for the target offenses was 29, out of a possible 12,468. (See Yokota, Fujita, Watanabe, Yoshimoto, & Wachi, 2007, for a more recent reevaluation of the system using sexual assaults.)

Ewart, Oatley, and Burn (2005) carried out a similar analysis. They compared the crime-matching ability of Yokota and Watanabe's (2002) random choice probability algorithm (RCPA), which was based solely on MO behaviors, with two other crime linking algorithms. The second algorithm, referred to as RPAL, ranked suspects based on spatial–temporal similarity between target offenses and other offenses. This algorithm was based on recency (the time between a previous crime and a target crime), prolificness (the number of previous crimes committed by an offender before he committed the target crime), and actual location (RPAL; the distance between a previous crime and a target crime). The third algorithm, referred to as COMBIN, essentially combined the RCPA and RPAL models.† Each of these algorithms was tested using a database of 966 domestic burglaries committed by 306 British offenders. Unlike the study by Yokota and Watanabe (2002), this sample represented crimes committed at a fairly local (vs. national) level, which better reflects how crime linkage analysis is actually done. One by one, each of the crimes was identified as the target crime and the database was searched for good matches. Crimes (offenders) were given a rank based on across-crime similarity, with closer matches given lower ranks. The RCPA model generated ranks with a range from 1 to 336. This algorithm generated a perfect match (a rank of 1) for 3% of crimes, 25% of crimes had a rank of 10 or less, and 62% of

* For more details of the random probability method, see Yokota and Watanabe (2002).

† For more details of the algorithms that were tested, see Ewart et al. (2005).

cases had a rank of 50 or less. The RPAL model generated ranks with a range from 1 to 519. This algorithm generated a perfect match for 24% of crimes, 52% of crimes had a rank of 10 or less, and 53% of crimes had a rank of 50 or less. Finally, the COMBIN algorithm generated ranks with a range from 1 to 341. This algorithm generated a perfect match for 24% of crimes, 59% of crimes had a rank of 10 or less, and 94% of crimes had a rank of 50 or less. These findings suggest that combining MO behaviors with spatial–temporal information increases matching performance and may be a better approach when attempting to establish accurate crime linkages in practice.

Bayesian Modeling

Perhaps the most recent procedure to be used to study the role of individual MO behaviors is Bayesian modeling. This analytical approach underpins the sort of computer systems examined above, but has recently been examined more explicitly by Salo et al. (2012) and Winter et al. (2013).

Salo et al. (2012) coded 92 offender behaviors (dichotomously) for 116 solved homicide cases committed by 19 offenders in Italy. A Bayesian approach for studying crime linkage issues was developed and tested using a leave-one-out cross-validation procedure (LOOCV).* More specifically, as described by Salo et al., they

> examined the data using a Bayesian model that assigns different probabilities on observing specific behaviours depending on the series to which the crime belonged [and] [b]ased on these probabilities, the decision can be made to link a new crime to the series for which a shared offender is most likely. (pp. 362–363)

The model achieved a classification accuracy rate of 83.6% using LOOCV, which is significantly higher than the level of classification accuracy that would be accomplished by chance (5.3%). Salo et al. also showed that this level of classification accuracy could be accomplished even when they reduced the number of behaviors upon which linkage decisions were based. For example, the accuracy rate accomplished with the full Bayesian model (92 behaviors) was preserved even when only 15 carefully selected behaviors were present in the model. These results suggest that there may be some potential utility in carrying out crime linkage analysis using Bayesian probabilities and that this analytical approach may also be useful for determining which MO behaviors carry the most predictive power.

* The LOOCV procedure is a relatively efficient validation procedure. Essentially, individual crimes are systematically removed from the dataset to act as test cases with the remaining crimes acting as training data to develop the statistical models. The performance of the models on the test cases estimates the degree to which the models would be effective at identifying crime linkages with yet to be observed cases. For more details of the Bayesian approach that was adopted by Salo et al. (2012), see Appendix S1 in the online version of their article.

Winter et al. (2013) conducted a similar study, although they were also interested in comparing the multivariate Bayesian approach with another approach, which relates to a method discussed below in the section on psychological themes (what Winter et al. refer to as a "theory-based, dimensional approach"; p. 28). Using 219 cases of solved serious sexual assaults committed in the United Kingdom by 159 offenders (including 30 serial offenders who were responsible for 90 of the assaults) they tested (1) a dimensional approach, whereby they identified seven dimensions via Mokken scaling (see below for more details) that were then used as predictors in discriminant function analysis (DFA),* and (2) a Bayesian approach, or a naïve Bayesian classifier. Like the study conducted by Salo et al. (2012), LOOCV was used to cross-validate the results. Additionally, in order to compare the two procedures, a common accuracy metric was used by calculating the area under the curve (AUC), as derived from receiver operating characteristic curve (ROC) analysis.† The dimensional approach they tested was found to predict 28.9% of crime series correctly, compared to 34.5% for the Bayesian approach. The inclusion of nonserial offenses in the analysis caused a significant decrease in linking accuracy when using the dimensional approach (8.9%), but had little impact on the Bayesian approach (32.2%). With respect to the AUCs, the Bayesian approach (AUC = 0.84) was found to significantly outperform the dimensional approach (AUC = 0.74).

Methods for Examining Functional Domains

A variety of researchers have adopted a slightly different approach compared to the approach described above. Rather than basing their analysis on unaltered MO behaviors, these researchers have opted to combine MO behaviors

* Like logistic regression analysis, which will be discussed in Section Multidimensional Scaling, DFA allows for linkage predictions (i.e., assignment of a particular case to a crime series) to be made based on a set of predictor variables. Using a sample of cases in which series membership is known, and using those predictor variables that contribute the best discrimination between groups, a set of discriminant functions are formed to classify cases into crime series.

† As discussed previously in this volume, an ROC curve can be produced in these contexts by calculating the hit rates (predicting that crimes are linked when they are) and false alarm rates (predicting that crimes are linked when they are not) that emerge across a range of decision thresholds (e.g., different *p*-values, which reflect the likelihood that a given crime belongs to a specific crime series). When these rates are plotted on a graph (hit rate on the *x*-axis and false alarm rate on the *y*-axis) and the points are connected, a concave downward ROC curve usually results. The AUC is the area of the graph falling beneath this curve. The AUC can theoretically range from 0 (none of the graph falls below the curve) to 1 (the entire graph falls below the curve). Basically, the larger the hit rate to false alarm rate ratios along a ROC curve, the higher the curve falls in the ROC graph. Higher AUCs reflect more accurate linkage decisions (0 = no accuracy, 0.5 = chance accuracy, 1 = perfect accuracy).

to form functional domains (i.e., groups of behaviors that relate to a common function, such as securing access to a dwelling for the purpose of committing a burglary). Across-crime similarity scores, which are calculated for each domain separately, serve as the basis for further analysis when taking this approach. The approach was originally proposed because it was thought that different domains of MO behavior may prove more (or less) useful for crime linkage purposes (Bennell & Canter, 2002).

Logistic Regression Analysis

The analytical method used most often when adopting this approach is logistic regression analysis (Bennell et al., 2014). Like other forms of regression, logistic regression analysis is used to determine the relative power of a set of variables for predicting a criterion variable. However, in the case of logistic regression analysis, the criterion variable is dichotomous. When studying crime linkage assumptions, the criterion variable is the linkage status for each pair of crimes under consideration (i.e., whether a pair of crimes was committed by the same offender or different offenders). The predictor variables in linkage research that uses logistic regression analysis typically consist of similarity scores derived from pairs of crimes across a range of functional domains (e.g., entry methods, internal behavior, property stolen, and dwelling characteristics in cases of residential burglary). Logistic regression analysis not only allows the researcher to assess the predictive power of specific behavioral domains, but also various domain combinations.

Bennell and Canter (2002) were the first to use this approach. They examined whether readily available information at burglary crime scenes in the United Kingdom could be used to link burglaries to a common offender. They randomly selected two burglaries each from the crimes of 43 serial residential burglars. For each burglary, they had access to a wide range of crime scene behaviors, which they categorized into the following domains: entry behaviors (e.g., whether the offender entered through the front door of the property), target characteristics (e.g., whether the offender burgled a property with an external alarm), items stolen (e.g., whether the offender stole cash from the property), and the distance in kilometers between burglary locations. Using a program called B-LINK, Bennell and Canter calculated similarity scores (Jaccard's coefficients) for each behavioral domain across every possible pair of burglary offenses in the sample. For cross-validation purposes, the sample was then split to form a development (training) sample and a test sample. Logistic regression models were developed from the similarity scores in the development sample and these models were then used to predict whether pairs of burglaries in the test sample were committed by the same or different offenders (i.e., whether the burglaries should be considered linked or unlinked). Bennell and Canter found that each of the behavioral domains had some value in establishing links between crimes, but certain domains were associated with significantly higher levels of predictive power. The optimal regression model was found to consist of inter-crime distances and entry behaviors, with inter-crime distances being the best predictor overall. The model including inter-crime distance and entry behaviors had an AUC of 0.81 when it was applied to the test sample. The model including just inter-crime distance had an AUC of 0.80. These results suggest that behaviors that are largely under the control of the offender (e.g., deciding on crime locations) potentially have more predictive power than behaviors that are more situation dependent (e.g., what property is stolen). These results have been replicated in other studies of burglary since Bennell and Canter's study (e.g., Bennell & Jones, 2005). These findings have also been replicated in studies of other crime types, such as vehicle thefts (e.g., Tonkin, Grant, & Bond, 2008; see Chapter 6).

Classification Trees

Classification trees are often used to examine decision making in diagnostic contexts (e.g., risk assessment; Monahan et al., 2000). Recently, they have been used by researchers to examine crime linkage assumptions. Thus far, the input to these classification trees has been the same as the input to logistic regression analysis—across-crime similarity scores calculated for various functional domains. However, once the input data are submitted to classification tree analysis, the analytic procedure differs from regression analysis.

The organization of a classification tree is determined by applying a statistical algorithm to the data used to construct the tree. In instances where researchers are trying to predict the linkage status of crime pairs (i.e., a categorical classification), the chi-squared automatic interaction detection (CHAID) algorithm is used. As the name suggests, this algorithm relies on the chi-square test of independence to split the tree into branches using the various predictor variables (Magidson, 1993). The tree first begins with all crime pairs at what is commonly called the *root node*. The algorithm then runs a chi-square test of independence for all predictors and the outcome and selects the predictor (e.g., entry behaviors) holding the most significant chi-square value to split the data into subgroups (i.e., linked and unlinked crime pairs). Each resulting subgroup is comprised of the cases that fall into the different categories of this predictor variable (e.g., Jaccard's coefficients that are $<$ or ≥ 0.30 for entry behaviors). These subgroups are referred to as *child nodes* because they arise from an earlier node, or a *parent node*. Next, for each child node, this splitting process continues until the cases can no longer be further distinguished from one another on the basis of the predictor variables. Once no additional predictors can differentiate between the cases in a given child node, the search for group differences ends and that child node is labeled a *terminal node* or *end node*. As discussed below, in some cases, crime pairs that remain unclassified in these terminal nodes can be analyzed again to create iterative classification trees.

One of the first attempts to use classification trees for crime linkage purposes was a study conducted by Gerlach, Bennell, Woodhams, and Beauregard (2011). A total of 347 sex offenses committed by 69 offenders in Canada were examined. MO behaviors were categorized into five functional domains: control, escape, sex, style, and target selection. All possible linked and unlinked crime pairs were constructed and across-crime similarity scores were calculated for each functional domain. The sample was then split to form a model development (training) sample and a test sample. The similarity scores from the development sample were submitted to both CHAID analysis and stepwise logistic regression analysis.

With respect to the CHAID analysis, the initial classification tree that was produced contained 30 terminal nodes. Crime pairs within each end node were classified. The crime pairs were deemed *linked* if the base rate of linked pairs in the node exceeded twice the base rate of linked pairs in the total sample (i.e., >6.4%) and *unlinked* if the base rate of linked pairs in the node was less than half the base rate of linked pairs in the total sample (i.e., ≤1.6%).* All other crime pairs were deemed unclassifiable. Out of the 30 terminal nodes, four could be classified as linked, 21 as unlinked, and five as unclassified. The unclassified crime pairs were pooled and submitted to further CHAID analysis. The second tree contained six terminal nodes (one linked, four unlinked, and one unclassified). The unclassified crimes were pooled again and subjected to CHAID. This final iteration resulted in a tree with two terminal nodes (zero linked, one unlinked, and one unclassified). This iterative classification tree, when applied to the test sample, resulted in an AUC of 0.97. The logistic regression analysis run on the test sample produced an AUC of 0.98.

Tonkin, Woodhams, Bull, Bond, and Santtila (2012) used the same methodology to examine classification tree and logistic regression analysis. They used two samples: 160 residential burglaries committed by 80 serial burglars in the Greater Helsinki region of Finland between 1990 and 2001, and 376 vehicle thefts committed by 188 serial car thieves in Northamptonshire, UK, between January 2004 and May 2007. After combining MO behaviors into functional domains, similarity scores were calculated, development (training) and test samples were formed, and the data were submitted to the analysis. For the burglary analysis, the domains consisted of inter-crime distance,

* This is consistent with how diagnostic decisions have been made in other contexts where classification trees have been used (e.g., Monahan et al., 2000).

type of property burgled, method of entry, search behavior, and type and cost of property stolen. For the car theft analysis, the domains consisted of intercrime distance, temporal proximity, type of car stolen, age of vehicle, how the vehicle was entered and started, and the physical state in which the vehicle was recovered. For the burglary data, the AUCs for the classification tree were 0.96 (development) and 0.80 (test). The AUCs for the optimal logistic regression model were 0.92 (development) and 0.87 (test). For the car theft data, the AUCs for the classification tree were 0.84 (development) and 0.78 (test). The AUCs for the optimal logistic regression model were 0.83 (development) and 0.80 (test). These results led the researchers to conclude that the level of linkage accuracy associated with each method was similar, but the reliability of the classification tree model was inferior to the logistic regression model given the greater change observed in the AUCs between the development and test samples for the classification tree analysis.

Methods for Examining Psychological Themes

The final approach we will discuss relies on psychological themes. When using this approach to study the principles of crime linkage analysis, statistical methods (e.g., MDS) are used to group or cluster crime scene variables into themes. Information about these themes (e.g., scores indicating the degree to which offenders exhibit behaviors from each theme) are then submitted to further analysis (e.g., DFA) to gauge the extent to which the themes can be used to potentially identify crime linkages. The theoretical basis of the thematic approach, as in the functional domain approach, surrounds the hypothesis that MO behaviors may group together in meaningful ways that will prove useful for crime linkage purposes. However, in contrast to the functional domain approach, the basis for grouping behaviors when adopting a thematic approach is empirically driven, typically based on behavioral co-occurrence rather categorizations determined by the researcher. Because this chapter has already discussed in detail various ways of assessing linking accuracy once inputs are determined, this section will focus primarily on the various methods that have been used to develop thematic inputs. Three methods in particular will be focused on (1) MDS, (2) principal components analysis (PCA), and (3) cluster analysis.

Multidimensional Scaling

We have mentioned MDS already when discussing linking studies based on MO behaviors. In that case, behavioral data were submitted to the analysis and the MDS plot (of crimes) was used to represent, in visual form, the degree of behavioral similarity between all crimes included in the analysis. The proximities between crimes were then used to determine potential linkages. In the approach we are describing now, MDS is used in quite a different way, to represent the degree to which crime scene behaviors co-occur. The closer two behaviors are to one another in an MDS plot, the more often they co-occur. As such, the plot can be used to identify groupings or clusters of co-occurring behaviors, which represent regions of overall similarity, or *themes* of behavior.

It is important to note when using MDS in this way that the partitioning of behaviors into particular themes is not based on any sort of statistical division, but instead on a theoretical or even intuitive basis. As such, the adoption of the term *theme* is reflective of the fact that these variable groupings are not to be thought of as distinct factors or constructs. Instead, themes are considered to have potentially overlapping and fuzzy boundaries (see Goodwill et al., 2013). It is also important to stress, as we did above, that the identification of psychological themes within a dataset represents only the first step in the analysis when adopting a thematic approach. Once psychological themes have been identified, they are then used to characterize crimes in some way, and those characterizations are used to assess across-crime similarity for the purpose of establishing series membership.

A clear example of this approach can be seen in the study conducted by Santtila et al. (2005). They explored the potential of using a thematic approach to describe Finnish stranger rape cases (43 offenses belonging to 16 different series) for the purpose of studying crime linkage analysis. Santilla and his colleagues used an MDS-based thematic approach, which resulted in two major themes of victim contact: *hostility* or *involvement*. However, within the involvement theme, two more subthemes emerged: an *expressive* offender that engaged in verbal behaviors during the act, such as revealing information about himself and threatening the victim not to report the attack, and a *deceptive* offender that used confidence approaches, such as persuading the victim to join him voluntarily. Two themes also emerged within hostile offenders: a *sexual* offender that approached the victim outdoors, achieved penetration more than once, and performed numerous sexual acts; and an *aggressive* offender that was found to commit behaviors such as manually gagging the victim while inflicting injury. Their MDS analysis was followed by DFA, where the predictor variables were scores characterizing the thematic *make-up* of each crime in the dataset. Using the LOOCV procedure described earlier, each case in Santtila et al.'s dataset was classified by functions derived from all other cases minus the one being classified. The classification accuracy they observed exceeded that expected by chance, with 25.6% of the cases being classified without any error and for 86.1% of the cases the series to which it belonged being included within the 10 most probable series.

The authors concluded that crimes committed by an offender in their sample were both similar enough and distinct enough to allow for good discrimination between crimes committed by different offenders.

Principal Component Analysis

In a similar way to the study just described, Santtila, Fritzon, and Tamelander (2004) investigated the possibility of linking arson cases based on the statistical factoring of behaviors into components through the use of PCA. Although not exactly themes of behavior, components generated through PCA represent groupings of correlated variables and as such the methodology is similar to MDS-based approaches. Using 42 series of arson, containing a total of 248 arson cases, Santtila and his colleagues assessed the linking effectiveness of component factor scores entered into a DFA using the LOOCV procedure. In this study, 33% of the arson cases could be correctly linked. Additionally, for over 50% of the sampled cases, the series they actually belonged to was among the top 10 series identified by the statistical analysis.

Cluster Analysis

Perhaps the best example of cluster analysis being used to derive psychological themes of behavior for crime linkage purposes is a study conducted by Grubin, Kelly, and Brunsdon (2001). The study was actually based on two datasets, although the dataset from the United Kingdom will be focused on here.* This dataset included 468 sex offenses that occurred between 1965 and 1993. The offenses were committed by 210 offenders, 81 of which would be considered a serial offender (committed two or more crimes). Grubin and his colleagues used cluster analysis, which is conceptually similar to both MDS and PCA, to identify various offense types within four behavioral domains: control, sex, escape, and style.† By cluster analyzing behaviors within each domain, four types of offenses could be identified (per domain).

Grubin et al. refrained from labeling these types, preferring instead to simply refer to them as Type 1, 2, 3, and 4 (e.g., Control Type 1, 2, 3, 4). However, thematic labels could have been used given that the types each had a distinctive character. Instead of submitting this information to DFA, as was done in the previously mentioned studies, the researchers developed a

* The other dataset came from Canada and represented 840 sex offence cases. One hundred and two of the cases were part of a crime series, which were committed by 36 offenders.

† Grubin et al.'s (2001) study may be more accurately viewed as a mixture of two approaches to crime linkage—the functional domain approach and the psychological theme approach. The four domains that were examined were derived by the researchers based on existing literature on sexual offences. However, once those domains were determined, cluster analysis was used to identify themes of behavior within each domain.

computer algorithm to compare crimes with respect to their thematic (or type-based) similarity. As described by Grubin et al., "for each offence in the databases, the 10 per cent of cases 'most similar' to it were identified ... [and] examined to determine how many, if any, were part of the same offence series as the index offence" (p. viii). Although the results varied as a function of series length, the number of matched offenses was significantly better than what would be expected by chance (with the exception of crime series involving just two offenses). The results could be improved even further (by reducing the number of false positives) by filtering out crimes that were spatially and temporally distant from the index offenses.

Issues to Consider

Across all of the approaches (e.g., MO behaviors, functional domains, and psychological themes) and statistical methods (e.g., similarity coefficients, logistic regression analysis, and MDS) we have discussed, there are a number of important issues that researchers might wish to consider when setting out to study the principles of crime linkage analysis. In this section, we discuss six issues. Many of these issues are general ones that researchers will want to keep in mind regardless of what approach/method they are using. Other issues may be useful for actually deciding what approach/method to use. The six issues we discuss are (1) reliability of data; (2) ecological validity, including sample and task characteristics; (3) cross-validation; (4) decision thresholds; (5) measurement of predictive accuracy; and (6) pragmatism.

Data Reliability

As we have tried to make clear in this chapter, a variety of sophisticated statistical methods can be used to examine the assumptions underlying crime linkage analysis. However, researchers need to keep in mind (and most clearly do) that no level of statistical sophistication can produce meaningful results if the data being relied upon are not reliably coded (Bennell, Snook, Macdonald, House, & Taylor, 2012). Data reliability should be a big concern for crime linkage researchers because the data that most researchers rely on were not collected for research purposes (the data were typically collected during the course of a police investigation for the purpose of facilitating that investigation). Because of this, many of the safeguards that researchers traditionally put in place to ensure the quality of their data (e.g., the use of well-defined coding dictionaries, training on how to code data using those dictionaries, checks for satisfactory inter-rater reliability) do not often exist within policing contexts. Of course, there are many reasons for police officers to collect and code data in an accurate and reliable fashion but, as others have pointed out (e.g., Alison et al., 2001), there are numerous obstacles to collecting such data within naturalistic settings.

In most cases, there will be little that researchers can do to improve the reliability of their data; they simply need to recognize that their statistical methods do little to correct this potential problem and make sure this is clear to readers of their work. Of course, when things can be done to improve the situation, they should be done. For example, it may be that certain coding practices could improve the reliability of the data (e.g., coding behaviors dichotomously, as having occurred or not occurred, rather than continuously, such as how often something occurred), that certain statistical methods can be used that are more forgiving of messy data (e.g., nonmetric methods that do not consider the absolute value of data, or methods that can accept dichotomous input), or that strong tests of inter-rater reliability can be imposed at certain stages in the research process (e.g., when coding victim statements). Well-validated data collection protocols also exist for certain types of studies (e.g., Salfati's Homicide Profiling Index-Revised; Salfati, 2006) and, when possible, these coding schemes should be used. Police agencies can also assist with this task over the long term, by ensuring that their coding schemes are well validated and/or that they put meaningful quality assurance checks in place that are specifically designed to improve the accuracy and reliability of the data they are collecting (and ultimately sharing for research purposes).*

Ecological Validity

Another issue that needs to be considered when using the approaches and methods described in this chapter is ecological validity. Like data reliability, no amount of statistical sophistication will improve the value of results (with respect to their applicability or generalizability) if the samples upon which the statistical tests are based lack high levels of ecological validity. There are a variety of issues that should be considered to increase the ecological validity of studies in this field.

Some of these issues have been raised in previous chapters (e.g., see Chapter 6) so we will not focus on them too much here. The most obvious issues are the heavy (or exclusive) reliance on *solved/convicted* crimes and *serial* crimes in published studies. As discussed elsewhere (e.g., Bennell & Canter, 2002), a reliance on such data may result in inflated reports of linking accuracy in research studies that are not generalizable to naturalistic

* Such quality assurance checks appear to be in place in some police organisations, such as those that rely on the Violent Crime Linkage Analysis System (ViCLAS; Bennell et al., 2012).

settings where samples include many unsolved and/or one-off crimes (i.e., the kinds of samples crime analysts and investigators typically work with). Importantly, studies are now emerging that deal with these issues. Generally speaking, these studies suggest that linking accuracy levels reported in previous studies are not seriously inflated because of their sample characteristics (e.g., Winter et al., 2013; Woodhams & Labuschagne, 2012).

Other important issues have largely been ignored by researchers to date despite the fact that these issues may seriously skew studies to such a point that their results are not generalizable. For example, crime linkage research is heavily biased toward the analysis of UK data. This is true of the examples discussed in this chapter and the research literature more broadly (Bennell et al., 2014). Given that serial offenders committing crimes in different jurisdictions have been shown to exhibit differences in their offending behaviors (e.g., Woodhams & Labuschagne, 2012; see Chapter 7), it is not clear whether the analysis of UK data will necessarily generalize to other countries. The examination of crime type is also biased heavily toward property crimes (Bennell et al., 2014). Again, it is unclear whether studies of serial burglaries, vehicle thefts, or commercial robberies say anything meaningful about how serial rapes or homicides might be linked.

The generalizability of linking *tasks* has also been largely ignored by researchers in this area. Although various types of linking tasks have been studied by researchers, it is not currently clear that these tasks generalize to the sorts of tasks crime analysts and investigators typically encounter. For example, a relatively large number of studies in this area have examined whether it is possible to use logistic regression models to discriminate between crime pairs that have been committed by the same offender versus different offenders (see Chapter 6). Yet, practitioners have argued (see Chapter 8) that this task bears little resemblance to the work that they do. As other contributors to this volume have argued (see Chapter 11), much more effort needs to be put into determining the sorts of challenges that practitioners actually face so that studies can be set up to examine practically relevant tasks. The choice of statistical methods that researchers use will obviously be heavily influenced by the task characteristics, so care should be taken in choosing appropriate methods when future studies are conducted.

Cross-Validation

Related to the above issues is the issue of cross-validation. Cross-validation refers to a process of determining the extent to which results from a statistical analysis generalize to an independent dataset (Efron & Gong, 1983). This is a particularly important issue in cases where predictive models are developed, as they often are in the studies cited above (e.g., Bennell & Canter, 2002). In these cases, the goal is not to show how useful a prediction model is for making decisions on the set of crimes used to develop that model. Instead, the goal is to demonstrate how useful the model might be for predicting crime linkages on *yet to be observed* cases. Cross-validation helps determine whether the study's results, particularly the reported rate(s) of predictive accuracy associated with a statistical model, are valid and generalizable. Without cross-validation (i.e., when prediction models are developed and tested on the same set of data), it will be difficult to determine if the accuracy of a prediction model is simply due to the success of a very well-fitted model, or the predictive ability of the underlying aspects of the model itself (e.g., the particular set of variables the model relied on or the methodology).

As illustrated in this chapter, people who conduct crime linkage research generally recognize the need to cross-validate their results. Indeed, attempts to assess cross-validation are often, though not always, made in this area (Bennell et al., 2014). The method of cross-validation used by researchers varies, however, and some forms of cross-validation are probably better than others. In early studies, split-half validation was often used (e.g., Bennell & Canter, 2002). Using this procedure, 50% of a sample is randomly selected and held back for the purpose of model development and the model is then tested on the remaining 50% of cases. Although this is a better approach than ignoring cross-validation altogether, it is still relatively inefficient (especially when small samples are being analyzed) given that only half the crimes are used to develop and test the model. More recently, LOOCV has been used by researchers in this area. LOOCV is a much more efficient procedure than split-half validation given that all cases but one are used to develop the prediction models, and the models are systematically tested on all cases within a sample. At this point, our recommendation to crime linkage researchers is to use LOOCV to validate their models.

Equally important, and related to the issue of cross-validation, are attempts to carry out replication studies in this area. Several theoretical replication studies have been conducted to date. For example, attempts have been made to replicate early findings, such as those reported by Bennell and Canter (2002), Bennell and Jones (2005), and Goodwill and Alison (2006), which showed the dominance of geographical and temporal proximity as predictors of crime linkage (e.g., Markson, Woodhams, & Bond, 2010). In addition, several methodological replication studies have been conducted. Good examples include Ewart et al.'s (2005) replication of Yokota and Watanabe's (2002) work, and Tonkin, Bull, and Santtila's (2012) replication of Bennell and Canter's (2002) linking approach. It is important that these types of studies continue to be conducted because it is only through such studies that we can truly determine the generalizability of research findings.

Decision Thresholds

In virtually all methods that have been used to study crime linkage assumptions to date, the decision to link one crime to another crime (or a crime to a crime series) is based on some sort of continuous output from the statistical method. These outputs provide an estimate of the likelihood that crimes are linked and could include (among others) across-crime similarity scores, probability estimates, or even proximities on an MDS plot. To decide if two crimes are potentially linked, or whether one crime belongs to a particular crime series, one must identify a point, or threshold, along the continuous output that will signal when linkage decisions should be made. Values on one side of the decision threshold (e.g., higher probabilities) will indicate probable linkages, whereas values on the other side (e.g., lower probabilities) will not.

The choice of what threshold to use for this purpose is an important decision because outcomes will vary dramatically as a function of where this threshold is set. Unfortunately, the decision can also be a difficult one to make because it is not usually clear which threshold to use. Consider the previously described study by Canter et al. (1991). For each pair of crimes in their sample, some of which were committed by the same offender and some which were committed by different offenders, they calculated across-crime similarity scores. They then selected a threshold (i.e., a specific similarity score) for deciding when two crimes should be linked. The threshold they adopted was ≥0.30. This allowed them to correctly classify 7 out of 12 (58.3%) crime pairs that were committed by the same offender (hits) and 49 out of 54 (90.7%) crime pairs that were committed by different offenders (correct rejections).* This represents an overall accuracy rate of 84.8%. But those results are specific to the threshold that Canter et al. adopted. If another threshold had been chosen, the level of linking accuracy would change (Bennell, Jones, & Melnyk, 2009). For example, had Canter et al. applied a threshold of ≥0.10 to their data, their overall accuracy rate would have been 40.90%. In contrast, a threshold of ≥0.50 would have resulted in an accuracy rate of 0%.

* Although not necessarily a standard way of talking about decision outcomes in this context, one common approach is to talk about hits (linking crimes when they have been committed by the same offender), misses (not linking crimes when they have been committed by the same offender), false alarms (linking crimes when they have not been committed by the same offender), and correct rejections (not linking crimes when they have not been committed by the same offender). When using this terminology we can also talk about the rates with which decision outcomes are made. For example, hit rates can be calculated by dividing the number of hits made for a given sample of crimes by the sum of hits and misses (the miss rate is equal to 1—the hit rate). False alarm rates can be calculated by dividing the number of false alarms made for a given sample of crimes by the sum of false alarms and correct rejections (the correct rejection rate is equal to 1—the false alarm rate).

There are currently no concrete rules for setting decision thresholds, and it is an issue that requires more detailed exploration by crime linkage researchers (and practitioners, given that similar decisions may have to be made in practical contexts). One possible approach is to try and identify a threshold for a given dataset that allows linking accuracy to be maximized in the sense of increasing the hit rate as much as possible, while simultaneously reducing the false alarm rate as much as possible. It appears that this is the approach that Canter et al. (1991) adopted, even if they did so in a relatively ad hoc fashion. However, this approach is potentially too simplistic in that it does not take into account the plethora of factors that are likely to be important when setting decision thresholds.

For example, it may be that the benefits of achieving hits outweighs the costs of making false alarms in the general crime linkage context, and thus, a procedure that assigns equal weight to these outcomes would not be desirable. Decisions around costs and benefits may also relate to other factors (e.g., the crime type under investigation, offense seriousness, the resources available to follow up leads), which will necessarily involve discussions with practitioners.* Other approaches may avoid detailed consideration of these types of issues and involve the determination of an acceptable hit or false alarm rate (e.g., limiting the false alarm rate to 0.10). The probability of encountering linked and unlinked crimes should also be factored into the decision of what threshold to use. For instance, if the probability of encountering linked crimes varies across two settings (e.g., based on crime type), the threshold that is set across these two settings should reflect this fact (Swets et al., 2000).

Of particular importance to our discussion of available methods for researching crime linkage analysis is that the methods themselves are unable to tell the researcher what the appropriate decision threshold might be. Other analytical approaches, such as ROC analysis, need to be used to assist with setting decision thresholds (see below). We discuss this procedure next.

Using ROC Analysis to Produce Valid Measures of Linking Accuracy

Crime linkage researchers have made advances in determining how to set appropriate decision thresholds, while at the same time developing more valid measures of linking accuracy (Bennell et al., 2009). These advances have come about through a reliance on ROC analysis, which is commonly used

* Of course, deciding on costs and benefits can be a tricky business, especially when some of the costs and benefits are not tangible (e.g., what is the human cost of a miss or a false alarm in the crime linkage context?). However, methods exist for dealing with these issues, and as Swets, Dawes, and Monahan (2000) have said, it is often more preferable to explicitly consider costs and benefits, even when they are difficult to set, rather than "sweeping them under the rug" (p. 22).

in other contexts to assist with diagnostic decision making (e.g., radiology; Swets et al., 2000). The problem with many measures of linking accuracy, as discussed above, is that the measures are threshold specific. In other words, the level of accuracy reported by the researcher is specific to the threshold they adopted in their study, and it will vary as different thresholds are applied to the data. However, output coming from each of the methods discussed in this chapter can be submitted to ROC analysis to produce a measure of accuracy—the AUC—that is not threshold specific (see footnote in p. 346 of this chapter for a discussion of the AUC). At the same time, ROC analysis retains information about the linking outcomes associated with all possible decision thresholds, which enables the researcher (theoretically at least) to identify appropriate thresholds for crime linkage purposes.

One of the primary advantages of the AUC as a measure of linking accuracy is that it is independent of any specific threshold; the AUC relates to the position of the entire ROC curve in its graph rather than any single point (threshold) along the curve. Thus, the AUC indicates how useful a method is, *in general*, for identifying linked crimes. Additionally, this measure is relatively flexible in that it can be used to assess the level of linking accuracy that is achieved using a wide variety of statistical methods. Recent studies, for example, have used the AUC to compare the results of logistic regression and classification tree analysis (Tonkin, Woodhams, et al., 2012) and to compare approaches that rely on MO behaviors versus psychological themes (e.g., Winter et al., 2013). The AUC is also not impacted by base rates (of linked crimes). Thus, it can be used to compare the performance of different linking methods even if the base rates of linked crimes varies across datasets (as it might, e.g., if serial homicide and serial burglary were being examined; Bennell et al., 2014). As highlighted above, although still a relatively underexplored aspect of ROC analysis, the technique can also be used to help identify optimal (or at least empirically determined) decision thresholds. For example, a range of formulae exist for identifying thresholds along a ROC curve that achieve specific outcomes (including scenarios where costs and benefits, and the probabilities of encountering linked and unlinked crimes, can and cannot be estimated; Swets et al., 2000). For all of these reasons, we recommend that crime linkage researchers consider the use of ROC analysis as they develop and test various methods for studying crime linkage analysis.

If researchers use ROC analysis, there are a number of issues they might want to consider. First, when using ROC analysis researchers often report only a single AUC value for their analysis, instead of presenting the entire ROC curve. The problem with this approach is that the AUC represents an aggregate level of accuracy (across decision thresholds), but not every threshold is equally important (McClish, 1989). For example, investigators may not have the necessary resources to cope with an extremely high false alarm rate, which makes thresholds falling along the upper end of ROC curves (in research studies) practically irrelevant. Potential solutions to this problem are to present entire ROC curves so that readers can make their own informed decisions about the efficacy of the proposed models. Alternatively, researchers could report AUC values for a range of thresholds that are practically relevant. This issue is also important when comparing ROC curves to one another to determine whether certain methods result in superior linking performance. Although it has not been done to date, researchers may want to consider using techniques that allow them to compare specified portions of ROC curves (vs. comparisons of entire ROC curves). If certain thresholds are practically irrelevant, then ROC curves should only be compared using the portions of the curves that matter. Software programs, such as R,* can easily accommodate such analyses.

Second, researchers need to consider how linking accuracy results are communicated to practitioners (Bennell et al., 2014). For example, despite how it frequently seems to be interpreted, the AUC does not simply reflect the percentage of times a correct linking decision will be made. In actuality, in most contexts where the AUC has been used to study crime linkage issues, the AUC indicates the percentage of times a randomly selected linked crime pair will be associated with a particular piece of evidence (e.g., larger similarity scores) compared with a randomly selected unlinked crime pair. Therefore, an approach needs to be developed to translate the AUC into a more meaningful measure of accuracy for other researchers, investigators, and analysts. This is particularly important because, under certain conditions, large AUCs can still be associated with an enormous number of decision errors. To address such matters, one of the things we urge researchers to consider is providing information about the frequencies of the various decision outcomes (i.e., hits, false alarms, misses, and correct rejections) that result when particular decision thresholds were used (Bennell et al., 2014). This information will give others a better sense of how accurate the linkage decisions actually are.

Third, alternatives to the AUC should be considered by researchers given that this accuracy metric might be influenced by factors that may vary within a crime linkage context. For example, although the AUC does seem to be generally unaffected by variability in base rates (e.g., of linked crimes; Rice & Harris, 1995), there is some limited research suggesting that the AUC may be sensitive to restriction of range in the predictor variable(s) included in statistical models (i.e., how much variability exists in the across-crime similarity scores used as input for a logistic regression analysis; e.g., Hanson, 2008). This same research suggests that alternative measures, such as odds ratios, may end up being more suitable for our purposes than the AUC because they

* http://www.r-project.org/

are not only unaffected by base rates, but they also appear to be relatively immune to the level of variability associated with predictor variables.

Pragmatism

Finally, a discussion of the above issues necessarily leads one to consider what is probably the most important issue facing crime linkage researchers—pragmatism. From its early beginnings (e.g., Green et al., 1976), crime linkage research has been consistently rooted in pragmatism—research has been conducted with real-world application in mind—and there are a variety of issues that researchers may want to consider when thinking about the potential practical utility of the methods they are using. Several of these issues will be discussed here.

Complexity versus Parsimony

The first issue that may be important to consider is the trade-off between complexity and parsimony. In its simplest form, complexity can be expressed as the number of variables used to arrive at linkage decisions; complex models include many variables, whereas parsimonious models remove variable redundancies and include only salient variables. Within the literature we have cited, there is a wide range of variables that have been used to predict linked offenses. This ranges from studies modeling just one variable (e.g., inter-crime distance; Tonkin et al., 2008) to studies modeling many MO (crime scene behaviors) variables at once (e.g., 92 MO behaviors; Salo et al., 2012).

Although debate around this issue still needs to take place, there may be some value in trying to identify parsimonious approaches to linkage analysis, even if it means forsaking some degree of predictive accuracy. For example, a model based on the presence or absence of over 300 variables may be far less pragmatically useful than a model based on just 30, even in cases where the former may result in slightly higher levels predictive accuracy. When dealing with particularly complex models, one must also factor in considerations of user-friendliness, fatigue in coding, and potential increases in missing or unreliable data, all of which may affect a model's reliability. In sum, when assessing the practical utility of a statistical method, or crime linkage model, one must consider not only predictive accuracy, but also the balance between complexity and parsimony.

Accuracy versus Precision

A second issue that might be important to think about when considering pragmatism relates to the trade-off between accuracy and precision (i.e., bandwidth and fidelity; Alison, West, & Goodwill, 2005). For example, it is possible to create crime linkage models that are highly accurate (the vast majority of linked crimes are identified by the model), but not very precise (many unlinked crimes are also identified by the model), just as it is possible to create crime linkage models that are fairly precise (very few unlinked crimes are identified by the model), but not particularly accurate (relatively few linked crimes are identified by the model). Ideally, what is needed in practical contexts is an understanding of the appropriate balance between accuracy and precision. At the very least, researchers and practitioners need to recognize that accuracy and precision are systematically (and typically inversely) related.

This issue of bandwidth and fidelity relates to a variety of decisions that crime linkage researchers (and practitioners) must make. For instance, it relates to decisions about what level of analysis to adopt when examining crime scene behaviors. If one defines behavioral similarity very broadly (e.g., increases bandwidth by relying on higher-order psychological themes), it is likely that many correct linkages will be made, but at the cost of possibly making many false alarms (e.g., Bennell, Gauthier, Gauthier, Melnyk, & Musolino, 2010). Alternatively, if one defines behavioral similarity in stricter terms (e.g., decreasing bandwidth by relying on one to one behavioral matches), we may be able to minimize false alarms, but we increase the chance of misses. The decision around accuracy versus precision also relates directly to the threshold setting exercise. Indeed, even when taking a consistent approach with respect to level of analysis, by making decision thresholds more or less lenient, accuracy and precision will vary systematically (i.e., strict thresholds will decrease accuracy, but increase precision; lenient thresholds will increase accuracy, but decrease precision).

Nomothetic versus Idiographic

A third issue that needs to be considered is the degree to which crime linkage methods can take into account the idiosyncratic nature of crimes and offenders. Practitioners across a range of contexts clearly think it is valuable to take into account idiographic factors (Swets et al., 2000), and practitioners in the area of crime linkage analysis appear to be no different (see Chapters 8 and 9). Idiographic factors, such as the behaviors exhibited by specific offenders or the potential impact of situational factors on a specific offender's behavior, are viewed with importance by practitioners in this field. Thus, at the very least, a method's ability to be used in an idiographic fashion may impact the degree to which the method is ultimately accepted by practitioners. Yet, it is questionable whether many of the statistical methods that researchers are currently using to study crime linkage analysis can be applied in this fashion. Although some of the methods discussed in this chapter (e.g., clustering crimes based on MO behaviors) are clearly idiographic in nature, many of the most common approaches (e.g., developing logistic regression models that can then be applied to new, yet to be observed cases) are not.

It seems that the nomothetic versus idiographic debate is particularly relevant to the discussion of linking tasks (see above). Indeed, it is possible that certain types of linking tasks require very different types of crime linkage methods. For example, Rainbow (see Chapter 8) discusses two separate linking tasks. One is a reactive task, which involves a discrete set of crimes being brought to an analyst for the purpose of determining whether the crimes are linked. The second is potentially a proactive task, which involves trolling through large datasets to identify potential crime linkages. The former task appears to be biased toward an idiographic approach, whereas nomothetic methods appear more suited to the latter approach. Alternatively, both scenarios may be handled best by a nomothetic (or idiographic) approach, or even a merger of the two approaches in what is often called a structured professional judgment approach (idiographic considerations are anchored to a quantitative prediction made by a nomothetic model; see Chapter 12). Little thought has been put into this issue by researchers who study crime linkage analysis despite the fact that it has been debated extensively in other contexts (e.g., risk assessment; Grove & Meehl, 1996). Ultimately, the question about which approach is best is an empirical one and searching for an answer to this question will likely be a productive line of future research.

Automated versus Practitioner Oriented

Directly related to the previous issue is another important issue that researchers may want to consider: The degree to which analysts or investigators are involved in the crime linkage decisions made by the methods we have discussed. Traditionally, end users have been reluctant to hand over decision-making power to automated systems, often because they feel these systems cannot take into account idiographic factors or because the decision maker feels that they need to be accountable for any decisions that are made (Swets et al., 2000). Clearly, the methods discussed in this chapter vary in this regard. When relying on clustering approaches, for example, not only will the end user choose the MO behaviors to enter into the analysis, but they will often be required to interpret the output and decide whether the crimes are close enough in space (i.e., similar enough) to warrant being linked. Other methods, however, such as the algorithm-based linking system proposed by Yokota and Watanabe (2002) appear fairly autonomous. Although the precise application of these types of systems is often not made explicit in research papers, there is an implicit notion that these systems could be automated, with or without the need for an operator to input data or determine potential links. In certain cases, automated crime linkage systems may have high pragmatic utility (e.g., for high volume crime), although in our view, practitioners will always have a role to play in the crime linkage process. Ultimately, the practical value of any method will be determined by the actual uptake, confidence in, and continued use of the method by end users.

Given our view that practitioners will always play a key role in making linkage decisions, it is important to highlight a recent method that has the potential to directly use investigator knowledge in creating a crime linkage model, that of Bayesian modeling (e.g., Salo et al., 2012; Winter et al., 2013). In the vast majority of methods discussed throughout this chapter (e.g., logistic regression analysis), linkage predictions (i.e., probabilities) are derived from variable inputs that have all been considered to have the same reliability, relevance, and statistical importance (i.e., weight) to the model. This is particularly true for methods that use Jaccard's coefficient to determine the similarity between two cases, based on a set of variables. In contrast, when using Bayesian approaches to study crime linkage, researchers have the ability to create prior probabilities of the linking *environment* appropriate to the context (e.g., jurisdiction and/or database), which gives them the means to increase the ecological validity of their models and their potential pragmatic utility (e.g., real-world application). Moreover, in Bayesian analysis, an investigator could potentially use their expert knowledge to create prior probabilities or weights for variables based on, for example, their judgment of which variables are more important or salient for crime linkage purposes. Thus, these methods are much more compatible with a practitioner-oriented approach than many of the other methods that we have discussed and we believe that the Bayesian approach will receive much more attention in the future by researchers who are interested in crime linkage analysis.

Conclusion

A wide range of methods have been used by researchers to examine how well crimes from the same series might be identified through statistical means. Generally, these methods can be categorized into different levels of analysis depending on whether they have been used to study MO behaviors, psychological themes, or functional domains. Though each of the methods we have discussed in this chapter has certain pros and cons associated with them, we believe that each of the methods has value for examining important issues within specific contexts. Rather than focusing on these pros and cons when conducting research in this area, it is probably more valuable to consider a variety of broader issues, some of which will lead researchers to select certain statistical methods over others. Specific issues that may be useful to consider include the reliability of the data we are using in research, the ecological validity of our study design, the issue of cross-validation, the importance of decision thresholds, developing and relying on valid measures of linking accuracy, and the pragmatic utility of specific methods. We believe that a consideration of these issues will lead to higher quality research and to methods that are more likely to have an impact on crime linkage analysis as it is conducted in real investigative settings.

References

Alison, L. J., Snook, B., & Stein, K. L. (2001). Unobtrusive measures: Using police information for forensic research. *Qualitative Research, 1*, 241–254.

Alison, L. J., West, A., & Goodwill, A. M. (2004). The academic and the practitioner: Pragmatists' views of offender profiling. *Psychology, Public Policy, and Law, 10*, 71–101.

Bateman, A. L., & Salfati, C. G. (2007). An examination of behavioral consistency using individual behaviors or groups of behaviors in serial homicide. *Behavioral Sciences & the Law, 25*, 527–544.

Bennell, C. (2013). Linking crimes in criminal investigations. In D. Youngs (Ed.), *Behavioural analysis of crime: Studies in David Canter's investigative psychology* (pp. 219–232). Aldershot, England: Ashgate.

Bennell, C., & Canter, D. V. (2002). Linking commercial burglaries by modus operandi: Tests using regression and ROC analysis. *Science & Justice, 42*, 1–12.

Bennell, C., Gauthier, D., Gauthier, D., Melnyk, T., & Musolino, E. (2010). The impact of data degradation and sample size on the performance of two similarity coefficients used in behavioural linkage analysis. *Forensic Science International, 199*, 85–92.

Bennell, C., & Jones, N. J. (2005). Between a ROC and a hard place: A method for linking serial burglaries by modus operandi. *Journal of Investigative Psychology and Offender Profiling, 2*, 23–41.

Bennell, C., Jones, N. J., & Melnyk, T. (2009). Addressing problems with traditional crime linking methods using receiver operating characteristic analysis. *Legal and Criminological Psychology, 14*, 293–310.

Bennell, C., Mugford, R., Ellingwood, H., & Woodhams, J. (2014). Linking crimes using behavioural clues: Current levels of linking accuracy and strategies for moving forward. *Journal of Investigative Psychology and Offender Profiling, 11*, 29–56.

Bennell, C., Snook, B., MacDonald, S., House, J., & Taylor, P. J. (2012). Computerized crime linkage systems: A critical review and research agenda. *Criminal Justice and Behavior, 39*, 620–637.

Canter, D. V., Heritage, R., Wilson, M., Davies, A., Kirby, S., Holden, R., … Donald, I. (1991). *A facet approach to offender profiling*. London, England: Home Office.

Douglas, J. E., & Munn, C. (1992). Violent crime scene analysis: Modus operandi, signature, and staging. *FBI Law Enforcement Bulletin, 61*, 1–10.

Efron, B., & Gong, G. (1983). A leisurely look at the bootstrap, the jackknife, and cross-validation. *The American Statistician, 37*, 36–48.

Ewart, B. W., Oatley, G. C., & Burn, K. (2005). Matching crimes using burglars' modus operandi: A test of three models. *International Journal of Police Science & Management, 7*, 160–174.

Fosdick, R. B. (1915). The modus operandi system in the detection of criminals. *Journal of the American Institute of Criminal Law and Criminology, 6*, 560–570.

Gerlach, A., Bennell, C., Woodhams, J., & Beauregard, E. (2011, June). *Using iterative classification trees to link serial sex offences.* Poster presented at the annual conference of the Canadian Psychological Association, Toronto, Canada.

Goodwill, A. M., & Alison, L. J. (2006). The development of a filter model for prioritizing suspects in burglary offences. *Psychology, Crime & Law, 12,* 395–416.

Goodwill, A. M., Stephens, S., Oziel, S., Sharma, S., Allen, J., Bowes, N., & Lehmann, R. (2013). Advancement of criminal profiling methods in faceted multidimensional analysis. *Journal of Investigative Psychology and Offender Profiling, 10,* 71–95.

Green, J., Booth, C., & Biderman, M. D. (1976). Cluster analysis of burglary M/O's. *Journal of Police Science and Administration, 4,* 32–38.

Gross, H. (1906). *Criminal investigation.* Madras, India: G. Ramasawmy Chetty.

Grove, W. M., & Meehl, P. E. (1996). Comparative efficiency of informal (subjective, impressionistic) and formal (mechanical, algorithmic) prediction procedures: The clinical-statistical controversy. *Psychology, Public Policy, and Law, 2,* 293–323.

Grubin, D., Kelly, P., & Brunsdon, C. (2001). *Linking serious sexual assaults through behaviour.* London, England: Home Office.

Hanson, R. K. (2008). What statistics should we use to report predictive accuracy? *Crime Scene, 14,* 15–17.

Jaccard, P. (1908). Nouvelles recherches sur la distribution florale. *Bulletin de la Société Vaudoise des Sciences Naturelles, 44,* 223–270.

Magidson, J. (1993). The use of the new ordinal algorithm in CHAID to target profitable segments. *The Journal of Database Marketing, 1,* 29–48.

Markson, L., Woodhams, J., & Bond, J. (2010). Linking serial residential burglary: Comparing the utility of modus operandi behaviours, geographical proximity and temporal proximity. *Journal of Investigative Psychology and Offender Profiling, 7,* 91–107.

McClish, D. K. (1989). Analyzing a portion of the ROC curve. *Medical Decision Making, 9,* 190–195.

Monahan, J., Steadman, H., Robbins, P., Silver, E., Appelbaum, P., Grisso, T., … Roth, L. (2000). Developing a clinically useful actuarial tool for assessing violence risk. *British Journal of Psychiatry, 176,* 312–319.

Rice, M. E., & Harris, G. T. (1995). Violent recidivism: Assessing predictive validity. *Journal of Consulting and Clinical Psychology, 63,* 737–748.

Salfati, C. G. (2006). The homicide profiling index (HPI)—A tool for measurements of crime scene behaviors, victim characteristics, and offender characteristics. In C. Gabrielle Salfati (Ed.), *Proceedings of the 2005 Meeting of the Homicide Research Working Group: Homicide Research—Past, Present and Future* (pp. 150–166). Chicago, IL: Homicide Research Working Group.

Salo, B., Sirén, J., Corander, J., Zappalà, A., Bosco, D., Mokros, A., & Santtila, P. (2012). Using Bayes' theorem in behavioural crime linking of serial homicide. *Legal and Criminological Psychology, 18,* 356–370.

Santtila, P., Fritzon, K., & Tamelander, A. L. (2004). Linking arson on the basis of crime scene behaviour. *Journal of Police and Criminal Psychology, 19,* 1–16.

Santtila, P., Junkkila, J., & Sandnabba, N. K. (2005). Behavioural linking of stranger rapes. *Journal of Investigative Psychology and Offender Profiling, 2,* 87–103.

Swets, J. A., Dawes, R. M., & Monahan, J. (2000). Psychological science can improve diagnostic decisions. *Psychological Science in the Public Interest, 1*, 1–26.
Tonkin, M., Bull, R., & Santtila, P. (2012). The linking of burglary crimes using offender behavior: Testing research cross-nationally and exploring methodology. *Legal and Criminological Psychology, 17*, 276–293.
Tonkin, M., Grant, T., & Bond, J. W. (2008). To link or not to link: A test of the case linkage principles using serial car theft data. *Journal of Investigative Psychology and Offender Profiling, 5*, 59–77.
Tonkin, M., Woodhams, J., Bull, R., Bond, J., & Santtila, P. (2012). A comparison of logistic regression and classification tree analysis for behavioural case linkage. *Journal of Investigative Psychology and Offender Profiling, 9*, 235–258.
Winter, J. M., Lemeire, J., Meganck, S., Geboers, J., Rossi, G., & Mokros, A. (2013). Comparing the predictive accuracy of case linkage methods in serious sexual assaults. *Journal of Investigative Psychology and Offender Profiling, 10*, 28–56.
Woodhams, J., & Labuschagne, G. N. (2012). South African serial rapists: The offenders, their victims and their offences. *Sexual Abuse: A Journal of Research and Treatment, 24*, 544–574.
Yokota, K., Fujita, G., Watanabe, K., Yoshimoto, K., & Wachi, T. (2007). Application of the behavioural investigative support system for profiling perpetrators of sexual assault. *Behavioral Sciences & the Law, 25*, 841–856.
Yokota, K., & Watanabe, S. (2002). Computer-based retrieval of suspects using similarity of modus operandi. *International Journal of Police Science & Management, 4*, 5–15.

Crime Linkage Research
Where to From Here?

15

CRAIG BENNELL AND
JESSICA WOODHAMS

Until recently, a book such as this one would not have been possible. But, now, a critical mass of individuals exists who are conducting high-quality crime linkage research. The chapters we have collated for this book represent fairly well the diversity of issues that these individuals are examining, and the chapters have been written by some of the most active individuals in this field. Although we were not able to focus on all of the interesting issues being explored at present, nor include chapters from some active researchers and practitioners, we believe that this collection of chapters allows us to reflect in a meaningful way on the current state of crime linkage research. Such reflection indicates how far we have come over the last decade or so. However, it also shows us that much work still needs to be done. In this concluding chapter, we briefly summarize what the current state of research is and we consider where this field might be heading in the future.

Over the past 10 years, researchers have clearly learned a lot about crime linkage. As made clear in Chapters 1 and 2, there appears to be a high level of agreement about what assumptions underlie crime linkage analysis, although the terms used to refer to these assumptions often vary from study to study (e.g., behavioral consistency, temporal stability, intra-individual variation). In order for the field to move forward in an efficient way, we think it will be important for some degree of consensus to be reached regarding how these assumptions are referred to (and how crime linkage itself is defined; Chapter 8). This will help to reduce confusion in the literature and between researchers and practitioners.

There also seems to be some level of agreement (among both researchers and practitioners) that the assumptions underpinning crime linkage analysis are based in personality and social psychology, and to some degree in environmental criminology (e.g., Chapters 2, 5, and 8). Clearly, there has emerged a significant body of research that has examined these assumptions within the specific context of investigative psychology (e.g., Chapter 6). However, there is also recognition that this body of research is characterized by some potentially serious limitations (e.g., Chapters 5 and 6). Generally speaking, there appears to be some evidence supporting these assumptions (Chapter 6); however, it is also apparent that the assumptions do not hold true for all offenders all of the time (e.g., certain types of offending behaviors appear to be exhibited more consistently than other types of behaviors).

We and our contributors have also hypothesized as to the drivers of behavioral consistency, variation, and distinctiveness. For example, sexual fantasy (Chapter 3), mental disorder (Chapter 4), culture (Chapter 7), and situational influences (Chapters 2 and 13) have all been proposed as potentially important factors. New and innovative research is starting to explore the role that these factors might play in crime linkage analysis. Some important new work has also shown that crime linkage analysis can be successfully applied to versatile offenders who commit a range of crime types (Chapter 12). Finally we have learned a great deal about how a wide range of statistical and computational methods can be used to explore various aspects of crime linkage analysis (Chapter 14).

In our view, these are all very impressive accomplishments, especially given how young this field of research is. But, as we said above, books such as this one also show us what is left to be learned; and there is certainly no shortage of issues that require further exploration. For example, although there is some indication that the core linking assumptions discussed throughout this book are generally supported, we know very little about whether these assumptions are supported across different cultures, or how cultural influences might impact the expression of crime scene behaviors (Chapter 7). Bearing in mind the relatively strong bias toward the use of UK data in crime linkage studies, much more research needs to explore the cultural expression of behavioral consistency, variability, and distinctiveness. Without such research, it is impossible to know how universally applicable the results from existing studies are.

Although it is clear that crime linkage analysis is finding its way into the courts in some jurisdictions (Chapter 9), this is clearly the exception rather than the rule (Chapter 10). We currently know little about why differences exist around the world with respect to the admissibility of crime linkage evidence. Although the *Daubert* criteria were given explicit attention in Chapter 10, these criteria do not apply to all jurisdictions and we need to develop a better understanding of international admissibility standards. Once the relevant legal standards have been identified, consideration needs to be given to whether it is possible to conduct research that will allow these standards to eventually be met. Further, in collaboration with practitioners, we need to consider (across jurisdictions) whether the necessary resources are available to meet these standards (e.g., establishing base rates of behavioral occurrence for specific crime types). If they are not, we need to think about what can be done to eventually reach this ideal.

While it is important to have research that supports the assumptions underlying crime linkage analysis, it is not clear currently that this research provides evidence that accurate linking decisions can be made in naturalistic investigative settings. Although most of the research cited in Chapters 2 and 6 (and elsewhere in the book; e.g., Chapter 14) rely on statistical models to predict the likelihood of crimes belonging to the same series, statistical models of the sort that have been tested are not currently used in most jurisdictions to make real linking decisions (as far as we are aware). Practitioners with varying backgrounds and levels of support typically make these decisions, and there is currently very little research that can be relied on to assess whether these practitioners can perform their job well (Chapter 11). The small amount of research that does exist suffers from important limitations (e.g., low levels of ecological validity; Chapter 11). Additional research in this area will be useful, but only if it realistically models the conditions under which crime linkage decisions are made (e.g., by examining linkage tasks that bear some similarity to the tasks real practitioners encounter).

To carry out such research, we clearly need to better understand the sort of tasks practitioners encounter, and it is not clear at present that researchers are sufficiently aware of what these tasks are (Chapter 8). What is clear is that closer collaborations between researchers and practitioners are likely needed to ensure that future crime linkage research is more relevant to practice. Given the desire of many crime linkage researchers to have an impact on the *real world*, the criticisms of existing research (with respect to its lack of practical relevance) that have been outlined in Chapter 8 potentially represent the most notable gap highlighted in this book. On this note, it is interesting upon reflection that the discussion of certain topics, which are of obvious importance to the crime linkage field, is completely absent from this book.* Consider, for example, the fact that a large amount of linkage work around the world is being done with the assistance of computerized systems such as the Violent Crime Linkage Analysis System (ViCLAS).† Yet, none of the chapters in this book deal directly with issues that would be of immediate assistance to ViCLAS analysts. That statement may be equally true for approaches adopted by other practitioners who do not rely on such computer systems, such as the methods described in Chapters 8 and 9.

We think this speaks to the absence, to date, of any sort of systematic strategy for bringing academic researchers and police practitioners together to discuss the state of this field. It is difficult to think of ways in which the practical relevance of crime linkage research can be improved without establishing more open and direct lines of communication between these two groups. Given our views on this issue, we are pleased that this is slowly starting to change. Indeed, at the time of writing this conclusion, an international group of researchers and practitioners involved in this area have just finished meeting in Birmingham, UK, in what will be the first of a series of workshops

* This is not necessarily because we intentionally or unintentionally omitted this material, but because the research does not yet exist (or if it does, we are unaware of it).

† ViCLAS was developed by the Royal Canadian Mounted Police (RCMP), but it is now in use within many countries, including Belgium, the Czech Republic, France, Germany, Ireland, the Netherlands, New Zealand, Switzerland, and the United Kingdom (RCMP, n.d.).

that are designed specifically for the purpose of developing a more practitioner-informed research agenda for the crime linkage field.* Nearly all of the contributors to this book were in attendance at this workshop, in addition to several other crime linkage practitioners from around the world. Although it is still early days, the work of Crime Linkage International NetworK (C-LINK) thus far has shown us that academic researchers can achieve much by working more closely with our practitioner colleagues. Such collaborations are needed to shape a responsive research agenda. Practitioners know the questions to which they need answers and the expertise of researchers will be needed to design studies that can answer the pertinent questions. Collaborations such as C-LINK allow us to learn from one another,† and this is what is needed to move this field forward in a truly meaningful and efficient way.

We can well imagine that another book dealing with crime linkage will be published a decade from now. In addition to reporting on higher-quality basic research studies being conducted in this field, our hope is that this future book will show that the gaps identified within this book have been (at least partially) filled. In particular, we hope that the practical relevance of future work being conducted by researchers in this field cannot be questioned to the same degree that it can be now. Through collaborations with practitioners, this is a very achievable goal and the impact will be important. Such research should have the potential to allow police practitioners to link crimes more effectively and efficiently, which will lead to enhanced public safety. That is the ultimate goal of both practitioners and researchers working within this area.

Reference

Royal Canadian Mounted Police. (n.d.). *Violent crime linkage system*. Retrieved November 10, 2013 from http://www.rcmp-grc.gc.ca/tops-opst/bs-sc/viclas-salvac-eng.htm

* These workshops form part of a successful grant application by Jessica Woodhams at the University of Birmingham, UK, to the Leverhulme Trust. This grant has made possible the creation of C-LINK. As part of this grant, researchers and practitioners from around the world who are involved with crime linkage work will meet three times over the course of 2 years to discuss strategies for advancing research in this field; particularly strategies for making the research more practically relevant. The grant will also fund a number of collaborative research projects carried out by the founding members of C-LINK.

† Interestingly, it became very clear in our first meeting that C-LINK not only provides a forum for academic researchers to learn from police practitioners and vice versa, but it also provides a useful forum for researchers to exchange ideas with other researchers and to learn from one another, and for practitioners to do the same thing with other practitioners.

Index

Note: Locators followed by "*f*" and "*t*" denote figures and tables in the text

A

Absolute behavioral consistency, 18
Academic–practitioner collaboration, 5
Adaptive toolbox, 95
Aggressive offender, 351
Algorithmic approaches, MO behaviors
  COMBIN, 344–345
  RCPA, 344
  RPAL, 344
Analysis of variance (ANOVA), 89
Area under the curve (AUC), 19, 62, 115, 119, 159, 285, 346
Australia trends in serial homicide, 152–153
Automated crime linkage systems, 121–122

B

Bad character evidence, 188
Bayesian approach, 345–346
Bayesian probability of crimes, 243
Behavior
  aggressive, 25, 145, 181, 184
  bizarre, 57–58
  crime scene, 35–37, 46, 59, 66*t*, 120, 162, 307, 362
  crime-switching, 34, 37–38
  criminal, 15, 19, 90, 142, 181
  domains, 352
  modus operandi (MO), 38–40, 88, 119, 126, 178–179, 202, 363
    functional domains, 349
    methods for examining, 340–346
  rapist, 22
  ritualistic, 40, 159, 179, 194, 233–234
  serial homicide. *see* Serial homicide
  sexual, 42–44, 150, 156, 204, 313, 323
  signature, 36, 40, 47, 144, 155, 161, 202, 229, 233
  spatial. *see* Spatial behavior
  temporal, 86, 121, 291, 298
  type in situational similarity, 22–23
  victim, 21–22, 67, 313, 316–317
Behavioral component of sexual fantasy script, 42
Behavioral consistency, 12–13
  cross-situation, 35
  and distinctiveness, 36
    degree of, 60
    empirical tests of. *see* Empirical tests of behavioral consistency and distinctiveness
    evidence on discrimination accuracy, 122–123
    influence of situations on, 310–312
    principles of crime linkage, 109–110
  rapists with mental disorder, 63*t*
  research to date in serial homicide. *see* Behavioral consistency research in serial homicide
Behavioral consistency research in serial homicide, 154–166
  international studies
    Germany, 161–162
    Italy, 162–163
    Republic of South Africa, 163–166
  US cases, 155–161
    individual behaviors, 156–157
    themes, 157–160
    victims, 160–161
Behavioral evidence, 189
Behavioral investigative advice, 175
Behavioral investigative advisers (BIAs), 174, 176, 179, 181, 187–188, 304
Behavioral investigative support system (BISS), 121
Behavioral science, 198
  behavioral similarity missing instances, 213–214
  behavioral themes, 320–321
  change and evolution, 203–205
  consistency, 240–241, 314

Behavioral science (*Continued*)
 examining behaviors, 213
 if...then contingencies in crimes, 303–329
 influence of situations on distinctiveness, 310–312
 offenders signature behavior, 233
 themes similarity, 201–203
 using linkage analysis, 211–212
Behavioral Science section of Surrey Police developed a database (BADMAN), 182, 184
Bennell and Canter (2002) study of spatial behavior, 84–85
Bennell and colleagues (2010) study of spatial behavior, 87–88
Bennell and Jones (2005) study of spatial behavior, 85–86
Bennell approach, 113–121, 114*f*, 116*t*–119*t*
BIAs (behavioral investigative advisers). *see* Behavioral investigative advisers (BIAs)
Binary logistic regression, 284
Bizarre behavior, 57–58
B-LINK, 347
Blitz approach, 318
Blitz attack, 183–184
Bottom-up approach, 241
Bounded rationality, 95–96
Brigadier Gérard Labuschagne, 217
Burrell and colleagues (2012) study of spatial behavior, 89–90

C

Canada trends in serial homicide, 152, 152*f*
Canter et al. (1991) study of human performance on linking task, 253–255
CAPS, 13, 13*f*
 applying to criminal events, 20–25
  age of individual, 24–25
  expertise, 23–24
  psychopathology, 25
  situational similarity, 20–22
  time elapsed, 24
  type of behavior, 22–23
 cool cognitive system, 15
 framework
  crime linkage, 308
  if...then offender profiles, 309
  Mischel and Shoda (1995), 310*f*
  offender's behavior (*if*), 315
  victim's response (*then*), 315
 hot emotional system, 15
 Mischel and Shoda's (1995), 13–15, 59
 predictions about personality disorders, 59
 types of units or mental representations, 14
Car key burglary, 127
CHAID (chi-squared automatic interaction detection) algorithm, 348
Child nodes, 348–349
Chi-squared automatic interaction detection (CHAID) algorithm, 348
Clinical approach, 180
C-LINK (Crime Linkage International NetworK). *see* Crime Linkage International NetworK (C-LINK)
Cluster analysis, 202
Clustering procedures, MO based, 341–342
Cognitive–affective personality system (CAPS). *see* CAPS
Cognitive bias, 237
Cognitive scripts, 145
Comparative case analysis (CCA), 173–175
Consistency, 143
 behavioral. *see* Behavioral consistency
 international studies in serial homicide
  Germany, 161–162
  Italy, 162–163
  Republic of South Africa, 163–166
 issues of, 143–144
 series, 158
 studies on US cases of serial homicide, 155–161
  individual behaviors, 156–157
  themes, 157–160
  victims, 160–161
Cool cognitive system, 15
Court cases
 evidence analysis, 199–201
 murder cases, 200
Crime linkage, 1–2, 35–36
 academic–practitioner collaboration, 5
 basic steps to, 4–5
 Bayesian analysis, 131
 Bennell approach, 113–121, 114*f*, 116*t*–119*t*
 cautionary issues, 211–215
 cognitive bias risk, 237
 confirmation bias risk, 238–239

court opinions in cases, 229–237
evidence
central cases, 230*t*
Daubert standard, 245
legal principles, 205–211
evolution of, 34–35
experience, 260
expert evidence, 225–246
Bayesian probability, 243
behavioral consistency, 240–241
frequency, 243–244
reliable database, 241–243
expert opinions, problems, 237–239
issues, 353–364
cross-validation, 355–356
data reliability, 353–354
decision thresholds, 357–358
ecological validity, 354–355
pragmatism, 361–364
produce valid measures of linking accuracy using ROC, 358–361
MO, 242
neural network models, 131
offense plasticity in, 36–38
principles, 1
behavioral consistency and distinctiveness, 109–110
importance of testing, 108–109
research, 337–365, 369–372
testing assumptions with mentally disordered rapists, 60–64
umbrella term, 2–5
uses, 199–201
Crime linkage analysis (CLA), 173–175, 179, 189–190, 194, 235, 243
evidence, 191
process assumptions, 36
tiers of priority to cases, 187
Crime Linkage International NetworK (C-LINK), 2, 372
Crime linkage research, limitations, 123–135, 262–273
CAPS framework, 308–310
comparison purposes, 270–271
definitions of experience, 266–267
examined linkage task type, 271–272
eye movements, 269
generic process, 124*f*
human judgment, 263
linking decisions using linking model, 265
measurement of decision-making process, 267–269
moving beyond theoretical tests, 134–135
person × situation interactions, 134
stage 1: identifying sample and behaviors
homogenous samples of crime, 125
number of crimes selected for each offender, 126
operationalized offending behavior, 126–127
over-reliance on solved crime, 123, 125
stage 2: form domains/themes, 127–128
stage 3: creating crime pairs, 128–129
stage 4: calculate similarity coefficients, 129–130
stage 5: statistical analyses to test discrimination accuracy
inappropriate comparison groups, 131–133
limited comparison, 130–131
stage 6: limited by geography, time, and methodology, 133
stimuli studies, 262–266
Crime pattern theory, 94–95
Crime(s)
aspects of, 158
domains relevant to presence of behaviors, 85
pairs, type of, 91
scripts, 35
types, 85–86, 260
Crime-switching behavior, 34, 37–38
Criminal investigation, 251–252
Criminal investigative analysis (CIA), 33
Cross-crime linkage, 125
crime category, 281–282
crime pair subsets, 283*t*, 284
decision thresholds, 287*t*, 289, 295*t*
discrimination accuracy, 284–285
DNA sample, 298
future direction for research, 297–299
Home Office framework, 299
importance, 280–281
inter-crime distance value calculated, 284
offender behavior, 298
police force, 298
research studies, 281–297
conclusions and implications, 288–290, 296
findings, 284–288, 293–296

Cross-crime linkage (*Continued*)
future directions, 297–299
limitations of Tonkin, Woodhams, et al. (2012), 296–297
methodology, sample, and data, 281–284, 292–293
Tonkin et al. (2011) limitations, 291–292
ROC analysis results
with solved crimes, 286*t*
with unsolved and solved crimes, 294*t*
temporal proximity values calculated, 284
Cross-validation, 89–90, 355–356
Crown prosecution service (CPS), 292

D

Data coding, 322–323
Data reliability, 353–354
Daubert–Joiner–Kumho trilogy. see Daubert standard
Daubert standard, 205, 226–229, 236, 240, 245
crime linkage evidence, 245
guidelines, 228–229
standard decision, 227
Davies and colleagues (2012) study of spatial behavior, 90
Deceptive offender, 351
Decision-making accuracy, 258
Decision thresholds, 357–358
Demographic component of sexual fantasy script, 42
Deoxyribonucleic acid (DNA), 198, 304
crime scene, 297
forensic science, 198
linkage analysis, 198
physical evidence, 252
Detectives, 254
DFA (discriminant function analysis), 346
Dimensional behavioral linking, 181
Discriminant function analysis (DFA), 346
Discrimination accuracy, 110–111, 115, 296
evidence on behavioral consistency/ distinctiveness and, 122–123
one-cue model, 85
statistical analyses to test, 130–133
inappropriate comparison groups, 131–133
limited comparison, 130–131
Distinctiveness. *see* Behavioral consistency, and distinctiveness
DNA (deoxyribonucleic acid), 198, 304
crime scene, 297
forensic science, 198
linkage analysis, 198
physical evidence, 252

E

Ecological validity, 242, 354–355
Empirical linking model, 271
Empirical tests of behavioral consistency and distinctiveness, 110–122
automated crime linkage systems, 121–122
Bennell approach to crime linkage, 113–121, 114*f*
research evidence, 116*t*–119*t*
thematic approach to crime linkage, 111–113
Environmental criminology, 369
Evidence, 198
bad character, 188
behavioral, 189
on behavioral consistency/ distinctiveness and discrimination accuracy, 122–123
CLA, 191
in court cases, 200–201
DNA, 292
expert, 176, 188–189
forensic science, 198
opinion, 205–206, 226
other crimes, 207–210
requirements of behavioral linkage, 209
similar fact, 226
legal guidelines for use of, 210–211
and other crimes, 207–210
Evidential approach, 188–190
current practice, 189–190
legal context, 188–189
Expectancy effect, 238
Expert evidence, 176, 188–189
crime linkage, 225–246
practical considerations, 239–244
Expert witness, role, 206–207
Expressive offender, 351

F

False alarms, 287
False negative errors, 122

False positive error, 122
Fast and frugal heuristics, 95
Federal Rules of Evidence 702, 206, 237
Forensic sciences, 198
Freedom of Information Act (1966), 212
Frye standard, 205
Functional domains, examining methods
    classification trees
        AUC, 350
        crime linkage assumptions, 348
        crime pairs, 348
    logistic regression analysis
        B-LINK, 347
        optimal regression model, 348

G

Global positioning system (GPS), 99, 101
Goal-oriented wounding, 164
Goodwill and Alison (2006) study of spatial behavior, 86
Grounded theory, 312

H

Hazelwood, Roy, 209
Her Majesty's Inspectorate of Constabulary (HMIC), 176
Her Majesty's Inspectorate of the Crown Prosecution Service (HMICPS), 176
Home Office, 282, 290, 299
Homicide investigation tracking system (HITS), 231
Homology, 35
Hot emotional system, 15
Human performance on linking task, studies, 252–262
    Bennell et al. (2010)
        decision-making accuracy, 258
        ROC analysis, 258
    Canter et al. (1991)
        performance of human judges, 253
        phases, 253–254
        relevant behaviors, 254
    Santtila et al. (2004)
        decision-making process, 256
        degrees of experience, 256–257
    Tonkin (2012)
        crime types, 260
        experience variation, 260

I

Ideal investigative strategy, 34
If... then contingencies, 303–329
    based proximity coefficients, 320–321
    crime linkage purposes, 321
    lag sequential analysis, 320
    offender's behavior (*if*), 315
    offender–victim interaction, 312–316
    in serial sexual assaults, investigating, 316–317
    signature, 305, 325
    victim's response (*then*), 315
Interactive offender profiling system (IOPS), 121
Inter-crime distance, 86, 88–89, 91, 114
Inter-rater reliability analysis, 100–101
Intuitive approach, 241
Investigation, forensic science, 198
Investigative approach, 176–188
    further considerations, 187–188
    methodological considerations, 178–179
    practice, 179–182
    report extract example, 182–187
    theoretical considerations, 176–178
Investigative experience, 257
Investigative psychology
    Brigadier Gérard Labuschagne, 217
    similarities and differences between personality and, 15–20
        concepts, 16
        data, 16–17
        methodology, 17–20
ipse dixit, 237

J

Jaccard (*J*) coefficients, 19, 23, 61–62, 85, 87–88, 129–130, 187, 342–343
Japan trends in serial homicide, 153
Journal of Investigative Psychology and Offender Profiling, 2

K

Kumho standard, 205–206

L

Leave-one-out cross-validation (LOOCV), 293, 345
Likelihood ratios (LRs) method, 7, 190–193

Linkage analysis, 217
behavior similarity, 201–202
bottom-up approach, 241
caution issues, 211–215
computer databases, 212
dissimilarities, 214–215
evidence
in court cases, 200–201
requirements, 209
investigation, 198
research, 201–205
thematic approach, 202–203
top-down approach, 241
trial phase, 199–200
uses, 199
Linkage blindness, 146
Live victims, 165
Logistic regression analysis, 19, 85–91, 130
LOOCV (leave-one-out cross-validation), 293, 345

M

Markson and colleagues (2010) study of spatial behavior, 88
MDS (multidimensional scaling) techniques. *see* Multidimensional scaling (MDS) techniques
Mean area under the curve (mean AUC), 258
Mean interpoint distance (MID), 86
Mental disorder, 56
incidence in sex offender population, 56–60
personality disorder and sexual offending, 58–60
schizophrenia and sexual offending, 57–58
serial sex offenders. *see* Mentally disordered serial sex offenders
testing assumptions of crime linkage with rapists, 60–64
Mentally disordered serial sex offenders
change in offending behavior of, 64–77
diagnostic profile of, 61*t*
factors affecting stability, 64–77
Methodological concerns and explanations, linking research, 96–101
threats to reliability, 99–101
threats to validity, 96–99
Mischel and Shoda's (1995) CAPS, 13–15
Modus operandi (MO), 35, 69, 73–74, 88, 119, 161–162, 178, 202
behavior methods, 340–346
algorithmic approaches, 343–345
Bayesian modeling, 345–346
clustering procedures, 341–342
functional domains, 349
similarity coefficients, 342–343
offenders', 23, 68
in sex crime linkage, 38–40
MSA (multidimensional scalogram analysis), 254, 342
Multidimensional scaling (MDS) techniques, 113, 325, 350–352
Multidimensional scalogram analysis (MSA), 254, 342
Multivariate behavioral linkage, 181

N

Naïve Bayesian classifier. *see* Bayesian approach
Narrative action system (NAS) model, 298
National Center for the Analysis of Violent Crime (NCAVC), 142

O

Objective variables, 97
Offenders
behavior, 198, 204
correct rejections, 357
crime scenes evidence, 198
decision making, 321
forensic science, 198
investigation, 229
linkage analysis, 201, 211
MO, 23, 202
profiling activity, 177
profiling techniques, 229
serial offenses, 244
sexual assault, 254
signature, 201
Offense-focused fantasy and temporal shift, 44–47
Offense plasticity
in crime linkage, 36–38
sexual fantasy and, 41–44
Offense script, 35, 42
Opinion evidence, 205–206, 226

P

Parent node, 348
PCA (principal component analysis), 352
People v. Prince (2007), 236
Perceptual component of sexual fantasy script, 42
Personal factors affecting serial sex offenders stability, 69–77
  arranged lower-order themes, 66*t*
  attitudes and beliefs, 75–77
  experience, 72–74
  motive/mood, 71–72
  physiological, 74
  planning/preparation, 74–75
  sexual fantasy, 69–71
Personality disorder
  and sexual offending, 58–60, 63*t*
  types of, 65
Personality paradox, 12
Personality psychology
  interactionism in, 13
  similarities and differences between investigative and, 15–20
    concepts, 16
    data, 16–17
    methodology, 17–20
  social and, 12–13
Personality, theory of, 92–93
Post-offense behavior, 41, 46, 72
Practitioner's perspectives
  evidential approach, 188–190
    current practice, 189–190
    legal context, 188–189
  investigative approach, 176–188
    further considerations, 187–188
    methodological considerations, 178–179
    practice, 179–182
    report extract example, 182–187
    theoretical considerations, 176–178
  proposed approach, 190–193
    example, 191–192
    further considerations, 192–193
  research agenda, 193–194
Pragmatism
  accuracy *versus* precision, 361–362
  automated *versus* practitioner oriented, 363–364
  complexity *versus* parsimony, 361
  nomothetic *versus* idiographic, 362–363
Principal component analysis (PCA), 352
Process-oriented wounding, 164
Proposed approach, 190–193
  example, 191–192
  further considerations, 192–193
ProxCalc (Proximity Coefficient Calculator), 323
Proximity coefficients (*P*), 320–321, 326*t*
Pseudo-relationship acts, 218
Psychological themes, examining methods
  cluster analysis, 352–353
  MDS, 350–352
  principal component analysis, 352

R

Radford Serial Killer Database, 146
Random choice probability algorithm (RCPA), 344
Rape model (RM), 313
Rational choice theory (RCT), 93–94
RCMP (Royal Canadian Mounted Police), 212
RCPA (random choice probability algorithm), 344
Receiver operating characteristic (ROC) analysis, 85–87, 89, 115, 258, 284, 346
  to produce valid measures of linking accuracy, 358–361
  results for cross-crime linkage, 284, 286*t*, 293–294, 294*t*
Relational component of sexual fantasy script, 42
Ritualistic behaviors, 40, 159, 179, 194, 233–234
RM (rape model), 313
Robbery types, 282
ROC (receiver operating characteristic) analysis. *see* Receiver operating characteristic (ROC) analysis
Root node, 348
Royal Canadian Mounted Police (RCMP), 212
R. v. Arp (1998), 210
R. v. Clune (1993), 208
R. v. Handy (2002), 210

S

Sample-level analysis, 19
Santtila and colleagues (2004) study of spatial behavior, 85

Santtila et al. (2004) of investigative experience
  decision-making process, 256
  degrees of experience, 256–257
Schizophrenia and sexual offending, 57–58, 63*t*
Sequence analysis
  in crime linkage
    data coding, 322–323
    exploratory results, 326–327
    offense series, 327
    sample description, 322
    statistical analysis, 323–325
  if…then contingencies based proximity coefficients, 320–321
  of interpersonal crimes, integrating time, 317–321
  offense styles, 319
  potential issues, 327–329
  rape victim statements, analyzed, 318–319
  sexual assault using lag, 318–319
  thought unit, 322
Serial homicide
  behavioral consistency research to date. *see* Behavioral consistency research in serial homicide
  cultural influences on, 144–145
  trends across countries. *see* Serial homicide across countries, trends
Serial homicide across countries, trends
  comparing behavior patterns, 147–154
    non-US trends, 149–153
    US trends, 148–149
  setting Worldwide context, 146–147, 147*t*
Serial sex offenders
  Beauregard et al. (2007) sequential phases, 314
  crime scenes of, 38
  mentally disordered
    change in offending behavior, 64–77
    diagnostic profile of, 61*t*
    factors affecting stability, 64–77
  South Africa, 125
Serial sexual assaults
  crime type, 311
  Grubin et al.'s (2001) types of, 311
  if…then contingencies, investigating, 316–317
  MDS plot, 325*f*
  rapists, 312
Serious acquisitive crime, 280
Sex offenders, 351
  diagnostic profile of serial, 61*t*
  mentally disordered serial. *see* Mentally disordered serial sex offenders
  population, incidence of mental disorder in, 56–60
    personality disorder and sexual offending, 58–60
    schizophrenia and sexual offending, 57–58
  treatment programs, 77
Sexual acts, 218
Sexual assaults
  average proximity coefficients, 326*t*
  offender, 254
  offender–victim interaction, importance
    categories, 323
    cognitive and affective determinants decision making, 312–314
    crime linkage purposes, 321
    environmental constraints in decision making, 314–315
    state transition diagram, 324*f*
    victim resistance, influence, 315–316
  sequential coding, 323*t*
  serial. *see* Serial sexual assaults
  sexual gratification, 313
Sexual fantasy
  components evident within script, 42, 46
  and offense plasticity, 41–44
  relapse process, 47
  tripartite model of, 45–46
Signature analysis, 200
Signature behaviors, 36, 40, 47, 144, 155, 161, 202, 229, 233
Similar fact evidence, 226
  legal guidelines for use of, 210–211
  MO, 207
  other crimes and, 207–210
Similarity coefficients
  calculation in crime linkage research, 129–130
  MO behaviors, 342–343
Situational component of sexual fantasy script, 42
Situational factors affecting serial sex offenders stability, 67–69
  arranged lower-order themes, 66*t*
  employment, 68
  offense environment, 67–68
  presence of co-offender, 68–69

social network, 68
third party interruption, 69
victim behavior/characteristics, 67
Social psychology, 12–13
Spatial behavior
empirical linking studies review, 84–92
Bennell and Canter (2002), 84–85
Bennell and colleagues (2010), 87–88
Bennell and Jones (2005), 85–86
Burrell and colleagues (2012), 89–90
Davies and colleagues (2012), 90
Goodwill and Alison (2006), 86
Markson and colleagues (2010), 88
Santtila and colleagues (2004), 85
Tonkin and colleagues (2008), 87
Tonkin and colleagues (2011), 88–89
Tonkin and colleagues (2012a), 90
Tonkin and colleagues (2012b), 91
Tonkin and colleagues (2012c), 91–92
Woodhams and Toye (2007), 86–87
methodological concerns and explanations, 96–101
threats to reliability, 99–101
threats to validity, 96–99
theoretical explanations, 92–96
bounded rationality, 95–96
crime pattern theory, 94–95
rational choice theory, 93–94
theory of personality, 92–93
SPJs (structured professional judgments), 252
SPSS (Statistical Package for the Social Sciences), 325
Staging of crime scene, 41
State of Louisiana v. Code (1994), 208
State of New Jersey v. Fortin (2000, 2007), 209
State v. D (1991), 215
State v. Fortin (2000), 233–237
State v. Russell (1994), 231–232
State v. Williams (2009), 213
Statistical analysis, 323–325
Statistical approach, 180
weaknesses of, 189–190
Statistical clustering techniques, 19
Statistical Package for the Social Sciences (SPSS), 325
Structured professional judgments (SPJs), 252
Subjective variables, 97
Sunday serial rapist, 216–222
linkage analysis
approach method/location, 217–218
offender description, 218
pseudo-relationship acts, 218
sexual acts, 218
souvenir, 218–219
victims head cover, 218
state evidence, 216
trail, 220–221
Surprise attack, 183–184

T

Taken into consideration (TIC), 97, 99
Template analysis, 66
Temporal proximity, 114
Terminal node, 349
Thematic approach, 111–113, 157, 202–203
Theoretical explanations, spatial behavior, 92–96
bounded rationality, 95–96
crime pattern theory, 94–95
rational choice theory, 93–94
theory of personality, 92–93
Thought unit, 322
Tonkin and colleagues studies of spatial behavior
2008, 87
2011, 88–89
2012a, 90
2012b, 91
2012c, 91–92
Tonkin (2012) study of human performance on linking task, 260–262
Top-down approach, 241
Tripartite model, 45–46

U

US Supreme Court, 227
US trends of serial homicide
behaviors, 148–149
non-, 149–154
Australia, 152–153
Canada, 152, 152*f*
Japan, 153
transnational comparisons, 149–151
victims, 149

V

ViCAP (Violent Criminal Apprehension Program), 209
ViCLAS (Violent Crime Linkage Analysis System), 100, 212, 242, 318, 371

Victim behaviors in maintenance stage, 21
Victim(s), 17, 155, 165
  behavior, 21–22, 67
  behavior/characteristics in factors affecting sex offenders ability, 67
  head attempts to cover, 218
  influence of resistance offense outcome, 315–316
  live, 165
  –offender situation interaction in sexual assaults, 312–316
  in serial homicide
    behavioral consistency research, 160–161
    US trends, 149
Violent Crime Linkage Analysis System (ViCLAS), 100, 212, 242, 318, 371
Violent Criminal Apprehension Program (ViCAP), 209
voire dire, 211, 216

W

Woodhams and Toye (2007) study of spatial behavior, 86–87
Wordsmith© computational program, 134

Y

Youden's Index, 287–288

A Call for Authors

Advances in Police Theory and Practice

AIMS AND SCOPE:

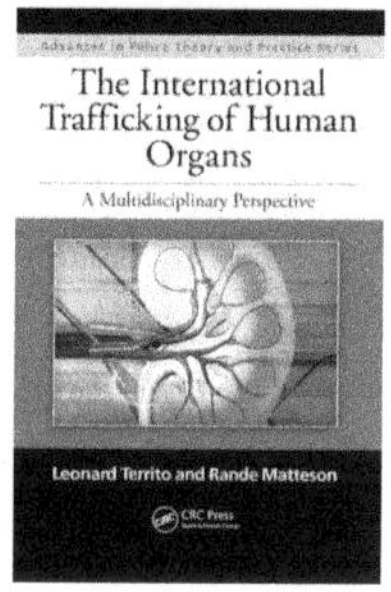

This cutting-edge series is designed to promote publication of books on contemporary advances in police theory and practice. We are especially interested in volumes that focus on the nexus between research and practice, with the end goal of disseminating innovations in policing. We will consider collections of expert contributions as well as individually authored works. Books in this series will be marketed internationally to both academic and professional audiences. This series also seeks to —

- Bridge the gap in knowledge about advances in theory and practice regarding who the police are, what they do, and how they maintain order, administer laws, and serve their communities
- Improve cooperation between those who are active in the field and those who are involved in academic research so as to facilitate the application of innovative advances in theory and practice

The series especially encourages the contribution of works coauthored by police practitioners and researchers. We are also interested in works comparing policing approaches and methods globally, examining such areas as the policing of transitional states, democratic policing, policing and minorities, preventive policing, investigation, patrolling and response, terrorism, organized crime and drug enforcement. In fact, every aspect of policing, public safety, and security, as well as public order is relevant for the series. Manuscripts should be between 300 and 600 printed pages. If you have a proposal for an original work or for a contributed volume, please be in touch.

Series Editor
Dilip Das, Ph.D., Ph: 802-598-3680
E-mail: dilipkd@aol.com

Dr. Das is a professor of criminal justice and Human Rights Consultant to the United Nations. He is a former chief of police, and founding president of the International Police Executive Symposium, IPES, www.ipes.info. He is also founding editor-in-chief of *Police Practice and Research: An International Journal* (PPR), (Routledge/Taylor & Francis), www.tandf.co.uk/journals. In addition to editing the *World Police Encyclopedia* (Taylor & Francis, 2006), Dr. Das has published numerous books and articles during his many years of involvement in police practice, research, writing, and education.

Proposals for the series may be submitted to the series editor or directly to –

Carolyn Spence
Senior Editor • CRC Press / Taylor & Francis Group
561-317-9574 • 561-997-7249 (fax)
carolyn.spence@taylorandfrancis.com • www.crcpress.com
6000 Broken Sound Parkway NW, Suite 300, Boca Raton, FL 33487

For Product Safety Concerns and Information please contact our EU representative GPSR@taylorandfrancis.com
Taylor & Francis Verlag GmbH, Kaufingerstraße 24, 80331 München, Germany

www.ingramcontent.com/pod-product-compliance
Ingram Content Group UK Ltd.
Pitfield, Milton Keynes, MK11 3LW, UK
UKHW020023200926
475702UK00014B/2033

* 9 7 8 0 3 6 7 8 6 7 0 7 2 *